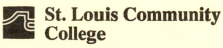

Television in America

**LOCAL STATION
HISTORY
FROM ACROSS
THE NATION**

Television

in America

LOCAL STATION
HISTORY
FROM ACROSS
THE NATION

Edited by **Michael D. Murray**
and **Donald G. Godfrey**

Iowa State University Press / Ames

Michael D. Murray, professor and chair of the Department of Communication at the University of Missouri–St. Louis, has B.A. and M.A. degrees from St. Louis University and a Ph.D. from the University of Missouri–Columbia. He founded the communication program at the University of Louisville and has taught at Virginia Tech University, where he received the university award for teaching excellence. Dr. Murray also has received the Missouri Governor's Award for Outstanding Teaching, the Distinguished Broadcast Educator Award from the Radio-Television Division of the Association for Education in Journalism and Mass Communication, and the Frank Stanton Fellowship from the International Radio-Television Society. He is currently the John Adams Fellow, Institute for U.S. Studies, University of London.

Donald G. Godfrey, professor, Walter Cronkite School of Journalism and Telecommunication, Arizona State University, holds a Ph.D. from the University of Washington. He also has taught at the University of Washington, Southern Utah State, and the University of Arizona. Dr. Godfrey operated a consulting firm that specialized in corporate communications, television syndication and advertising, and he worked in production for 10 years at KIRO-TV, Seattle. He has received national recognition by the NAB/BEA for his contributions to historical scholarship.

© 1997 Iowa State University Press, Ames, Iowa 50014
All rights reserved

Authorization to photocopy items for internal or personal use, or the internal or personal use of specific clients, is granted by Iowa State University Press, provided that the base fee of $.10 per copy is paid directly to the Copyright Clearance Center, 27 Congress Street, Salem, MA 01970. For those organizations that have been granted a photocopy license by CCC, a separate system of payments has been arranged. The fee code for users of the Transactional Reporting Service is 0-8138-2969-0/97 $.10.

⊗ Printed on acid-free paper in the United States of America

First edition, 1997

Library of Congress Cataloging–in–Publication Data

Television in America: local station history from across the nation /
    edited by Michael D. Murray and Donald G. Godfrey.
        p.   cm.
    Includes bibliographical references and index.
    ISBN 0-8138-2969-0
    1. Television broadcasting—United States—History. 2. Television
stations—United States—History.   I. Murray, Michael D.
II. Godfrey, Donald G.
PN1992.2.T48   1997
    384.55'4'0973—dc20   96-31730

Dedicated to our wives,
Carol Murray and
Christina Maria Godfrey,
and our families,
and to
those unsung pioneers
of local television
across the nation

Contents

III. THE CENTRAL HEARTLAND

IV. THE WESTERN FRONTIER

Preface

On the eve of the nation's first half century of television, *Television in America* looks at the unsung pioneering of local stations across the nation. We have commissioned a team of scholars to research the stations, the people, and the programming that made a difference in local communities and in our industry. We have drawn on local-station resources, oral history, and the people who pioneered the stations as our primary sources.

Little has been written about the history of local television, unless the station has had some national significance or a national personality attached to it. The tendency in media history has been to write about prominent people, usually men, and often the industry is examined without giving the general historical context. Broadcast historians tend to examine the field from a national perspective, perhaps due to the national focus of scholarly journals.

We know of no collective work on local television station history. Ted Nielsen, who wrote about early television in Chicago, notes Chicago's first stations, The Chicago Daily news stations: W9XAP; Zenith Radio Corporation's station W9XZV; WBKB; WGN; WENR; and WNBQ.[1] His primary focus is discussion of the factors that led to the decline of Chicago as a national center of television production. Robert R. Smith and Paul T. Prince chronicled the milestones of WHDH from 1947 to 1973.[2] A case study of the Cox Broadcasting Corporations, by Herbert H. Howard, deals with "one of the oldest and largest group owners" in the United States.[3] Howard presents one of the more outstanding historical works as he discusses how the development of Cox has influenced the present, how management's local-station philosophy brought success, and the advantages of group own-

1. Ted Nielsen, "Television: Chicago Style," *Journal of Broadcasting,* 9, 4 (Fall 1965): 305–312.

2. Robert R. Smith and Paul T. Prince, "WHDH: The Unconscionable Delay," *Journal of Broadcasting,* 18, 1 (Winter 1973–74): 85–96.

3. Herbert H. Howard, "Cox Broadcasting Corporation: A Group Ownership Case Study," *Journal of Broadcasting,* 20, 2 (Spring 1976): 209–232.

ership in Cox. In addition, there are several doctoral dissertations and master's theses focusing on local television.

In the *Bibliography of Theses and Dissertations in Broadcasting, 1920–1973*, compiled by John M. Kittross, there are some 56 station histories, but most of them are radio stations. Only 10 of the total focus on *local television* stations: Billeaud, KLFY-TV; Buell, WSAZ-TV; Dewhirst, KSD-TV; Farber, KLPR-TV; Gill, WNYC-TV; Liao, WQED; Lyson, WWJ-TV; Portes, DXTM-TV (Philippines); and Tichter, WTTV-TV.[4] Among the more prominent would be Edwin L. Glick's dissertation on WGBH-TV.[5] Since 1973, dissertation abstracts list several additional studies of local-station news operations. Indeed, news seems to be the topic of local station analysis, but few of these studies are historical.[6] There is only one recent local-station history listed. In it, Mark Williams provides an overview of local television in Los Angeles,[7] a topic he revisits in this work. Earlier, Samuel Smart wrote a descriptive history of the Outlet Corporation in which there are two chapters on WJAR television and radio. It is a chronological history of a corporation that includes television.[8] Lynn Hinds has written on the early years of KDKA television. Although Hind's work focuses on local news, there is a good deal of station history reflected in his important work.[9]

Despite the fact that a few scholars are conducting local-station history in conjunction with dissertation research, little of this work has made its way into the scholarly journals. Yet the development of television has been both local and national. Many successful innovations at local stations have made it to the national scene, where the networks and larger corporate operators often take the credit. For example, one of our authors (chapter 17) points out

4. John M. Kittross, *Bibliography of Theses and Dissertations in Broadcasting, 1920–1973* (Washington, D.C.: Broadcast Education Association, 1978).

5. Edwin L. Glick, "WGBH-TV: The First 10 Years," unpublished Ph.D. dissertation, University of Michigan, 1970.

6. See, for example, John C. Pauly, "Producing Local Television News: An Observational, Historical and Theoretical Study," unpublished Ph.D. dissertation, University of Colorado at Boulder, 1994. Also Joseph Anthony Russomanno, "The Tyranny of the Majority: The Culture of Conformity in the Local Television Newsroom," unpublished Ph.D. dissertation, University of Colorado at Boulder, 1993. Also Choi Yangho, "Process of Parasocial Interaction in Local Television News Watching," unpublished Ph.D. dissertation, University of Florida, 1995.

7. Mark J. Williams, "From Remote Possibilities to Entertaining Difference: A Regional Study of the Rise of Television Industry in Los Angeles, 1930–1952," Ph.D. dissertation, University of Southern California, 1993.

8. Samuel Chipman Smart, *The Outlet Story, 1894–1984* (Providence: Outlet Communication, 1984).

9. Lynn Boyd Hinds, *Broadcasting the Local News: The Early Years of Pittsburgh's KDKA-TV* (University Park, Pa.: Pennsylvania State University Press, 1995).

that Don Lee's system on the West Coast used the first public suitcase remote equipment on March 6, 1940, predating the NBC network remotes by three months. Less than a decade later WMAL offered the NBC network affiliates President Harry Truman's live television debut on October 5, 1947, even though the station was just three days old. The next year WPTZ's remote telecast of the 1948 political convention in Philadelphia provided network coverage for the NBC network.

In *Television in America* you will read about some stations you never realized had significance. Although you may look for some pioneering stations that are not present, there are chapters on some stations we suspect will surprise you. At opposite ends of the spectrum, for example, KTLA, Los Angeles, telecast A-bomb tests from Nevada in April and May of 1952, whereas less than a decade later WHAS, Louisville, telecast open-heart surgery performed by nine doctors from the University of Louisville. Shortly after the WHAS telecast, KSL, Salt Lake City, participated in the first live telecast to Europe, and KING, Seattle, telecast the nation's first locally produced documentaries.

This book identifies and documents pioneering local television stations. It examines some stations that have historical significance locally, extending at times nationally. It provides a brief glimpse of pioneering characters and their characteristics and documents the innovative news, programming and general history within local markets setting the stations within a national context. Our primary objective is the promotion of scholarship on these all important topics.

Preparing this publication was not without its challenges. First, many of the records that could document a station's local history no longer exist. As a result the authors have relied heavily on oral histories, the local press, and whatever documentation was available. The second challenge was one of geography and of accessing primary sources and industry pioneers. Because it could take years for a single author to conduct research in so many regions of the country, the editors turned to scholars, asking them to contribute original essays. The authors were asked to reach beyond the stations identified in today's textbooks to those stations that have truly been pioneers within their locales. Some authors have worked individually, others collectively, exchanging materials wherever they were located. The third challenge was an editorial one—deciding which stations to include and which to exclude. Although these decisions have at times been difficult, in some cases there was not enough information on stations we wanted to include, the editors have worked to assure a broad representation, selecting a cross section of stations with interesting pioneering foundations.

Finally, we faced the challenge of organization. In an effort to meet this challenge the authors were provided with a set of guidelines designed to create uniformity and an effective overall organization for the manuscript. However, each local station presented unique research problems, strategies, and opportunities, and each author approached these problems from a unique perspective. Thus specific guidelines proved, finally, to be of limited value. In general each author has covered station history, first-day broadcasts, pioneer personalities, programming, and news operations. In some cases individuals placed under the microscope in a local context went on to become major national figures. This happened often—for example, WPTZ's Ernie Kovacs and WBBM's Frank Reynolds. The California stations described here, Paramount's KTLA and Don Lee's KCBS of Los Angeles, were network feed stations, as were WBBM in Chicago and WABC in New York, due to market size and advertising-agency involvement.

As the work progressed, it became apparent that there were more commonalities regionally than there were organizationally. The editors have, therefore, organized the material geographically—Part I, The Eastern Establishment; Part II, Southern States; Part III, The Central Heartland; and Part IV, The Western Frontier. We believe this organization provides the greatest ease in reading, as well as the most effective structural continuity.

The editors wish to thank those who made this project possible—in particular, the authors, who have contributed original materials and put up with the editors for the years this project has been in the making.

We acknowledge Janet Soper, Director, Publication Assistance Center, in the College of Public Programs at Arizona State University. Janet and her team have provided the camera-ready copy for this publication as well as much advice along the way. Lori Morgan at the University of Missouri–St. Louis also aided in preparing much of the original copy.

We acknowledge the administration and our colleagues at our respective universities. Their input has always been important. Special thanks to Dr. Douglas Anderson, Fritz Leigh, and ElDean Bennett at Arizona State University, and to Blanche Touhill, Roosevelt Wright, Tom McPhail, and Terry Jones at the University of Missouri–St. Louis.

The authors also wish to thank the staff at Iowa State University Press.

DONALD G. GODFREY
MICHAEL D. MURRAY

Introduction:

Origins of Innovation

Theoretically and technically television may be feasible, [but] commercially and
financially I consider it an impossibility, a development of which we need waste
little time dreaming.

LEE DE FOREST, 1926[1]

The "Inventors" of Television

The evolution of television began over 100 years ago. It was not the
invention of a single individual, but the evolution of theory and technology
mixed with fierce competitiveness as some developers recognized the experiments as potentially profitable.

In 1873 Englishmen Joseph May and Willoughby Smith discovered
that light falling on photosensitive elements produced a small amount of
energy. G.R. Cary, in 1887, developed an electronic proposal paralleling
systems of the human eye. Not far from Cary's work in Boston, Alexander
Graham Bell first tried to use light in the transmission of human voice. Bell's
experiments produced a system that was a forerunner to the facsimile.[2] It was
the French who first used the principle of "scanning." Scientist Maurice
Leblanc developed the scanning system to improve picture quality. In 1883
a German scientist, Paul Nipkow, developed the mechanical scanning device. The idea of scanning produced several mechanical apparatuses, some
of which hung around until the mid-1940s.

---

1. Lee de Forest, "Bad Predications," reprinted in *Parade Magazine*, September 10, 1995, p.
16.
2. "Far-Off Speakers Seen As Well As Heard Here in a Test of Television," *New York Times*,
April 8, 1927, p. 1.

The inventors primarily responsible for today's system were Baird, Jenkins, Farnsworth, and Zworykin. These people were our 20th-century pioneers.

According to George Shiers, the first public demonstration of television was conducted by John Logie Baird of Great Britain.[3] The demonstration, conducted in March 1925, was held at Selfridge's Oxford Street department store. It was a crude but exciting display, which attracted attention in the United States.[4] A science reporter in attendance noted the "rather blurred, image of simple forms." Baird himself called it "astonishingly crude," but he also described it as an "outstanding miracle."[5] He named his apparatus the "televisor." Baird had conducted numerous tests, starting in the early '20s, with a mechanical scanning apparatus. His work almost became the English standard, but it was turned aside by the British government in favor of an electronic scanning system.[6]

Charles Francis Jenkins was not far behind Baird in his television experimentation. Jenkins was an independent inventor and known in the United States as founder of the Society of Motion Picture Engineers.[7] In the early 1920s Jenkins was experimenting with what he called "Prismatic Rings." These were rotating disks similar to Baird's. Jenkins referred to his work as "radio photographs, radio movies and radio vision."[8] Jenkins's first public demonstration came just three months after Baird's, in June 1925. This demonstration, according to Shiers, was not as crude as was Baird's.[9] Jenkins had arranged for an influential gathering of visitors from the Washington area to witness the events in his laboratory on Connecticut Avenue. The result produced glowing reviews in the press.[10] He continued with further demonstrations over the next few weeks, giving his work a good deal of publicity.

3. George Shiers, "Television 50 Years Ago," *Journal of Broadcasting*, 19, 4 (Fall 1975): 387–399. For a detailed "prehistory" of television see Albert Abramson, *The History of Television, 1880–1941* (Jefferson, N. C.: McFarland, 1987), pp. 1–23.

4. Shiers, p. 389.

5. J.L. Baird, "Television, or Seeing by Wireless," *Discovery*, 6, 142 (April 1925): 143.

6. Christopher H. Sterling and John M. Kittross, *Stay Tuned: A Concise History of American Broadcasting*, 2nd ed. (Belmont, Calif.: Wadsworth, 1990), p. 100. See also Ronald Tiltman, *Baird of Television* (London: Seeley Service, 1933), and Tom McArthur and Peter Waddell, *The Secret Life of John Logie Baird* (London: Century Hutchinson, 1986).

7. See his autobiography: C.F. Jenkins, *The Boyhood of an Inventor* (Washington: Jenkins Laboratories, 1931).

8. See numerous articles authored by C.F. Jenkins in *Transactions of the SMPE* 1922–25.

9. Shiers, p. 390.

10. See C.A. Herndon, "Motion Pictures by Ether Waves," *Popular Radio*, 8, 107 (August 1925): 113. Also W.B. Arvin, "See With Your Radio," *Radio News*, 7, 278 (September 1925): 384–387.

In the early 1920s Baird and Jenkins set the stage. At this time television reached a critical point in its development—it was becoming recognized as a potentially profitable technology. As a result the larger electronic media began to take an interest: General Electric, AT&T, Philco, RCA, and later Farnsworth Radio and Television would all eventually overshadow television's earlier individual inventors.

Philo Taylor Farnsworth and Vladimir Kosma Zworykin have both been contestants for the title "father of television." Who should be credited as "father" of the invention is a discussion left to other scholars.[11] It is sufficient for this discussion to note that the real competitive battles for television and patent rights were yet ahead for both of these pioneers, and they would both make substantial contributions to the American system of television. Again, television was not the invention of an individual, but the evolution of technology and competitive business entrepreneurs.

Farnsworth's story is a fascinating one. He first drew an electronic schematic for his high-school chemistry teacher. That drawing was later a turning point in a patent suit between RCA and Farnsworth Television. Farnsworth's experiments began in 1926 in San Francisco, where his company, Farnsworth Television, was first organized. While in San Francisco, Farnsworth electronically scanned and telecast, in the laboratory, the image of a photograph of a young woman.[12] The demonstration took place September 7, 1927. It might have taken place earlier, but when an investor learned Farnsworth was going to use a line picture of a triangle and a dollar sign, he persuaded the inventor to postpone the experiment until a "real photograph" could be utilized.[13] Today, though all of the Farnsworth patents have long expired, the Farnsworth papers claim that every set sold in America has over six of his patents in some form.[14]

---

11. See T. Ropp, "Philo Farnsworth: Forgotten Father of Television," *Media History Digest,* 5, 2 (Summer 1985): 42–58; Stephen F. Hofer, "Philo Farnsworth: Television's Pioneer," *Journal of Broadcasting,* 23, 2 (1979): 153; George Everson, *The Story of Television: The Life of Philo T. Farnsworth* (New York: W.W. Norton, 1949). Popular-press debate over the title is illustrated by Frank Lovece, "Zworykin v. Farnsworth," *Video,* 9 (September 1985): 96–98, 135–138. See also "Open Mike" letters in *Broadcasting,* January 13, 1992, p. 108; February 3, 1992, p. 46; February 17, 1992, p. 53; Albert Abramson, *Zworykin: Pioneer of Television* (Urbana: University of Illinois Press, 1995), pp. 1–5.

12. Philo T. Farnsworth and Larry Lubcke, "The Transmission of Television Images," *California Engineer,* 8, 5 (1930): 12–33.

13. Everson, p. 94.

14. Farnsworth Prospectus, p. 17. In the Farnsworth/Meeks Papers at the Arizona State University, Hayden Library Special Collections.

Farnsworth's career and business enterprises put him in direct competition with the giant Radio Corporation of America. He, with his associates, organized Farnsworth Radio and Television for purpose of research, manufacture, and sale of radio and television receivers. They set up two television stations in Philadelphia and Fort Wayne, Indiana (see Chapter 3, WPTZ Philadelphia). Farnsworth was not only an inventor—he was a forward thinker. Unfortunately, the competition between Farnsworth and RCA was, as described by Farnsworth's wife, Elma, a "David and Goliath" confrontation—only in this situation Goliath won the free-enterprise war for corporate dominance of television.[15] Farnsworth was struggling against the well-entrenched media corporations of the time. He had little financial backing, whereas RCA had the much larger budget, laboratory, and public-relations machinery. For example, in 1935, while Farnsworth was reorganizing for the third time since 1927, RCA announced it was setting aside $1 million for public demonstrations of its television system.[16]

Vladimir K. Zworykin was Farnsworth's chief competitor. In charge of RCA's television development, he worked with the support of David Sarnoff and the substantial backing of RCA. Zworykin was a Russian immigrant who was first employed by Westinghouse but moved to RCA when the company showed greater interest in the development of a television system. The backing of Sarnoff and the RCA corporation provided Zworykin with a strong foundation for his work through the difficult years of the Depression and World War II. In 1929 Zworykin met with Sarnoff and convinced him that he, Zworykin, could complete television in two years and for a hundred thousand dollars. This was a significant underestimate, but Sarnoff concluded that such a development would place RCA well ahead of competitors.[17] Zworykin's idea was, in reality, the beginning of an extended and costly research-development program in electronic television. He visited the labs of both Baird and Farnsworth.[18] Because Zworykin and Farnsworth were both working with electrical scanning systems, they later found themselves embroiled in patent-interference cases. Again, it was a David-and-

15. Elma G. Farnsworth, *Distant Vision: Romance and Discovery on an Invisible Frontier* (Salt Lake City: Pemberly Kent, 1989), pp. 128–134, 153–158. See also Kenneth Bilby, *The General: David Sarnoff and the Rise of the Communications Industry* (New York: Harper and Row, 1985), p. 128.

16. Erik Barnouw, *Tube of Plenty: The Evolution of American Television* (New York: Oxford University Press, 1975), p. 76.

17. Abramson, pp. 76–77.

18. Hofer, p. 153.

Goliath situation but David won this smaller battle. Zworykin's work was demonstrated at the 1939 New York World's Fair and, with the force of RCA behind him, became the most powerful innovator in the history of television.

The Industry Investment and the Government

As technology began promising the prospect of profitability, competition increased among developers and major growing corporations. Farnsworth Television's first proposed signal, a dollar sign, is symbolic of the prospects everyone believed lay ahead. Zworykin himself had left Westinghouse for RCA because of the promise of stronger financial backing. However, the capital investment required for television was significant, and throughout the Depression development was somewhat inhibited. The market crash of 1929 and its aftermath made financing a difficult task. Still, there were those who wanted to "cash in" on this new gadget called television. General Electric, with Ernst F. W. Alexanderson as chief television engineer, experimented with the mechanical scanning system. AT&T warned its competitors about the sole proprietorship of AT&T patents.[19] The company was experimenting under the leadership of Herbert E. Ives, one of the Bell Laboratories' scientists. RCA had no laboratory until the late 1920s but was active in research and did take out licenses for three experimental stations. Philco started its own television work in 1928, but activities were modest until Farnsworth was hired in 1931. The Allen Du Mont Laboratories were organized in 1931.[20]

Television evolved as radio began to mature. Headlines of the popular press touted the marvels of a number of new inventions—telegraphy, the telephone, phonograph, and radio. Television was the latecomer trying to obtain a position on the "roaring '20s prosperity bandwagon." All of this was to television's advantage—the new technologies were at least somewhat related and later provided significant financing for television's developments. This is especially true at the local-market level, where it was often

---

19. Barnouw, pp. 48–49.
20. Andrew F. Inglis, *Behind the Tube: A History of Broadcasting Technology and Business* (Boston: Focal Press, 1990), pp. 165–166. See also Abramson, p. 60. See William E. Denk, "An Elusive Frame of Television History," *The AWA Review*, 4 (1989): 99–109; and Allen B. Du Mont Papers at the Library of Congress and National Museum of American History, Archives Divisions.

the AM radio station that took out the television license and funded its earliest operation.

Television in the '20s and '30s was first and foremost experimental. It existed in the labs of RCA, Farnsworth Television, Philco, Bell Telephone, Du Mont, and later CBS. From the labs it moved on to the experimental-station phase—operating with experimental call letters. Sarnoff wanted FM as a television sound system, not something to replace his AM radio network stations.

Regulatory efforts and discussions preceding proposed regulation—the 1927 Radio Act and the 1934 Communications Act—focused primarily on radio and sought to organize the spectrum and establish technological standards. At the same time the radio industry requested legislation to "clear the air." Radio was growing rapidly and developing operational patterns—the patterns we take for granted today. Most of the media attention of the 1920s and 1930s went toward radio as the new entertainment medium, as governmental debate sought to establish the rules and regulations for its operation. The radio industry continued to grow rapidly.

The Federal Radio Commission's interest in television was purely technical, as was that of the Federal Communications Commission. In 1927 the FCC was busy parceling out a balanced system of frequency distribution for radio, but there was consideration of what was ahead for television.[21] By 1937 interest and development had grown significantly, and the commission held frequency-allocation hearings to determine where this new technology would be placed on the spectrum. It decided that although applications for experimental stations would still be accepted, television was far from ready for national distribution. In other words, the FCC wasn't moving at the same pace as experimentation; it desired slow and studied introspection before the commercial development of television. The industry reacted, with RCA in the lead, by pressing the FCC for standards and terms.

The adoption of these standards was important to industry because such guidelines would dictate how equipment would be manufactured. Developers were reluctant to invest capital in a system that might not be adopted. The FCC's slow pace resulted in considerable frustration. Developers criticized the commission for being slow to establish television standards; those ready to manufacture and distribute television were stymied while others were

---

21. Federal Communications Commission, "The Evolution of Television 1927–1943," *Journal of Broadcasting*, 4, 3 (Summer 1960): 199–207. The journal editor prefaces this article by noting the bias it shows toward RCA.

given the opportunity to catch up. Farnsworth, for example, at the end of the
'30s, had won the patent interference case with RCA, thus forcing RCA to
agree to Farnsworth's terms in the acquisition of his patents. Some considered this a significant victory for Farnsworth, and indeed it was. However,
it was also a success for RCA: With access to Farnsworth's patents, RCA
was ready to push forward again toward standardization with the FCC.

RCA was ready to go. Not only did it have the system prepared to push
into commercial operation, it had also been competitively successful in
persuading the Radio Manufacturer Association to adopt its standards for
production manufacturing. This development did not sit well with RCA's
competitors. Farnsworth Television accused RCA of refusing to sell it parts
for manufacturing. The company saw RCA's actions as a competitive move
to put it out of the manufacturing business.[22] Here, again, RCA was aggressive, and its rivals were intimidated.

The FCC did not move with the speed and optimism of the inventors
or the manufacturers. In 1939 the commission recommended a delay in the
adoption of television standards. It wanted to study the situation further to
assure itself that the adopted system would be in the public interest. In 1940,
under increasing pressure from the industry, FCC chairman James Lawrence
Fly appointed the National Television System Committee to study the
standards and make recommendations to the commission. One year later the
commission adopted the recommendations of the NTSC for industrywide
operation.

World War II Brings a Halt

World War II virtually halted the development of television. As the
war approached, the companies that had been developing television switched
their emphasis from development to wartime sales. One hundred percent of
their efforts went into the production of precision military-communications
equipment, a far more profitable enterprise.

Before the war the FCC had authorized the operation of 32 experimental stations.[23] However, station construction, along with the manufacturing
of receivers, was restricted by wartime regulation, and by the end of the war

---

22. Elma G. Farnsworth, pp. 128–134; 153–158.
23. Inglis, p. 185.

only six stations were on the air, with a total of only nine authorized.[24] Most of these stations operated a few hours a day, if that, as there were few receivers on the market. It was almost impossible to acquire either parts or trained personnel, most of whom were involved in the production of defense materials.

The Freeze, and the Sixth Report and Order

At the end of the war there was renewed enthusiasm and competition to get on the air. The influx of television-license applications from 1946 to 1948 grew from the nine authorized stations to 303 pending applications and 123 authorized applications (12 licensed, 25 on-air construction permits, and 86 outstanding CPs).[25] Realizing that the current frequency-allocation system was insufficient, and taking note of other pressing issues, such as educational allocations, UHF, and color television, the FCC issued its "freeze." The order, coming September 20, 1948, again halted further expansion of television stations while the FCC considered allocation issues. This was a brief boon to the existing stations as they operated without competition, but frustrating to those who anxiously awaited FCC decisions before they could go on the air. According to Pepper, "By the end of the freeze there were only 108 authorized television stations, all on the air, 96 of which were fully licensed. In 1972, 106 of these original 108 were still telecasting ... two of the stations were taken over by educational broadcasters.... These 108 were distributed in 63 markets ... [and] all but three ... were in the top 100 markets."[26]

Of all the major corporations CBS gained the most from the hiatus, including competitive equilibrium with RCA. Although the decisions to be rendered from the freeze were primarily those of allocation, the issue of color television was also of importance. The CBS engineers, with Peter Goldmark as senior, put forward a mechanical color-reproduction system just as RCA was beginning to place monochrome receivers on the market. However, because of the incompatibility of the CBS color system with RCA's mono-

24. Robert Pepper, "The Pre-Freeze Television Stations," in Lawrence W. Lichty and Malachi C. Topping, eds., *American Broadcasting: A Source Book on the History of Radio and Television* (New York: Hastings House, 1975), pp. 140, 148.

25. Pepper, p. 140.

26. Pepper, p. 141.

chrome sets, CBS reasoned that, with RCA black-and-white sets already in the marketplace, its color system would be precluded. The CBS strategy was to acquire FCC approval for its color system, thus blocking RCA's sale of receivers. This approach resulted in a second battle for broadcast standards—color standard versus black and white. Although CBS played the role of underdog, RCA already had the support of the manufacturers, and its public-relations and manufacturing machinery was in place. RCA knew well how to compete and win in the marketplace.

Eventually, however, the FCC approved CBS's color system (October 1950), then rescinded its order approving the RCA system (December 1953). Although CBS had lost the initial battle for the adoption of its color system, it did gain the time it needed to become competitive with RCA once the standards were announced. The technological and regulatory foundations for television had thus been laid. In 1952 there were 108 commercial stations on the air, and growth was rapid. By 1954 the number had more than doubled to 354.[27]

The freeze was lifted April 11, 1952, after nearly four years of frustration and contentious debate. The FCC's Sixth Report and Order lead to the establishment of standards that form the foundation of the system we have today. The spectrum space was allocated for commercial television, with special channels set aside for educational telecasting. The number of VHF (very high frequency) channels allocated to most cities was increased (Channels 2–13), and the FCC opened an additional 70 UHF (ultrahigh frequency) channels for commercial licensing. Individual allocations were made on a city-by-city basis, providing both VHF and UHF assignments. The end of the freeze was a major turning point in television's history. The industry was now on its way, with somewhat of a firm footing and business operational patterns in place as well. The issues of technological development, financing, and regulation were for the most part resolved. Programming for a growing audience was the next challenge.

From Local-Station Programming to the Network

Television had a significant advantage in the development of its programming—existing radio programs and local radio stations. The busi-

---

27. Sterling and Kittross, pp. 632–633.

ness of radio set the patterns of operation for television, both locally and nationally. Radio networks became radio-TV networks. Television's personnel were largely trained in radio. Radio stations became combined AM-TV-FM operations as radio stations took out television licenses and provided financial support for both the early networks and individual stations. The local operational patterns of radio were adapted to and superimposed on early television stations. According to Pepper, "of the 108 pre-freeze television stations [on the air] ... 82% were held by radio licensees."[28] Many radio pioneers were also television pioneers. The next-most-important source of income and support was from the manufacturers. "Nine ... manufacturers owned 18 of the pre-freeze stations."[29]

Early television-programming innovations are legion—demonstrations, motion pictures, cooking, sports—and, of course, radio's golden age was a national program resource. Shiers referred to Baird's early experiments as "the first television show."[30] Actually, this "show" was a demonstration arranged for members of the British Royal Institution.[31] Programming that existed during the experimental stages was limited largely to demonstration and display—people were simply interested in the new marvel of television—and demonstration usually consisted of little more than the transmission of a photograph or an object in motion, displayed for purposes of attracting publicity and financial backing.

Programming had a long way to grow to hold its audience. One person who was questioned about his reaction to the 1939 World's Fair television demonstration responded "Who wants to watch people make speeches? That's not entertainment."[32] As development moved from laboratory-styled experiments to staged public demonstrations, the first experimental television stations became established. Their programming hours were limited to a few hours each day, including the transmission of a lot of test-pattern and still imagery, but grew along with transmission capability and the number of receivers in the homes.

The design of the early television studios reflects the considerable awareness that television, like radio, was to be first and foremost an enter-

---

28. Pepper, p. 143.
29. Pepper, p. 144.
30. Shiers, pp. 393–394.
31. "Inventor Describes His Radio Motion Pictures. Televisor Lets Radio Fans Look In as Well as Listen," *New York Times,* April 25, 1926, sec. 9, 17:1–3.
32. Orrin E. Dunlap, Jr., *The Future of Television* (New York: Harper and Brothers, 1947), pp. 118–119.

tainment business. The first studios were large and, like most radio facilities, elaborate. Constructed to produce live programming, they emphasized audio control, lighting and smooth camera movement. Writing in 1942 and again in 1947, Dunlap talks about the "television programs that click." Citing a BBC study of the time, he declared the audiences of London to be "quite similar" to those throughout the United States. The Londoners, he argued, wanted "plays and variety programs direct from the theatres, news reels ... the weekly topical magazine and light entertainment.... Outside broadcast of sporting and other events come next, followed by full length plays, cartoon films, demonstrations and talks."[33] Early studios and technology were designed basically to meet these programming needs, as well as to perfect picture quality.

Much of what has been written about the early years of television makes it appear that programming was instituted from the top down—that is to say, it descended from the networks to the local stations. We too easily forget that a network is merely the contractual relationship between local stations. In truth the local stations were innovative. Many network programs were not borrowed from the Hollywood movie reels or radio, but were taken from local success stories. Local stations experimented and were often successful. Their programs grew, and some eventually became the network programs we have come to know, such as KSL's "The Mormon Tabernacle Choir," now a CBS-network broadcast. "Boston Blackie" became the first locally produced dramatic show originating with WLWT.[34] Local as well as national programs were an important part of a television station's operation. Although some programs appealed only to local audiences, others would move on and succeed nationally.

There were several mainstays in early programming: talk, kids' programming, sports and the motion picture.[35] Samuel Goldwyn reported in 1949 that the motion-picture industry was on the verge of its third era: "First there was the silent period, then the sound era. Now we are on the threshold of the television age."[36] Many local stations, and experimental ones as well, used the motion picture, especially shorts, to fill time within their brief program schedules. KCBS, Los Angeles—during Don Lee television years

33. Dunlap, pp. 48–49.

34. See Chapter 9 in this volume.

35. Harrison B. Summers, "Programming for Television," *Quarterly Journal of Speech,* 31 (1945): 44–47.

36. Samuel Goldwyn, "Hollywood in the Television Age," *New York Times Magazine,* February 13, 1946, pp. 15, 44, 47.

—programmed over 10 million feet of motion-picture film the seven years it was on the air.[37]

In the case of many local stations those on the air first had the distinct advantage to develop a strong affiliate relationship, a talent base, film resources, and live local programming—something beyond a test pattern. The actual expansion of the broadcast program schedule usually coincided with efforts to promote the sale of television sets. Local bars invested in sets to broadcast sporting events and to lure potential male viewers. A sometimes disproportionate number of first-day broadcasts from around the country featured wrestling or professional boxing matches surrounded, of course, by a lot of talk and ceremony. Sports grew from these local beginnings to national telecasts of football, baseball, and even bowling.[38]

Programs for homemakers and children were usually next in priority. Cooking shows were the first offerings and predate the soap-opera genre. Cartoons for the children were from Hollywood and were ready-made resources for stations in need of children's programming. The syndicated cartoons were mixed with a local clown or a colorful, fun-loving host who entertained a live children's audience and provided transitions between cartoons. These first children's programs introduced today's baby-boom generation to cartoons and comedy shorts "Our Gang," the "Three Stooges," or "Bugs Bunny" were introduced by someone called Bozo, Cookie, Corkie, Captain, Cowboy Bill, or Texas Joe. These were augmented by the national programs such as "Howdy Doody," "Kukla, Fran and Ollie," and eventually "The Mickey Mouse Club." The local program riveted the attention of its audience to the "idiot box," watching live performances and sometimes going in as a group of scouts or a school class to participate firsthand in the program. These programs produced interaction between the community and the local station long before the word "interactive" was popular.

In most markets television news programs today account for a substantial element of the station income. This has not always been the case, but television news is an important part of most stations' histories as well as their involvement in the community. According to Nielsen, news programming began with the experimental stations of the 1930s.[39] He claims that the first television news special was broadcast on WCBW, New York—a nine-hour

---

37. See Chapter 17 in this volume.
38. Barnouw, pp. 347–350.
39. Ted Nielsen, "A History of Network Television News," in Lawrence W. Lichty and Malachi C. Topping, eds., *American Broadcasting: A Source Book on the History of Radio and Television* (New York: Hastings House, 1975), p. 421.

report on Pearl Harbor. "At that time the CBS station was the only TV subscriber to the United Press radio wire and had a news staff of two."[40] Nielsen doesn't elaborate on how the station accomplished that feat but does note that it broadcast two news programs daily on a regular basis. Not until 1948 did a network schedule a regular news program in its lineup—CBS-TV News with Douglas Edwards. The "NBC Newsreel," featuring John Cameron Swayze, began in 1949 and was soon followed by similar network offerings on ABC and Du Mont. At the local level, television news was usually conducted by just one or two people. These folks made up the news departments, shot the film, edited the wire copy, kept the assignment-desk files current, and produced and anchored the news programs.

News began to be financially successful at a local level during the '60s. WABC was instrumental in developing a format that spread to local stations throughout the nation—"action news." It was known by different titles—"Eyewitness News," "Action News," "Happy Talk"—but introduced a faster-paced, localized format to the audience. Critics today call it tabloid and often blame the social science research news consultants for its spread. However, clearly this local development has today become a major program genre.

The '60s and '70s marked the beginning of a number of trends that transferred the power base from the network to the local station. Technology and deregulation placed emphasis on the marketplace—a marketplace both local and national. The technology of satellite, electronic news gathering (ENG), and electronic field production (EFP) helped pass the control from the network to the local stations. Heretofore the local station had been dependent upon the network to cover a nationally breaking news story. The local station acquired its visual material from the network via the evening news and material fed to the station as delayed electronic feeds (DEFs). Occasionally a local station would provide a news feed to the network—you see these reports credited at the end of a network news feed. Today, however, the local station, via satellite and ENG/EFP technology, can cover a story no matter where it occurs. For example, almost every major-market local station in the country had a reporter "live" in Los Angeles at the O.J. Simpson trial—the control was local.

Local stations today use their elaborate production facilities not only to produce news, but to create material for syndication. The talk shows, "produced in the facilities of ...," are delivered via satellite rather than

---

40. Nielsen, p. 421.

through the network. In effect, an alternative "network" is established contractually—contracts to produce, contracts to perform, contracts to deliver and distribute, all link local independent and traditional affiliate local stations.

Summary

As the nation approaches its first half century of television, scholars have often overlooked the importance of the local station in the foundations of our history. Television began as an individual's scientific theory. People such as Cary, Bell, Leblanc, Nipkow, Baird, Jenkins, Farnsworth, and Zworykin developed experiments based on the transmission and reproduction of electromagnetic energy. Their experiments often received a great deal of press attention—they were described as crude, yet miraculous.

As these scientists began to realize the potential profit in their experiments, large corporations began to take an interest and provided the necessary financial backing. The experiments grew from simple demonstrations to the establishment of experimental stations—those stations with an X in their call letters. These experimental stations were key stations, and they were local stations. They served a local audience as they experimented with technology and programming in the hope of expanding. Key stations owned by the networks (RCA/NBC, CBS, and ABC) became production centers for the network as well as stations licensed to, and serving, their own communities. Key stations were not always experimental or network owned and operated (O&Os). WPTZ, Philadelphia, was a key station in the development of Philco television. WGL, Fort Wayne, was a key station in the development of Farnsworth Television. WABC, New York, was a key station in the development of the ABC network. KSD was key to Pulitzer Broadcasting, just as KSL was to Bonneville. These stations acted as experimental and developmental operations for those with a vested interest in television. Here, again, they served as centers of experimentation as well as local stations serving local interests.

Radio played an important role in the development of television. Radio was the new medium of the era, maturing as television was just beginning to evolve. The technologies were obviously related, and as a result of radio's interest in television many of the first local stations across the nation were underwritten by the profits from a successful radio operation. Radio stations took on the burden of financial support for both the early stations as well as the networks. The local operational patterns of radio were superimposed on television; they became AM-FM-TV combined operations. Early talent, technology, and business operations were easily adapted from radio to television.

The government also played an important role in the development of television, although not at the pace many experimenters had hoped. The FCC was slow to adopt television standards; it wanted to make sure its actions would result in the public's best interest. The FCC's pace resulted in considerable frustration. Corporations ready to manufacture and distribute sets were stymied while others were given the opportunity to catch up. RCA was clearly ahead of CBS, but by the end of the freeze CBS had caught up and was ready to compete.

The programming innovations of local television are legion. Much of what has been written about those early years would make it appear that everything emanated from the network and was passed on to local stations. In reality, however, many programs and personalities were successful at the local level before they were nationally distributed.

As we approach our first half century of television, *Television in America* looks at the history of an industry from a local point of view. There are some interesting ramifications: What would have happened to the ABC network without the support of its key station, WABC? What effect did KSL television have on the Mormon Church communication empire? Can stations in Atlanta and Orlando be credited with promoting a civil-rights agenda before it was politically correct? Would the Kefauver hearings have taken on as much national significance had it not been for the local coverage of WMAL-TV? Without the efforts of WEWS's Dorothy Fuldheim and Nancy Craig at WABC, would women have been welcomed in the nation's newsrooms?

These questions represent surface inquiry. Some are addressed here; for others we have worked to set the stage of scholarly inquiry.

DONALD G. GODFREY
MICHAEL D. MURRAY

The Eastern Establishment

1

Tackling the TV Titans in Their Own Backyard: WABC-TV, New York City

Craig Allen

WABC-TV (Channel 7) in New York City made a difference in television history because without it the American Broadcasting Company may not have survived. Beginning as a stepchild in the early development of radio and television, ABC went on to become the world's largest broadcast organization, with assets valued at $15 billion at the time of its merger with the Disney corporation in 1995. The story behind ABC's success begins with WABC, its flagship station, which contributed creative and financial energy during many troubled years at this network. ABC began television operations in 1948 as a footnote to the then vastly larger and more sophisticated activities of CBS and NBC. Well into the 1970s what many called the "Almost Broadcasting Company" had yet to emerge competitively. However, while the ABC network trailed nationally during this period, WABC-TV flourished in New York City. WABC was the company's first, and for a time only, significant profit center. In the late 1970s and early 1980s WABC had the largest audience of any television station in the United States. Year after year WABC generated the revenues that helped keep alive ABC's unprofitable network operations. On two occasions it helped the network surmount potentially catastrophic financial crises. Perhaps more important, WABC was a psychological oasis for the people of ABC. In New York, where all three networks were based, ABC employees saw themselves not as hopeless underdogs, but as figurative Davids capable of leveling the two TV Goliaths, an outcome they eventually accomplished. In no small way

WABC's success made it possible for viewers everywhere in the country to have three television alternatives from the inception of the medium.

Only recently have authors found relevance in ABC's rags-to-riches evolution. For years Sterling Quinlan's *Inside ABC* stood alone against dozens of histories hailing CBS and NBC. Then, in 1991 Ken Auletta inspired new thinking when his best-selling book *Three Blind Mice* characterized ABC as an emerging beacon of stability next to the two pioneer broadcast networks, which were experiencing audience erosion and seemed unprepared during a period of widespread industry upheaval. More was learned that year when ABC chair Leonard Goldenson published his memoirs, appropriately entitled *Beating the Odds*, and detailed the network's intense interest in cultivating relations with local broadcasters. Whereas CBS and NBC, years earlier, had rapidly enlisted affiliates, ABC had to work to build its affiliate chain, the ensuing struggle, according to Goldenson, proving the key to ABC's dominance. Starting with WABC, the network touted a shirtsleeves corporate culture and a willingness to assume risks, which made ABC seem to its affiliates as much a local operation as a major national network. In the late 1970s a former WABC general manager named Richard Beesemyer would effect one of ABC's major corporate maneuvers when he coaxed several key CBS and NBC stations to drop their affiliations and join ABC. Both Auletta and Goldenson gave considerable attention to ABC's merger with Capital Cities in 1985, a year that saw both CBS and NBC merge with nonbroadcast entities. That Capital Cities, like ABC, was a group owner of local TV stations and possessed a similar grassroots orientation accounted for ABC's stability in the years preceding the 1995 merger with Disney.

For most of ABC's history WABC was a lively slice of the company's grassroots traditions. WABC's sister local stations in Chicago, Los Angeles, Detroit, and San Francisco, also were integral to the network's emergence, yet particularly WABC reflected the spirit of this maverick organization. Its competitors having entered television as inventors of the medium, the ABC network sprang not from laboratories but from the studios of its first station in New York. Austerity forced the early WABC to depart from the path taken by New York's CBS and NBC stations, then involved in nationalizing programs for network distribution, and to opt for local programs. Although it eventually did absorb much national fare, and its image changed after Capital Cities' arrival, for a long time WABC was to New Yorkers the "home station." This status was best illustrated by WABC's pathbreaking local news programs, which abandoned the national-international "big journalism" priorities of CBS and NBC and stressed events that unfolded on the streets of New York, although dubiously, in the view of many critics.

Early Ingenuity

It is safe to say that no American television station was associated with more inventiveness than WABC. It demonstrated some of this ingenuity before it had even gone on the air, when engineers arranged for its FCC license. It also would set trends in the selling of local programs to sponsors. WABC's programming, though, was its signature. Few of its early programs were award winners. Indeed, as the local television station that critics loved to hate, WABC may have been in a class by itself. Yet WABC's programs meant something to the New York audience, notably the millions who lived in Brooklyn, Queens, and the Bronx, who by and large were of the working class and diverse ethnically and in many other ways. Although the entire history of WABC was one of moving toward the establishment, it left an antiestablishment tradition. It was exactly this tradition that New Yorkers, throughout the 200-year evolution of mass media in their city, had always been quick to embrace.

All of this had begun in the late 1940s, when a nascent ABC faced not two, but three, network television rivals. Each of them—CBS, NBC, and Du Mont—had moved into television from an engineering direction, their owned stations in New York having started as experimental facilities for the testing and eventual manufacture of television sets and videotechnology. With no laboratories or production lines, no network division, no affiliates, and few television assets, the first dollars ABC spent on television were used to construct WABC. WABC was outfitted with equipment purchased from RCA, NBC's parent company, and thus, as ABC scraped to make the payments, the proceeds helped boost one of its primary competitors. WABC did begin with some engineering foresight, although not the type CBS, NBC, or Du Mont had envisioned. Its first key figure was chief engineer Frank Marx, who perceived the importance of local television in ABC's eventual fortunes. With ABC, formerly the NBC Blue radio network, only four years old, Marx requested from the FCC the licenses for what would become WABC and its four sister stations. When these applications were submitted in 1947, Marx had not consulted ABC owner Edward Noble and was fired for insubordination, Noble fearing these TV licenses would sink the flagging radio network. Yet, as Marx told the story, he was soon rehired once his coup was realized.[1] Noble had been angry at Marx mainly for his failure to negotiate for channel positions at the low end of the television dial. Instead, Marx took an easy course of applying for Channel 7 in New York and elsewhere. This seemed risky even to Marx, who was wagering the FCC would transfer to the military all the low-end frequencies through Channel 6, thus leaving Channel 7 as "Channel 1" in all five cities. Although the FCC backed away from the military designation of Channels 2–6, Marx's quick action gave ABC control of TV stations in five of the six largest markets, together covering 25 percent of the national audience. CBS and NBC never were able to achieve comparable local coverage with their owned stations. Besides WABC, the other ABC-owned stations included WLS (initially WBKB) in Chicago, KABC (initially KECA) in Los Angeles, WXYZ in Detroit, and KGO in San Francisco. Marx completed the feat by having all five on the air by the end of 1949.

ABC's advantage from these licenses at first existed only on paper. Ultimately, a crippling expense to Noble was the $8.5 million needed to start the far-flung television operations. Three million dollars was earmarked for WABC, the envisioned origination point of network programs. WABC began by renting studio and warehouse space at a dozen Manhattan locations before consolidating as best it could into four buildings on West 66th Street near Central Park. Hardly ultramodern, the main building was previously the horse stable for the Manhattan Riding Club.[2] Channel 7 initially beamed from a 43-story hotel, its signal blocked by taller structures. It was not until late 1949 that WABC could afford transmitter placement at the Empire State Building, even then not at the top, where NBC was located, but on the 86th floor.[3]

Symbolic of the station's obstacles was the humdrum reception New Yorkers gave its premier on August 10, 1948. WABC, until 1953 with the call letters WJZ, may have been the lone TV station, among the 30 in the United States to sign on in 1948, not to be received with excitement and fanfare. WABC staged its opening festivities on a Tuesday night, when three-fourths of New York's 350,000 television owners regularly tuned to

---

1. Leonard H. Goldenson, *Beating the Odds* (New York: Charles Scribner's Sons, 1991), pp. 98–99.
2. "TV Center Rising off Central Park," *New York Times*, Oct. 28, 1956, p. VIII-8.
3. "Inside Television," *Variety*, Oct. 12, 1949, p. 33.

the Milton Berle comedy show on Channel 4. Moreover, there were five other stations already on the air. NBC-owned Channel 4 was the top-rated station—at first with the call letters WNBT, later WNBC. A close second on Channel 2 was CBS-owned WCBS—initially WCBW. On Channel 5 was the base of the Du Mont network, WNYW—initially WABD. On Channel 11 was WPIX, the New York's first independent station. In addition, on Channel 13 was the second independent, an off-and-on outlet called WATV. A seventh New York station, WOR, began a year later on Channel 9.[4]

At few points in its history was ABC's free-wheeling managerial philosophy more evident and productive than when WABC stepped onto this competitive minefield in late 1948. As near as can be determined, the network's decentralized chain of command was not preordained. To the contrary, Noble had given orders expressing his desire to establish WABC as a staging facility for national attractions, as had WNBC with Berle and Phil Silvers, and WCBS with Ed Sullivan and Arthur Godfrey. Yet, as Noble would concede in 1951 and 1952 in hearings that preceded his sale of ABC, he lacked the resources to direct his station that way.[5] In the meantime Noble and most top network officials, including Mark Woods and Robert Kintner, the first ABC presidents, were so consumed by efforts to raise capital that they allowed those closest to the programming process to do fairly as they pleased. Network executives apparently sensed they had little to lose. "Fear of failing was never ABC's problem," recalled Sterling Quinlan, one of its first local managers. "You were already third among three and had only one way to go and that was up."[6] That the first management team at WABC made good in this liberal corporate environment helped guarantee its longevity.

This team consisted of general manager Murray Grabhorn, sales manager Clarence Doty, program manager Alex Stronach, and Marx. While these figures were instrumental in implanting ABC's build-from-the-bottom corporate philosophy, weaknesses had left them no alternatives. Although WABC was responsible for ABC's anemic prime-time schedule, and would continue to be blamed until network production shifted to the West Coast a few years later, the station's biggest dilemma was not this, but rather dead air. In 1949 it carried no programs prior to 5 p.m. and none on Monday and Tuesday. Not wasting time, WCBS and WNBC were well along in assembling particularly daytime schedules for national distribution, taking the high

---

4. Sidney Lohman, "Three New Stations for New York," *New York Times*, June 12, 1948, p. 16.

5. "Ambitious ABC Planning," *Broadcasting*, Feb. 16, 1953, pp. 27–29.

6. Sterling Quinlan, *Inside ABC* (New York: Hastings House, 1979), p. xii.

road with entries such as "The Today Show" and "House Party With Art Linkletter." WABC was consigned to the low road, which meant local programs unsuitable for the network, but which could be produced for next to nothing.

None of WABC's early programs won critical approval. Nevertheless, beginning with a frenzy of activity in mid-1949, WABC within two years had succeeded in piecing together a program schedule equal in length to those of WCBS and WNBC. Against the expectations of practically everybody the year before, the station, after just two years of operation and five years ahead of schedule, turned a profit. WABC joined Detroit's WXYZ, in the black by 1949, as ABC's only profit centers. Impressed, the editors of *Broadcasting* magazine in a 1950 issue drew national attention to this industry surprise. WABC was characterized as an exception to the fiscal uncertainty that reigned elsewhere at the network. The article credited Grabhorn's "experimentation," especially with the "station's daytime operation, which is entirely local." Local fare allowed WABC to perfect a sales strategy that made it possible for advertisers to buy airtime at discounts jointly on Channel 7 and its sister radio station, WABC-AM. A forerunner of "co-op" advertising, eventually a standard procedure in local sales, this tactic was shunned as unnecessary by WCBS and WNBC. "Although other sales executives may not agree with this theory, it's hard to quarrel with its results," the article stated. Owing to the audience WABC had fostered from its "good local programming," all of its locally produced offerings, albeit often at bargain-basement rates, were sold out.[7]

Because Grabhorn, unlike his counterparts at WCBS and WNBC, was not under inordinate pressure to turn local productions into network hits, a high level of creativity blossomed. Although WABC's programs usually were panned, critics frequently conceded a flair for the unusual. Part of the creative impulse was WABC's knack for finding new ways of transforming what essentially were local radio shows into television programs. In 1949 WABC's most ambitious undertaking was a daytime show called "Market Melodies," which for two hours featured a combination of music and demonstrations of new food and consumer products. Not quite as ambitious but more popular through the early 1950s was the "Television Telephone Game," the first sustaining local quiz show. Up to 500 prizes were awarded each day to viewers whose telephone numbers matched digits announced in

---

7. "Good Local Programming for New York," *Broadcasting*, Mar. 13, 1950, pp. 46–47.

the manner of a bingo game.[8] Another new concept was "Nancy Craig Interviews," one of the first local talk shows with a female host.[9]

Through the 1950s further ideas were unveiled. "Looka Here" was a filmed urban travelogue, in which host Roy Heatherton toured such things as new construction sites around Manhattan.[10] Somewhat similar was the "Arnold Constable Show." In this program cameras took to New York streets and wound up at department stores and supermarkets, usually to spotlight retailers who were running sales promotions.[11] In "I Cover Times Square" a cast of young actors recreated the day-to-day activities of Broadway newspaper columnists.[12] In "A Couple of Joes" a New York disc jockey and a piano player, both named Joe, chatted and offered musical numbers while directing viewers in scavenger hunts in the midtown district. The first viewer to arrive at the Channel 7 studios with such articles as an eight ball and a burned-out lightbulb won a daily prize. Additional prizes were available elsewhere in the program to viewers not wanting to participate in the scavenger hunt but who could phone in a song title that the two Joes could not perform.[13] With the exception of the Nancy Craig broadcast, which anchored WABC's daytime schedule through most of the 1950s, none of the station's early programs lasted for more than two seasons. Nevertheless, they served their needed purpose of filling the station's schedule. As a by-product, they advanced at low cost WABC's early reputation as the "eyes and ears" of New York, in contrast to WCBS and WNBC, which had nationalized virtually their entire schedules, and also in contrast to the four independents. The independent stations, which in 1955 included Channel 5 after the Du Mont network collapsed, had economic constraints worse than WABC's. One of these independents, WPIX, had sustained the nation's first large-scale local newscast, a program "Telepix Newsreel." Even so, WPIX and the other independents tended to offer sports coverage or syndicated film features that lacked a "street" flavor. It was inevitable from WABC's output of short-duration clinkers that at least some of its concepts would have more enduring applications.

One was roller-derby, WABC's most notable early invention. The sport of roller-derby was devised by Stronach and his programming staff as

8. "WJZ-TV Debuting Daytime Airing," *Variety*, May 18, 1949, p. 26.
9. "Nancy Craig—Interviews," *TV Guide*, Apr. 3, 1953, p. A-16.
10. "Looka Here," *Variety*, Jan. 25, 1950, p. 40.
11. "Arnold Constable Show," *Variety*, Apr. 5, 1950, p. 36.
12. "I Cover Times Square," *Variety*, Oct. 11, 1950, p. 40.
13. "A Couple of Joes," *Variety*, Aug. 17, 1949, p. 34.

WABC's answer to another made-for-TV creation, professional wrestling, which in 1949 was seen on three of the other six New York channels. Another motive behind roller-derby was an opportunity to employ WABC's expensive remote equipment and give it a role in sports programming, then the most popular local offering of the New York stations. At the time, WABC lacked the money to negotiate for legitimate sports events, including Yankees, Dodgers, and Giants baseball games, which in the late 1940s were headline attractions on the other channels. WABC hired the roller-derby players and organized the teams.[14] Legend had it that WABC managers also determined the outcomes of the matches. Championship matches were held at Madison Square Garden.[15] A halftime feature at some of the matches was a competition that saw skaters ascend vertical ramps and then jump over numbered barrels placed side by side on the arena floor. A few years later barrel jumping on ice would help usher in the "ABC Wide World of Sports."[16] WABC's roller-derby contests were so popular that they were carried in prime time by the full network in the early 1950s.[17] After losing its appeal in the mid-1950s, roller-derby reappeared in syndicated form in the 1960s and was still being telecast on local stations and cable networks in the 1990s.

In addition to roller-derby WABC was responsible for "The Adventures of Superman," one of the most popular children's programs ever developed. "Superman," starring George Reeves, was a theatrical serial augmented for the small screen by a group called Flamingo Films. It was rejected by the networks as too limited in appeal and appeared headed for demise until Paul Mowrey, Grabhorn's successor as WABC general manager, hit on the idea of using the series adjacent to the network's afternoon "Mickey Mouse Club," and thus forming a continuous block of children's offerings. This tactic interested the Kellogg cereal company, which supported WABC's "kids block," the first ever attempted by a local station.[18] "Superman" debuted on WABC in 1953 and by the following year was being syndicated all over the country. WABC also had a major role in the network program that would precede "Superman" on Channel 7's afternoon schedule. In 1950, to fill its Saturday-night schedule, WABC had premiered a two-hour

14. Richard Beesemyer, oral-history interview with author, June 29, 1995, Walter Cronkite School of Journalism and Telecommunications, Arizona State University.

15. "Roller-Derby in Hypo as ABC-TV Exclusive," *Variety*, July 27, 1949, p. 35.

16. Marc Gunther, *The House That Roone Built* (Boston: Little, Brown and Company, 1994), p. 19.

17. "Roller-Derby," *TV Guide*, Feb. 6, 1977, p. 17.

18. "Adventures of Superman," *Variety*, Apr. 1, 1953, p. 29.

program called "TV Teen Club." Produced by Skipper Dawes and hosted by Paul Whiteman, the "TV Teen Club" was moved to WFIL in Philadelphia, where facilities were available to originate a version of the two-hour broadcast each afternoon.[19] In 1957 a WFIL disc jockey named Dick Clark succeeded Whiteman as host of the show, by then renamed "American Bandstand." While the show continued to originate at WFIL, WABC engineers facilitated "American Bandstand," which, like Clark, became an ABC institution.[20]

While free to initiate carefree fare such as roller-derby and "A Couple of Joes," WABC managers were not oblivious to the increasing stakes those at the network level ascribed to their efforts. As undistinguished (at least from a critical standpoint) as most of its programs were, WABC's status as a profit center had major implications during the first two landmark events in ABC's history (its later 1985 sale to Capital Cities being the third, the 1995 sale to Disney the fourth). ABC faced its first crossroads in 1953, when Noble finally gave up and effected a merger with Goldenson's United Paramount Theater company. Goldenson recalled that WABC and its Detroit sister station were the only profitable assets ABC had, and, as such, they enabled Noble to drive up the asking price to a then astronomical $25 million. Not only did this infusion of cash from UPT allow ABC to press on with network operations, had UPT not agreed to pay this sum, according to Goldenson, Noble would have sold the network to CBS, which presumably would have folded ABC in order to obtain ABC's local stations in Chicago, Detroit, and San Francisco.[21] The 1953 crisis, though daunting, proved less catastrophic in portent than the one that began to unfold a decade later.

"Eyewitness News" Watershed

The timing could not have been worse. ABC, managing annual profits of around $10 million in the early 1960s, suddenly was faced with a $100 million capital investment to commence color telecasting. ABC's network programs, which had been competitive with those of CBS and NBC briefly, became mired in last place as the decade wore on. ABC barely surmounted

19. "John Reed King to WJZ-TV Daytime," *Variety*, Feb. 18, 1953, p. 27.
20. "ABC Opens Probe of Disc Jockeys," *New York Times*, Nov. 18, 1959, pp. 1, 18.
21. Goldenson, pp. 99–100.

hostile-takeover bids by Norton Simon and Howard Hughes. Its single prospect, a friendly merger with ITT, was upended in 1968 after two years of negotiations and court maneuvers, when ITT backed out. Goldenson and the existing regime were forced to proceed alone, and they endured ABC's darkest days, in time with a full-color schedule, mainly because WABC and the other owned stations became powerhouse operations. By the mid-1970s the owned stations were making substantially more money than the entire ABC programming division was losing. They accomplished this by falling back on ABC's twin traditions of localism and unrestrained innovation, and by coordinating their efforts in a single new program called "Eyewitness News."

"Eyewitness News," a new style of television newscasting, was as important to the evolution of television news as it was to the emergence of ABC. Perfected at WABC, "Eyewitness News" was emulated by television stations all over the country. Prior to the unveiling of "Eyewitness News" at WABC in November 1968, that station and almost all others had carried 15-minute newscasts, in which viewers saw lone anchors reading out loud the day's stories. In local news the use of film was irregular. "Eyewitness News" ushered the expansion of local newscasts, soon at WABC to a full hour, and introduced viewers to the "field reporter." Before "Eyewitness News," reporters could not be seen on camera because only the main anchors, as professional "talent," were considered sufficiently appealing to the viewer. WABC's decision to put its reporters in front of the camera dramatically altered television news presentations. While WCBS and WNBC continued with lone newscasters who gave third-person accounts of New York events, WABC featured a half-dozen additional news personalities, the reporters, whose accounts were first person and accompanied not by a random, but by a coordinated, use of film.

The key figures in the development of "Eyewitness News" were WABC news director Al Primo, who had pioneered earlier versions of the "Eyewitness" concept at Westinghouse stations in Cleveland and Philadelphia, and Richard O'Leary, a network executive who as head of the Owned Stations Division supervised all five ABC stations, including WABC. In his third year at Philadelphia's KYW in 1968, Primo at first refused the opportunity to join WABC, believing its news department a "rag-tag outfit." But he agreed to make the move that year after WABC general manager Richard Beesemyer promised Primo a free reign for enacting sweeping changes.[22] In

---

22. Al Primo, oral-history interview with author, July 22, 1993, at Walter Cronkite School of Journalism and Telecommunications, Arizona State University.

addition to making way for the "Eyewitness" reporters, attention was given the newscasts' aesthetic effects. Primo enlarged and made more eye-catching WABC's studio set, designed on-screen graphic elements, and instituted distinctive news theme music adapted from the 1967 motion picture *Cool Hand Luke*.[23] These measures, which now are standard in local television news, were radical in 1968. Even more radical had been O'Leary's idea of having two newscasters present the news, in what became known as the "coanchor" format. O'Leary encouraged an informal, on-camera dialogue between the news figures. Newscasters Fahey Flynn and Joel Daly at Chicago's WLS, O'Leary's former station, had been the first to communicate news in this fashion. An influential article by Morry Roth in the trade publication *Variety* had labeled this practice "happy talk."[24] This phrase—"happy talk"—endured in local TV news and was widely used to describe the "Eyewitness News" presentation on WABC. "Things were changing in the 1960s and people were confused," O'Leary would explain. "Under the old school, you had to deliver the news from Mt. Olympus in a way that was totally abstract to the audience." O'Leary's idea was not to be "happy" but to personalize the news presentation and to "communicate in human terms with the audience."[25]

New York critics rightfully saw "Eyewitness News" as a total departure from the principled newscasts seen, in O'Leary's words, "on the mighty WCBS and WNBC." Jack Gould of the *New York Times* assailed WABC's "Eyewitness News" as "ratings bait."[26] Paul Klein of *New York* magazine condemned the concept as a "wind-in-the-hair technique."[27] Unlike the critics, however, New York television viewers appreciated "Eyewitness News." WABC added a half-million new viewers within two years. By 1972 WABC was number one in the New York television market, a distinction it had never before had. The attraction of "Eyewitness News" was the formula Primo and O'Leary prescribed: latitude given to anchors and reporters toward appearing less as serious newscasters and more as familiar people with interesting stories to relate. The consummate objective was to provide

23. "Inside Eyewitness News," videotape, WABC-TV, Oct. 18, 1980, Alan Weiss Collection.

24. Morry Roth, "O'Leary's (Sacred) Cow Updated as Flynn and Daly Duo Start Another Great Chicago Fire Under Chi News Via WLS-TV," *Variety*, Feb. 11, 1970, pp. 37–38.

25. Richard O'Leary, oral-history interview with author, Aug. 4, 1994, at Walter Cronkite School of Journalism and Telecommunications, Arizona State University.

26. Jack Gould, "TV: Six-Part Prostitution Report Begins," *New York Times*, Feb. 25, 1969, p. 87.

27. Paul Klein, "Happy Talk, Happy Profits," *New York*, June 28, 1971, pp. 60–61.

the nation's largest city with a "news of the neighborhood." Ratings began to climb, maintained Av Westin, a CBS and later ABC news executive, when New York viewers began to say to each other, "You wouldn't believe what I saw on Channel 7 last night."[28] The original anchor team included a curmudgeonlike but witty anchor named Roger Grimsby, a younger coanchor named John Shubeck, a flamboyant weathercaster named Tex Antoine, and a salty sportscaster named Howard Cosell, known for the controversies he stirred. In September 1970 ABC News London correspondent Bill Beutel joined Grimsby as WABC's coanchor; they appeared together on "Eyewitness News" for the next 16 years. Others seen on "Eyewitness News" were sports reporters Jim Bouton and Frank Gifford, entertainment editor Rona Barrett, field reporters Melba Tolliver, Gloria Rojas, Gil Noble, and John Johnson. Anchor Ernie Anastos was believed to be the first person in local TV news to command a million-dollar annual salary.[29] One of the most popular figures ever to report news in New York was anchor-reporter RoseAnn Scamardella, known nationally in the 1970s from the "Roseanna Danna" impersonations of her by comedienne Gilda Radner on NBC's "Saturday Night Live."[30]

WABC's enlistments of Tolliver, Rojas, Noble, Johnson, and Scamardella represented the first attempt by a local television station to put large numbers of women and minorities on the air. Geraldo Rivera, one of the first "Eyewitness" reporters, likewise personified this objective. Rivera had been a public defender in Harlem whom Primo recruited and groomed upon a recommendation by Rojas. Although Rivera was unpolished and quickly associated by critics with "improper" reporting techniques that allegedly pandered to the audience, he nevertheless was responsible for bringing WABC its first measure of critical acclaim. This came in 1972 in a series of reports on the living conditions of the mentally retarded at the Willowbrook hospital on Staten Island. Rivera's exposé for WABC, photographed by Bob Alis, earned both a Peabody Award and a national Emmy Award, the first time a local television station ever had been so honored. Investigations inspired by Rivera's reports led to reforms in New York's

---

28. Av Westin, *Newswatch* (New York: Simon and Schuster, 1982), p. 210.

29. Marvin Kitman, "Another Day, Another Million," *Washington Journalism Review*, Sept., 1983, pp. 39–42, 58.

30. See excerpts "Eyewitness News," WABC-TV, May 9, 1972, in film "TV News: Behind the Scenes," Encyclopedia Britannica, 1973, KUSI collection, San Diego, Calif.; and excerpts, "Eyewitness News," WABC-TV, May 19, 1977, in film "Six O'Clock and All Is Well," 1977, Museum of Radio and Television, New York City.

mental-health system. "The quick flashes" of the mentally retarded in the hospital wards and the "incredibly accurate sound track made the whole thing seem as though it was taken from the movie *The Night of the Living Dead.* The comparison was uncomfortably close to the truth," Rivera had reported.[31]

As noticeable as its new style of news presentation were ABC's promotional ads on billboards, in newspapers, and on TV. One promotion depicted an NBC peacock with its feathers clipped and tears issuing from a CBS "eye."[32] In these promotions WABC had attempted to create the impression that WCBS and WNBC were overly serious with their news presentations. Research had shown that obscure, "grim," and generally negative news content on the larger CBS and NBC stations was alienating many average viewers.[33] To convey that WABC had a more positive approach, Grimsby, Beutel, and other "Eyewitness" team members were seen attending a huge Puerto Rican wedding hosted by Rivera. "The 'Eyewitness News' family," this promo had announced. "The reason people like them so much is because they like people so much."[34] A WABC news promotion with an even larger cast was filmed in Central Park, in a setting designed to look like a scene from the popular Broadway musical *Hair.* Dozens of people held hands and sang "Let the Sun Shine In."[35]

Particularly after these promotional ventures, the ratings of "Eyewitness News" continued to grow. According to Arbitron estimates in February 1977, "Eyewitness News" was regularly viewed in 3 million of New York's 7 million homes.[36] In the meantime a research report circulated that year by the McHugh and Hoffman consulting company found not only that WABC was the favorite or second-favorite station of nearly 80 percent of the audience, but that its main anchor team of Grimsby and Beutel were recognized by 87 percent of the survey's respondents, a remarkable display of public support.[37] This research also suggested that the strides of WABC, because it was the flagship station, finally were preparing the full network

---

31. Geraldo Rivera, *Willowbrook* (New York: Random House, 1972), pp. 34, 56.

32. "We're No. 1," film, WABC news promotion, 1970, Howard Burkat Collection, New York City.

33. "WABC-TV, New York City," News Research Consultants Report, McHugh and Hoffman, McLean, Va., Mar. 6, 1969, pp. 41–44.

34. "The Eyewitness News Family," film, WABC-TV, 1971, Howard Burkat Collection.

35. "We Let the Sun Shine In," film, WABC-TV, 1970, Howard Burkat Collection; also see *Television/Radio Age,* June 29, 1970, p. 74.

36. Arbitron ratings, New York City, Feb. 1977, Arbitron Archive, Athens, Ga.

37. "WABC-TV, New York City," News Research Consultants Report, McHugh and Hoffman, McLean, Va., Aug. 11, 1977, p. 30.

for its ascension late that decade. As a result of the success of "Eyewitness News," the ABC-owned stations by 1979 were generating $100 million in profits each year, more money than that earned by the CBS and NBC local stations put together.[38] Many believed "Eyewitness News" had pretested a number of the journalistic concepts Arledge would advance in the ABC's network news division.[39] Arledge's "World News Tonight," unveiled in 1978, eventually would hold a commanding advantage in the size of its audience over the news broadcasts seen on CBS and NBC. Grimsby believed WABC helped "save" ABC because it destabilized the other networks in the nation's largest market, the "backyard" of CBS and NBC, in Grimsby's words. "You could tell they [CBS and NBC] were off balance," Grimsby recalled, "when they brought in their big-name network stars to do the local news, as our competition, and they bombed."[40] Among the nationally recognized CBS and NBC figures who appeared on local newscasts in New York, and who eventually were taken off the air apparently because of their stations' failure to make headway against WABC, were Robert Trout, Frank McGee, Sander Vanocur, Edwin Newman, Bob Teague, Jim Hartz, and Lem Tucker. Perhaps the best sign of WABC's success was the July 1972 ratings, which showed "Eyewitness News" with a 40 percent share of the audience. This was striking because the same Nielsen figures had shown the local news on WNBC with no measurable audience—in effect, a "zero" rating.[41] By this time "Eyewitness News" had been emulated at 80 additional television stations around the country.[42]

Sadly, to those who had seen it evolve, WABC's maverick tradition did not live on. As if by a premonition of what was to come, an owned-station promotional campaign in the 1970s touting the exodus of local viewers from CBS and NBC rhetorically posed the question, in so many words, "Will success spoil ABC?"[43] To many, it did. ABC's 30-year struggle against CBS and NBC culminated in its own entry into the broadcast establishment. The results were first visible at WABC.

38. *FCC Annual Reports 1979*, Records of the Federal Communications Commission, Washington, D.C.

39. Gary Deeb, "At ABC, the Net's Set for Happy Talk," *Chicago Tribune*, Feb. 4, 1976, p. 10.

40. Roger Grimsby, oral-history interview with author, May 3, 1994, at Walter Cronkite School of Journalism and Telecommunications, Arizona State University.

41. Robert Daley, "We Deal With Emotional Facts," *New York Times Magazine*, Dec. 15, 1974, p. 62.

42. "Happy Talk," *Newsweek*, Feb. 20, 1972, p. 46.

43. "Will Success Spoil?" film, ABC-owned stations promotions, 1969, WLS/Capital Cities Archives, Chicago, Ill.

A New Corporate Culture

By the mid-1980s the energy behind WABC's once-inventive local news ventures had dissipated and was shifting back to WCBS and WNBC, which then were developing even livelier and more innovative presentations. In 1980 WNBC premiered a local news broadcast called "Live at Five," which was copied by local stations all over the country. A revealing sign that WABC's momentum had stalled was its decision in late 1982 to replace anchors Scamardella and Anastos with Tom Snyder, whose late-night network talk program had been canceled so NBC could make way for David Letterman. WABC management, having ignored the lessons of WCBS and WNBC, which had placed network figures on New York local newscasts and failed, realized the mistake and put Scamardella and Anastos back on the news. This came, however, after a public outcry that caused many New Yorkers to question WABC's "home station" reputation. A similar type of distress was felt among some New York viewers when WABC's pioneering and locally oriented "kids block" fell prey to syndicated talk shows, including, by 1985, the "Oprah Winfrey Show." Winfrey's program originated at WLS, and though it was key to the ongoing ratings dominance of the ABC's owned stations, as a national program it zapped more of WABC's local identity. Then came ABC's merger with Capital Cities in 1985. At the corporate level this merger was essential in order that ABC have the financial backing needed to confront new competition from cable TV and other sources. The merger was friendly and gave ABC an advantage over CBS and NBC, which simultaneously were forced into less-than-cordial takeovers. Yet at both the local and network level the merger, at first, was painful. Capital Cities entered by laying off 2,000 employees and instituting a top-down corporate scheme alien to those who remained. Although Capital Cities would reinstate stability by the end of the 1980s, a general decline in network television never was reversed.

Still, parts of WABC's legacy endured. Many veterans of the glory days were observed at "Eyewitness News" reunions, including one held in May 1995 just weeks before Grimsby's death.[44] This station not only underscored rewards available to broadcasters by advancing the unusual, but made it impossible for Goldenson and his successors to dismiss the importance of

---

44. "Eyewitness News Twenty-fifth Anniversary," videotape, May 17, 1995, Alan Weiss Productions.

localism and local stations in sustaining a network. Capital Cities placed a
heavy emphasis on owned local television stations in the course of bolstering
ABC's TV-distribution capabilities, and it was this strength that had made
ABC attractive to Disney in 1995. "A network is no stronger than its weakest
local station," Goldenson had urged. "Without the success of our owned and
operated stations," he would add, "we never would have had any chance."[45]
If WABC became a more orthodox television station under Capital Cities
and then Disney, it was to New Yorkers an alternative through most of its
history. As WABC's concepts moved into the mainstream, they left a broad
trail of change in their wake.

45. Goldenson, p. 374.

2 The Hustler: WTNH-TV, New Haven

Margot Hardenbergh

The history of WTNH-TV, aka WNHC-TV, reveals many of the paradoxes of television broadcasting. WNHC started as a community television station, covering the whole state of Connecticut. Then, when it became licensed as a full-power station with statewide coverage, it was known as the New Haven station to its competitors. It was one of the first stations on the air, and the first to get into the black, yet those who worked there always feared their jobs might be gone the next week. It started out as locally owned and then was group owned. One characteristic has always been true of the station from the very beginning: It has always been hustling—hustling for programming, for sales, for viewers. It hustled first by getting on the air, then throughout the tenure of its first three owners. This history will cover the changes in technology, the programming emphases, and a few major stories the station covered.

Beginnings

In 1946, after starting the second AM radio station in the community, two men convinced four others to join them in Elm City Broadcasting and start an FM station. Their AM radio station, WNHC, was doing well, especially on Sunday mornings, when they aired Italian programming. The owners sent co-owner Mike Goode on the train to Washington, D.C., to apply for the FM license. While they were at it, they decided to investigate getting a construction permit for a television station.[1]

Only one television channel was allocated for the entire state of Connecticut—Channel 3 in the city of Hartford—and it was unclaimed. Although no one else seemed interested in starting a television station in the state, the Elm City owners sensed they should not go after that one. So they applied to the Federal Communications Commission for another channel, arguing for a community channel for New Haven, Connecticut. Even today Ed Taddei, who helped complete the application, is amazed that the FCC agreed.[2] As one engineer recalls, "Mike [came] back off the train, grinning, waving the CP for both the FM license and the television station." The FCC granted Elm City Broadcasting the license for Channel 6 as a community channel for New Haven, Connecticut.

The six owners shared an appropriate combination of attributes and abilities, including sales skills, political connections, and engineering and production backgrounds. Aldo DeDomenicis is credited with being the driving force behind the group. DeDomenicis sold Italian products in New Haven and had been selling time for foreign-language broadcasting for the only radio station in New Haven, WELI-AM. Michael Goode, a political commentator for WELI-AM, produced a Sunday program called "The People's Lobby." Michael's brother, Patrick J. Goode, was postmaster for the city of New Haven; Vincent DeLaurentis and Garo W. Ray were engineers; and David Harris, who joined at the last minute, was a young man interested in any and all aspects of radio production.

As WNHC-AM, they used a house in the center of town that had previously been a funeral home. It was an old town house on Chapel Street that had been resided in glass and remodeled into radio studios by WICC of neighboring Bridgeport. WICC had intended to have a satellite operation in its neighboring city, but that plan had a short life. Elm City adapted the studios, and aspects of the funeral home would offer unique opportunities in the station's future.

---

1. Oral-history interview with Emery Schmittgall, conducted by Margot Hardenbergh, December 2, 1994, tapes 12 and 13. Unless otherwise stated, all subsequent Schmittgall quotes are from this interview. All the interviews for this history were tape-recorded and are in the possession of the New Haven Colony Historical Society.

2. Oral-history interview with Edward Taddei, conducted by Margot Hardenbergh, November 18, 1994, tape 10. Unless otherwise stated all subsequent Taddei quotes are from this interview. See also *Broadcasting Yearbook 1950* (Washington, D.C.: Broadcasting Publications), p. 104.

Each person invested from $5,000 to $30,000. They purchased equipment from Du Mont and in 1946 bought land on Gaylord Mountain in Hamden, 11 miles from the station. A road to the site was built within a year, and in August 1947 they started constructing the transmitter building. The FM signal was in by the end of the year. A five-kilowatt Du Mont TV transmitter was put up in the winter of 1947–48 and was allotted only 600 watts of power. Press accounts described the equipment as a "150-foot antenna tower topped by [an] RCA super-style triplex antenna which rose another 51 feet toward the heavens."[3] They figured out a way to relay the signal automatically from Du Mont's Channel 5, WABD, in New York City, to Huntington Long Island, to a fire tower in Oxford, Connecticut, and then to WNHC's site on Gaylord Mountain. The first television pictures transmitted from Connecticut were of the transmitter, surroundings, and the station officials on the air from 11:30 p.m. until 2:30 a.m. on June 2–3, 1948.

Press Coverage

The headlines all noted that WNHC was to be New England's first television station. Although there would be no recognition of the existence of radio or television by the New Haven newspapers, the papers of the other Connecticut cities and towns carried stories promoting the television station, and the radio station helped promote it. "Hear stories about television," read one upbeat news article, "behind the scenes in Connecticut TV operations" on Monday evenings on WNHC-AM and FM.[4] There were advertisements urging people to get to their radio dealers and buy a television. The *Yale Daily News* reported there were 2,500 sets in New Haven, 500 of which were in public places.[5] The least expensive sets cost just under $200, and articles reported that the sets would be useful for years to come. Any changes would only be "evolutionary, rather than revolutionary."[6]

---

3. Wartime shortages prevented purchase of equipment. "New Haven Station Hopes to Start State's First Television June 1," *Bridgeport Post,* May 23, 1948, p. 12.

4. "WNHC-TV Test Pattern a Success," *Milford Citizen,* June 10, 1948, p. 4.

5. "WNHC-TV Begins Television in June: Autumn Football Programs Possible," *Yale Daily News,* May 29, 1948, pp. 1, 4.

6. Lewis L. Doolittle, "WNHC's Television Arrival Remarkable Achievement," *Bridgeport Herald,* June 20, 1948, n.p. (held in scrapbook at WTNH-TV, New Haven, Conn.). Also see "16,000 Fans Use Tele in County," *Bridgeport Sunday Herald,* June 27, 1948, p. 14.

There were predictions of great programming: sports, news, and theater. Sports would include the World Series, college football games, and hockey. Boxing and wrestling would run at least four evenings a week. WNHC was the first station to sign an affiliate contract with Du Mont. In its promotion of daytime programming Du Mont boasted it would provide "a Television Baby Sitter to entertain junior while mother does her work ... and then 'School Reporter' to entertain pupils when they return home from school."[7]

Political programming received the most publicity. WNHC was one of 18 television stations that aired coverage of the 1948 national political conventions, televised direct from Convention Hall in Philadelphia with Drew Pearson, from 8:55–9:00 p.m.[8] The first local production from the studios in New Haven on Tuesday, November 2, 1948, would also feature political personalities. A local paper warned there would be more interest in looks, 5 o'clock shadow, extemporaneous speaking, and more women.[9]

The programs that aired from June through October came from the transmitter where engineer Emery Schmittgall was learning on the job. Schmittgall, an amateur radio buff, had been in the Army Signal Corps and had come out looking for a job. He learned about WNHC's position by talking on the radio with engineer/co-owner Vincent deLaurentis. He was hired for the weekend shift, working on the AM transmitter, whose antenna was on an old oil rig an owner had brought up from Texas.[10]

Once they had the FM station and built the FM transmitter and antenna on Gaylord Mountain, Schmittgall was hired full-time to cut the electrical transmission at the transmitter. Then came the Du Mont television transmitter. Schmittgall had to come up with a way of switching between cameras at the transmitter and the slide projector. He also had to "go down to Jack Young's photography studio and tell him how to shoot the slides with safe zones." Everything was brought up to the transmitter for the first five months; then only film had to come from the transmitter. He had to devise a method

7. Rocky Clark, "TV Begins Daytime Schedule," *Bridgeport Post,* September 22, 1948, p. 36.
8. "Stay at Home to See Conventions," *Hartford Times,* June 19, 1948, p. 18.
9. "Conventions Will Be Televised," *Waterbury American,* June 15, 1948, p. 5.
10. Schmittgall spent much of his time fixing things. The equipment was Army surplus.

whereby those in the studio, 11 miles away, could let him know while he was at the transmitter when they needed the film shown.[11]

WNHC was initially set up to play back Du Mont's programming, but soon it could choose from all four networks. Lee St. Martin can remember having to keep all the wires straight.[12] As Ed Taddei says, "We selected the best for each evening ... but there was a lot of boxing and wrestling."[13] Here is a typical evening program schedule Monday through Friday:

6:00 p.m. Small Fry Club with Bob Emery, interview and movies

6:30 p.m. Russ Hodges Scoreboard; a pictorial résumé of the day's leading sporting events across the nation

6:45 p.m. Film shorts

or

Direct from Washington SEE, roundup presented by Walter Compton

7:30 p.m. Camera headliners, see pictures you'll see in next day's papers

7:45 p.m. Film shorts

8:00 p.m. Fashions on Parade

8:30 p.m. TBA

9:00 p.m. Wrestling from Jamaica Arena

There was no programming on Saturday; programming started at 5 p.m. on Sunday.[14]

---

11. Schmittgall recalls that the film projectors were very troublesome. The pull-down mechanism would shake the projector, and sometimes the noise went out over the air. One night, when the microwave went out between the studio and the transmitter, Schmittgall had to sustain the evening with films from the transmitter. He spliced the commercials in as quickly as possible, and the projector went all evening. The next day the projector stopped completely. Schmittgall interview, tapes 12 and 13.

12. Oral-history interview with Lee St. Martin, conducted by Margot Hardenbergh, November 18, 1994, tape 4. St. Martin has worked at the station from 1956 to 1959, and 1969 to the present, and at the time of the interview was executive assistant to the president, general manager, director of personnel, and director of viewer relations. All subsequent St. Martin quotes are from this interview.

13. Taddei recalls that later, when there were more choices to make, the station would select the best for an evening and take a kinescope of its second choice for an air date a week later. Taddei interview, tape 10.

14. This is actually a composite of the publicity pieces that appeared in the *Bridgeport Telegram,* June 18, 1948, p. 21, and *Milford Citizen,* June 10, 1948, p. 4.

New Haven

WNHC-TV had made it through the first year; it was on the air before the freeze on new stations set by the FCC; it had set the pattern for how the station would operate, showing a mix of network and locally produced programs; it had started some commercially sponsored local programs. All this in spite of its location—or perhaps because of it. New Haven, Connecticut, is located on Long Island Sound, between New York City and Boston, home to Yale University. As the third-largest city in the state, its population was 155,000 in 1950. As did other northeastern cities, it had a large industrial base that became quite prosperous, but in the '40s the city started losing jobs and population to the suburban towns.[15]

The location of the city of license would have a strong influence on how the station was run, and how it would react to competition as it came along. Half of its coverage area was lost on a large body of water, Long Island Sound, and one side of the coverage area was also covered by New York City stations. Says Taddei, "If there were as many as 400 receivers in the state when the station went on the air, they were probably all in Fairfield County"[16] within the New York City market.

New Haven was not geographically in the middle of the state, but it was perceptually. The city claims to be the gateway to New England and is proud of its early history. It was founded in 1638, served as the state capital for a year, and is home to many technological inventions, writers, and trends. In the 1940s New Haven was a two-newspaper town run by one family. The Jackson family published both the morning and evening papers and could not abide competition. Their policy toward both radio and television in the '40s and early '50s was very restrictive: "They would not publish any call letters in news stories. They would not run ads with call letters in them. The papers' photographers were to exclude any radio person in a photograph, and if it happened the person or the mic with call letters made it to the photograph,

---

15. Ira Leonard, "The Rise of Metropolitan New Haven, 1860 to 1980," in *New Haven: An Illustrated History,* ed. Floyd Shumway and Richard Hegel (New Haven, Conn.: Windsor Publications, 1981), pp. 44–61.

16. Taddei interview, tape 10.

they would be blackened out."[17] This restrictive policy meant that no local radio station logs would be printed, much less the fledgling television program schedule. Yet, by some mistake, the readers of the New Haven papers could learn about the arrival of this new medium: the radio dealers' ads congratulated WNHC on offering a new window to the world.[18]

As part of its hustling nature, the station was constantly trying to gain further support from the appliance dealers. They asked for sponsorship of the test pattern, arguing that the dealers needed something on their television screens in the stores. Then they urged further support of local programming. The appliance-trade press noted that all were watching to see how successful WNHC's efforts would be in promoting local programming, instead of New York programming, as a way to get the dealers to sell more receivers with less expensive antennas. The detractors noted that customers would be dissatisfied if their equipment couldn't pull in the better, distant programs.[19]

Local Programming

News was not a major effort for the first twenty years of the station, although those hired to cover the news did their best. And the station hired a remarkably well-trained staff, probably due to the determination of the applicants. The first news director had graduated from college and studied English and journalism. The first sports announcer had founded his college's sports-broadcasting network, been to radio school, and had already been a DJ. The first photographer had had his own studio for a few years. The first news director, John Quinn, wrote the hourly news for the radio stations and three 15-minute newscasts for the television station: early morning, noon, and evening. "What we did was awful," he has said. He had a wire service,

17. Oral-history interview with Daniel Kops, conducted by Margot Hardenbergh, September 26, 1994, tape 6. This description was supported by Edward Taddei, tape 10. The restrictive policy of the paper was one of the reasons Kops chose New Haven to start his radio station, WAVZ. Kops notes that the policy changed because the paper began making a lot of money from the TV appliance dealers' advertising. Kops was the owner of the third radio station in New Haven, WAVZ, which would win national recognition for its editorials. Kops also held many national positions in the profession.

18. For example, see the *New Haven Evening Register,* June 16, 1948, p. 14.

19. "Opinions Differ on New Haven Plan to Promote Local Video Programs," *New England Appliance and Radio News, Boston,* January 1949, n.p. (held in scrapbook at WTNH-TV, New Haven, Conn.).

which he admits to rewriting for the newscasters, supplementing with local news from phone calls. For the 6 p.m. newscast he would use still photos from wherever he could steal them.[20] He would pay newspaper photographers, utility public-relations people—anyone he could find—$2 a shot for a photograph. Sometimes the readers had so little preparation time that Quinn would write the newscasts phonetically to ease the reading, and the scripts were put in large type on easels. After two years he was such a bundle of nerves that he went to work for a newspaper. However, in hindsight Quinn had to admit that the year-end reviews he produced were an interesting look at the foregoing year.

There was no attempt to find sponsors for the newscasts, nor did the management put many of its own resources into gathering the news. However, one of the owners, Mike Goode, maintained an interest in political programming. Goode went on the air November 2, 1948, with the first TV spot program in the state. The station carried the Du Mont Network coverage, then went on at 11 p.m. with the local election returns, the Republican town chairman conceding on camera to the New Haven Democrats.[21] It stayed on the air until 4:35 a.m. and was back on by 7 a.m.[22] The program was sponsored by General Electric Supply Corporation, the state distributors of GE products. In 1949 the station covered the state elections with remotes from Hartford.

Syd Jaffe applied for the position of TV sports announcer and actually started his job before the station went on the air. He would produce and announce two sportscasts each evening. He took movies of the Yale football games, spliced them together and hoped that the film wouldn't fall apart. The New Haven arena supplied many events and people to cover, including Joe DiMaggio, Rocky Marciano, and Jackie Robinson. At first, jealous of his Western Union ticker and his ability to put the statistics on at 11 p.m., those at the Connecticut Sportswriter Alliance saw him as their enemy, infringing on their area. But one sportswriter, Bob Casey, befriended him, and eventually he was accepted.

---

20. Oral-history interview with John Quinn, conducted by Margot Hardenbergh, December 5, 1994, tape 13. Quinn went on to become the editor of the *Bridgeport Herald,* and after that paper folded, he became a columnist, the Elm City Clarion, for the *New Haven Register.*

21. "WNHC Stages First TV Spot Program in State," *Bridgeport Herald*, November 14, 1948, n.p. (held in scrapbook at WTNH-TV, New Haven, Conn.).

22. The station was carrying programming from 10 a.m. to noon and 5 p.m. to sign-off, in an effort to help sell the sets. Leo Miller, "Takin' the Air," *Sunday Bridgeport Herald,* November 14, 1948, p. 29.

Jack Youngs had come back from the war and opened a photography studio with a partner. They had produced stills for the station to use as flip cards, for news and advertising. In 1950 Youngs asked for a job at the station. DeDomenicis's response was, "Why, what use does a television station have for a photographer?" Youngs replied, "Well, if I came on maybe I could figure out something. I could take publicity pictures."[23] DeDomenicis decided to give it a try and hired Youngs. Youngs worked for the station as news photographer for 29 years. "I was a one-man band. I did anything to learn more, just to be involved in the stories." He used a Bell and Howell with 100-foot magazines. Engineer Ray devised a drum to process the film on their own. First he covered events only in the city of New Haven but eventually went throughout the state. Later he was assisted by a full-time staff member, Frank Hogan, and always had the help of the AP stringer, John Mongillo. They covered all the parades in the city, after they made sure all parades passed their studio. Later "Sidewalk Interview," with the news anchor Larry McNamara, would go out on the street with a camera, live, and offer a silver dollar to the person who answered his current-events questions correctly.

Inside there were two studios: one a news set and the other a kitchen.[24] The cooking shows included "Cooking with Roz," "Cooking with Philameena," "The Bon Tempi's," and others.[25] There was an interview/crafts show with Joan Crowther. One show clearly indicated desperation in filling airtime: "Stay up Stan," during which someone would spend at least an hour flipping records, introducing them, then playing them.[26] On the more serious side, Albert D. Burke, Ph.D., from Yale University, produced and hosted a weekly contemporary issues program that drew on sources from the CIA and the Naval War School.[27]

---

23. Oral-history interview with Jack Youngs, conducted by Margot Hardenbergh, December 4, 1994, tapes 14 and 15.

24. Oral-history interview with Ruth Purvis, conducted by Margot Hardenbergh, December 5, 1994, tape 17. Purvis was the station's first receptionist hired in 1948, and she then moved on to other positions until she left in 1960. Unless otherwise stated, all subsequent Purvis quotes are from this interview.

25. "The Bon Tempi's" show is recalled by all: Fedora did the cooking, Pino sang with an accordion, and there was a large dog.

26. Oral-history interview with David Harris, co-owner, conducted by Margot Hardenbergh, September 12, 1994, tape 1.

27. Personal interview with Richard Tino, October 11, 1994. Tino worked with Burke in 1959 after he moved his show to Channel 30 in New Britain, Conn. It was a program that David Harris as production director was proud to be airing on WNHC.

Joey Russell with his Happy Sticks, simple wooden dowels, entertained the children daily. Kit Adler, who worked in the traffic department, produced and hosted a daily show called "Kadoodle the Clown."[28] Syd Jaffe produced a daily variety show called "Date at Six," and a sports-review show, which he always closed with "A good sport today makes a better American tomorrow."[29] David Harris, the production manager/co-owner, became bored with all in-studio programming and came up with the idea of producing a children's show that incorporated film segments: "The Outdoor Adventure Club." He sold the idea to the station, then left the station to set up the production company to produce it.

Trouble

The station management was always concerned that the FCC look kindly on them. Sometimes the FCC needed to remind the station of proper behavior; other times the station immediately let go anyone they found guilty of questionable behavior. Their very first run-in came as a result of the station's nature—hustling. Schmittgall recalls suggesting they sell the test pattern. From six months to a year the test pattern was a commercial for companies such as Iron Right Ironer, until the FCC informed them that the test pattern had to be free. They quickly stopped selling the test pattern, but Schmittgall's idea had made some money in the meantime.

Another time the station was running through preparations for a fashion show. The models were using one studio as a changing room. The crew turned the camera to the changing studio, covered the tally light, and watched the models change. The scene didn't go out over the air, but management fired everyone even possibly involved, from the production manager to the entire crew, afraid someone might make a complaint.[30] One program host

28. Purvis interview, tape 17.

29. Oral-history interview with Syd Jaffe, conducted by Margot Hardenbergh, December 5, 1994, tape 17. Unless otherwise stated, all subsequent Jaffe quotes are from this interview.

30. Oral-history interview with Len Sanna, Bill Ellison, and Mike Warren, conducted by Margot Hardenbergh, September 12, 1994, tapes 2 and 3. This was part of an interview with three people together: Bill Ellison (from 1964 to 1980 he had held positions of program, news, and/or public-affairs director at the station), Len Sanna (film editor from 1959 to 1985), and Mike Warren (talent from 1962 to 1980).

referred to the color of a handmade afghan as "nigger brown." She was not allowed on the air again.[31]

The news crew was given a lecture by the station's attorneys based on a letter from the FCC warning them that they would lose their license if they did not stop their practice of "news by arrangement." Youngs gives a description of the news story that caused this reprimand: "I was covering a strike in Ansonia. It was cold and the strikers were all sitting there, leaning against the fence, or something, you know? I would get them all lined up and say, 'Now, I want you to march around the gate here, ... and then go over and warm your hands by the fire, hold your signs up and shake 'em and yell' ... otherwise they looked like a bunch of slobs, just sitting there. I was trying to make 'em look good, but that was news by arrangement, and I was told I couldn't do that anymore."[32]

WNHC-TV was the only television station on the air in Connecticut for five years, and the staff enjoyed the monopoly. They chose among the networks for the best programming; they produced as much local programming as they could; they were a growing family trying out television production and transmission all on their own. By 1955 there were from 150 to 200 employees, including dolly pushers, cable pullers, assistant camera operators, and three different shipping/mail positions. In the film department there were four people to preview the 60 hours of film before they aired and three people to "butcher them and splice in the commercials."[33]

Channel Change

When the freeze was lifted, there were changes. WNHC-TV was a community station on Channel 6, and in 1952 the FCC offered them Channel 8 in the hyphenated market of Hartford–New Haven. The transition from 6 to 8 meant not only that they would have more power, but their power would also have to be directed to avoid the Springfield, Massachusetts, market to the north. They still had the obstacles of half their signal going out over the water, and one-quarter being lost to the New York City market. But they retained some advantage: They were a VHF station in a two-VHF market.

31. St. Martin interview, tape 4.

32. Oral-history interview with Jack Youngs, conducted by Margot Hardenbergh, December 5, 1994, tape 16.

33. Len Sanna interview, tapes 2 and 3.

Eight UHF channels were allocated to Connecticut: Channel 30 in New Britain went on the air in 1953 and was owned by an NBC subsidiary; Channel 18 in Hartford went on the air in 1956 and was owned by CBS; and the Hartford Traveler's Insurance Company, which was running the powerful WTIC-AM and FM stations, went on the air on Channel 3 in 1956.[34]

Competition was coming, and Aldo DeDomenicis was not sure how to face it. He was very friendly when the owners of Channel 3 came to visit, to learn how to run a TV station.[35] But DeDomenicis worried. Engineer Emery Schmittgall warned, "You better go down to ABC and sign a contract with them."[36] DeDomenicis did, but he became more nervous about being able to maintain his station, staff, and investment, and asked Edward Taddei to find a buyer for the stations.

Under Triangle

In 1956 Triangle Publications purchased WNHC-AM and FM and WNHC-TV for $5.5 million. The WNHC-TV staff were sorry to see the change. They had benefited from profit sharing of a week's salary every six weeks, a family atmosphere at work, and plenty of help to get the programming on the air and sold.[37] Others in New Haven were eager to see a more professional attitude. The station could benefit from people who had experience elsewhere.[38]

Triangle came in with the new vice president and general manager, Howard Maschmeier. They told the staff there would be very few changes. Within a month 15 percent of the staff had lost their jobs, and within a year 50 percent had lost their jobs.[39] Triangle was a highly centralized organization where all decisions were made by the offices in Philadelphia. All hiring had to be approved by one person after a very lengthy process; all editorials had to be approved by one person.

---

34. Charles S. Aronson, ed., *International Television Almanac, 1958* (New York: Quigley, 1958), p. 19.

35. Harris interview, tape 1. Other reports were that DeDomenicis tried to have Channel 3 moved to a UHF channel.

36. Schmittgall interview, tapes 12 and 13.

37. Syd Jaffe notes that DeDomenicis had worked to keep the unions out of the station, and thinks he was fired because he had tried to bring in AFTRA, December 5, 1994, tape 17.

38. Kops interview, tape 6.

39. AFTRA and NABET unions came in with sale.

Triangle did make capital improvements: It improved the transmitter, moved the station to a new and larger building, and added some programming changes. With an attempt to broadcast in color in 1956 came a new transmitter. The height of the tower was increased, and more land was purchased to avoid FAA complaints and to put in a new transmitter.[40] The original building on Chapel Street had become too tight for the station.[41] The station moved only four blocks away to the site of the first settlers' landing in 1638. The bottom line was the determining factor for many of the programming decisions. Triangle put more people in the business office than in the news department.[42] The news department could be only as large as the economy would allow. If sales slumped, people in news were let go. The department was regarded as the money pit of the station.[43]

Entertainment

WNHC-TV had its own teenage "Bandstand" program with a group of regulars every afternoon and high-school students coming in by the bus load. The station continued its variety shows and its children's programming. Titles would vary. During one era they had "Captain Sea Whiskers" with a Shakespearean actor, Mitch Agruess, as the master of ceremonies. With full red beard, very soft-spoken, the captain was very popular with those five years and under. There was a drawing program with Ralph Kanna on the weekends. Admiral Jack was another host, but he had problems with payola and was fired.[44]

Although "Bandstand" was a very popular show, it was cut in November 1962 because the kids were buying only the records and very few of the products advertised. The host, Mike Warren, then came up with another

---

40. Schmittgall interview, tapes 12 and 13. The station returned to black-and-white broadcasting and reintroduced color for local origination in 1965. Bill Ellison noted it was a big transition in 1965. Ellison interview, November 21, 1994, tape 11.

41. WNHC had taken advantage of all the building had to offer: the ghosts in the old morgue, the roundtable in one of the garages for showing off the new Edsel, and the central location.

42. Ellison interview, September 12, 1994, tapes 2 and 3.

43. Youngs interview, December 4, 1994, tapes 14 and 15.

44. He would plug his own appearances at other places, both the paid appearances and the benefits. When program director Bill Ellison became sleuth, he found many of Admiral Jack's appearances were paid ones. Jack replied he didn't know he was doing anything wrong. Ellison and Sanna interview, September 12, 1994, tapes 2 and 3.

children's program, "Mr. Goober": "It took quite a while convincing management to go with it. I would talk to the station manager every time I had a
chance, follow him to lunch, etcetera, till he agreed to my only alternative. I
said I would start the show using a slide of Mr. Goober with voice-over
introductions to the film clips and other parts of the show. The deal was that
if I could make that successful, then the station would go for the show with
me on camera as Mr. Goober. He would see the results in the next rating
period. That was a long wait ... from November until May. The numbers
were good, and I went on camera as Mr. Goober for a two-hour ... taped
show on Saturdays."[45] Triangle also produced programs for syndication, and
Mike was hoping "Mr. Goober" would be one of them. But Triangle, instead,
went with car racing. Roger Clipp, Triangle's chief of broadcasting, loved
car racing, and he would have all the races filmed, except for the Indianapolis
500, to which he could not get the rights.

In 1965 WNHC filmed in color and nationally syndicated an exercise
program, "Exercise with Gloria." They also ran a music show from Triangle
called "Big Boss with the Hot Sauce," but the host was using such risqué
language that it did not last long. And Walter Annenberg had the station
produce a number of programs with Yale University called "Yale Reports,"
but there was so little production value that very few people found the
programs watchable.[46]

Public Affairs and News Under Triangle

The station manager, Howard Maschmeier, was very interested in the
image of the station. He started an advisory board called the Connecticut
Service Council, which would become a model in the FCC's eyes. Leaders
from all over the state would meet at the station on a monthly basis, discuss
their organization's efforts, and hear the station's remarks. It was a good way
of gathering information for the station, and for the leaders to feel as if they
had some impact.[47] In 1965 Triangle had all its stations produce a weekly
series called "Community Salute" for all the stations to sell. It would also be

---

45. Warren interview, tapes 2 and 3.
46. Sanna interview, tapes 2 and 3.
47. Ellison interview, November 21, 1994, tape 11.

a way for the stations to make use of their investment in the new "slant-head" tape-recording machines.[48]

Maschmeier encouraged the station staff to go out into the community, join community organizations, speak at functions. He thought that the role of the station manager was to be seen in the local elite clubs, delegate to the station's staff the work needed to be done, and read editorials. The station's editorials were not political endorsements, but rather encouraged the viewers to do positive things to help their community, especially in the areas of social unrest and inner-city efforts.[49] One editorial series, which led to the appointment of a statewide task force on lead paint, won the award for the best editorial series in the country.[50]

The Sixties and Beyond

There are conflicting messages about the station's policy on coverage of civil unrest in the city. Some say there was a policy *not* to cover the riots, and others say there was no explicit policy. Coverage did occur, and there were differences on what the station's response should be, due to concern about inciting further rioting. News anchor/producer Bob Norman can recall covering the riots in New Haven for three to four days straight, with no break, all on film. Photographer Youngs would get himself right in the middle: "I was stupid. I went to see what was happening, the lights had been knocked out. I wasn't scared and I got pictures. I called back to the station and got four people on the line wanting to hear what was up, but not one of them came out to join me. The police were lined up on one side, and you could hear the cops cocking their rifles ... but nothing happened. That was 4 or 5

48. Ellison as news and public-affairs director had reporters cover communities as far away as possible yet still in the coverage area: Pittsfield, Mass; Suffolk; Long Island; New London—places that would take one to three hours to reach. They would spend a couple of days there, then return to edit the footage by the end of the week.

49. Ellison suggests the reason: "You have to really know what you're doing. You have to have a real editorial board that would be prepared to interview candidates, and reach some conclusions together, and be able to justify, in your own mind, those conclusions. Triangle didn't want to carry the editorial process that far. And if you endorsed the wrong candidate it could hurt the station in the future. It's safer to stay away from endorsing candidates. Some stations might do it well, but it would be safer to just not endorse candidates at any of the Triangle stations." November 21, 1994, tape 11.

50. Ellison interview, November 21, 1994, tape 11. The station won the national award in 1970 largely because it showed how the state had changed the laws about lead paint.

nights in a row."[51] The station, as others in the country, was trying to respond to the unrest in various ways. Maschmeier asked Ellison, program and news director, to produce a documentary about the positive events going on in the cities of Connecticut. In the first one, entitled "It's What's Happening," Ellison followed activist Ned Coll, who had started a job-training program in Hartford. One of the viewers was so impressed that he got his company, the Hartford Insurance Group, to sponsor a series of half-hour, prime-time editorial documentaries from 1968 through 1972. They included "The Cool Side of a Connecticut Summer"(after the summer of 1967); "A Couple of Guys Named Smith and Jones" (community activists); "It's Your Rights and My Rights" (the Connecticut Human Rights Commission); "And Some New Kids Come to School" (about Project Concern); "The Little Red School House, Color It Modern" (alternative high schools); "Police Are Made Not Born" (police-community relations); and "Teaching the Inner City Teacher."[52]

The civil-rights issues came to a head for New Haven in 1970 when members of the Black Panthers were tried for the murder of Alex Rackley. The city was flooded with the National Guard, and the station was closely watched by the FBI, as it had been identified as a target. The news crew parked themselves in the hotel on the green where the people were holding a rally. Both reporter Norman and photographer Youngs will never forget covering the evening the National Guard met the demonstrators with tear gas. Norman reports that Youngs said he was afraid of tear gas, but the two egged each other on to cover the clash. Youngs could see the tear gas coming from the Guard, but there wasn't enough light, so he moved to the middle of the green. As Norman says, Youngs got brave all of a sudden, and Norman ran. Youngs turned around to shoot Norman reporting on the scene, but Norman had disappeared.[53]

It was a frightening time for the station staff. They could hear and see the Guard's tanks coming up the street; the FBI came to clear them out of the station because of a bomb threat—that is, all but those in the control room. Another evening, during this long weekend of demonstrations, there was an explosion at Yale's hockey rink. Norman rushed over with the police and saw all the glass-front doors shattered and the floor covered with smoke. There had been a concert in the rink that evening to keep people occupied,

51. Youngs interview, December 4, 1994, tape 14.
52. Ellison interview, October 24, 1994, tapes 7 and 8.
53. Oral-history interview with Bob Norman, conducted by Margot Hardenbergh, December 12, 1994, tape 19; and Youngs interview, tapes 14 and 15.

and no one knew whether there were any victims of the explosion. The police detective asked Norman for his light. Norman said sure, "and I'll follow you with our camera." Fortunately, no one had been in the rink at the time of the explosion. Norman and photographer Pat Childs got excellent film footage, but, of course, it wouldn't be ready for the 11 p.m. newscast. As Norman says, it was a major story—the top story—but the station broadcast it as the sixth story.[54] Norman believes those in charge were concerned about inciting further unrest, though perhaps they were anticipating the future, when all lead stories would have visuals.

Changes in news were occurring throughout the country, and Channel 8 was there too. Ellison describes the changes by the late 1960s: "There were so many events, from the Vietnam War to King's assassination. The people wanted more news, and television was there ready to cover it. Triangle hired a news consultant, Magid, which came in and told them how to produce the news and sell it. And they purchased the Action News package. People did respond to the name." Triangle had started formatting its news program in Philadelphia as "Action News" by 1970, and the WNHC staff were there to observe how it was done. "Action News was the first to integrate sports, weather, and news. It required 15 pieces of film, three packages a day for the one-half-hour program."[55] But management still would put very few resources into the news department. It would take a new owner to make news the largest department in the station.

Capital Cities

In 1971 Capital Cities Communications purchased the television stations of Triangle Publications. As a result of the sale, the station call letters changed to WTNH, the radio stations were split off and sold to another owner, and new management came in. As part of the sales agreement Capital Cities created the Minority Advisory Committee and contributed $350,000 for minority-related programming for three years. *Broadcasting Magazine* summed up the arrangement in this way: "$1 million pledged by CapCities

---

54. Norman interview, tape 19.

55. Oral-history interview with Kenn Venit, conducted by Margot Hardenbergh, September 26, 1994, tape 5. Venit gave an interesting description of how having the reporters win the right to cut the film—not splice, but make the cuts—made the news faster paced. The film editors who cut and spliced made fewer cuts.

for minority programs to scrub 'citizen' protests against its Triangle buy."[56] General manager Pete Orne described the committee as interesting and vital to the development of the station. It was made up of community people, who recommended other community people. Bill Ellison as public affairs and news director found the council frustrating, with nothing happening for at least a year: "People [were] so accustomed to criticizing and needling, and being negative about things that were going on in the established media.... It's good to complain about newscasts, about the hiring. But do something with that money."[57] All agree that the council provided constant communication between station management and the minority communities in the state, just as women's groups did later.

The National Organization for Women organized the Feminist Committee for Media Reform, addressing themselves to all media in the New Haven area, not just to the TV station. When they asked to meet with station management, particularly to complain about news coverage, Orne was pleased to meet with them. He describes the women's group as "not ... tactful," and ineffective because nobody could define what a women's program was. Ellison considered the group more of an educational source about women's issues. But the station had a strong record in the area of women's issues, so there wasn't as much to talk about. Ellison, as public-affairs director, found that changes in women's-issues coverage did occur over the long term.[58]

When Capital Cities took over the station, it made a commitment to news. The station already had a good track record of editorials and urban-affairs involvement.[59] The new management recognized that entertainment programming was being provided by other delivery systems, so the future of the station, lay in local news. Tape was also replacing film, which would allow for an expansion of the news operation. Now that management planned to emphasize local news, they began to hire better people, and more people, and committed more airtime to the station. As Orne says, "Fortuitously the

56. Walt Hawver, *Capital Cities/ABC The Early Years: 1954–1986; How the Minnow Came to Swallow the Whale* (Radnor, Pa.: Chilton Book Company, 1994), p. 126.

57. Ellison interview, October 24, 1994, tape 7.

58. Ellison notes how he had to keep reminding the news staff not to argue, get offended, or take complaints personally, but to try to consider points in their larger context. October 24, 1994, tape 7.

59. Oral-history interview with Peter K. Orne, conducted by Margot Hardenbergh, November 14, 1994, tape 9. Orne was vice president and general manager of WTNH-TV from 1971 until 1986, the time that Capital Cities owned the station.

advertising community also saw news as a better advertising opportunity. So it all fit very nicely."

After many requests from the staff, the decision to boost the equipment and personnel was made very apparent by one event: Orne was interviewing former colleague Dick Williams from WTEN in Albany, New York, for the position of news director. The current news director, Bill Ellison, was also meeting with Williams when they were interrupted by a message of a plane crash at the New Haven airport. Because they wanted to be sure the story was covered, Ellison went out to the site with Williams and producer, Bill Harris. But all the deficits in the news operation made coverage of one of Connecticut's biggest stories almost impossible. There was no two-way radio, no way for the station to get one of its reporters to the site. The staff did not have reliable cars; it had only the UPI wire service. When Williams came to be co–news director with Ellison, the station hired more reporters and photographers, bought station cars, radios, and scanners, and added new wire services.

WTNH also increased its efforts in political programming. In 1976 Capital Cities decided to put a major effort into election-year programming at all the stations. WTNH produced six debate programs every Sunday for six weeks, with two hosts, local newspaper and radio reporters, and all candidates for both state and federal offices. The station continued its political programming efforts through 1979.

The tug of new technology was always part of the station's life. It had slowly changed over to videotape in the late '70s,[60] then started using microwave and satellite feeds to go live more often. Once in the late '70s the station produced a promo claiming that it now had the capability to go live from Hartford. Their major competitor, Channel 3,[61] called and warned they had better prove their advertising true, or they would have to take the promo off the air. General manager Orne directed the news team to go live that day, whatever it took. Kenn Venit describes what happened: "I was assigned to write a story, which was about the state police and the legislature. So I wrote that story in New Haven, drove to Hartford (about one hour away), where a photographer had the dish on the truck pointed to the top of the Gold Building ... a Channel 8 engineer was hand holding a dish pointed to East Peak in Meriden ... [and] another engineer had a hand-held dish ... that was hitting the dish at the transmitter site on Gaylord Mountain in Hamden. It was a

---

60. Orne interview, tape 9.
61. Orne referred to Channel 3 as their "hate object," tape 9.

rainy night and the picture was scratchy, but we went live for 45 seconds, and there was tremendous response from the other media. That spot was run at a far greater frequency after those 45 seconds."[62]

In 1983 the station moved for the third time to the new studios and offices that Capital Cities had built, still in the center of the city. They offered greater flexibility in producing the next major efforts in community programming: telethons. The station had been carrying the muscular-dystrophy telethon and an auction for a local charity on an annual basis, but it started producing more locally. In 1979 it held a telethon for the Bradley airport museum, which had suffered losses from a tornado. In 1980 it held one for the victims of the Italian earthquake and raised $250,000. By the mid-'80s it was producing four annually, for the Easter Seals Rehabilitation program, the Newington Children's Hospital, the Leukemia Society, and the United Negro College Fund. The latter had local informational, nonentertainment, inserts.

Changes

In 1985 Capital Cities announced its merger with ABC, which meant that WTNH would be sold again. Capital Cities had done well with WTNH-TV and as a farewell gift gave employees who had been with the station during its ownership two weeks pay for each year there. WTNH was sold to Cook-Inlet, Broadcasting and Whitney Communications in 1986, which has since gone bankrupt and sold the station to Lin Broadcasting. The station is now making more money than ever.[63] WTNH is affiliated with ABC and continues to provide news, special community-programming efforts, and opportunities for many advertisers. The station continues to hustle for viewers and advertising dollars, as it has since 1948.

---

62. There was some discussion of the danger involved, and the hand-held aspect was replaced by a permanent relay system. Venit interview, tape 5.

63. Ellison interview, tapes 2 and 3.

3 Forgotten Pioneer: Philco's WPTZ

Michael Woal and Linda Kowall Woal

No champagne corks popped at Philadelphia's old Philco plant on October 17, 1941, to celebrate the event. It failed to rate even a few lines in local newspapers; reports of an increasingly grim drama unfolding in Europe took precedence. America's first commercial-network telecast—the real beginnings of commercial television—went virtually unnoticed. The "network" undertaking this historic telecast was the National Broadcasting Company (NBC)—all two stations of it: New York City's WNBT and the new network's first affiliate, Philadelphia's Philco-owned WPTZ. They had just been granted the nation's first two commercial-television licenses by the Federal Communications Commission.[1] The first network program seems to have gone quite unremarked, but that was hardly surprising, considering its tiny audience. A handful of WPTZ technicians manned the station's control room at Philco's C and Tioga streets factory in north Philadelphia as WNBT's signal came in over the television industry's first coaxial-cable hookup. Relayed from the factory into the homes of the Philco and RCA engineers who were testing the quality of early television receivers, the fleeting electron-images of Arturo Toscanini and the NBC Symphony Orchestra materialized on the snowy screens of Pennsylvania's fewer than 100 and New York City's fewer than 500 sets.

The creators of what was then a live medium saw little reason to record their efforts for posterity, and so most of the programs like this ephemeral

---

1. "The History of Channel 3," unpublished manuscript, n.d., Station History File, KYW-TV, Philadelphia, Pa.

telecast, much of the documentation, and many of the memories of television's beginnings have disappeared. Sorting through the remains, broadcast historians Erik Barnouw and William Boddy are among the first to chronicle the industry's beginnings seriously. Their studies focus on New York City as the hub of broadcasting activity during the time the big issues relating to television technology, programming development, sponsorship, and creation of the three major commercial-television networks were played out, giving network television its final form. References to Philco's role are few and brief.

Today Philco is a name that evokes nostalgic images. One of America's leading radio and television manufacturers from the late '20s through the '50s, its streamlined, art-deco radios and formidable television consoles are collector's items now, charming relics of the nation's first love affair with broadcasting. All but forgotten, however, is the extent of the Philco Corporation's pioneering technical, commercial, and artistic roles at the center of the creation and early development of the television industry. The history of Philco and station W3XE/WPTZ offers a rare opportunity for a closer look at the evolution of the television industry for a number of reasons: Under the direction of Philo T. Farnsworth the station was a major contributor to the development of television technology; it was RCA's chief competitor in the manufacturing and sales of early television sets; it was the nation's second commercially licensed television broadcaster and a key participant in the formation of the first television network; and it was a nursery for formidable broadcasting talent and innovative program development.

Early TV Broadcasting by Philco

Informal company histories point to 1928 as the year of Philco's big shift from emphasizing storage batteries to becoming a leading manufacturer of radios. James Carmine emerged as the key figure, who also led the company into television experimentation that year.[2] While RCA and the NBC radio network, under the flamboyant leadership of David Sarnoff, conducted television experiments and negotiated with AT&T and Westinghouse over patents and fees, Philco brought the eccentric television pioneer,

---

2. "The History of Channel 3"; William Balderston, *Philco: Autobiography of Progress* (New York: Newcomen Society, 1954).

Philo T. Farnsworth, to Philadelphia in 1931. With backing from Philco, Farnsworth, who held important patents for his electronic television system, continued his research in Philadelphia from 1931 to 1933 and established Philco as the only serious competition to Sarnoff and RCA.[3] Under Farnsworth's direction Philco engineers completed a TV control room and erected a workable, if not always reliable, television transmitter.[4] In 1932, the year RCA installed its television station in the Empire State Building, Philco officially started broadcasting from its own W3XE, the nation's second experimental television station licensed by the FCC. W3XE went on the air June 28, 1932; and, according to correspondence with the FCC, its "usual hours of operation" were 9 a.m. to 5 p.m. and 7 p.m. to 9:30 p.m.[5] "Experimental" was, indeed, the operative word.

According to one of the station engineers, William N. Parker, "Early 'studio' programs originated in the space next to the control room with a single Iconoscope camera and a couple of flood lights."[6] The studio was on the fifth floor of the Philco factory, which, according to Parker, created an intolerable audio rumble. A. H. Brolly, Farnsworth's former chief engineer, devised an ingenious solution to the rumble: a new studio using the "room within a room" principle, with the concrete-floor slab floating on a bed of coil springs.[7] Early W3XE programming was as experimental as the studio. "Most of the studio presentations consisted of variety shows and plays by amateur dramatic groups.... The television department secretary frequently acted as 'script girl,' giving cues to the director regarding camera changes, etc."[8] Committed to programming development as well as to technological improvement, W3XE hired a full-time program director, Nick Alexander, one of the nation's first television program directors. W3XE was on the air

3. Erik Barnouw, *Tube of Plenty: The Evolution of American Television,* 2nd rev. ed. (New York: Oxford University Press, 1990), p. 83; Lawrence W. Lichty and Malachi C. Topping, *American Broadcasting: A Source Book on the History of Radio and Television* (New York: Hastings House, 1975), pp. 60–61.

4. William N. Parker, "Early Philadelphia Television," unpublished paper, May 13, 1986, p. 1, W3XE File, Free Library of Philadelphia, Theatre Collection.

5. National Archives, RG 173, Federal Communications Commission, Office of the Executive Director, General Correspondence 1927–1946, Box 415, File 89-6, Philco Radio and Television Corporation. See "Outline of Experimental Work Accomplished at Station W3XE Since It Was First Licensed."

6. Parker, p. 7.

7. Parker, p. 7.

8. Parker, p. 7.

150 hours in 1933, and by 1936 the station's airtime had grown to 463 hours.[9] In 1936 the coaxial cable between New York City and Philadelphia was developed by AT&T and was ready for use, setting the stage for tests in television networking.

Despite these technological developments, the '30s was a decade of slow progress and unrealized potential. The industrywide technical standardization that would have opened the door to commercial-television broadcasting was stalled as the FCC continued to waiver over the number of scan lines and other specifications to which television broadcasters and manufacturers would have to conform.[10] Meanwhile, Philco and RCA followed parallel courses, using their profits from radio manufacturing to finance experimental television through years of development in fits and starts. "Demonstrations were part of the life of early television," Parker remembered: "One important demonstration was held at the Franklin Institute in downtown Philadelphia in 1936, and represented the first on-the-air showing of a 441 line picture.... The picture quality was excellent and seemed to greatly impress R. D. Kell and other engineers from RCA (our competitors)."[11]

A 10-day exhibition that actually started August 25, 1934, this was the first public demonstration ever of a complete electronic television system. Philo Farnsworth and his engineers set up an improvised studio in the Franklin Institute with the camera on the roof. An approximately 12-by-13-inch receiver provided a view to 200 people.[12]

Parker also recalled another series of demonstrations. A Philco "road show" was presented at department stores in a number of Midwest cities, designed to pique public interest in television.[13] With the groundwork for networking already in place in radio, an inkling of the new medium's potential to entertain and inform came the following year with television's escape from the studio in 1937, when Philco and NBC put the first mobile television units into action and expanded programming to include sports and

---

9. National Archives, RG 173, Federal Communications Commission, Office of the Executive Director, General Correspondence 1927–1946, Box 415, File 89-6, Philco Radio and Television Corporation. See "Outline of Experimental Work Accomplished at Station W3XE Since It Was First Licensed."

10. Parker, pp. 10–11.

11. Parker, p. 9; Philo T. Farnsworth, "Television by Electronic Image Scanning," *Journal of the Franklin Institute* (October 1934), pp. 411–44.

12. Albert Abramson, *The History of Television, 1880–1941* (Jefferson, N.C.: McFarland, 1987), p. 209.

13. Parker, p. 10.

live news events.[14] Experimenting with broadcasts originating from outside the studio, W3XE scored a technical breakthrough with its telecast of the first college night football game, Temple University versus the University of Kansas in 1939. It used video monitors in the mobile control room, which permitted the director to choose from a selection of available camera shots.

According to station veteran Andrew McKay, WPTZ was also possibly the first television station to introduce a "color commentator," Sam Stewart, to enhance sports telecasts for its viewers.[15] Meanwhile, NBC made public-relations history that year with David Sarnoff's demonstration telecast of President Franklin D. Roosevelt speaking from the New York World's Fair. Finally, in 1939 Philco's W3XE and RCA's forerunner to station WNBT made an agreement to exchange programming, an experimental alliance that formed the basis for creation of the NBC television network, with W3XE becoming the fledgling network's first affiliate.

The Republican National Convention, which opened on June 24, 1940, marked another major breakthrough when W3XE became the first television station to air a national political convention. Its 60-hour remote telecast from Philadelphia of the convention, in which Wendell Wilkie was nominated as the Republican candidate for president, was an engineering feat that required elaborate preparations. A 300-megahertz transmitter was located in a room built on top of Philadelphia's Convention Hall to relay the program to receiving equipment located at the Philco plant. The convention facilities included a camera platform attached to the left-hand balcony and a control room under the balcony. NBC occupied a second platform attached to the right-hand balcony, remembered W3XE's engineer Parker.[16] From Philadelphia the signal was relayed over the coaxial cable to the NBC control room in the Empire State Building. From there it was broadcast to New York City's estimated 500 television sets, and on to the NBC experimental network's second affiliate in Schenectady, New York. Although immediately recognized as a significant technical triumph, this W3XE-NBC telecast also foreshadowed television's future impact on the American political process.

---

14. "The History of Channel 3"; oral-history interview with Leonard Valenta, conducted by Linda Kowall, August 6, 1986, transcript on file at the Free Library of Philadelphia, Theatre Collection.

15. Mary Gannon, "WPTZ, Philco Station Operations," *Television*, November 1946, n.p.; Andrew C. McKay, telephone interview, August 7, 1986, transcript on file at the Free Library of Philadelphia, Theatre Collection.

16. Parker, p. 8.

To assist in the long-awaited setting of standards for American TV, Philco conducted important tests relating to the optimal number of television-picture scanning lines, transmission frequencies, and other technical aspects of TV broadcasting. After a decade of hesitation, in 1941 the FCC finally set the technical standards for television, following most of the recommendations made by RCA and Philco. With the primary technical roadblock to commercial development cleared, in August 1941 the FCC issued RCA station WNBT the nation's first commercial television license, marking the advent of commercial television broadcasting in the United States. Following WNBT, W3XE was granted the nation's second commercial license on September 3, 1941, and changed its call letters to WPTZ. A month later the two stations participated in America's first commercial-network telecast. Commercial status in these early years of the television industry, however, still did not mean commercial success—indeed, far from it.

On the eve of television's hard-won technical viability and public acceptance as a significant entertainment and communications medium, World War II suddenly shifted the spotlight back to radio. By the end of 1941 most of the nation's 23 television stations had left the air; only six, including WPTZ and WNBT, remained.[17] In 1942 manufacturing of TV receivers was halted and programming was sharply curtailed for the duration of the war. Television was forgotten.

Philco Incubates Programming During World War II

Although the war years were quiet ones in television history, they were not years of total hibernation. Citing Lee DeForest's criticism of dependency on New York as a laboratory for early television programming in his 1942 "Television Today and Tomorrow," historian William Boddy also overlooks Philco as he writes, "Due to commercial television's abortive prewar start and subsequent suspension during the war, the only television broadcast service through the mid-1940s came from a handful of New York stations."[18] In Philadelphia, however, WPTZ not only continued broadcasting but

17. Barnouw, p. 92.
18. William Boddy, *Fifties Television: The Industry and Its Critics* (Urbana: University of Illinois Press, 1990), p. 101.

charted new "firsts" in television programming and provided valuable production experience for a number of talented individuals. Thanks to their years
of "television school" at WPTZ, by 1946 they had already developed into
seasoned pros who would be instrumental in helping guide television programming through its postwar period of explosive development. It's necessary to turn to oral histories and the few surviving photos and program
schedules to sketch a rough picture of these largely unchronicled years.

"You wouldn't believe how it was then!" recalled veteran actor-
director Leonard Valenta, whose television career has spanned a half century
and included directing such venerable network soap operas as "The Edge of
Night," "Search for Tomorrow," "One Life to Live," and "The Guiding
Light." Valenta joined WPTZ in the fall of 1941. It all began when he spotted
a notice on a Temple University bulletin board seeking volunteers for
television work at Philco, Valenta recalled, "I didn't know anything about
TV, but I did know I wanted to be an actor, so I went. I won the part of the
narrator in *Quarter Century*, a blank verse play they were putting on by N.
Richard Nash who went on to write *The Rainmaker*. During the production
I remember thinking, 'Hey, this is going to be a new industry someday!'"[19]
Valenta traces his long career in "soaps" to his starring role in American
television's first domestic drama series, produced and aired by WPTZ in
early 1942. Taking its cue from the mood of the times, "Last Year's Nest,"
written by Claire Wallis and directed by WPTZ stage manager Ernest
Walling, was more socially conscious than sultry. "I guess you could
describe it as early Waltons," Valenta remembered. "It was a wartime drama
about the trials and tribulations of a German refugee and the family that took
him in as a kind of second son. I played the young immigrant—my name
was Blackie—and the story seemed to imply that I had left Germany to
escape from the Nazis because I was Jewish. The episodes covered everything from Blackie's first love—tame compared with how we'd handle it
today—to an episode with me being hunted by a Nazi."[20]

Actors and stagehands for WPTZ's wartime dramatic telecasts frequently came from Philadelphia's lively community of little theater groups.
In addition to acting, many like Valenta found themselves called upon to fill
every role from director and stage manager to property master and even
camera technician. Reflecting on the difference between television acting

---

19. Interview with Leonard Valenta, conducted by Linda Kowall, August 6, 1986, transcription,
p. 3, Free Library of Philadelphia, Theatre Collection.
20. Valenta interview, p. 6.

then and now, Valenta smiles at memories of the spirited antics that characterized the early years, and at the relative leisure of yesterday's so-called
"hectic" pace compared with today's high-pressure production schedules. "I
remember how the actors all complained about the impossibility of having
to learn a half-hour script every week. Now, our actors routinely learn the
equivalent of a Broadway second lead overnight!" Live telecasts presented
other challenges, however, as every veteran of live broadcasting has a
stockpile of anecdotes to illustrate. Relating indelible memories of one
fateful telecast of "Last Year's Nest," in which the actor playing his father
saw that he was going to be written out of the script and decided to exit a
little sooner than planned, Valenta recalled, "He just didn't show up. We all
had to wing it. We made up something about father being 'ill' and made up
ways around his lines as we went along. After live television, you're ready
for anything!"[21]

Televised dramatic productions like "Never Too Old" (broadcast May
17, 1942) and written-for-television series like "Last Year's Nest," were
regular highlights of a surprisingly full WPTZ wartime evening schedule.
The following program schedule of the Monday, February 23, 1942, shows
is typical:[22]

7:00–7:15	"Last Year's Nest," episode 5
7:15–7:30	Film Short
7:30–8:00	Elizabeth Jane Taylor, Noted Philadelphia Coloratura Soprano
*8:00–8:30	WNBT Retelecast—Air Raid Warden Instructional Program
*8:30–9:00	WNBT Retelecast—"America Prepares"
9:00–9:20	Philadelphia Council of Defense Presents "Women in Emergency Relief"
9:20–9:30	Film Short
9:30–9:45	Hale America Presents a Boxing Exhibition
9:45–10:00	"See the Skies Tonight" by Armand Spitz of the Franklin Institute
*10:00–10:15	WNBT Retelecast—President Roosevelt's Speech
10:15–10:30	The Philco News Analyst

*Special test programs originating through the facilities of WNBT, New York

21. Valenta interview, p. 6.
22. Philco-WPTZ Television Program Schedule, February 23–March 1, 1942, personal collection of Andrew C. McKay, Philadelphia, Pa.

In response to wartime demands the Philco plant was heavily involved in the research and manufacturing of airborne radar systems and other war-related electronics. The practical demands of wartime were also reflected in WPTZ's broadcasting of special NBC-network programs originating from WNBT, which were designed to test network television's potential as a public-communications link in national defense. As did the nation's defense plants, at WPTZ the wartime television industry owed a substantial debt to its own "Rosie the Riveters." A casual glance at the program credits during the war years—from "Last Year's Nest" writer, Claire Wallis, and Elizabeth Jane Taylor, soprano, to the casts for WPTZ's dramatic telecasts—indicates the important role women played in sustaining WPTZ's television programming during these years. A wartime photo taken inside the control room of the WPTZ transmitter, entirely staffed by women, further illustrates the major role women played in keeping the station on the air.

WPTZ Develops After World War II

In 1945 James Carmine, Philco vice president and the man instrumental in involving the company in television research back in 1928, commented, "Probably never before has a product of a great new industry been so completely planned and highly developed before it was offered to the public as has television."[23] As the war ended, television at WPTZ was well prepared to enter the most important phase of development. It was during this period, from 1946 to 1953, that its programming formats, business practices, and institutions were borrowed from radio and shaped for television. This was the period now nostalgically referred to as television's Golden Years.

As Americans again focused their lives around home and family after the war, 1946 marked the turning point for television's final acceptance as the nation's favorite home-based entertainment and information source. However, the viewing audience had still not grown large enough to make television a commercially viable medium. As WPTZ's commercial manager, Rolland Tooke, told *Television* reporter Mary Gannon that year, "There's nothing wrong with television in Philadelphia that 100,000 receivers won't cure overnight."[24] Returning war veteran Harold J. Pannepacker, one of the

23. Quoted in Boddy, p. 16.
24. Gannon, n.p.

nearly dozen returning war veterans who joined the WPTZ staff in 1946, laughed as he recalled, "You're not going to believe this, but my first job at the station was addressing postcards telling what we were going to be showing the next week to the only 500 or so people in the Philadelphia area with television sets. Our entire week's programming fit on a three-by-five penny postcard!"[25]

Early television continued to be subsidized by radio profits. The real test of its commercial viability came as Philco, Farnsworth, and RCA rushed to put television sets on the market in 1946. Potential TV purchasers needed something to watch, and, as in New York, activity at WPTZ picked up dramatically that year as the station began rapidly expanding its programming and hired more technicians and production personnel. In 1947 the FCC began requiring commercial stations to air a minimum of 28 hours of programming per week. Questions of how and with what to fill that much airtime were suddenly urgent. Reaching for expedient ways to fill the airtime, NBC and CBS quickly began offering program schedules that relied heavily on sports, supplemented by 15-minute news summaries, "Kraft Television Theater" (which debuted in May), "Hour Glass" (the first commercially sponsored network variety show), "Meet the Press," and, for young viewers, "Howdy Doody" and "Kukla, Fran and Ollie."

Building on the programming foundation it had laid during the '30s and early '40s, WPTZ televised a similar mix."We'll wear the tires off that mobile truck," predicted program manager Paul Knight when outlining WPTZ's plans to fill the gap by relying heavily on remote telecasts relayed from the station's traveling control room.[26] "They didn't waste much time making a cameraman out of me," Pannepacker remembered with more than a trace of amusement. "I've always suspected the real reason they hired me was because I happen to be six-foot-four, and those early cameras weighed nearly a couple of hundred pounds. Not everyone could manage them."[27] Going out on remotes in those days was quite a production. Permanent cable and even some equipment were left at several regular broadcast sites, including Philadelphia's old Franklin Field and Shibe Park. A crew needed considerable time to lug in the remaining gear and finish setting up. Positioning the mammoth trailer truck housing WPTZ's mobile control room (and constructed to hold two camerapeople and an announcer on the roof)

25. Oral-history interview with Harold Pannepacker, conducted by Linda Kowall, August 2, 1986, transcription, p. 1, Free Library of Philadelphia, Theatre Collection.

26. Gannon, n.p.

27. Pannepacker interview, p. 1.

was sometimes more like docking a giant tanker. "It was a little like staging an invasion," Pannepacker laughed.[28]

Sports accounted for most of WPTZ's programming, advertising revenue, and viewers. The station's—and Pennsylvania's—first television commercial, for the Atlantic Richfield Company, was aired during a 1946 Penn football telecast. Pannepacker was one of the camera operators on the first Army-Navy game network telecast, as well as on remote telecasts of baseball (the Phillies and the Athletics), football (the Eagles), hockey (the Ramblers), college sports, boxing, bowling, and wrestling. Add NBC network telecasts of the "Gillette Cavalcade of Sports" to these "Philco Sports" offerings, and it's easy to see why neighborhood tavern owners were the first to gamble on some of the earliest commercially available television sets. Sets that then cost the rather considerable sum of about $400 were an investment justified by the number of patrons who gathered to share a few drinks and the novelty.

Other WPTZ remotes brought more television firsts. Telecasts of Philadelphia theater productions accounted for another sizable number of WPTZ's remotes and much of its programming. In 1947 Leonard Valenta costarred with Katharine Minehart in "The Taming of the Shrew," American television's first complete Shakespearean production, broadcast live from Philadelphia's Germantown Theater Guild.[29] Blocking, lighting, camera placement, and covering the time between scene changes for these live dramatic telecasts presented formidable technical challenges that often called for more improvisational skills from the production crew than from the actors.[30]

A milestone in broadcasting history was marked by WPTZ's remote telecast of the 1948 Democratic and Republican national conventions, held in Philadelphia, for which the station provided the NBC network coverage. Television and WPTZ, in fact, were the reasons behind the selection of Philadelphia as the site for both the Democratic and Republican national conventions, because of WPTZ's experience in remote telecasts and the coaxial cable already linking WPTZ, Philadelphia, to New York and Washington. With the cable's scheduled summer expansion of an additional 14 eastern stations, the expected audience potential was millions.[31] WPTZ's Harold Pannepacker was one of the camerapeople on that historic telecast.

28. Pannepacker interview, p. 3.
29. "History of Channel 3"; Valenta interview, p. 7.
30. Oral-history interview with Leonard Valenta, conducted by Linda Kowall, August 14, 1986, transcript, p. 2, Free Library of Philadelphia, Theatre Collection.
31. Barnouw, p. 111.

It was exciting to cover such an important national event, he reflected, "but I don't think many of us in the business then had any idea that we were making a kind of history, too. We weren't that aware yet of television's influence. We were still wondering if anyone out there was even watching. But the politicians were quick to catch on. Truman, the first President to sit in the White House and watch the nomination of his rival on TV, was skeptical of broadcasting and the power of its advertisers. He chose to campaign in person, but Dewey actually sought us out and would do anything we'd say! That came as a total surprise."[32]

Out of the Red

Television was on its way. In October 1946 WPTZ and WNBT signed a formal agreement to exchange programming and began working out the financial arrangements for this pooling of programming and viewers, which formed the keystone of the NBC television network. WPTZ's—and television's—commercial viability appeared finally to be in sight. Expansion was taking place at WPTZ within the studio as well. Originally crammed in a corner of Philco's C and Tioga streets factory, and sharing the premises with a major manufacturing operation that included everything from research labs to the glass-blowing plant where Philco radio and TV picture tubes were made, WPTZ moved temporarily to Philadelphia's Architects Building and, in 1947, expanded to more permanent facilities at 1619 Walnut Street.

Television was expensive and still being sustained by profits from radio. Although WPTZ's programming expenses in 1947 totaled $180,332.59, its advertising revenues came to only $11,500.00. In Philadelphia, as in New York, the question of the hour was, Who will pay for and who will control program content—the station/network or the sponsor? Although the question was the same everywhere, the answer in Philadelphia was unique.[33]

In New York, television sponsorship began falling into the pattern previously established by radio, with individual advertisers sponsoring entire programs and taking direct responsibility for content and production. The

---

32. Pannepacker interview, p. 4.
33. National Archives, RG 173, Federal Communications Commission, Annual Financial Reports of Broadcast Stations, 1937–1947, Box 213, Station WPTZ, Philco Television Broadcasting Corporation.

result was that by 1949 five of the 10 most popular television shows were produced not by WNBT or the networks, but by a single ad agency, leaving the networks faced with the problem of trying to regain program control.[34] NBC's Pat Weaver is given credit for introducing an alternative, "magazine advertising," or the sale of several commercial spots on a single program, the "Today" show, in 1951.[35] However, sponsor-program relationships in Philadelphia were already breaking new ground.

With the postwar expansion of WPTZ, account executive Robert Jawer, another of the ex-veterans recruited in 1946, found himself faced with the double challenge of enlisting commercial sponsors and developing new programming for them. Although Pat Weaver is credited with the introduction of spot advertising on the "Today" show in 1951, in reality WPTZ set the precedent in 1946. Special program sponsors such as Atlantic Richfield and Gillette weren't overly enthusiastic to buy airtime, and Jawer's first efforts to sell short commercial spots were often greeted with the suspicion due a con artist. "We're pretty sure I was the first TV ad salesman in the country, and do you know who I sold my first twenty second spot to? Jawer's Auto Supply—my dad! I think it cost him about thirty dollars."[36] Unlike sales practices in New York, from the very outset of commercial sales at WPTZ, potential advertisers were offered a choice between sponsoring an entire program or buying individual spots. Programming suggestions from sponsors were welcomed, but final responsibility for program development and production remained in the hands of the station.

Daytime programming became the next challenge. Appliance dealers complained that it was impossible to sell television sets in the middle of the afternoon, with nothing on the air but the test pattern. To meet the growing demands of potential sponsors and appliance salesmen, as well as the new FCC requirements for more programs, WPTZ adopted an ambitious strategy to supplement its remotes with stepped-up in-studio production or, in Jawer's words, "Live Anything!"[37] "Live anything" came to include dramatic and variety shows developed by WPTZ staff, then sold. Other shows were specially created at a particular sponsor's request. The result was a kind of

34. Boddy, p. 94.

35. Boddy, p. 104.

36. Oral-history interview with Robert Jawer, conducted by Linda Kowall, July 27, 1986, transcription, p. 1, Free Library of Philadelphia, Theatre Collection.

37. Jawer interview, p. 3.

primordial sea of evening and daytime programming, some of which worked and some of which didn't.[38]

WPTZ's innovative "Video Ballet" series, an evening program directed by Paul Nickell, was repeatedly singled out as an outstanding popular, as well as artistic, success. The series offered a variety of presentations ranging from a special-effects production of "Danse Macabre," to a modern adaptation of "Gaietie Parisienne" called "GI Blues" and a special Christmas presentation of "Cinderella." One of television's first talk shows, WPTZ's "Pleased to Meet You," hosted by a future space program's favorite commentator, Roy Neal, was also well received and, judging from its description by *Televiser* and station veterans, featured an intriguing assortment of guests that would be the envy of David Letterman, ranging from magician Harry Blackstone to "the Chinese delegate to the United Nations who told how he designed a three-hole golf course in Vatican City during the war."[39] Big-name sports figures, meanwhile, regularly appeared on "Sports Scrapbook."

Unlike New York, where much early television programming was produced by ad agencies directly for the sponsors, thereby cutting the stations out of the process, television sponsorship and program production at WPTZ was a collaborative effort. Gimbels Department Store became a daytime television advertising pioneer in 1946 by sponsoring "All Eyes on Gimbels," the first fully sponsored program series.[40] The store quickly followed this success with long-running sponsorship of "The Handyman," a cross between a how-to show and an infomercial that blithely muddled the distinction between program and commercial by presenting Jack Creamer offering home-improvement tips that usually just happened to call for Gimbels merchandise.[41] The Philadelphia Electric Company sponsored television's first cooking show, "TV Kitchen," with resourceful Florence Hanford, who, sometimes forced by the fierce studio heat to substitute unlikely ingredients during her demonstrations, became famous for her melt-proof mashed-potato "ice cream." Pleased with its tentative advertising forays on WPTZ, Atlantic Richfield also continued as a major sponsor of televised sporting events. The successful examples set by these early advertisers, and the efforts

---

38. See Mary Gannon, "WPTZ: Philco Station Operations," *Television*, November 1946, and E. D. Lucas, Jr., "WPTZ Trying Out Varied Program Ideas," *Televiser*, March 15, 1948. These offer a valuable behind-the-scenes account of the kinds of programming experiments tried, and television formats forged, at WPTZ during these important formative years.

39. Lucas, p. 16.; also McKay interview, p. 2.

40. Lucas, p. 17; also Valenta interview, August 14, 1986, p. 4; McKay interview, p. 3.

41. Jawer interview, p. 3.

of Bill Jawer and the WPTZ sales department, gradually helped television turn the corner from experimental to commercial broadcasting. By 1948 WPTZ proudly reported that although it wasn't making a profit yet, half of its programming was finding sponsors.[42]

Before Nielsen ratings and sophisticated audience-share analysis, just how many viewers were actually "out there" watching was anybody's guess. The number of viewers in 1946 requesting Florence Hanford's free recipes provided the first less-than-scientific indication of WPTZ's daytime "ratings."[43] The following year *Television* reported that WPTZ had developed its own system for keeping a rough tally of viewers—establishing a mailing list of television-set owners. "Before a television viewer is added to the list, they insist that the person supply them with information on the type of set, name of manufacturer, size of screen and where purchased. In return, the viewer is mailed a free program schedule for the week."[44] From a total of approximately 500 sets in 1946, by 1947 *Television* reported, "Their WPTZ records average about 125 new names a week, which they believe covers practically all purchases of sets in the area."[45]

The postwar mood of the country was one of renewed economic confidence. The general public was ready to be entertained and willing to take chances on new consumer goods and the latest novelties, like the costly new television sets. "Owning a television set became a status symbol, and a surprising number of status-seekers to adorned their roofs with TV antennas despite the fact that they didn't own a television set," recalled Andy McKay.[46] The age of consumerism was dawning, and the television industry stood poised to reap the windfall. By 1948 full-page ads for Philco and RCA television sets began appearing in *Life, Look,* and the *Saturday Evening Post.* Up from six in 1942, by 1949 television had 87 commercial broadcast licensees, and manufacturers like RCA and Philco were reporting big profits in equipment sales.[47]

A measure of television's growing popularity was also suggested that year by increasing concern within the film industry about the tube's effects on box-office receipts. Seventy movie-theater closings were reported in

42. Lucas, p. 17.
43. Jawer interview, p. 4.
44. "Audience Statistics," *Television*, March 1947, personal collection of Andrew C. McKay, Philadelphia, Pa.
45. "Audience Statistics."
46. McKay interview, p. 5.
47. Boddy, p. 30.

eastern Pennsylvania alone.[48] Concern stimulated ideas about big-screen television projection in movie theaters and, in Philadelphia, inspired a novel film/television collaboration. With considerable fanfare in a cover story headlined "Television From the Stage Offered Something for Exhibitors to Ponder," a major motion-picture trade journal described the cooperation of WPTZ, Philadelphia's Roosevelt Theater, and their sponsor in promoting and staging a live broadcast remote of WPTZ's "Telekids" series from the theater's stage as the first half of a double feature that concluded with the evening's film. The "Philadelphia Experiment" hoped to demonstrate that by pooling their resources and their promotion, the film and television industries were not necessarily in competition but could both profit by stimulating audience interest in each other.[49] The experiment was short-lived.

The Golden Age at WPTZ: A Bunyip and the Mad Hungarian

After nearly 25 years of struggling to lift off, the television industry finally took flight in the early 1950s with programs that captured the imagination of viewers and were hailed by critics for the brief promise they offered of an intelligent form of popular entertainment. At WPTZ the studio from which many of these programs emanated was, its pioneers all recall, very small and very, very hot. As Valenta remembers, "There was hardly any room to move and I remember more than one occasion when we'd be doing a show with the sets tumbling down around us. Bill Smith—who went on to Hollywood and designed the sets for Blake Edwards' *S.O.B.* and *Victor/Victoria*—was our art director. He came up with the idea of constructing sets-within-sets that peeled away like the layers of an onion to give us more room and make scene changes easier."[50]

In addition to his contributions to early television scenery and production-set design, Art Director W. Craig "Bill" Smith conducted some of the industry's first color tests for the tube—with garish results, Valenta recalled.[51] "To give the most pleasing look on the black and white home

48. Barnouw, p. 114.

49. "The Philadelphia Experiment: Televising From the Stage Offered Something for Exhibitors to Ponder," *Exhibitor*, April 20, 1949, pp. 6–7.

50. Valenta interview, August 6, 1986, p. 3.

51. Gannon, n.p.; Valenta interview, p. 3.; McKay interview, p. 5.

screens, sets and costumes were outrageous colors. We had to wear yellow make-up on our faces, black lipstick, and paint black shadows around our eyes. We got used to it, but it gave anyone who came to visit us a hell of a fright. Every day was Halloween!"[52]

Dealing with the intense heat wasn't so easy. "The lights they had in there were so powerful, I'm not kidding when I say the temperature in the studio often got above one hundred degrees," Pannepacker remembered.[53] "There were a couple of times when I honestly thought I was going to pass out," Valenta added. "It was so hot, they kept a salt tablet dispenser around to help keep us from getting too dehydrated. Between the sweat and our make-up, we were a sight!"[54]

Despite the rough edges, WPTZ was one of the country's early state-of-the-art television facilities, both in terms of its technical sophistication and its experienced personnel. "In the 1940s and early 1950s, WPTZ was really PBS before PBS. We were broadcasting live ballet, drama, musical and scientific programs—TV material which commercial stations rarely present anymore," reflected Andrew C. "Andy" McKay, another member of WPTZ's "class of '46," who joined the station as an actor and makeup artist prior to becoming chief production assistant for Ernie Kovacs. "During those years, WPTZ was blessed with two exceptionally innovative people—both stage-trained—Program Manager and director Ernie Walling, and director Paul Nickell who went to the CBS network in New York in late 1948 to become one of the directors of their famed *Studio One* series."[55] In interviewing veteran WPTZ actors like Valenta and McKay, one is immediately struck by their extraordinary familiarity with the technical aspects of television hardware and production. In its November 1946 article describing the station's production philosophy and methods, *Television* reported,

> While they believe in ultimate specialization in each job category, the best method of training anyone for a particular niche is to familiarize him with every phase of studio operations. By doing this, each member of the staff has a realization of the other's problems and can dovetail his particular task into the composite teamwork that's necessary to smooth video programming....[Executive Producer/Director] Ernie Walling's best trick along these lines is to put in a stand-in and take the

---

52. Valenta interview, p. 3.
53. Pannepacker interview, p. 2.
54. Valenta interview, p. 3.
55. Oral-history interview with Andrew C. McKay, conducted by Linda Kowall, September 19, 1986, p. 3, Free Library of Philadelphia, Theatre Collection.

actor into the control room to show him the picture he wants to get on the monitor. It's important that the actor knows what the director is trying to do; he must be conscious of the camera, where it will be, its scope, etc. And only by taking him behind-the-scenes can a director train his cast in developing a television technique.[56]

Without exception WPTZ veterans, like Leonard Valenta, Andrew McCay, Katherine Minehart, and Harold Pannepacker, who learned the craft of television acting, writing, directing, stage managing, videography, and even sound effects at WPTZ, credited the station's crossover training for the unusual versatility and high level of professionalism they were able to bring to decades of work in the industry.

In addition to training its own staff, WPTZ can also be credited with serving as an important early "TV school" where other prospective stations sent their personnel to be trained. As McCay later recalled, "Before ABC had its own first station or network, arrangements were made with WPTZ for a "shake-down" trial and training period at WPTZ's facilities from May 1946–March 1947. ABC trained their production personnel in various TV formats—dramatic plays, cooking shows, variety shows, game shows, etc., plus pick-ups of sporting events from remote locations in Philadelphia."[57]

The majority of ABC's dramatic offerings in those years were staged by the Television Workshop in New York, a TV school sponsored by *Televiser* magazine. McKay appeared in and helped produce a number of these programs, which were rehearsed in New York before the Television Workshop crew was sent to Philadelphia, where WPTZ furnished scenery, props, technical facilities, and personnel.

After two decades of technical and artistic innovation, WPTZ finally owed much of its long-awaited commercial success to a "bunyip" and a wild, cigar-waving Hungarian. Thanks to the post–World War II "baby boom," children's programming quickly became a major factor in the phenomenal growth of the television industry after 1950. The enormous popularity of "Howdy Doody," "Kukla, Fran and Ollie," and WPTZ's own "Bertie the Bunyip," the fanciful creation of Australian-born puppeteer Lee Dexter, demonstrated the special chemistry that resulted when the intimacy of television camera work suddenly bestowed life-size, screen-filling believability and independence to formerly diminutive, proscenium-bound puppets.

---

56. Gannon, n. p.
57. McKay interview, September 19, 1986, p. 4.

On March 20, 1950, with its introduction of Ernie Kovacs to television, WPTZ unwittingly gave the nation its first "television personality." In singer-comedienne-actress Edie Adams, Kovacs found a perfect television foil and a wife. Her memories of their first meeting at WPTZ offered a preview of the fascination viewers would also share with this wild man who was exotic and somehow "dangerous": "I saw this man sitting there with a mustache—which was unheard of in those days—a big cigar stuck in his mouth, a hat crushed on his head and a foreign last name. All this was totally alien to my blonde-haired, blue-eyed, white-bread heritage. I was twenty-one and I took one look at him and said to myself, 'I want one of those.'"[58]

WPTZ had no idea what it was in for when it hired Kovacs as the world's most unlikely host of a cooking show, "Deadline for Dinner," which, in Ernie's hands, immediately became known around the studio as "Dead Lion for Breakfast." From there the creative, totally unpredictable comedian whose motto was "Nothing in moderation" launched the station—and early television—on a wild series of looking-glass adventures beginning with "3 to Get Ready," "It's Time for Ernie," "Ernie in Kovacsland," and "Kovacs on the Corner." Tuning into WPTZ, viewers might find Ernie hanging a cardboard control panel over his chest and using his face as a picture tube as he instructed them in the use of the horizontal and vertical knobs, or see him fighting with a street vendor and being escorted to the studio by a policeman.

Combining his admiration for the great silent clowns Buster Keaton and Charlie Chaplin with his fascination for the technology of television, Kovacs successfully drew upon the past to change the existing landscape of television comedy, thereby influencing its future. His parodies of television programming conventions, his improvisations, his zany characters, his video special effects and other technical innovations that later became a familiar part of TV comedy, had their origins at WPTZ between 1950 and 1952, magical years when Kovacs was given free reign to do anything that came to mind.[59] "When people around him were doing old vaudeville material—Alan Young or Ed Wynn were still doing old gags—Ernie was the first one to see the visual possibilities of television. He was the first surrealist in television," wrote critic and columnist Harriet Van Horne.[60] WPTZ's little stock company, crew, and studio engineers were more-than-willing accom-

58. Oral-history interview with Edie Adams, conducted by Linda Kowall, September 11, 1986, transcription, p. 1, Free Library of Philadelphia, Theatre Collection.

59. "The Vision of Ernie Kovacs," Exhibition Schedule and Program Notes, May 30–September 4, 1986, Museum of Broadcasting, New York.

60. David G. Walley, *The Ernie Kovacs Phile* (New York: Simon and Schuster, 1987), p. 117.

plices as Kovacs played with the Orthicon camera controls to create the split screen, and superimposed images that enabled him to hold interviews and even stage sword fights with himself. On the heels of engineer Carl Weger's creation of an inverter lens that produced upside-down images, Andy McKay designed a skit with Kovacs vacuuming the studio ceiling. Through film editing worthy of Buster Keaton, another Kovacs-WPTZ tour de force was a baseball game in which Ernie was all the players, the spectators, the umpire, and even the hot-dog vendor. Production at WPTZ was flexible enough to allow Kovacs to give full vent to his genius for improvisation, Adams remembered: "Sometimes Ernie wrote his scripts on the way to the studio. Sometimes he'd still be in his apartment on Rittenhouse Square and he'd hear his introduction music, yell 'Oh my God!' and take off down Walnut Street. He'd give us some idea of what was going on, just barely. He might call me before the show and say, 'We're doing a spy sketch. Bring a trench coat.' But that was about as much structure as we had."[61]

"We had latitude to use the TV medium then, something which couldn't happen in today's formula-ridden world of TV," McKay reminisced. "There was a fresh and, above all, adult approach which was inspiring and gave us all a sense of creativeness, of having furthered the medium along its true course, not aping radio or the stage."[62]

An artist creatively and temperamentally in tune with the medium in which he worked, Kovacs saw his career come to mirror the fate awaiting that medium as well—a good thing spoiled by success. Kovacs's popularity with Philadelphia-area TV audiences resulted in his show's being chosen for broadcast on NBC. Through "Ernie in Kovacsland" (August 1951), Kovacs's second WPTZ network program for NBC, the network was already growing increasingly concerned with the idea that Ernie ran the whole show. It hired writers whose scripts he either rewrote or ignored. "Kovacs on the Korner," also a network-conceived program, proved to be another frustrating experience. Only his not-ready-for-prime-time morning show, "3 to Get Ready," continued to offer the freedom from inhibiting sponsor and network involvement that nourished Kovacs's creativity. After two years in Philadelphia, on March 28, 1952, Kovacs did his last show for WPTZ and went to New York to work for CBS.

Television was playing to larger audiences and was highly visible now. Increasingly dominated by the networks, and under siege by sponsors in fear

61. Adams interview, p. 2.
62. Andrew C. McKay, quoted in Walley, pp. 78–79.

of offending public taste, television had outgrown its childhood and was entering what Erik Barnouw describes as "an adolescence traumatized by phobias. It would learn caution, and cowardice."[63] It was no longer a place for Ernie Kovacs. CBS dropped him on April 14, 1953. Looking back on the freedom that television once offered, former WPTZ program manager Rolland Tooke observed with more than a trace of regret, "The industry no longer offers such an opportunity. It is now a world of time, budgets, ratings, sponsors, pressure groups and play-it-safe programming. The result of the change is simple: an Ernie Kovacs coming along today wouldn't be allowed in front of a camera."[64]

Legacy

The networks' centralization of national program scheduling, and the advertising revenues necessary to support the costs of television production, resulted in the inevitable consolidation of the television industry. With the phenomenal success of "I Love Lucy" in 1951, Desilu Studios proved that television programming did not need to be produced by the stations and networks in-house. When CBS opened TV City in Hollywood in November 1952, the die was cast for the center of programming to move from New York (and Philadelphia) to Hollywood. WPTZ's years as a vital television-production center were drawing to a close. In 1953 Philco sold WPTZ to the Westinghouse Electric Corporation for 8.5 million dollars.[65] WPTZ's reliance on personnel from Philadelphia theater groups and returning war vets with no formal show-business experience, rather than on established radio performers, may underlie some of the originality, even radical genius, of its early programming. Looking back to 1941 and the naive young man who answered a notice on a university bulletin board, Leonard Valenta marveled, "We weren't paid and we didn't care. It was fun. I think after a year we were given a Philco portable radio. In fact, I think it was several years before I did a show that actually had a sponsor. I had finally made the 'big time'; I got paid five dollars for playing Abraham Lincoln!"[66] WPTZ's broadcast

---

63. Barnouw, p. 112.
64. Rolland Tooke, quoted in Walley, p. 79.
65. "Westinghouse Will Buy WPTZ for $8,500,000," *Evening Bulletin,* Philadelphia, Pa., February 22, 1953, n.p.
66. Valenta interview, p. 6.

pioneers, now seasoned veterans and respected professionals in the industry they helped create, all hold especially fond memories of the camaraderie and shared sense of excitement they experienced during their early years in live television. Speaking for them all, Harold Pannepacker added, "We were young people in a young business loving what we were doing."[67]

---

67. Pannepacker interview, p. 4.

4 Capitalizing on the Capital: WMAL-TV

David Weinstein

Applying for a Washington, D.C., television-station license was risky business in early 1946. There were approximately 100 television sets in the nation's capital. Over half of these prewar models sat in the offices of government officials.[1] However, a paucity of home viewers did not prevent six corporations—NBC, Du Mont Laboratories, Philco Products, Bamburger Broadcasting, Capital Broadcasting, and the Evening Star Broadcasting Company—from submitting bids for a VHF station construction permit. The applicants invested significant amounts of money to convince the FCC that they were ready to run a commercial-TV operation. In April 1946 the commission issued construction permits to NBC, Du Mont, Bamburger, and Evening Star. For the two applicants that did not receive licenses, Philco and Capital Broadcasting, the gamble was costly. Philco, for example, had invested $150,000 in a relay system connecting Washington and Philadelphia. It had also purchased land for a transmitter and studio in Arlington, Virginia.[2]

Two of the original six applicants, Du Mont and Philco, were electronics manufacturers with plans to produce TV sets after the war. Three other companies—Bamburger, Capital Broadcasting, and Evening Star—had nothing to do with electronics but owned radio stations in the nation's capital

1. Chris Mathisen, "Television's Magic Carpet Beckons Eager Washingtonians," *Washington Sunday Star*, March 18, 1946, p. 3C.

2. Federal Communications Commission, "Bamburger Broadcasting Service, Inc., et al.," *Federal Communication Commission Reports* (Washington, D.C.: Government Printing Office, 1946), p. 221.

or elsewhere. NBC's parent company, RCA, was a power in both the manufacturing and broadcasting industries. Of the six bidders only the Evening Star Broadcasting Company, whose parent company owned the *Washington Evening Star* newspaper, was based in D.C.

What did these corporations hope to gain from owning a TV station in the nation's capital? At the end of the war metropolitan Washington was the 10th-largest retail trade area in the country, with over a billion dollars in sales; 96.2 percent of all families in the Washington area had radios. These facts suggested that Washington's relatively affluent, media-hungry consumers would support television. In fact, a March 1946 *Evening Star* feature claimed that television suppliers would not be able to keep up with demand for several months.[3] For NBC (RCA), Du Mont, and Philco, makers of consumer electronics, a Washington-owned and -operated station could feed news, public affairs, and special events from the capital to other owned and affiliated stations. Consumers around the country would then buy televisions to watch this Washington programming. *Broadcasting Telecasting* ranked Washington "second only to New York as a video center" because of the city's position as a "national as well as a so-called world capital."[4] In its preliminary station-allocation decision the FCC explicitly recognized the importance of Washington, D.C., as a network center in awarding a license to NBC: "The Commission is of the opinion that the effective operation of a nationwide television network would be greatly aided by network ownership of a television station in Washington." None of the other applicants promised to reach as many viewers as NBC.[5]

Throughout the late 1940s and early 1950s television-industry executives trumpeted the new medium's ability to present activities originating from the nation's capital: elections, congressional hearings, inaugurations, speeches, and political interviews. In an October 1953 speech Du Mont president Allen B. Du Mont presented a list of shows on all four networks that helped sell televisions. Three were political programs that originated in Washington: "American Forum of the Air," "Meet Your Congress," "Meet the Press." Du Mont also praised "happenings of historical importance, such

---

3. Mathisen, p. 3C.

4. Bill Thompson, "The Washington Radio Market," *Broadcasting Telecasting*, March 29, 1948, p. 33.

5. Federal Communications Commission, "Before the Federal Communications Commission in the Matter of Bamburger Broadcasting Service Inc. et al," Proposed Decision, March 7, 1946, Du Mont Collection, Box 38, Library of Congress, p. 16.

as the nominating conventions of the two major political parties, the inauguration ceremonies of our presidents."[6]

National corporations (NBC, Bamburger, and Du Mont) owned and operated three of the capital's first four TV stations.[7] This chapter focuses on the activities of the only local operator, the Evening Star Broadcasting Company, both before and after it was allocated Channel 7. WMAL's position as the capital's only locally owned station, an ABC affiliate, presented it with a variety of opportunities and problems.

Although Evening Star did not have television experience when the FCC granted it a construction permit in April 1946, the company was no stranger to the mass media. WMAL-TV added to the firm's powerful radio (WMAL-AM) and newspaper (the *Evening Star*) holdings in the city. WMAL-AM went on the air on October 12, 1925, as the 15-watt voice of the Martin A. Leese Optical Company. It was affiliated with CBS from 1928 to 1932, when it joined NBC's Blue network. After the Evening Star Broadcasting Company bought WMAL radio in 1938, it continued to lease the station to the network. When NBC was forced to give up control of the Blue network stations in 1942, Evening Star chose to operate WMAL, using much of NBC's old staff. The company placed Kenneth H. Berkeley in charge. WMAL became part of the new ABC radio network in 1943. Star's TV station kept both General Manager Berkeley and its ABC affiliation when it went on the air in 1947.[8]

Samuel H. Kauffmann, the newspaper's publisher and broadcasting company's president, was also a trustee at American University. In 1945 Kauffmann struck a deal that allowed Star to build a transmitter at the university, one of the highest points in the city. At least one other applicant, Du Mont, had also approached American. "The association of a reputable school on the application for a Commercial Operation will carry tremendous weight," wrote chief engineer Julian Armstrong in a 1945 memo to Allen B. Du Mont.[9] In exchange for the favorable tower location and alliance with a

6. Allen B. Du Mont, "The Electrical-Electronic Manufacturing Industry—How It Operates," Address to the Industrial Council, Troy, New York, October 30, 1953, Du Mont Laboratories Collection, Box 139, Library of Congress, p. 16.

7. In August 1950, after scuttling its plans for a network, Bamburger Broadcasting sold its Washington station to a partnership of the *Washington Post* and CBS. The new owners changed Channel 9's call letters from WOIC to WTOP.

8. Harry MacArthur, "Television-Radio," *Washington Sunday Star,* October 15, 1950, p. 9C. Thompson, p. 44. "Telefile: WMAL-TV," *Broadcasting Telecasting,* July 9, 1951, pp. 84–85.

9. Julian Armstrong, memo to Allen B. Du Mont, August 21, 1945, Du Mont Laboratories Collection, Box 78, Library of Congress.

prominent local educational institution, Star agreed to build a completely equipped television studio next to the transmitter for the university's use. The broadcaster also promised to provide at least 50 hours of airtime annually for programming produced by the university.[10] After receiving its construction permit Star claimed that due to zoning restrictions, it could not locate a commercial TV studio at American. In 1950 Kauffmann agreed to American's request that Star build a studio for the university's students. It took another three years to break ground on the state-of-the-art radio and television facility. The $250,000 studio opened on American's campus in time for the 1954 school year.[11]

Star used the nation's first high-band transmitter to operate Channel 7. At first the signal "was inadequate but as good as you could get, because at the time they applied for their license, there wasn't such a thing as a high-band transmitter. The only transmitters extant were for channels 2 through 6," said Fred Houwink, who joined WMAL-TV in 1954, replacing Berkeley as general manager. "The Star got its license without knowing when it could get a transmitter. High band transmitters were finally being built and the first ones were all channel seven because Frank Marks, who was head of engineering at ABC, had all ABC-owned TV stations on channel seven."[12] In September 1947 a four-ton antenna was positioned on the tower.[13] Channel 7 made its successful debut less than three weeks later, on October 3, 1947.

On the Air

When WMAL started broadcasting, Du Mont's WTTG (Channel 5) and NBC's WNBW (Channel 4) were already on the air. However, the

---

10. Letter from American University president Paul Douglass to Kenneth Berkeley, October 15, 1945, E. F. Colladay Files, Box 9, American University Archives, Washington, D.C. Letter from Samuel H. Kauffmann to Robert Fletcher, December 26, 1945, American University Archives, Washington, D.C.

11. "New Era Foreseen as AU Begins Work on Radio-TV Center," *Washington Evening Star,* December 2, 1953, p. 29A. "Washington Baltimore Dateline," *TV Guide,* Washington-Baltimore edition, December 18, 1953, p. A-1.

12. Fred Houwink, transcript of personal interview conducted by David Wilt, December 1, 1978, Broadcast Pioneers Library, College Park, Md., p. 8.

13. "Antennas for Television, FM, Placed on Tower by WMAL," *Washington Evening Star,* August 17, 1949, n.p.

station's debut was heavily promoted in the *Evening Star*, which had been keeping readers apprised of WMAL's progress over the past two years. The newspaper announced the station's debut on its October 3 front page, and the next day it carried an article, with two photos, on Channel 7's "action-packed start."[14] Company president Kauffmann started the broadcast with a speech hailing WMAL-TV as the latest development in the *Evening Star*'s long and respected history of serving as the city's news and information source. After Kauffmann's talk the station went to its featured attraction: a football game between Georgetown and Fordham universities. Popular football, boxing, and wrestling remotes from local arenas were to become a programming staple for the next several years.

WMAL's early live studio consisted of a cramped room in the downtown Commonwealth Building, located a few blocks from the White House at 1625 K Street. Film projection and master control operated at the American University transmitter several miles to the northeast.[15] The station had two cameras at first and later added a third. With low ceilings in the converted downtown office building, lighting presented a challenge. "We had one announcer, Lee Dayton, who I guess was 6'4" or 6'5". We couldn't use him very often because we couldn't clear him because of the lights. He was just too tall," remembered Bryson Rash, an early WMAL newscaster and program host.[16] Engineer Stan Egbert recalled banks of reflector floodlights scattered throughout the studio.[17] By May 1951 the station had acquired bigger facilities in a Connecticut Avenue building about four miles uptown. Employees called their new home the Ice Palace because of its former occupant: an ice-skating rink.

In its early days this adventurous local station had lots of programming hours to fill. It was on the air for two months before it became the capital's "first and only seven day a week station."[18] By January 1948 it was airing 28 hours of programming a week. In April of that year it became Washington's first station with regular daytime telecasts. Its network, ABC, originated a handful of shows through Philadelphia's WFIL-TV.[19] WMAL welcomed the

---

14. "WMAL Launches TV Service," *Washington Evening Star*, October 4, 1947, p. 12A.

15. "Telefile: WMAL-TV," p. 84.

16. Bryson Rash, transcript of personal interview conducted by Nick Duncan, November 10, 1976, Broadcast Pioneers Library, pp. 71–72.

17. Stan Egbert, transcript of personal interview conducted by Joanne Beardsley, April 17, 1978, Broadcast Pioneers Library, p. 7.

18. WMAL-TV advertisement, *Television*, January 1948, p. 9.

19. "Henry Morgan Broadcast to Open Television Chain," *Washington Evening Star*, April 18, 1948, p. 17A.

new programming from ABC's New York flagship, WJZ-TV, in the summer of 1948. The Washington station aired most of WJZ's August 9 opening-night broadcast, interrupting it only for the regularly scheduled local program: hypnotist Robert L. Friend's "On Wings of Thought."[20] The Washington affiliate continued to carry ABC material as it became available from the struggling network.[21] WMAL also showed popular CBS programs before CBS's WOIC went on the air in January 1949.

Between 20 and 40 percent of WMAL's programming in the late 1940s and early 1950s consisted of film acquired from various distributors and syndicators.[22] In addition to instructional movies, WMAL's early schedule included old serials and B movies, with detective films and westerns the most common genres. Better features were reserved for prime time. In July 1948 WMAL began airing a series of 26 Alexander Korda British productions. Safeway Supermarkets later sponsored a series of first-run movies, "Safeway Theatre," every Saturday night.

Daytime Programming

Less prestigious movies found their way to "Hollywood Matinee," a daily show with Ruth Crane, WMAL's director of woman's activities. At the end of each "Hollywood Matinee" program, Crane conducted Guest Time, a segment unrelated to the day's film, in which Crane interviewed authors, actors, and other "outstanding individuals." Crane, who presided over

20. "WMAL-TV to Carry Programs of New ABC Video Station Tonight," *Washington Evening Star,* August 10, 1948, p. 2A.

21. For example, WMAL's application for FCC license renewal dated December 1, 1950, indicated that in a composite week 59 percent of its programming came from a network. A few non-ABC programs originating from Chicago may have been included in this tally. The amount of network programming fluctuated from year to year. It was as low as 21.4 percent in 1953, according to the renewal application dated June 28,1954. The applications are in the National Archives, Suitland, Maryland. For more on ABC's early programming, see James L. Baughman, "The Weakest Chain and the Strongest Link: The American Broadcasting Company and the Motion Picture Industry," in Tino Balio, ed., *Hollywood in the Age of Television* (Boston: Unwin-Hyman, 1990), pp. 91–114.

22. The applications on file at the National Archives start in 1950, although a scan of earlier newspaper TV listings indicate that this figure is accurate for the years 1947–50. Twenty-three percent of WMAL's programming time was filled with film, according to the renewal application dated December 1, 1950. In 1951, according to the November 11, 1951, application, the figure was 22 percent. In 1952, according to the July 2, 1953, application, film constituted 41 percent of WMAL's programming day. In 1953, application dated June 28, 1954, the figure was 41.8 percent.

several WMAL programs from 1947 to 1955, didn't like the one-hour matinee show. "The movie was cut to the point of being absolutely senseless. I don't know why anybody ever watched the program. And my interviews had to be so short and incomplete that I couldn't consider them at all well done."[23] "Hollywood Matinee" was on Channel 7 for three years, starting in June 1952.

WMAL's primary afternoon personality from 1947 to 1955, Crane has fonder memories of her other two shows: "The Modern Woman" and "Shop by Television." A combination of household hints, fashion tips, current-events discussion, and public-service features on the local community, "The Modern Woman" was Washington's longest-running daytime series when Crane retired from broadcasting in 1955. In 1944 the Missouri native started "The Modern Woman" on WMAL-AM after 15 years at Detroit's WJR, where she was known as Mrs. Page. When WMAL-TV went on the air in 1947, station management "didn't want to put on another staff to operate TV—we all doubled up," according to Crane. She remembered sales manager Ben Baylor calling her into his office and telling her to start a TV program: "I said, 'Well, all right, I guess so, what do you plan to have me do?' He said, 'What do I plan to have you do? That's your job. You put on a program—that's all I'm requiring—you put on a program.' So I had a week to plan it. Well, Christmas was approaching and I decided to do a sort of burlesque on Christmas shoppers. I borrowed the materials from a department store and it was real good, actually, for a first program."[24] As the show's producer, Crane selected the topics and segments for each program, chose guests, placed commercials, and planned homemaking demonstrations.[25] Jackson Weaver, who appeared on several early WMAL shows, served as Crane's comic foil.

Like other former WMAL staffers, Crane remembered that the Commonwealth Building studio where the show started was poorly equipped. However, the new Ice Palace included a kitchen in each of the three studios. Furniture was courtesy of Goodwill and Crane's creativity. Her program covered the community and enticed Washingtonians to buy TV sets by regularly featuring representatives from local women's social groups, politi-

---

23. Ruth Crane Schaefer, personal interview conducted by Valerie Renner, April 29, 1978, Broadcast Pioneers Library.

24. Ruth Crane Schaefer, transcript of interview conducted by Pat Mower, November 18, 1975, Broadcast Pioneers Library, p. 13.

25. "Behind 30 Minutes of TV, 50 Hours of Preparation," *Washington Sunday Star*, Pictorial Supplement, July 1, 1951, pp. 14–15. Schaefer interview by Mower, p. 13.

cal associations, and charities. "Members who could not be invited [due to] space limitation in the studio were required to hold TV teas for twenty members or more in each home," Crane explained. "Many of the members, you see, had to buy TV sets for their own families to see them on TV, as, of course, did the members who were asked to give the teas for the members in their homes."[26]

In much of its public service "The Modern Woman" covered the activities of the government and nonprofit agencies located in the nation's capital. For example, Crane had a working arrangement to advise the Department of Agriculture and allow the department to test ideas on "The Modern Woman." After fine-tuning their recommendations for "chickens of tomorrow" or "the care of African violets" on WMAL, the department distributed programming suggestions to other local and network stations.[27]

The nation's capital also served as fertile ground in Crane's hunt for guests from the world of politics and diplomacy. Distinguished visitors from abroad were especially fascinated by early television, according to Crane. "I had an embassy program once a week and featured the ambassador or in some cases the ambassador's wife. We featured some of their practices, some of their foods and their costuming."[28]

"Shop by Television," which ran for 3½ years starting on November 8, 1949, bears a strong resemblance to today's home-shopping fare. Sponsored by Hechts, a department-store chain, "Shop by Television" was one of the first demonstration-type programs that featured department-store merchandise. The programs indicated to local advertisers across the country that television was a viable sales medium. "Shop by Television" had a novel twist. It employed up to 40 telephone lines, which viewers used to order featured products and open Hechts charge accounts. The Hechts Company's Joseph Rotto wrote that "many shows produce $2,000 in direct phone calls the night of the show, and there is usually an equal response the next day in the departments themselves." Hechts made money on the program: Rotto

26. Schaefer interview by Mower, pp. 15–16.

27. Untitled WMAL-TV press releases in vertical files, Broadcast Pioneers Library. One of the releases is dated April 24, 1952. The other two releases do not have dates. Also see Schaefer interview by Mower, p. 21.

28. Schaefer interview by Mower, p. 19.

estimated that the combined cost of "Shop by Television" and another Hechts program, WOIC's "Fashion Story," was $500–700 a week.[29]

Through 1955 WMAL featured afternoon productions in several genres: game shows ("Just for Fun"), variety ("The Milton Ford Show," "The Jerry and Jimma Show"), children's programs ("Ruth Anne's Kindergarten"), and music shows ("Sherm's Showplace," "Bandstand Matinee"). A 60-minute program that featured teenagers dancing to popular records, "Bandstand Matinee" represented a local innovation and sparked strong community reaction. The show premiered on Monday, April 6, 1953, with Sherman Butler as host. Bill Malone occasionally filled in for Butler.

The program was apparently popular with capital-area teens. According to Berkeley, the Bandstand Matinee Club boasted 6,000 members at the end of August 1953.[30] Some of these fans practiced more than the jitterbug on the way to WMAL's Ice Palace. A *Washington Post* article informed readers of the police patrols dispatched around the station's studios to deal with the teenage hoodlums: "The harassed merchants reported they were threatened by switchblade knives. Windows were broken, merchandise was stolen, cashiers were defied by teenaged customers who refused to pay, and general rowdyism and vandalism prevailed in the area each afternoon."[31]

Berkeley issued a response that didn't deny the allegations. However, the general manager claimed that "not more than twenty youths have caused any serious difficulty." He further said that the station had taken measures to keep rabble-rousers off the program. Through its Bandstand Matinee Club the station established stricter screening procedures and a dress code, which teens had to follow before they would be allowed on the show. "As far as we know," said Berkeley, "all troublemakers have been eliminated."[32]

The show was taken off the air in October 1953. Fisher remembers that the "transit company asked us to stop the program, or at least complained, because the people on the buses were getting these kids en masse after the program was over."[33] "Bandstand Matinee's" lack of commercial support probably contributed to the show's cancellation. Before any published

---

29. James Rotto, "How to Advertise a Department Store on TV," *Television*, June 1952, pp. 31–32. In the Mower interview Crane remembered the show as generating about $6,000 worth of direct sales. In the later Renner interview, she said the figure was between $6,000 and $10,000.

30. "TV Station Continues Bandstand Program," *Washington Post,* August 27, 1953, p. 21A.

31. "TV Station Continues Bandstand Program," p. 21A.

32. "TV Station Continues Bandstand Program," p. 21A.

33. Kay Fisher, personal interview conducted by Carmela Kube, March 14, 1978, Broadcast Pioneers Library, Washington, D.C., p. 8.

reports of rowdyism, an April 1953 *TV Guide* article noted that the program was unable to secure a sponsor: "'Bandstand Matinee' has no gimmick for the advertiser. It is a new approach, and advertisers shy away from the new and different."[34]

Sports

Jim Gibbons dominated the evenings of WMAL's early schedule. Gibbons was the sportscaster at the station's boxing, wrestling, and football games. He also hosted a weekly program, "Sports Cartoon-a-Quiz," the nightly sports news, and an evening variety show, "The Jim Gibbons Show." In the late 1940s Gibbons's programs would sometimes fill over half of the seven- or eight-hour broadcast day. "There wasn't that much to televise," Gibbons explained. "The network wasn't offering that much, so they [WMAL] filled in with whatever they could get."[35]

Like the other primary on-air personalities from Channel 7's first decade, Gibbons was a regular on WMAL-AM before the TV station went on the air. He started as a staff announcer and worked his way to morning man in 1946. Since most of his television work was in the evenings, Gibbons was able to keep doing the morning radio show for 10 years. He was popular with listeners and viewers. In a 1950 poll readers of *Teleguide* magazine voted Gibbons their favorite local personality and favorite sports announcer.[36] The sports man remembered that "most of the shows we had were sold out."

It was at WMAL radio in the early 1940s that Gibbons began working the Washington Redskins games as a commercial announcer. By the time that television came around, he was a color commentator, with Harry Wismer handling play-by-play.[37] The broadcast team's first telecast was a Redskins-Steelers remote from Griffith Stadium on October 5, 1947. The Redskins

---

34. "The Week's TV Program: 'Bandstand Matinee,'" *TV Guide,* Baltimore-Washington edition, April 24, 1953, p. A-3.

35. Jim Gibbons, personal interview with author, August 23, 1994, Broadcast Pioneers Library. Subsequent Gibbons quotations are from this interview.

36. Harry MacArthur, "News of Television and Radio," *Washington Sunday Star,* January 29, 1950, p. 8C.

37. "WMAL-TV Covers the Game," *Washington Sunday Star,* Pictorial Magazine, December 7, 1947, p. 18.

had four consecutive losing seasons from 1948 to 1952. Still, future Hall of Famer Sammy Baugh and his replacement, the Little General, Eddie LeBaron, provided excitement as quarterback for the fans and viewers. According to Gibbons, for the first several years the station conducted radio and television simulcasts, rather than employ separate crews for each broadcast. These presented problems for the play-by-play man, who had to paint a descriptive picture for radio listeners without telling viewers too much.

In its early broadcasts WMAL's 17-man crew followed the action with two cameras. The station periodically cut away from its game coverage to telecast live commercials for Amoco gasoline, the sponsor for several years. "We had a mock-up gas station in the studio. A couple of actual gas pumps. The announcer was dressed as a station attendant," remembered remote engineer Gilbert Bentley.[38]

Through the mid-'50s WMAL periodically showed boxing on Monday nights and wrestling on Wednesdays from local venues Turner's Arena and Uline Arena. Gibbons said that compared to football, boxing and wrestling were easy to telecast because "you had a smaller area and you could cover it with one camera." Egbert recalled that these sports were also popular with the public.

One of the city's first regularly scheduled programs, "Sports Cartoon-a-Quiz," aired 7:30 to 8 p.m. on Tuesdays from January 1948 through April 1950. The program pitted three whiz kids against different adults from the community, including athletes and members of civic organizations. Cartoonist Bill Willison sketched clues to Gibbons's questions on an easel next to the contestants. Like Ruth Crane, Gibbons considered the commercial potential of his guests. "A lot of business people belonged to Kiwanis and Rotary. And a lot of those business people were sponsors," remembered the host. "Anybody that wanted to get anywhere and have commercials wanted to know the advertisers." "Cartoon-a-Quiz's" prizes were not very lucrative. "We gave away a lot of Briggs [meat] products. We used to give away hams; and the hot dogs were easy. You could display them and hold them. They were very visible," Gibbons said.

"Sports Reel" started as an occasional five-minute supplement to the news in 1948. By the summer of 1949 it was up to 15 minutes daily. Gibbons read scores, interviewed athletes and featured local and touring golf pros. In September 1952 "Sports Reel" was replaced by "The Jim Gibbons Show," a half-hour variety program that aired every evening for four years. In

38. Gilbert Bentley, personal interview with author, July 27, 1994.

addition to including sports news, Gibbons's program featured singers and other performers geared to a more general audience.

Covering the Nation

In WMAL's early days Bryson Rash was the main newsman. He anchored a daily news program and hosted all major remotes. Born in 1913, Rash got his start in radio at the age of 12. He was the voice of Buster Brown on St. Louis's KWK. Rash graduated to announcing positions at other stations in St. Louis, Cincinnati, and Washington, D.C. (WTOP). In 1937 Rash joined the announcing staff of NBC in Washington, where he was heard on WMAL and WRC. When the NBC network split five years later, Rash joined WMAL as director of special events and public affairs. Rash made daily broadcasts as ABC's White House correspondent until he moved to NBC-WRC in 1956.

Rash's "Telenews Daily" began to air regularly in October 1949. The 15-minute evening "Telenews" followed what *Evening Star* TV columnist Harry MacArthur identified as the TV news formula, "a sort of blend of techniques involving motion pictures, occasional still pictures and commentary accompanied by the image of the commentator."[39] Like most early local news operations, WMAL did not have a film crew. In order to satisfy the public's desire for timely news and create a program that took advantage of the visual medium, WMAL ordered footage from New York's Telenews company.

The process by which WMAL produced its daily news program illustrates the challenges local operations faced at a time when the public demanded more than stations were economically and technologically equipped to handle. The Telenews pictures were edited in New York late in the morning, processed and placed aboard an afternoon plane. By telephone Rash received descriptions of the stories. After this call he rearranged the stories and added local and national material. When the New York airplane arrived, it was met by a limousine, which brought the copy to Rash and rushed the film to master control at American University. Everything had to be accomplished by airtime: 7 p.m.

---

39. Harry MacArthur, "Television-Radio," *Washington Evening Star*, May 21, 1950, p. 8C.

News production became smoother with the 1951 move to the Ice Palace, where there was room to conduct all operations. Perhaps because of the bigger and better studio facilities, by the middle of 1952 the station apparently shifted its emphasis from Telenews to more local coverage. Rash sat at a desk reading the news and conducting occasional interviews, although the station still subscribed to Telenews.[40] Among Rash's local fans was J. Edgar Hoover, who commended the newsman for televising pictures of the FBI's ten most wanted fugitives.[41]

In its daily news and special-events coverage WMAL received little help from ABC. Until the early 1960s the network did not have a regular bureau in Washington. All capital news on the network—for example, elections, White House events, and congressional hearings—originated from WMAL. For a big production, such as an inauguration, ABC would supplement WMAL's remote crew with people and equipment from New York and Baltimore. In its early days WMAL looked to other Washington broadcasters as much as to the network for help covering national politics. The local stations set up a pooling system from the outset, whereby they shared equipment and sometimes personnel. They took turns covering smaller events, for which only one crew was needed.[42]

An early example of this cooperative coverage took place when WMAL was only two days old. On October 5, 1947, President Truman made his live television debut with a food-conservation speech. It was carried by the Washington stations and their network affiliates in the three other cities linked by coaxial cable: New York, Philadelphia, and Schenectady, New York.[43] White House correspondent Rash arranged to telecast the speech. "It was a joint effort," remembered Rash. "The technical equipment, cameras, etc. were supplied by NBC, the direction and production was performed by ABC WMAL-TV, and the director [WMAL's] Burke Crotty. The announcer

40. Frank Brewary, personal interview with author, April 13, 1994, Broadcast Pioneers Library.

41. Harry MacArthur, "Television-Radio," *Washington Sunday Star*, March 6, 1949, p. 8C. Harry MacArthur, "Television-Radio," *Washington Sunday Star*, June 18, 1950, p. 8C.

42. This local cooperation dates back to February 12, 1946, when CBS, Du Mont, and NBC inaugurated the new coaxial cable by sending transmissions from different Washington, D.C., locales to their New York affiliates. "This date [February 12, 1946] is commonly referred to as the birthdate of network television broadcasting," writes Stewart Louis Long in *The Development of the Network Television Oligopoly* (New York: Arno, 1979), p. 55. "Test of Cable Prepares D.C. for Television," *Washington Evening Star*, February 13, 1946, p. 1B.

43. A filmed speech by Truman was telecast in October 1945. Robert Underhill, *The Truman Persuasions* (Ames: Iowa State University Press, 1981), p. 156.

was from Du Mont."[44] The event was shown at the Hotel Statler on the first television sets installed in the city for public viewing. The *Washington Post* reported that "Truman's well-known features appeared with great clarity on the three screens," in the Statler's Veranda Room.[45]

In 1949 WMAL's coverage of Truman's inauguration involved the entire production staff. "There had been no full-scale inaugural festivities in Washington since before the war, and this [the 1949 inauguration] was to be the biggest, most costly inauguration on record, the parade the greatest in the city's history," wrote historian David McCullough.[46] The four networks pooled their sound and camera facilities. Through a random drawing among the networks, NBC's Adolph Schneider was chosen to coordinate the 15-camera broadcast, which was the most complex project the young stations had ever undertaken.

The out-of-pocket budget for the coverage was $25,000. The money seems to have been well spent. The six-hour telecast went off without any technical glitches. In addition, according to the *Evening Star*, the estimated 10 million viewers who watched in the East and Midwest represented "the largest number of persons in history to witness a single event as it actually happened."[47]

By Eisenhower's 1953 inauguration that national audience had grown to 75 million. The TV coverage also reflected the growth of local stations and their networks. Each network employed 15 cameras in mounting its own coverage, although the inaugural ball was a pooled affair. Since WMAL originated the ABC feed, it was positioned to stay on the air past the announced 6:30 network sign-off. To the delight of its viewers, who had flooded the station's switchboard asking for extended coverage, WMAL was the only station in the country to telecast the entire inaugural parade. The station ended its live coverage around 7 p.m. To facilitate the after-dark telecast, emergency lighting was set up, with equipment from a mobile unit and help from the D.C. police.[48]

---

44. Rash interview, p. 75. "Three D.C. Stations to Televise Truman Plea for Food Tomorrow," *Washington Evening Star* , October 4, 1947, p. 1A.

45. "Hotel Guests See Truman as He Addresses Congress," *Washington Post*, January 7, 1947, p. 6A.

46. David McCullough, *Truman* (New York: Simon and Schuster, 1992), p. 723.

47. "Five Sets of Television Cameras to Send Out Inaugural Scenes," *Washington Evening Star*, January 18, 1949, p. 4A. Harry MacArthur, "Video Experts Make History in First Inaugural Telecast," *Washington Evening Star*, January 21, 1949, p. 24A.

48. MacArthur, "Inauguration Believed Viewed by 70 Million on TV Screens," *Washington Evening Star*, January 21, 1953, p. 12A.

From the station's early days Congress received WMAL's attention. Starting in 1948, Rash hosted "Capitol Close-Up," an interview show like "Meet the Press," which featured congressmen. In fact, the program may have been too similar to the NBC program. Rash remembered, "Larry [Spivak] and Martha Roundtree accosted me and said if I didn't get that show off the air, they were going to sue us for infringement of their copyright, or whatever it was."[49] The show went off the air in 1950. Another Rash show, "Open Hearing," presented congressmen in a simulated hearing. The program was later taken over by the network, with John Secondari as host and moderator.

On November 11, 1947, after five weeks on the air, WMAL originated and produced the nation's first televised congressional hearing: the testimony of Secretary of State George C. Marshall on his controversial European economic-aid plan before the Senate Foreign Relations Committee. Of WMAL's many subsequent congressional telecasts, one event stands out. On April 22, 1954, WMAL began broadcasting the Army-McCarthy hearings before the Senate Investigations Subcommittee. Historians have identified the six-week coverage as a key episode in Communist hunter Joseph McCarthy's downfall. ABC broadcast the 37-day subcommittee hearings gavel to gavel, which "helped to no end in creating the network as a part of America's life," according to WMAL's Rash.[50] Du Mont network stations also picked up WMAL's live feed, while NBC and CBS aired regularly scheduled daytime programs, and kinescope highlights of the hearings at night.

WMAL drew the assignment because it was ABC's turn to provide coverage for the Washington TV pool. Rash acted as producer and commentator from WMAL's studios about five miles from Capitol Hill. Gunnar Back reported from the Senate floor. Twenty-five-year-old Ed Scherer directed. After the hearings ended, articles praised WMAL's coverage for its objectivity, technical proficiency, and ability to anticipate action.

While the remote crew covered the hearings, a second crew worked WMAL's studio productions during breaks in the hearings and after the coverage ended at 4:30. Engineer Frank Brewary remembers that the remote crew would report directly to the Capitol every day. "Back at the studio we

49. Rash, pp. 73–74.
50. Rash, p. 89.

got to do a lot of things that we normally couldn't do as 'shave-tails' because the big guys were down at the hearings."[51]

WMAL's coverage of the Army-McCarthy hearings symbolizes the level of maturity, independence, and importance that the Washington station had reached by the mid-1950s. Without extra personnel from ABC or any of the other local stations, WMAL conducted a network feed for six weeks, while maintaining studio operations. The coverage helped to demonstrate the power of TV to influence politics. Furthermore, it established ABC as a force in network television.

After Fred Houwink took over as WMAL's general manager in September 1954, the station replaced many of its live local programs with syndicated film and network fare. The three most important on-air personalities from WMAL's early days had all left the station by 1956. Crane retired from broadcasting in 1955. The following year Rash and Gibbons both moved to NBC's WRC-TV.[52] It is striking how much of the programming that these three broadcasters established and adapted, alongside their fellow pioneers at WMAL and other stations across the country, became generic norms in later television.

---

51. Brewary, personal interview.
52. Gibbons left WMAL in 1956 but didn't actually start at WRC until early 1957.

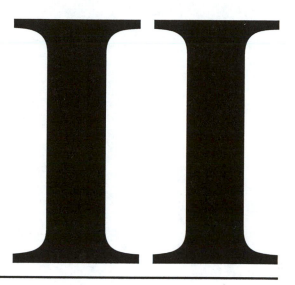

Southern States

5 WSB-TV, Atlanta: The "Eyes of the South"

Ginger Rudeseal Carter

For the people of Atlanta and the south, the initials *WSB* will always mean "Welcome South Brother." These call letters represent the first and largest of Georgia's radio and television stations. WSB-AM became the "Voice of the South," the south's first radio station, when it signed on at 100 watts May 15, 1922; within 10 years it was broadcasting at 50,000 watts and was a charter NBC affiliate. On September 29, 1948, the "Eyes of the South" opened, bringing the south's first television station, WSB, to the air on Channel 8. Nearing its golden anniversary, WSB-TV remains a strong, clear voice in southern broadcasting, a testimony to the faces and forces who shaped the development of the station.[1]

The story of WSB-TV begins in 1931 with an unsuccessful bid for a developmental television license. In 1939 a closed-circuit experimental broadcast on six sets at Rich's department store brought "The Modern Miracle—Television" to Atlanta. But this too was only experimental; it would be nine years and a world war before television returned to the south for good.[2] In December 1939 Ohio governor James Middleton Cox bought WSB radio and the *Atlanta Journal,* calling the purchase "the rounding out of a dream." Cox figured Atlanta would become "the geographic terminus for northern and southern economic interaction, and the leading city in the Southeast."[3] A few days later, at the Atlanta premiere of *Gone With the Wind,*

---

1. *Welcome South Brother* (Atlanta: Cox Broadcasting, 1974), p. 6.
2. *Welcome South Brother,* p. 34.
3. *Welcome South Brother,* p. 36.

the new owner of WSB was introduced with the comment, "Governor Cox has just shown in a very substantial way the faith he has in the future of Atlanta and this section." Cox squelched the rumor that he bought the radio station just to get tickets to the sold-out gala at the premiere, when the station provided radio coverage heard all over the United States.[4]

Shortly after he bought the station and newspaper in 1939, Governor Cox tapped J. Leonard Reinsch, a bright young broadcast executive in his employ, to head the Atlanta broadcast operation. Reinsch had quickly—and impressively—risen through the ranks of the governor's growing broadcast empire; Reinsch, in fact, was only 26 when the Cox family asked him to put WHIO in Dayton, Ohio, on the air in 1934.[5] In 1948 he authored *Radio Station Management*, one of the first radio textbooks.[6]

Reinsch's radio career paralleled the growth of the industry. Radio was officially six years old when Reinsch, age 16, became a full-time announcer at WLS in Chicago. In his autobiography, *Getting Elected*, Reinsch tells of the time in his early career when he was broadcasting a Northwestern University football game for WLS opposite another young broadcaster—Ronald "Dutch" Reagan, the voice of WHO in Des Moines, Iowa. Reinsch added that history was in the making in more than one way in that broadcast. In 1944 Reinsch began his own career in Democratic politics when tapped by Franklin D. Roosevelt to serve as communication adviser.[7] Reinsch wrote, "Governor Cox asked me to meet him in his Biltmore apartment [in Atlanta]. 'Would you be willing,' he said, 'to be the radio director of the Democratic Convention and the presidential campaign?' I couldn't say 'yes' fast enough. A formal announcement of my role was made on June 12, 1944. President Roosevelt had his 'radio man.'"[8]

Thus was born Reinsch's two-sided career as broadcast executive and political consultant. It served the Cox family in two ways: First, Reinsch's political consulting gave the Cox family a continued connection with Democratic politics in Washington D.C.; second, the connection offered a cooperative, cross-medium learning situation. Reinsch took his vast radio

---

4. *Welcome South Brother*, p. 36.

5. By 1944 Reinsch had been given responsibility for three radio stations: WSB, WHIO, and WIOD in Miami. During this time he lent his radio expertise to his alma mater, assisting in the development of Northwestern University's broadcasting program.

6. "What Now, Mr. Reinsch?" *Images* (Spring 1979): 4.

7. Roosevelt was Governor Cox's vice-presidential running mate in 1920; the democratic candidates were defeated by Warren G. Harding.

8. J. Leonard Reinsch, *Getting Elected* (New York: Hippocrene Books, 1988), pp. xiii–xiv.

expertise to Washington in 1944 to assist Roosevelt; once there, Reinsch was in a natural position to learn more about the burgeoning television industry. For instance, as coordinator for the Democratic party, Reinsch recommended television's use at the convention in Philadelphia during the summer of 1948. Three months later he put WSB-TV on the air.[9]

Elmo Ellis, one of the station's first television producers and later the vice president and general manager of WSB-AM and FM, said Reinsch knew that television was an up-and-coming innovation, which led Reinsch to advise the Cox family, primarily investors in newspapers up to that point, of the growth potential in television. Ellis said that Reinsch "realized, as a lot of smart people did, that television was going to be a gigantic new industry; he wanted to be in on the ground floor."[10] Marcus Bartlett, WSB-TV's first program director and second general manager, said Reinsch "was a dynamic, forethinking person" who was Governor Cox's "ear to Washington; he had his finger on the pulse of activity."[11]

T-Day

The FCC granted WSB's television-license application January 8, 1948, but plans for Atlanta television had been under way for most of 1947; Reinsch had directed Marcus Bartlett and Elmo Ellis, two of WSB radio's brightest stars, to prepare for the television operation in 1947. John M. "Johnny" Outler, general manager of WSB radio, became the television station's first general manager, running both operations; Jimmy Bridges, a familiar voice for WSB radio listeners, was named news director. Their mission? Bring first-class television news and entertainment programming to Atlanta viewers.

WSB radio and the *Atlanta Journal* had a reputation to uphold; WSB-TV would operate with the same high standards. Bridges said of the transfers,

9. Reinsch, who had participated in an experimental television effort in 1931 at WMAQ in Chicago, noted that only those who owned television sets between Boston and Washington would see this convention; national coverage of the conventions began in 1952. See Reinsch, *Getting Elected*, pp. 42–43.

10. Elmo I. Ellis, personal interview conducted by Ginger Rudeseal Carter, August 10, 1994, Atlanta, Georgia. Transcript in possession of Carter.

11. Marcus Bartlett, personal interview conducted by Ginger Rudeseal Carter, August 10, 1994, Atlanta, Georgia. Transcript in possession of author. See *Welcome South Brother*.

"I felt they were pulling the cream of the crop. We were excited to be a part of this change. We were so excited, we'd work for nothing. You can do almost anything you want to do, you just have to have the will. We had the will."[12]

Station history suggests that personnel were "selected and packed off to any place information was available about the new medium—other stations, networks and technical schools"; yet Ellis, Bartlett, and Bridges remember learning the business "by the seat of the pants." Their hands-on training came with the arrival of the equipment for the new station, ordered from RCA; studio materials continued to arrive in the summer of 1948. Station employees from the general manager down participated in the testing. According to the station's history, "when the equipment and mobile unit arrived in the summer of 1948, they were used immediately." The WSB staff began originating "closed-circuit" programs around Atlanta to show the public what television was all about.[13] The WSB-TV mobile unit, staffed by Emmitt Kelley, Oliver Heely, and Gordon Swann, traveled around Atlanta that summer originating practice programs.

Preparation for the transition from radio to television news meant relearning the technical side of the business. Bridges, who anchored the first televised newscast on WSB-TV, said it was a time of adapting. He added that moving to television was even responsible for his quitting smoking: Television didn't have a "cough button" to cover his smoker's cough.

Final preparation for "T-Day," the first day of television in Atlanta and the south, began in earnest in late August. Reinsch had returned to Atlanta full of new ideas from the Democratic Convention in Philadelphia, and now the *Atlanta Journal* joined in publicizing its television station.[14] One month to the day before T-Day, the *Journal* reminded readers of television's arrival with a photograph and a description of the station's test pattern.

Beginning September 1, 1948, the *Atlanta Journal* featured a page-one T-Day countdown. On September 5, 1948, the small box reminded readers that "T-Day is Sept. 29—just 24 days from today. Don't forget!" The box also introduced general manager Johnny Outler, calling him "the guiding

---

12. Jimmy Bridges, personal interview conducted by Ginger Rudeseal Carter, August 14, 1994, Atlanta, Georgia. Transcript in possession of author. See *Welcome South Brother*.

13. *Welcome South Brother*, p. 55.

14. Throughout the literature the *Journal* calls WSB "our radio station" and "our television station." The three are still owned by different divisions of Cox Enterprises.

hand behind video at WSB-TV." The article added that Outler, a native of Metcalf, Georgia, "is predicting big things for television in Atlanta."[15]

As the equipment was tested and the new station publicized, WSB-TV employed an innovative introduction to television in Atlanta: For one week in late August and early September, television was made available to a quarter million potential viewers via closed circuit from the third-floor bridge of the Rich's department store in downtown Atlanta. According to a front-page article in the *Atlanta Journal,* the programs were "typical examples of the shows to be broadcast by WSB-TV when it begins broadcasting."

Station and store executives took advantage of peak shopping times—11 a.m. to 1 p.m. and 2 p.m. to 4 p.m.—to air a sequence of 13 live shows; viewers watched on "sixty home-type television receivers placed throughout the store." Shows during the preview included "The Sunshine Boys," a musical group that would perform at the station's premiere; "Man on the Bridge," a man-on-the-street interview show; fashions from Rich's; news with Jimmy Bridges; and the Junior League Marionettes.[16]

Several of the performers received prominent coverage in the *Journal.* Pianists Margaret and Forrest Perrin, featured daily at 11:20 a.m. and 2:20 p.m., were praised for their "four nimble hands on a piano"; yet even the pieces the Perrins performed were carefully selected. "The pieces with the fast rhythms show up better in television," Miss Perrin said in the article. "Lots of finger action, such as is necessary in an exciting piece, is better picked up by the television camera."[17]

It was Leonard Reinsch, however, who predicted the hypnotic qualities of television in a September 2 news article covering the Junior League Marionettes; Reinsch, noting that children were transfixed by the puppets on the television screen, said prophetically, "It's going to be hard for Mom and Dad to get the children to meals if there's a television show they want to see. The kids are going to love television."[18] The children's love of the marionette show may have prompted program director Marcus Bartlett to sched-ule—and Elmo Ellis to produce—"The Woody Willow Show"; performed by Don and Ruth Gilpin, this show was a mainstay of WSB-TV's early children's programming.

The station cooperated with Rich's to mutual benefit, and Ellis added, "The shows at Rich's helped develop public interest in television. There was

15. "Only 24 Days Until T-Day," *Atlanta Journal,* September 5. 1948, p. 1.
16. "WSB-TV on Parade at Rich's This Week," *Atlanta Journal,* August 29, 1948, p. 1.
17. "Sister-Brother Talents in Video Close-Up," *Atlanta Journal,* September 3, 1948, p. 12.
18. "Best in Video Fare Promised by Reinsch," *Atlanta Journal,* September 28, 1948, p. 1.

another advantage. By September, we had practiced and done a lot of dry runs before going on the air. Producing a TV program was not a new thing for us anymore."[19]

Pre-T-Day publicity was not limited to Rich's; appliance stores across Atlanta filled the pages of the *Journal* with ads for television sets. The L.C. Warren, Jr., Company ran advertisements in the *Atlanta Constitution* for the Motorola Golden View Television set, priced between $189.95 for a table model and $629.95 for the VF 102 Console, one of the first complete home-entertainment centers. A few days later they touted the General Electric "Daylight Television" for $325; the advertisement boasted of the screen size, "It's this big! 3 sq. ft. in area." As a cost comparison, "3 cozy rooms" of furniture were advertised for $298.95; a three-piece living room group, including end and coffee tables and lamps, was $120.95.[20]

The preview month of September also featured sports coverage. Thad Horton, sports director of WSB radio, was named sports director of the television station. Regular live coverage of local sports, including the Atlanta Crackers baseball team, would be a fixture of the television lineup. A photo spread in the September 1 *Journal* showed Mrs. Jerry Juzek and Mrs. "Red" Mathis, wives of Crackers pitchers, watching their husbands on television. The station had aired the game, beginning at 8:25 p.m., in one of the first experimental broadcasts.[21]

To make "believers" out of Atlanta sports reporters, Reinsch and Outler brought television to Grant Field on the campus of Georgia Tech; they "set up a Philco in Row 1, seats 15 and 16, with its screen toward the reporters, its back to the game, just to prove it was no fake." Ed Danforth, sports editor of the *Atlanta Journal,* added that this introduction to televised sports "left some of us in a fine state," adding, "Frankly I am scared of the thing and may never have one in my house."[22]

Finally, just to make sure all the Atlanta bases were covered, WSB-TV broadcast a high-school football game to 500 Philco executives gathered in Atlanta for a convention. "Those WSB cameramen work as if they had been at it for years," one observer said.[23] Before T-Day there were at least three

19. Ellis transcript, p. 4.

20. Prices come from advertisements in the *Atlanta Journal* and the *Atlanta Constitution* between August 29 and September 29, 1948.

21. "Nashville and Atlanta Baseball Teams Televised at Ball Park," *Atlanta Journal*, September 3, 1948, p. 14.

22. *Welcome South Brother*, p. 55.

23. *Welcome South Brother*, p. 55.

more games broadcast; the games caught the attention of those in the home of *Journal* editor Wright Bryan, whose September 30 column reflected Atlanta's excitement at having television to watch. He wrote, "The 8-year-old son and his playmate from next door decorated the library with pennants, and word went out that the kick-off would be at 8 o'clock. At game time every chair in the room was occupied and children covered the floor." Bryan also predicted that television would replace the radio as a source of entertainment.[24]

On September 28, 1948, the *Atlanta Journal* proclaimed the beginning of television in Atlanta with a 64-page special section filled with articles on station personalities, show previews, and television-set advertisements. "WSB Gives Eyes to Dixie," proclaimed the lead article in the section. Reporter Robert H. McKee pointed out that more than half a million dollars had been invested by WSB-TV in the new installations at 1601 West Peachtree Street, N.E. McKee noted that the station would run around the clock, employing 26 full-time engineers and 25 production and promotion employees.[25]

J. Leonard Reinsch, now the managing director of Cox radio and television properties, assured the people of Atlanta "the best in television"; he credited Governor James M. Cox; his son, James M. Cox, Jr.; and *Atlanta Journal* company president George C. Biggers with the leadership needed to make television a success. Reinsch added that under their leadership WSB-TV had assembled a "splendidly trained staff" and all the equipment needed to bring the best of television to Atlanta. Reinsch also prophetically predicted that television would revolutionize American life, just as the automobile had.[26]

Johnny Outler, general manager of the new station, promised a standard equal to television in Chicago, New York, or elsewhere. The T-Day front-page article in the *Journal* said the evening's debut would be "informal, 8–10:30 tonight." An editorial promised, "The pleasures and the benefits thus offered are hardly to be numbered, they are so many and so various." The editorial outlined for Atlantans an economic assessment of television in America, noting that television was "America's fastest-growing industry"

24. Wright Bryan, "When Can We Look at Television? The Answer Is Now—on WSB-TV," *Atlanta Journal,* September 30, 1948, p. 28
25. Robert McKee, "WSB Gives Eyes to Dixie," *Atlanta Journal,* September 28, 1948, p. 1.
26. "Best in Video Fare Promised by Reinsch," *Atlanta Journal,* September 28, 1948, p. 1.

and was expected to reach an overall capital investment of some $7.6 million by 1953 and give employment to 950,000 persons.[27]

The people of Atlanta were ready for television; local television dealers estimated that between 750 and 1,000 sets were in operation the night of the debut, prompting one dealer to tell an *Atlanta Constitution* reporter on August 29, "The demand has far exceeded our fondest expectations. This far in advance of actual scheduled broadcasting the Atlanta market seems to be ahead of that of the other markets which have introduced television." This was high praise indeed from the competition; the *Constitution* had applied for a television license, but it had yet to be granted. Within two years the *Journal* and *Constitution* would both be owned by the Cox family. WCON-TV would never go on the air, and WCON radio would also be taken off the air forever.[28]

Open at Last!

The television screen on Channel 8 at 8 p.m flashed the letters "WSB-TV" as announcer John Cone boomed "WSB-Television is on the air." A small studio audience watched from the inside as television came to Atlanta. First, The Baptist Hour Choir, directed by John Hoffman, sang the national anthem as the screen showed a flag billowing in the breeze. The *Journal* exposed the truth of the scene in a September 30 article about the premiere. Reporter Margaret Shannon wrote, "By the studio door a rickety table supported a small flag, a cardboard background of clouds and a little electric fan, blowing like mad."[29]

The evening continued with the Reverend Monroe F. Swilley, Jr., who gave the invocation; Jim Cox, Jr., Leonard Reinsch, Governor M.E. Thompson, Mayor William B. Hartsfield, and general manager John M. Outler made welcoming speeches. In all there were 16 speakers that night. Elmo Ellis, who produced the evening's telecast with Brad Crandall, recalled that the event looked glamorous from the screen, but behind the scenes "things were tight." He added that there was one small studio space in the

---

27. "WSB-TV Begins Telecast Tonight," *Atlanta Journal,* September 29, 1948, p. 1, and "Inaugurating the South's First Television Station," *Atlanta Journal,* September 29, 1948, p. 19.

28. "Television Response Terrific, Say Dealers," *Atlanta Constitution,* September 26, 1949, p. 5-F.

29. Margaret Shannon, "How History's Made," *Atlanta Journal,* September 30, 1948, p. 1.

basement, with a little room to have an audience. The two cameras, both mounted on wooden dollies, were not very flexible, either.[30]

An article in the September 30 *Journal* noted that dark pancake makeup was applied to all the guests that evening. Shannon reported that "it gave, temporarily, the same complexion to Gov. M.E. Thompson, Mayor William B. Hartsfield, Fulton County Commissioner R.L. (Shorty) Doyal and numerous others." The article noted that the makeup was "better than a close shave."

Next came the station's first newscast. Walter Paschall, head of the news division, explained that television news was "a combination, really, of the sort of newscasts you're accustomed to on regular AM radio and the newsreels you're used to seeing in the movies." Paschall added the news operation would "use everything possible to make sure you are kept abreast of events, pictorially and newswise."[31]

Then news director Jimmy Bridges, using a six-page script and drop-card pictures from the Associated Press news wire and Wirephoto, delivered the news of the day. The lead story examined a meeting of the big three Western Allies before the United Nations in Paris. After headlines Bridges introduced the News in Pictures segment. There was a photo from the honeymoon of Stephany Saja and Francis Hitchcock, six woman rodeo riders in New York, and a photo of a baby who could walk when he was six months old (and who stood when he was eight days old). The weather called for a low of 58 and a high of 78; in sports the Cleveland Indians beat the Chicago White Sox 5–2.[32]

Bridges said that that first newscast was an adaptation of a radio newscast, enhanced with visuals. Bridges added that visuals came from a variety of sources. Newsreel footage was shipped to the station daily from Telepix and Telenews; however, these films were often dated and needed major editing for use on the air. For the most part the station used drop cards with still photos for the News in Pictures segment of the show. He added that these photos came from the Associated Press and United Press wires at the *Journal*, and that the station never knew what photos it would get.

After music and entertainment the station showed its first movie, "Cheers for Miss Bishop," starring Martha Scott and William Gargan. The

---

30. Ellis transcript, pp. 2–3. See also Shannon, p. 1-F.
31. Script of the first televised newscast on WSB-TV, September 29, 1948. From the files of Jimmy Bridges, Atlanta, Georgia, p. 1.
32. Bridges script, p. 5.

station signed off at 10:30 p.m., to return the next day at 4 p.m. with the "Pantry Party." [33]

Buried on page 22 of the September 30 *Constitution* was a nine-paragraph, two-column story. "Television Debut Here Marks First in Dixie," read the headline. "Atlanta today has the first television station in the South," read the lead. Those reading between the lines saw the real story: WSB, the *Journal*, and the Cox family were first again.[34]

On the Air

With WSB-TV in action Leonard Reinsch, through Johnny Outler, directed that there be three main concerns; news, entertainment, and community service. To make news a priority was difficult, as technology was still in its infancy. Bartlett recalled that by current standards the situation in 1948 was "pretty grim." For instance, for a remote broadcast to work, the 598-foot steel tower needed to be in a clear line of sight. News was shot on film, not videotape, and because of processing requirements there was no immediacy; in fact, it was 1951 before an entire local newscast was filmed for posterity. Don Elliot Heald, who joined the station in 1950 and became its third general manager in 1965, pointed out that "news had to happen early in the day for film of it to make an evening newscast. We were lucky if we got the film the next day."[35]

Bridges recalled a time when Bartlett gave him permission to cover a flood on West Paces Ferry Road with the station's new $1,500 Bell and Howell camera. Bridges said he persuaded two inebriated men to take him into the flooded river, then almost dropped the camera into the water when one of the men fell overboard. A local film lab developed the film, and Bridges rushed the prime footage to the station with minutes to spare. But with no time to write a script, he resorted to reading a copy of the "Pink Edition" (breaking-news afternoon edition) of the *Journal*.

The station was also able to offer election coverage live from the *Journal* office in downtown Atlanta; unfortunately, Ellis said, it was a

33. Robert McKee, "WSB-TV Raises the Curtain on Dramatic Era of Television," *Atlanta Journal,* September 30, 1948, pp. 1–2.

34. "Television Debut Here Marks First in Dixie," Atlanta Constitution, September 30, 1948, p. 22.

35. Don Elliot Heald, personal interview conducted by Ginger Rudeseal Carter, August 8, 1994, Atlanta, Georgia. Transcript in possession of the author.

nightmare logistically because the aisles weren't made for television, and "we had a terrible time getting the cameras around."[36]

When it came to entertainment, Elmo Ellis was the king at WSB-TV. Ellis had created game and quiz shows for radio, and now he used this creativity for television. Some of his inventions included "Lanky Planky," a home-improvement show sponsored by West Lumber Company; "Crossword Quiz," which put a puzzle on television with two players competing while working it; "Battle of the Ages," a show that allowed four adults and four teenagers to discuss and solve a dramatized home or family situation; "Mary Nell at Home," a prototype of Jay Leno or David Letterman, featuring Atlanta actress Mary Nell Santacroce. The set was the living room of her home, and she interviewed the guests who visited. But perhaps the most popular was "The Woody Willow Show," a marionette program performed by Ruth and Don Gilpin.

Perhaps Ellis's most creative programming came during the 1950 trolley strike; Rich's Department Store was devastated by the lack of shoppers, so WSB-TV brought a studio to the third-floor bridge and offered "Rich's in Your Home." This three-hour call-in show allowed viewers to see and purchase items from the store; even after the strike ended, it stayed on the air for two more years. Ellis said, "You couldn't name a generic type television program that we didn't do. They were primitive then, but the idea was original."[37]

As for other entertainment, there was sports from Georgia Tech, the University of Georgia, and Ponce de Leon Field, home of the Atlanta Crackers. And Atlanta received kinescope broadcasts, beginning with the first "Philco Television Playhouse," which aired October 3, 1948.

Public service became a hallmark of Cox properties, and WSB-TV was no exception. Bartlett said that, "Leonard Reinsch was supportive of public service, which was not only a good news opportunity, but it was also a chance to give something back to the community."[38]

Two major contributions to community and public service still active today are the WSB "Salute to America" parade, begun by Jean Hendrix in 1960, and the WSB/Atlanta Gas Light Company "Shining Light Award." The parade still rolls down Peachtree Street every Fourth of July, honoring a group or organization in the Atlanta community; a new recipient of the

---

36. Ellis transcript, p. 6.
37. Ellis transcript, p. 7.
38. Ellis transcript, p. 6.

"Shining Light Award" is named every year, and past recipients include former Atlanta mayor William B. Hartsfield.

Beyond Beginnings

For the next five years WSB-TV, now moved to Channel 2, ruled the airwaves in Atlanta; by February 1954 it was broadcasting shows in color. Unfortunately, this growth and development left sister radio station WSB in the dust. Radio general manager Frank Gaither, noting the decline of radio in late 1951, called on his former radio colleagues. Would they return to help revitalize the station?

For Elmo Ellis, who was offered the position of program director, it was a difficult decision. He said he didn't want to leave television, but "our radio station was languishing. They asked me to help put some life into it." Ellis discussed it with his wife, then decided to go back to WSB AM-FM, where he spent the rest of his career.

Ellis went on to write a "list of 100 pointers," which Broadcast Music published; Ellis also penned an article titled "Removing the Rust from Radio" for *Broadcasting* magazine. In it he preached what he had been practicing at WSB-TV and WSB radio for years: community involvement, audience participation, and attention to details. These articles brought Ellis speaking requests from radio stations all over the world. He later coauthored a radio textbook with Leonard Reinsch. Ellis, who won the station's first ever award in the 1940s, went on to win a Peabody Award and 14 Freedom Foundation awards.[39]

Another television mainstay, news director Jimmy Bridges, also answered the call to return to radio, prompted by a desire for a different news environment. Bridges wrote that he felt he was in a fishbowl a lot of the time, onstage or on camera no matter where he went. He added that he preferred radio's anonymity.[40]

On the air at WSB-TV, new shows continued to hit the air. One, called "Today in Georgia," followed the "Today Show." Hosted by Don Elliot Heald, it filled a one-hour spot between 9 and 10 a.m. Heald said the station told him "Don't try to be Dave Garroway"; so with a parakeet sidekick—

---

39. Ellis transcript, p. 4.
40. Jimmy Bridges, letter to the author, August 14, 1994.

rather than a chimp named J. Fred Muggs—Heald interviewed "everybody who came to town with a new book, a new campaign, or a new message" for the next five years.

During the '50s, the station offered an innovative children's show called "The Popeye Club with Officer Don Kennedy." The show was based on another show called "Officer Joe's Treehouse Club," but star Don Kennedy talked Jean Hendrix out of calling him "Officer Joe." The Popeye Club was *the* in place to celebrate a birthday in Atlanta; because of limited seats, only 10 children were in the audience at a time. Heald recalled that in preintegration Atlanta, these 10 children were always white; but station manager Marcus Bartlett had a rule. "Marcus Bartlett made it clear: we ask no questions. We will put black children on the show if they made their reservations. Period."[41] The show later seated children—and featured guests —of all races. In the '60s the station would continue to make history as it integrated its news and anchor staffs; Monica Kaufman, one of the first black anchors in the United States, joined the station August 25, 1973, and continues to anchor the 6 p.m. news today.

Epilogue

Through the turbulent '60s and '70s WSB-TV continued to grow and thrive. In 1972 the Cox radio and television concerns became Cox Broad-casting Corporation; J. Leonard Reinsch became its first chairman. In September 1980 WSB-TV, an NBC affiliate from the beginning, switched its network affiliation to ABC. Two years later Cox Broadcasting Corporation became Cox Enterprises; broadcast and newspaper operations were divided.[42]

For every show or individual featured in this essay, there are hundreds more in the history of WSB-TV. One of Heald's favorite stories involves a young reporter who was offered an anchor job in Los Angeles. Heald said he hated to tell the reporter, an ambitious young man named Thomas John Brokaw, "no way I can match" an offer of $25,000 a year. "The rest, as they say," Heald added, "is television history."[43]

---

41. Heald transcript, p. 3.
42. Biographical statement provided by Cox Enterprises.
43. Heald transcript, p. 4.

6 "Foremost in Service, Best in Entertainment": WHAS-TV, Louisville

John P. Ferré

An era ended when the Binghams of Louisville sold their local media properties for $440 million in 1986. The Binghams had run their media according to the notion that whatever is worth doing is worth doing right, even if doing right meant making a little less money. Influence and prestige mattered as much as profit to them.

Such paternalism applied to the *Courier-Journal,* nationally famous since Henry Watterson's distinguished editorials during Reconstruction, and it also applied to WHAS-TV. For most of the Bingham years WHAS-TV's slogan—"Foremost in Service, Best in Entertainment"—fit the station's aspirations. The Binghams lived where they broadcast, so they plowed much of their profits back into the station, paying top dollar for talent, deluxe equipment and facilities, and public-service programming that often had more substance than popularity.

The Bingham years ended because of family problems. To stop their children from quarreling over money and management, Barry and Mary Bingham sold their publishing and broadcasting properties. The Providence Journal Company bought WHAS-TV on May 30, 1986, for $87.75 million.

The history of WHAS-TV is a tale of two owners: the community-based paternalism of the Binghams and the distant corporate management of the Providence Journal Company. But the history of WHAS-TV is also a tale of the competition that both owners have faced. WHAS-TV has gone from producing a variety of local programs, to relying almost exclusively upon current and syndicated network programming, and most recently to emphasizing local news—changes that follow the station's ownership and the competitive environment of television broadcasting in metropolitan Louisville.

Hesitation

Just as he was about to add television to his Louisville newspaper, printing, and radio enterprises, millionaire Barry Bingham got cold feet. Would television divert necessary resources from his *Courier-Journal* or *Times,* the newspapers that supplied him with fortune, influence, and pride? "It seemed to me," Bingham recalled, "that probably it would be better for us to divest ourselves of our broadcasting station and try to put all of our resources into the newspapers to be sure that we were going to be able to continue with those on the level that we had always tried to operate on."[1] Worried that the responsibilities and costs of television would weaken his newspapers, Bingham began to search for a suitable buyer.

A buyer was easy to find. WHAS-TV's construction permit, which the Federal Communications Commission issued in September 1946, was the first television license in Louisville and one of the first in the south. Early in 1949 Bingham asked the FCC for permission to sell WHAS-TV to Crosley Broadcasting Company, the family business that owned Cincinnati radio station WLW. "Crosley would be the best one for us to sell to," Bingham said, "because they ... knew this part of the country. They were interested in Kentucky, among other things. They had operated in Kentucky a good deal, and [we felt] that they would run a very high-class operation here, as they had done in Cincinnati."[2] When the FCC blocked the sale to prevent excessive concentration of broadcasting power in the Ohio River Valley, Bingham decided to follow his original plan. He would run WHAS-TV. The night of WHAS-TV's debut he told viewers that the station would "adhere to a basic principle set down by my father. He wanted WHAS [radio] to serve and be a vital part of the progress and well-being of this community. This philosophy

---

1. Quoted in Samuel W. Thomas, ed., *Barry Bingham: A Man of His Word* (Lexington: University of Kentucky Press, 1993), p. 131.
2. Thomas, p. 131.

has guided us throughout the twenty-eight-year history of WHAS [radio]. And it continues to guide us as we go into television."[3]

By the time WHAS-TV went on the air, there were already 25,000 TV sets in the viewing area. WHAS-TV may have been the first television station in Louisville to receive a construction permit from the FCC, but Bingham's second thoughts made it the second television station in Louisville actually to broadcast.WAVE-TV Channel 5, an NBC affiliate that also showed Du Mont and ABC programs, had been on the air since November 24, 1948.[4]

WHAS-TV began broadcasting at 2 p.m. on March 27, 1950, with nearly four hours of news and weather. "Let's Go to the Circus," a 10-minute film, followed. Then came the CBS hour of music variety, "The Fred Waring Show." At 7 p.m. WHAS-TV aired a 1½-hour inaugural program, which introduced station officials, previewed CBS programs, and showed samples of such local programs as "T-Bar-V Ranch," a children's show; "Hi-Varieties," a teenage talent show; and "Good Living," a cooking show. Barry Bingham appeared on film, saying, "We will do considerable local programming on our television station. We want WHAS-TV to reflect and serve the interests of the people of Louisville and its environs. On this first night of telecasting, I am happy to dedicate WHAS-TV to that end. May it serve Kentuckiana well."[5] The evening continued with the comedy variety of "The Ken Murray Show" and the drama of "Studio One." News at 10:30 ended the first day's broadcast.[6]

With a 600-foot tower near its studios in the downtown *Courier-Journal* and *Times* building, WHAS-TV Channel 9 soon became the nation's first 50,000-watt television station. When it boosted its power to the FCC limit of 316,000 watts in 1953, WHAS-TV had to move from Channel 9 to Channel 11 to avoid interfering with television in Cincinnati.[7]

Throughout the 1950s Louisville had only two full-power VHF stations: WAVE-TV (NBC) and WHAS-TV (CBS). In 1958 the school board started an educational station, WKPC-TV, but its hours were limited, and it used UHF frequencies that very few TV sets were equipped to receive. That

3. Thomas, p. 132. For a history of WHAS radio, see Terry L. Birdwhistell, "WHAS Radio and the Development of Broadcasting in Kentucky, 1922–1942," *Register of the Kentucky Historical Society,* 79 (Autumn 1981): 333–53.

4. "Louisville TV Grows Up," *Louisville Magazine,* Fall 1950, p.19.

5. Thomas, p. 132.

6. Bill Ladd, "After a Slow Start and Lots of Troubles, WHAS-TV Begins to Get Out of the Doldrums," *Louisville Courier-Journal,* 2 April 1950, sec. 5, p. 11.

7. "WHAS-TV Is Cleared for Move to Channel 11," *Louisville Courier-Journal,* 27 November 1952, sec. 1, p. 28.

meant viewers in the Louisville metropolitan area had in effect only two channels to watch in the 1950s. To span the diverse interests of the local audience, WHAS-TV broadcast various CBS crowd pleasers like "Arthur Godfrey's Talent Scouts," "I Love Lucy," "The $64,000 Question," and "Gunsmoke," while also producing its own children's programming, crusades, and documentaries.

Localism

The first generation of children to grow up with television in greater Louisville watched "T-Bar-V Ranch," which began when WHAS-TV did, in March 1950, and lasted for 21 years. "T-Bar-V Ranch" entertained children and it taught them, but mostly it celebrated them, especially at the end of each program, when 20 or so birthday boys and girls had the chance to wave and say "hi" on television. The program was homespun, but it made up with warmth what it lacked in production value. And it was popular. In 1956, after announcing the availability of free "T-Bar-V Ranch" coloring books just three times, WHAS-TV received 22,500 requests for them in the mail.

"T-Bar-V Ranch" was hosted by Randy Atcher and "Cactus" Tom Brooks. Atcher had begun his career at WHAS radio, first as a teenage "Yodeling Wonder" and later as an announcer. He composed and recorded country-and-western songs and appeared on a variety of TV network programs, including "The Grand Ole Opry." But the children of Louisville knew Randy Atcher as "T-Bar-V's" singing cowboy, with a scarf, white cowboy hat, and guitar. No episode went by without Randy reaching into his trunk for the Circle Round Ranch storybook from which characters would appear —maybe Merlin Lee Bradley the cotton picker or the "incredibly evil" Squire McSneer, the mustachioed scoundrel who tried to stop Christmas by stealing Santa's reindeer. And they learned the "Brush Your Teeth Song," which Atcher sang to the tune of "Battle Hymn of the Republic" at the end of every episode: *Brush your teeth each morning, get lots of sleep at night. Mind your mom and daddy 'cause they know what is right. Get lots of exercise each day and eat up all your food. Always wear a great big smile; it makes you look so good. Be sure to look both left and right before you cross the street. And be with us tomorrow at nine when it's "T-Bar-V Ranch" time.*

Atcher's cohort was "Cactus" Tom Brooks, the brother of comedian Foster Brooks. Like Atcher, Brooks came to "T-Bar-V Ranch" from WHAS radio, where he had worked both as an announcer and as an actor. But from his "howDEEE" at the start of the show to his cornpone humor and his baggy bib overalls, pointy cowboy boots, and face splotched with white greasepaint and lined with eyebrow pencil, Cactus, the toothless prospector clown, became the delight of area children.

For 21 years "T-Bar-V Ranch" laced local entertainment with instruction. Randy and Cactus filled much of their hour with films and slides from *Encyclopedia Britannica,* safety tips given by a local police officer or fire fighter, a story read by a librarian from the Louisville Free Public Library, and demonstrations on how to make paper hats or airplanes or kites.

On every show a string of local children announced their birthday. This segment was usually routine—dull for almost everyone other than the birthday children and their families, neighbors, and friends. But the alchemy of children and live television made for some memorable exceptions. One four-year-old boy asked Randy if he could say something to Mommy. "Sure. Go ahead," Randy replied. "Mommy," the boy said, "I wet my pants." Another boy told Randy that he had stopped watching "T-Bar-V Ranch." When Randy asked why, the boy's sister interrupted: "Because Daddy hocked the TV set!" During a live commercial for a local dairy, a little boy said firmly, "Randy, I don't like milk." Freelance writer Ginny Fleming recalled the day she and her little brother appeared on the show—a live performance during which her brother got into a fight, another boy gave the finger to the camera, and she proudly asked Randy if he'd like to see her new rosebud panties.[8]

"T-Bar-V Ranch" was hardly a high-budget program, but it was more costly and less profitable than syndicated programs, so in June 1971 it was replaced by reruns of "My Favorite Martian." Atcher went into real estate, and Brooks found a part-time job at Kaelin's House of Liquors. WHAS-TV passed the responsibility for producing and broadcasting edifying children's programming to specialists who showed their well-crafted material through PBS.[9]

Besides its children's programming, WHAS-TV became noted for its crusades. In 1951 a WHAS Cancer Crusade raised more than $10,500 in 10

8. Ginny Fleming, "Of Rosebud Panties, Long Blond Curls and Cowboy Randy," *Louisville Courier-Journal Magazine,* 10 April 1988, pp.16–18.

9. Virginia Delevan, "'T-Bar-V' Herds Them In," *Louisville Times,* 9 April 1966, p. B1; Dick Gabriel, "They're Still His 'Customers,'" *Louisville Times,* 15 August 1977, p. B2.

hours, and in 1952 a telethon for children with cerebral palsy starring singer Rosemary Clooney and comedian Garry Moore raised $114,000 in 16 hours.[10] The following year's crusade, however, was a landmark of local programming. Not only did WHAS-TV help a Cancer Crusade raise $100,000, it also dramatized the importance of early detection by showing surgeons remove the right lung from World War II veteran John J. Durham, who had learned of his condition after volunteering for an X ray at a Home Show in the local armory. As surgeons removed Durham's lung, "Operation Cancer" periodically returned to the WHAS-TV studios for medical explanations. Later that night WHAS-TV devoted its forum show, "What's Your Question?" to telephoned queries on cancer and on the operation. Durham returned to television for a half hour on May 13 to demonstrate his recovery on a special entitled "Operation Success." Durham lived more than 22 more years after the operation. "Operation Cancer" won a Du Pont award as well as an award from the Ohio Institute for Education by Radio and Television "for a bold and effective treatment of a vital health problem."[11]

In 1954 WHAS television and radio started the Crusade for Children to help mentally and physically handicapped children in Kentucky and southern Indiana. The crusade won one of Variety's Showmanagement Awards two years later for being "one of the great public service features by a regional station keenly aware of its community responsibility." This citation was hardly exaggerated. The annual drive has grown year after year for more than 40 years—a rarity in television—because its design and execution have consistently delivered tangible public benefits throughout the region.[12]

The first twenty crusades were televised from Memorial Auditorium, which was filled with people who came to see such celebrities as singer Eydie Gorme, movie star Lee Marvin, and trumpeter Doc Severinsen, as well as local personalities and performing groups. There were 10 telephones on

---

10. "10-Hour Marathon Cancer Crusade on WHAS-TV Raises Thousands," *Louisville Courier-Journal,* 29 April 1951, sec. 1, p. 16; Leslie Scanlon, "7 Hooked on Crusade from the Beginning," *Louisville Courier-Journal,* 6 June 1993, p. A1.

11. "Televised Lung-Cancer Operation May Have Been 'World Premier,'" *Louisville Courier-Journal,* 23 April 1953, sec. 1, pp. 1, 7; "Man Who Had Cancerous Lung Cut out on TV Able to Go Home 14 Days Later," *Louisville Courier-Journal,* 7 May 1953, sec. 1, p. 1; "Cancer Patient to Go on TV," *Louisville Courier-Journal,* 12 May 1953, sec. 1, p. 6; Bill Ladd, "Citations Won by WHAS-TV and U. of K. are Real Honors," *Louisville Courier-Journal,* 6 April 1954, sec. 1, p. 9; obituary of John J. Durham, *Louisville Courier-Journal,* 6 January 1976, p. B11.

12. "WHAS-TV and WAVE Honored for Programming," *Louisville Magazine,* 20 May 1956, p. 19.

stage. In the "black hole of Calcutta" below, volunteer telephone operators, the "Southern Bell Girls Club," recorded telephone pledges beneath the thumping of dancers and drums as they dodged the dripping of spilled soft drinks from the planks in the floor overhead.

Pledges from individuals and community groups have been the driving force behind the crusade from the very beginning. In fact, in the early years the crusade minimized outside commercial involvement to such an extent that it refused Kentucky Fried Chicken's offer to sponsor the event. And although WHAS encourages commercial involvement now—Kroger commits $250,000—the lion's share of donations comes a dollar at a time.

Ever since the 1955 crusade, when the chief of the Pleasure Ridge Park Fire Department walked onstage with a boot full of money and said, "I'd love to challenge all the other volunteer fire departments to match it or beat it," volunteer fire departments have competed to collect money. Throughout metropolitan Louisville, fire fighters and other volunteers spend the full week before crusade weekend knocking on doors and holding fire-fighter boots out at intersections. Such effort has made fire departments the most important single volunteer group, donating more than half of the money raised by the crusade every year. Pleasure Ridge Park is still the leading donor among volunteer fire departments. In 1994 between 100 and 200 volunteers canvassed the 37-square-mile area of 100,000 residents and collected more than $150,000.[13]

At least one other on-air challenge had a similar effect. During the very first crusade movie star Pat O'Brien noticed that Protestants and Shriners and members of B'nai B'rith were contributing, but that very few Roman Catholics like himself were. So he shouted into the microphone, "All right, where are you Catholics, you K of Cs, you priests and nuns?" Since then Catholic parishes have made their donations collectively. In 1994 the Archdiocese of Louisville contributed over $150,000 to the crusade.[14]

WHAS promotes the Crusade for Children as "the most successful SINGLE station telethon in the country" for good reason. The 1954 crusade raised $156,725; now it raises at least $4.5 million year—more than five times as much after adjusting for inflation. Meanwhile, its expenses have steadily declined, from 10.9 percent the first year to less than 4 percent now.

---

13. Nikita Stewart, "Tested Tactics Keep PRP Firefighters Top Crusade Fund-Raisers," *Louisville Courier-Journal*, 7 June 1994, p. 1.

14. James Doussard, "'You Can't Print This, But...': Some Offbeat Crusade Stories," *Louisville Courier-Journal*, 24 September 1967, pp. G1, G4; Debbie Gray, Archdiocese of Louisville, telephone interview, 26 September 1994.

Interest earned between the time funds are deposited and the time they are dispersed pays this overhead, effectively freeing the crusade from all operating expenses.

The money collected every year is distributed in August to select agencies that apply between January and March. Money contributed from southern Indiana goes to organizations there, and money from Kentucky goes to Kentucky causes. How this money is dispersed is decided every year by the ecumenical panel of clergy from the WHAS-TV program "Moral Side of the News," which now airs at 6:30 a.m. Sunday between "News for Kids" and "Kenneth Copeland." Last year the panel chose nearly 200 projects, to receive well over $4 million.

The Crusade for Children has made very few changes through the years. It moved to the studios of WHAS-TV in 1975 to avoid disruption from a labor dispute. In 1969 it shifted from September to May to stop interfering with October's United Way drive, and it moved to June in 1986 because the crusade, together with the Derby and primary election in May, overwhelmed the station with overtime.[15] Mostly, though, it sticks to raising funds from individuals and community groups and dispersing the money it raises to area institutions. Its benefits can be seen throughout hospitals in the region where plaques read, "This equipment was donated by the Crusade for Children." Such plaques line the walls of the University of Louisville School of Medicine and Kosair Children's Hospital, which together have received more than a third of crusade funds. A plaque is also on the Ronald McDonald House in Louisville, which was built in 1984 with the help of crusade funds to house families with children in Louisville area hospitals.[16]

Beyond its uplifting children's programming and annual charities, WHAS-TV earned prominence in the community through its documentaries. In 1959 WHAS-TV broadcast "53 Miles From Death," which showed how local schools were unprepared for tornado warnings. Shortly after the program had been repeated twice, every school in Jefferson County had a Conelrad warning receiver.

The following year WHAS-TV broadcast "Operation Open Heart," a videotaped operation performed by nine doctors and four nurses from the University of Louisville School of Medicine. The team closed a 1½-inch hole in the heart of a five-year-old boy, Gussie Snyder of Ashland, Kentucky.

15. "Crusade for Children Is Moving to June," *Louisville Courier-Journal,* 14 January 1986, p. B2.

16. Scanlon, pp. A1, A7.

This program was aired on an evening dedicated to promoting advancements in heart research and technology. At 6:15 viewers saw Gussie's operating room at Children's Hospital and heard his doctors discuss the surgery.The 90-minute tape began at 8:30 p.m.: not for tender viewers, the tape showed (without sound) doctors dividing Gussie's breastbone with a hammer and chisel. The operation proceeded smoothly, except at one point when a surgeon exclaimed, "How can [his blood pressure] drop that fast?" Afterward "What's Your Question?" devoted its half hour to telephoned questions answered by the physicians.[17]

The most recognized person on WHAS-TV in those days was Phyllis Knight, who moved to Louisville from Peoria in 1955 to host a community show in which she would interview important visitors and help with Red Cross drives and March of Dimes campaigns. She interviewed more than her share of Hollywood stars, but she also covered issues of pressing importance. In 1957, for example, several thousand women had a Pap test for cervical cancer as a result of Phyllis Knight's relentless coverage. For this effort she received McCall's Golden Mike Award in 1958 for outstanding woman broadcaster in America.

Later, in the documentary "Doctor of the Hills," Phyllis Knight followed Dr. Paul Maddox through a typical day in which he—the sole physician in two Appalachian counties—saw more than 130 patients. The show dealt with his promotion of birth control as a means of raising the area's standard of living, a controversial issue at that time. She won the Golden Mike again in 1962 for her coverage of local child adoption. Her series of six programs attacked misconceptions and red tape in adoption procedures, with the result that adoptions increased 36 percent within the year and placements of problem children doubled. The series led area adoption agencies to establish an information exchange.[18]

17. "WHAS-TV Will Show Open-Heart Surgery," *Louisville Courier-Journal,* 21 February 1960, sec. 1, p. 27; Robert P. Clark, "'Gussie,' 5½, Has Lots of Questions," *Louisville Courier-Journal,* 25 February 1960, sec. 2, p. 2.

18. Betty Lou Amster, "News and Documentaries: Immediate Journalism and the Longer View," *Louisville Magazine,* 20 September 1967, p. 17; Yvonne Eaton, "Phyllis Knight's Career Wasn't Just Small Talk," *Louisville Courier-Journal,* 16 August 1981, pp. H1, H7; Phyllis Knight, personal interview conducted by John P. Ferré, 14 June 1994.

News

WHAS-TV's original programming began to disappear in the '60s. One by one WHAS-TV replaced such long-standing productions as "Hayloft Hoedown" and "Hi-Varieties" with syndicated programs, which were becoming more plentiful with every season.WHAS-TV discarded most of its local productions by the early '70s and satisfied itself with making its money as the local outlet for "The Andy Griffith Show," "The Beverly Hillbillies," "60 Minutes," and "All in the Family." Such complacency surfaced because the reservoir of inexpensive and time-tested syndicated programming was growing much faster than the station's competition. Indeed, by the end of the 1970s WHAS-TV faced competition from only two commercial-network affiliates, PBS, and one independent UHF station. Moreover, having PBS affiliates in town took pressure off WHAS-TV to produce public-interest programming; it's hardly a coincidence that "T-Bar-V Ranch" disappeared in 1971, just two years after PBS began broadcasting "Sesame Street."

Ironically, the cancellation of local shows was taking place when WHAS-TV moved out of the *Courier-Journal* and *Times* building into a state-of-the-art broadcasting center designed with video production in mind. Since 1968 WHAS-TV has occupied a building that has more than 100 offices and utility rooms, crystal clocks that correct themselves to the second each day, an emergency generator, a freight elevator that can hold a mobile home, and a 40,000-square-foot basement. To shut out noises and vibrations from street and air traffic, the building had 10 "floating" studios, rooms with a felt buffer between the floor,walls, and ceiling and the surrounding concrete structure.[19]

The affluence that WHAS-TV's move into such premium space signified would have been much greater had the station been allowed to replace its original 600-foot tower, which stood at Sixth and Broadway downtown, with a 2,000-foot tower east of Louisville that would reach Lexington, which had no television station at the time. The only other site was across the river in Floyds Knobs, Indiana, where WAVE-TV had built its tower. But whereas the Indiana location would limit the reach of WHAS-TV to the Louisville metropolitan area, an Oldham County site would unite Louisville, Frankfort, and Lexington into a much larger market.

---

19. *WHAS Radio-TV-FM,* four-page brochure, California, 1969.

The Federal Communications Commission approved the plan, but permission to build the tower was denied by the Federal Aviation Administration, which believed that it would pose a hazard to air traffic. According to Barry Bingham, Jr., WAVE-TV feared the advantage that WHAS-TV would gain, so it hired private planes to log enough hours flying over the fields of Oldham County to leave a worrisome paper trail for the FAA to use to block WHAS-TV's proposed tower. The plan worked. Reluctantly, in 1964 WHAS-TV broke ground for its tower near WAVE's in Floyds Knobs, Indiana.[20]

Even though it canceled one local show after another, WHAS-TV managed to maintain its local character by expanding its production of news. The increase can be seen clearly by looking at one day's broadcast in 10-year intervals. On the first Wednesday in August 1953, for example, WHAS-TV broadcast one hour of news, but in 1963 the news output for that same day doubled. Ten years later the output was still two hours, but news had increased significantly by 1983, and by August 4, 1993, WHAS-TV was routinely broadcasting at least three hours of news every day. A glance through WHAS-TV's program schedule indicates that now it broadcasts three to four times as much news as it did in its first year on the air.

The news department at WHAS-TV proved itself fertile training ground for network reporters. David Dick and Richard Threlkeld went on to become correspondents for CBS News; Peter Hackett joined NBC News, and Joe A. Gotte became its executive producer; Bill Small became president of both CBS News and NBC News; and James Walker went to work for ABC's "Nightline."

Many WHAS-TV news stories have been memorable. The two-part "Open City" series on vice in Louisville in 1971 reported on bookies, prostitutes, and police officers and showed that WHAS-TV could compete with and sometimes even beat the *Courier-Journal* and *Times,* even though the same family owned and operated all of them.[21] WHAS-TV won awards for its coverage of the devastating 1974 tornado and the school-busing crisis of the mid-1970s. And in 1975, before she left the news department to direct the Crusade for Children, Phyllis Knight finished the hardest story she ever reported: a six-part series on depression in which she discussed her own nervous breakdown that resulted in a seven-week stay at the psychiatric ward

20. Barry Bingham, Jr., personal interview conducted by John P. Ferré, 5 October 1994.

21. Rick Northern and John Finley, "WHAS Plays Tape It Says Is Talk Between Ex-Officer and Vice Figure," *Louisville Courier-Journal,* 20 February 1971, pp. A1, A12; "Louisville Observed," *Louisville Magazine,* March 1971, pp. 22–24, 71.

of Norton Hospital.[22] Such reporting drew attention and accolades to WHAS-TV. By 1978 WHAS-TV had the top-rated news in Louisville, capitalizing on WAVE-TV's shift to 5:30 p.m. news and Livingston Gilbert's retirement from WAVE-TV.[23] WHAS-TV still has the highest-rated local news programs in Louisville today.

Change

The last 15 years have presented WHAS-TV with stiff competition. Besides the traditional commercial networks and PBS, local broadcasting now includes Fox, Warner Brothers, and Paramount affiliates, religious stations, and a video jukebox. Cable television reaches two out of three local households, and the number of video-rental stores has swelled from nine in 1984 to 113 in 1994. As WHAS-TV's network affiliation has lost value, the onus of profit making has fallen more and more to local news.

This was the environment in which the Providence Journal Company bought WHAS-TV. In addition to the newspaper, the Providence Journal Company owns television stations, cable-TV systems, radio paging, and cellular telephony from Rhode Island to Hawaii. Its expectations for high profits and low overhead were evident from the first day it owned WHAS-TV. On that day it laid off one of every 10 WHAS-TV employees.[24]

The most dramatic change that WHAS-TV has undergone as a property of the Providence Journal Company occurred in June 1990, when the station switched network affiliations. Leaving CBS (which had been WHAS-TV's network for 40 years) for ABC came as a surprise. CBS may have become the least popular commercial network nationally, but it was still popular in Louisville. WHAS-TV had apparently little to gain by dropping CBS.

But switching to ABC offered WHAS-TV exclusive rights to the Kentucky Derby. Although the Derby was first televised by WAVE-TV in 1949, WHAS-TV televised it exclusively beginning in 1952. Its long-standing Derby Day production made that day the most profitable of the year for WHAS. Even after ABC won the contract to broadcast the Kentucky

---

22. Leah Larkin, "TV's Phyllis Knight Talks Openly of Her Mental Illness," *Louisville Courier-Journal,* 25 November 1975, p. A8.

23. Morgan Atkinson, "The News Wars," *Louisville Magazine,* December 1986, pp. 73–75.

24. Ric Manning, "WHAS Television: Once Stable Station Wracked by Turmoil," *Louisville Courier-Journal,* 14 July 1991, pp. E1, E4.

Derby in 1976, Churchill Downs required ABC to permit WHAS-TV to broadcast the race. This practice stopped in 1988, which meant that WHAS-TV could broadcast much of the festivities but had to put something else on the air when the actual Kentucky Derby was run.[25] WHAS-TV was hopeful that CBS would regain the rights to broadcast the Kentucky Derby in 1990, but they went again to ABC. A month after ABC broadcast the 1990 Derby, WHAS-TV left CBS for ABC.[26]

However much WHAS-TV may dominate local news, competition for advertising revenue among the four local newscasters is so keen that WHAS-TV sometimes blurs the lines between news and promotion, forgetting, as one former TV-news executive said, to "put some buffer between the news department and the guys in the plaid suits down the hall." In 1993, for instance, WHAS-TV promoted an exposé on the dangers of carbon monoxide, warning, "It's in your house. You can't see it. You can't smell it. But it's there." In actuality "CO, the Silent Killer" was a syndicated package that dozens of TV stations across the country tied into promotions at building-supply stores that sold carbon-monoxide detectors for $3.99. Indeed, WHAS-TV's broadcasts were cosponsored by Levy's Lumber and Building Centers, which stocked the CO detectors beside a promotional poster of WHAS-TV anchor Gary Roedemeier. WHAS-TV, in turn, featured the company's logo and price stickers in its newscasts.[27] Such chicanery led former anchor Jim Mitchell to say that the Providence Journal Company "bought the Starship Enterprise and they're turning it into Eastern Airlines."[28]

Tomorrow

Like commercial television stations across the country, WHAS-TV has responded to the steady increase in competition by replacing most of its local productions with syndicated programs. Its local productions have been pared down to periodic election coverage, news, sports, and the Crusade for

25. Tom Dorsey, "WHAS to Bow Out Before Run for the Roses," *Louisville Courier-Journal,* 28 March 1988, pp. C1–C2.

26. Local media critic Vince Staten offered this speculation in a personal interview conducted by John P. Ferré, 14 September 1994.

27. John Filiatreau, "Wrestling for Ratings," *Louisville Magazine,* May 1993, pp. 42–50.

28. Quoted in Manning, p. E4.

Children. As competition gets fiercer and fiercer, will the Providence Journal Company dilute the station's local commitment further? The answer to this question, of course, is to stay tuned. Dedication to local news will mean more than broadcasting a few hours of headlines, weather, and sports every day. It will mean investing financial and human resources in reporting information that the people of Louisville really need to know, and not relying on flashy packages to lure viewers during rating periods. Community commitment will also mean continuing to operate the annual Crusade for Children fully even if donations to this charity begin to taper off. The degree of local commitment will be a measure of the character of the owners, operators—and viewers alike.

7 WTVJ, Miami: Wolfson, Renick, and "May the Good News Be Yours"

Fran Matera

On April 26, 1952, one of the first remote television news reports in Miami, Florida, changed forever the lives of the people involved. Nine days before the broadcast, Miami had been shocked by a sensational crime. Charles Johnson had reportedly kidnapped the six-year-old son of Dan Richter, one of the Magic City's wealthiest families.[1] He successfully pulled off the $20,000 ransom drop, then escaped to Havana via Cubana Airlines flight 495. Tracking him to the island nation just 90 miles south of the mainland, the police with the aid of pre-Communist government officials captured the assailant and extradited him to the United States. Then Cuban president Fulgencio Batista signed the warrant ordering Johnson's return.[2] The return was such big news that the only television station in the state, Miami's WTVJ/Channel 4, broke tradition and sent a news crew to Miami International Airport to cover Johnson's arrival.

The reporter that afternoon was a freshman broadcaster named Ralph Renick. The 24-year-old journalist pushed his way through the crowd of newspaper reporters and photographers, dragging his cords behind him.[3] Johnson spotted the camera, determined which reporter was carrying a microphone instead of a pencil, and walked toward him. "Get me Ellis Rubin!" Johnson shouted. Ten miles away a 27-year-old defense attorney

---

1. "Richter Kidnap Suspect Returns Today," *Miami Herald*, 26 April 1952, p. 1A.
2. *Miami Herald*, 26 April 1952, p. 4A.
3. The technical aspects of such a decision were formidable. A bulky film camera had to be transported to the airport tarmac and planted in position. The audio was captured on a portable wire recorder tethered to a long extension cord.

named Ellis Rubin, who had represented Johnson on an earlier charge, heard
on the radio that Johnson had been apprehended in Cuba and was on his way
back to Miami on a Pan American Clipper. "I didn't own a television set, so
I rushed over to a department store, fought off the salesman, and waited for
the news," Rubin explained. "I nearly fell over. Here was Public Enemy
Number One, calling out my name for all the world to hear."[4]

WTVJ and Renick became institutions in south Florida. Renick was
called "the dean of Florida broadcasters," holding the anchor's chair for 35
years—a record that most likely will never be challenged in today's environment of rating wars, consultants, and disposable news personalities.[5] From
the moment WTVJ signed on in 1949, to its sudden and shocking network
affiliation change from CBS to NBC in 1988, WTVJ has been a station that,
probably more than any other in the nation, has mirrored television history.

WTVJ Beginnings

The prosperity and promise of the 1920s made Miami the "Magic City"
in 1925 when brothers-in-law Mitchell Wolfson and Sidney Meyer formed
their entertainment company. The Wolfson-Meyer Theater Company survived the Depression to become an industry conglomerate worth $1 billion.
As it evolved, the name was shortened to Wometco from the *WO* of Wolfson,
the *ME* of Meyer, the *T* of theater, and the *CO* of company. The company
built and opened its first motion-picture palace, The Capitol, at 300 North
Miami Avenue on June 25, 1926. This site became Wometco's permanent
corporate headquarters. The theater earned a reputation for its own firsts—it
was patterned after the lavish Capitol Theater in New York and featured a
$60,000 Wurlitzer organ, stage shows, the latest film releases, and even an
early form of air-conditioning.[6] In the 1930s and 1940s Wometco theaters
became famous by hosting movie premieres featuring Clark Gable, Ethel

---

4. Ellis Rubin, *Get Me Ellis Rubin: The Life, Times and Cases of a Maverick Lawyer* (New
York: St. Martin's Press, 1989), p. 5. Rubin made his own media history by defending a teenage
murder suspect in Florida's first cameras-in-the-courtroom experiment in 1977, using a novel
"television intoxication" defense.

5. See S. L. Alexander, "May the Good News Be Yours: Ralph Renick and Florida's First TV
News," *Mass Communication Review* 19 (Winter–Spring 1992): 57; Juan Carlos Coto, "Veteran
Anchor Ralph Renick Dies," *Miami Herald*, 13 July 1991, p. 1A.

6. Arva Moore Parks, *Miami: The Magic City* (Tulsa: Continental Heritage Press, 1981),
p. 211.

Merman, Joan Crawford, and Betty Grable. When Wometco began trading its stock publicly in the 1950s, Meyer sold his interest, but Wolfson retained his controlling shares.[7] Wometco grew, and Wolfson, ever the entrepreneur, extended his theater chain in a new venture—television.

On January 10, 1947, the Southern Radio and Television Equipment Company filed an application for a permit to construct a new television station in Miami to be operated on Channel 4. The application was granted by the Federal Communications Commission without hearing on March 12, 1947, and was assigned the call letters WTVJ.[8] Other companies were vying for the permit, among them five radio stations and Wometco. They charged that Southern in its application had concealed material facts relative to its ownership and financial status. On April 19, 1948, application for consent to transfer control of Southern to Wolfson-Meyer Theater Enterprises was filed. As a result of its initial investigation, the FCC revoked Southern's permit on July 29, 1948. On October 15, at Wometco's request, the FCC consolidated the proceeding with Southern's request for a hearing on the revocation order. A hearing on the two applications took place in Miami from October 25 through October 27, 1948.[9]

Southern was organized and its application filed through the efforts of Robert Venn. Venn had tried to secure financial backing through Edward Claughton and Edward Nelson. Although both offered initial support, they later withdrew from the investment. Venn learned of Claughton's withdrawal prior to the approval of Southern's application and began searching for other financiers. In May 1947 Venn talked to Mitchell Wolfson about the possibility of Wometco financing Southern's venture. Venn was employed by the Lincoln Operating Company, a subsidiary of Wometco, whose goal was to create a new AM station in Miami. Lincoln and Venn's efforts were successful. Venn was named general manager of WMIE-AM. Venn kept "Wolfson informed on the progress of the art of television." Negotiations between Venn and Wometco took place between May 1947 and March 1948. Venn received $300 monthly from Wometco for his expenses on behalf of the WTVJ venture, as well as $97,657.66 to purchase equipment for Southern and to meet the payroll.[10]

7. Carol E. Curtis, "An Entertaining Proposition," *Forbes,* 29 March 1982, p. 122.

8. Paul Walker, Preliminary Statement, *Federal Communications Commission Reports* (1949), 289, Docket 9114, File BTC-636, Decision, sec. 1.

9. Walker, 290, Decision, sec. 2, 3.

10. Walker, 292, Decision, sec. 7.

"The Commission [FCC] at no time was informed of this arrangement" or of changes in the financial structure. Wolfson testified that Wometco's reasons for advancing the money to Southern were "in order for them [Southern] to have sufficient funds to meet their commitments, both to the FCC as to getting television equipment to the public in the public interest and getting television for the Fall of 1948 for Miami; our desire to assist them and to hope that we would be permitted to take over control of this company by the FCC; we advanced them the money ... as a loan, to proceed to purchase the equipment, to proceed to do the construction that was necessary, and to proceed to try to bring television to the Greater Miami area."[11]

By the fall of 1948 Wometco had committed $300,000 to the construction of WTVJ in the hopes the FCC would sanction its efforts to bring TV to Florida. This amount represented a significant portion of Wometco assets. Wometco's reported assets after its investment in Southern were $319,770, in addition to $454,990 in stocks held by Wolfson family members.

On January 5, 1949, the FCC under the direction of commissioner Paul Walker concluded that Wometco was "legally, technically, financially and otherwise qualified to operate station WTVJ" and granted the transfer of ownership.[12] Venn was tapped to serve as WTVJ's first general manager.

On the Air

Television arrived in the Sunshine State on March 21, 1949, at 7 p.m., when Florida's first station, WTVJ, went on the air from a back room of the Capitol Theater. It was the first television station in the state,[13] and claims to be the 16th commercial station in the entire nation.[14] Shortly after the sign-on, it was estimated that there were about 2,000 television sets in Miami, and

---

11. Walker, 292, Decision, sec. 8, 9.

12. Walker, 299, Conclusions, sec. 8.

13. See "WTVJ Sets Dedication," *Miami Herald*, 21 March 1949, sec. A; Alexander, p. 57; John Dorschner, "Renick in the Rest Room, Diapers in the Refrigerator," *Tropic*, 11 March 1973, pp. 33–36.

14. See *Gale Directory of Publications and Broadcast Media* 1 (Detroit: Gale Publishing, 1994), p. 44 ; Tom Jicha, "WTVJ Looks Back at Its Many Firsts," *Fort Lauderdale Sun Sentinel*, 25 March 1995, p. 3D; Sydney W. Head and Christopher H. Sterling, *Broadcasting in America* (Boston: Houghton Mifflin, 1982), p. 182. Head and Christopher indicate that by 1948, 16 stations were on the air. WTVJ, which went on the air in 1949, would at least be in the first 20 stations on air.

most of those were in bars and businesses.[15] The unveiling of WTVJ was, however, a major attraction in local department stores such as Burdine's and Richard's. In fact, for its first few years most of WTVJ's audience got their first glimpse of the new medium in the stores. At times people could be seen huddling six and seven deep around televisions displayed in show-room windows.

WTVJ's early program schedule began with two hours of local programming a night, six days a week. The station was dark on Tuesdays so that engineers could repair the equipment. Initially, all programs originated locally. The coaxial cable that would join WTVJ to network service was not in place until June 30, 1952. Gradually, Channel 4 expanded into daytime hours. Early programs included "Brunch with Judy" (Judy Wallace), a morning show featuring interviews with celebrities, chefs, artists, and local leaders; a cooking show hosted by Helen Ruth; and a late-night movie hosted by Alec Gibson. Artist Lee Dickens served as the featured personality in two early WTVJ programs—an art show and later an evening adventure program in which she would walk on the wing of a plane at 3,000 feet, travel down the Amazon, or climb to the top of the WTVJ antenna tower.[16] Under its application to the FCC, Wometco developed a program in cooperation with the state agricultural experimental station to show the farmers methods of fighting insects, improving crops, and preventing blights and viruses. This program ran on the station for many years, highlighting the extension service. Following the lead of other stations across the nation, Wometco paid the University of Miami $1,800 in 1948 for the rights to broadcast its athletic events.[17] Wometco was also interested in "the development of local talent" in connection with the company's motion picture theater operation. Kinescopes sent by airmail, and later coaxial cable, enabled the station to expand programming to include shows produced by other stations.[18]

---

15. See Alexander, pp. 57, 58; Parks, p. 144: Erik Barnouw, *History of Broadcasting in the United States* (New York: Oxford University Press, 1968), p. 285.

16. See G. S. Nyne, "Wometco's WTVJ/Miami: 25 Years of TV Pioneering," *Historical Association of South Florida Update* 2 (December 1974): 2, 6–8; Dorschner, pp. 33–36.

17. Walker, 295, Decision, sec. 18.

18. See Alexander, p. 59; Dorschner, p. 33; Parks, p. 144.

WTVJ News

The 1949 WTVJ news presentations included a news tape; news briefs with slides; news on film; narrator, interviews, and film; feature treatment of news; and on-the-spot coverage. The news tape was a feed roller on a ballop, which moved a 3/8-inch paper strip across the bottom of either a test pattern or a commercial slide. WTVJ sold sponsors five- and 10-minute segments in the afternoon. The news brief consisted of an announcer reading five minutes of wire-service news behind accompanying slides. The station offered two programs daily, in the early evening and before sign-off, to provide viewers with spot news. News on film was filmed and scripted by Telenews Productions and aired on WTVJ twice nightly Monday through Friday. This particular program's sponsorship was purchased by the American Brewing Company for $150 per week. The *Miami Herald*'s unique joint venture with WTVJ resulted in a half-hour Sunday-night news program called "Televiews of the News" and "Monday Morning Headlines." The weekly expenditure on the program was about $500. WTVJ also created and aired a weekly panel quiz program called "What's the Story?" during which a moderator presented clues provided by viewers to a panel of newsmen. If the panel accumulated a certain number of points, they "told the story." If the panel failed, the viewer providing the entry received a prize. The mail response to this program was more than 100 entries each week. Newsworthy events were aired on WTVJ by remote pickup. This included election coverage, candidates' speeches, parades, and hospital dedications. The average cost was about $300, but according to Renick, "This is TV news presentation at its best. The instantaneous transmission of events of interest will always rank high in viewer interest."[19]

Although few viewers actually witnessed those early broadcasts, a newspaper writer dubbed WTVJ's existence as the "biggest event since the Florida land boom."[20] Back when the station signed on, however, no one had a clue what was in store. Nobody even knew if local programs or a local newscast would fly. Two other south-Florida UHF stations, WFTL in Fort

---

19. Ralph Renick, *News on Television: A Report of an Investigation Carried out Under the Terms of a Fellowship of the Kaltenborn Foundation* (Coral Gables, Florida: May 1950), pp. 8–10. A copy of this unpublished report is in the Book Section of the Florida Collection, University of Miami Library, HE 8694.R4, file 150164.

20. Jack Anderson, "Miami TV: In the Beginning," *Miami Herald* TV Preview, 16 June 1964, p. 3.

Lauderdale and WITV in Hallandale, briefly experimented with television, but for most viewers from 1949 until 1957, TV meant WTVJ and Ralph Renick.[21]

"The Ralph Renick Report"

On July 16, 1950, WTVJ aired its first live news report and its first "Ralph Renick Report," a 10-minute recap of the three-week-old Korean War.[22] The program also featured national and international news. Renick was the program's anchorman, camera operator, news producer, and writer. In fact, he was the entire news department.[23]

Renick's first film-projection facility was the station's bathroom. He screened newsreels and added narrative—all while having to compensate for the fact that his picture vanished every time someone opened the door. To bolster the limited filmed reports, Renick started a file of graphics comprising photographs cut from news magazines. It was television news at its beginning.

Renick was given his own camera operator a few months after kicking off his news program. In December 1950 the *Miami Herald* and its radio station, WQAM, sponsored a weekly 30-minute local newscast on WTVJ for which the two staffers shot local film footage.[24] The station's film-processing equipment consisted of a bucket and a clothesline. More staffers quickly followed as the concept of local news caught on. Renick spent the next seven years as the only news program in Miami. WTVJ had the entire 400,000-strong south-Florida market to itself.[25]

By 1951 "The Ralph Renick Report" had expanded to 15 minutes and was available to a sponsor for $250 a week. It offered daily coverage of local events, meetings of the Miami City Commission, and the spring session of the state legislature in Tallahassee. Renick and crew also found news material in the national conventions that were annually staged in Miami's beachfront

---

21. Alexander, p. 57.
22. See Alexander, p. 59; Nyne, p. 6; Coto, p. 7.
23. Alexander, pp. 58, 59; Renick, p. 9; Dorschner, p. 34.
24. See Alexander, p. 59; Renick, p. 9.
25. *Columbia Lippincott Gazetteer of the World*, 1950 Census: Final Figures for All States and Counties (New York: Columbia University Press 1952), p. 480. The population for Dade County, in which Miami is located, was 495,084 in 1950. See Jicha, p. 3D.

hotels. The happenings at these gathering often made their way to network news programs. The 1951 American Legion Convention was one of the first to be covered by WTVJ.[26]

Growth of Viewers and Programs

Slowly at first, then in torrents, the populace began buying television sets. By 1951 it was estimated that 34,000 families in Miami had taken the plunge. That figure would increase to the virtual saturation point by the end of the 1950s. Meanwhile, WTVJ's overall staff increased even faster than its budding news division. From the 21 pioneers who began in 1949, another 100 were added by 1951.

In 1952 WTVJ became a CBS-network affiliate, filling its evening hours with professionally produced entertainment programs and big-time stars—and providing a bigger lead-in audience to Renick's news.[27] On the eve of 1953 the station had the honor of returning the favor. WTVJ produced the state's first network origination with the broadcast of the Orange Bowl parade to CBS's 30 affiliates.[28] The construction of Florida's first 100-foot tower and an increase to 100,000 watts extended Channel 4's signal to 16 counties in 1954. By January 1955 WTVJ offered 26 hours of network programs. Its first local live-color program aired in 1956.[29] That same year WTVJ originated the national variety program, "Arthur Godfrey Show," from Miami Beach's Kenilworth Hotel for CBS.[30]

In 1955 Renick found himself involved in a story in which he was called upon to mediate a dispute at Delray Beach, just north of Miami. Delray Beach had barred African-Americans from swimming at local beaches, as had many other Florida cities. Over a period of three days Renick mediated more than 15 meetings and moderated a debate between blacks and whites

---

26. Alexander, pp. 59–60

27. Alexander, p. 58; Nyne, p. 6.

28. Christopher H. Sterling and John M. Kittross, *Stay Tuned: A Concise History of American Broadcasting* (Belmont, Calif.: Wadsworth, 1978), p. 515; Alexander, p. 61; Nyne, p. 7.

29. Nyne, pp. 7–8.

30. See Richard Wallace and Mary Voboril, "TV, Radio Personality Arthur Godfrey Dies: 79-Year-Old Entertainer and Aviator Made Miami a Household Word," *Miami Herald,* 17 March 1987, pp. 1A, 10A; Nyne, p. 7; Parks, p. 146.

to resolve the conflict.[31] Other major stories that year were the Kefauver/
Adlai Stevenson presidential primary debate in Miami and a five-day series
on the growing traffic problems of south Florida.[32]

In the 1960s WTVJ added a 15-minute "Six O'Clock News" program
and a 30-minute "News at Noon" as its program influence continued to grow.
Live cut-ins from neighboring Broward County, originating from the Yankee
Clipper Hotel in Fort Lauderdale, appeared daily on both news programs. In
1964 the station introduced scenic station breaks. From 10 to 60 seconds in
length, the breaks featured picturesque scenes of south Florida backed by
music.[33] In the same year Jackie Gleason decided to move his variety show
to Miami Beach from New York. WTVJ assisted CBS in the program's
production for its seven-year run, as there were no facilities provided at the
Miami Beach Convention Center.[34] Color programming appeared on a
regular basis in 1966. Richard Nixon was the first guest interviewed in color
for Channel 4's weekend news show. In the 1960s the WTVJ series "FYI"
(For Your Information) sent reporters to foreign regions, including Israel and
South America; however, the station's prime focus remained on local issues.
In 1969 and 1970 WTVJ won RTNDA Edward R. Murrow Documentary
Awards for programs on unwed mothers and pollution. Other documentary
awards included those for "Swift Justice," which dealt with Europe's justice
system, and "A Seed of Hope," focusing on a local drug-abuse program.
Weather reporting added another dimension in the early 1970s when WTVJ
claims it was the first station in the nation to use the National Oceanographic
and Atmospheric Administration's satellite motion-picture loop. The early
1970s also marked the WTVJ production of an hour-long series, "Great
Adventure," which was syndicated nationally. In 1973 a three-month-long
series, "Not on the Menu," exposed unhealthy food-service preparation in
area restaurants. The program resulted in a tough new county sanitation law
and won WTVJ a commendation from the Florida Department of Health and
Rehabilitative Services.[35]

31. See Alexander, p. 60; Nyne, p. 7; Sandra Earley, "The Ralph Renick Report," *Tropic*, 3
October 1982, p. 8.

32. Alexander, p. 60.

33. Nyne, pp. 7–8.

34. Dan Holly and Reinaldo Ramos, "The Great One Is Dead at 71," *Miami Herald*, 25 June
1987, pp. 1A, 10AA; Bill Cosford, "Gleason in Florida: How Sweet It Was," *Miami Herald*, 25 June
1987, pp. 10AA, 11AA.

35. Nyne, p. 8.

Kefauver Committee

One of WTVJ's most significant historical news programs revolved around the Kefauver Committee. In 1950 WTVJ canceled regular programming and aired one of the first live news specials. As a result of a series of newspaper stories detailing crime's increasing influence in south Florida, the Greater Miami Crime Commission teamed with U.S. Senator Estes Kefauver and his Senate Crime Investigation Committee to hold hearings on organized crime in Miami. WTVJ decided to televise the hearings.[36] The proceedings were chaired by Tennessee's Democratic senator Estes Kefauver, who became a 1952 presidential candidate on the strength of the publicity created by television's coverage. Before Kefauver's investigation began, he assured reporters that he would conduct a "let the chips fall where they may" examination with no allegiance to political parties or personalities.[37] To assure this, his special committee held hearings in 14 major cities with stops in two Florida cities, Tampa and Miami. Kefauver's committee held its first hearings in July 1950 in Miami, long considered the winter home of organized crime in the persona of Al Capone. The result was that many public officials, including Florida's governor Fuller Warren and Dade county sheriff "Smiling Jimmy" Sullivan, were exposed as aiding organized-crime figures and accepting payoffs.[38]

Among WTVJ's coverage in 1952 were broadcasts of the only presidential primary campaign joint appearances of Kefauver and Georgia's senator Richard Russell. Kefauver also challenged Florida governor Fuller Warren to a debate. WTVJ agreed to televise the oral sparring and stayed on the air with Kefauver even after Warren failed to appear. The incident became known as the "empty-chair debate," an early display of television's power to shape politics and create candidates. Kefauver handily won the primary.

---

36. Paul G. Ashdown, "WTVJ's Miami Crime War: A Television Crusade," *Florida Historical Quarterly* 58 (July 1979–April 1980): 427; Parks, pp. 143–145; Alexander, p. 60.

37. Joseph Bruce Gorman, *Kefauver: A Political Biography* (New York: Oxford University Press, 1971), pp. 77–80.

38. Gorman, pp. 81–85; Estes Kefauver, *Crime in America* (Garden City, N.Y.: Doubleday, 1951), p. 60; Parks, p. 144.

Public-Affairs Programs

In 1954 WTVJ broadcast its first local-election debate. Charley Johns, from northern Florida, was the acting governor following the sudden death of Governor Dan McCarty. LeRoy Collins, McCarty's opponent, credited his appearance on the WTVJ debate as the major reason for his victory ousting Johns.

Kefauver was back in Miami with his Senate investigative hearings in 1955, covering the topic of juvenile delinquency. WTVJ devoted 10 hours of live coverage to the proceedings.[39] That same year WTVJ unveiled a mobile unit that, among other things, enabled it to carry out undercover investigative reports. Its first foray into investigative pieces resulted in filming a payoff to a Miami police sergeant by an undercover agent posing as a bookie. The story found its way to *Life* and *Newsweek* magazines and won the top national award of the Headliners Club. *Newsweek* noted that it was "the first time such pictures have ever been shown on television."[40]

WTVJ Monopoly Ends and Editorials Begin

The WTVJ monopoly ended in 1957 when WCKT (now WSVN) signed on as an NBC affiliate. ABC and WPLG followed in 1958. The addition of the two new stations gave birth to another television truism— entrenched viewership. Thanks to its head start, WTVJ's news programs were able to maintain their ratings supremacy for the next four decades. It wasn't until 1984 that Renick's newscasts dropped in the local ratings to the number-two position.[41]

On September 2, 1957, WTVJ became the first television station to institute a daily editorial.[42] Renick's editorial urged the building of a fire station on Key Biscayne, an island that falls inside Miami's city limits.

---

39. See Ashdown, p. 427 ; Alexander, p. 60; Gorman, pp. 197–198.

40. "Watching Cops Strike It Rich," *Life,* 23 May 1955, pp. 49–50; "How TV Caught a Cop," *Newsweek,* 23 May 1955, p. 34; Nyne, p. 7.

41. Alexander, pp. 58–61; Coto, p. 1A; Associated Press Wire Service, 12 April 1985, AM cycle.

42. See William Wood, *Electronic Journalism* (New York: Columbia University Press, 1967), p. 62; Ashdown, p. 428; "Profile: The Long Arm of the News—WTVJ Miami's Ralph Renick," *Broadcasting,* 5 January 1976, p. 121.

Perhaps as an indication of television's still limited influence back then, the island community didn't build the fire station for another decade. The birth of the WTVJ editorial was most certainly the result of Renick's regard for H.V. Kaltenborn. He had studied Kaltenborn and his commentaries while an undergraduate student at the University of Miami and was awarded a Kaltenborn Foundation Fellowship to examine news presentation. However, the daily editorial policy may also have been prompted by the new competition for viewership and advertisers. Over the next 28 years Renick delivered more than 5,000 editorials while at WTVJ.[43] Each nightly program ended with his signature closing, "Good night, and may the good news be yours."[44]

Cuban Exodus

In the late 1950s WTVJ was the key station feeding the CBS network most of its news footage of the political turmoil in Cuba, events destined to shake the world and change the population landscape of Miami forever. In 1958 and 1959 the station was one of the first to cover prerevolutionary Cuba on a regular basis, funneling its reports to CBS.[45] Cuban refugees staged a hunger strike in WTVJ's lobby to call attention to the plight of other rebels. In 1959, when the Cuban government was overthrown by Fidel Castro, Renick and WTVJ reporters were the first to interview the new world leader and produced a documentary entitled "Cuban Revolution."[46] That same year Renick organized a tour of the Soviet Union for 45 newsmen and south Floridians. They spent one hour and 40 minutes with Premier Nikita Khrushchev. It was a tremendous scoop for a Miami reporter, considering the USSR's growing ties to Castro's Cuba and the interest of many WTVJ viewers in the region. A photo of Renick ran on the front page of the *New York Times* to document the meeting of East and West.[47]

---

43. Coto, p. 1A. Coto attributes 5,487 commentaries to Renick at WTVJ between 2 September 1957 and 10 April 1985. Renick continued his commentaries at WCIX/Channel 6 in Miami between 1988 and 1990; William Cotterell, "Ex-Miami TV Anchorman Files for Governor's Race," United Press International, 30 April 1985, AM cycle.
44. See Alexander, p. 57; Coto, p. 18A; Jicha, p. 3D.
45. See Nyne, p. 7; Alexander, p. 61.
46. Nyne, p. 7; Parks, pp. 153, 154.
47. See Earley, p. 8; Alexander, p. 61; Coto, p. 18A; *New York Times*, 20 March 1959, p. 1A, 1.

As WTVJ grew, so did Miami. It grew from a tranquil seasonal resort town to a major international city. This change was fueled by the exodus of refugees from Fidel Castro's regime. In 1960 Miami was an English-speaking town of 291,688.[48] However, Freedom Flights of 1960 and 1973 pushed the Cuban-refugee migration to an estimated 342,000 and forever changed the lives of Miami residents.[49] In 1979 *U.S. News and World Report* called Miami a new Hispanic power base: "A major metropolis is undergoing reincarnation, with an in-flow of Spanish-speaking people and their culture that has made it the 'foreign capital' of Latin America."[50] Recognizing the shift in population demographics, WTVJ hired Manolo Reyes as the first Spanish-language news anchor in South Florida. Cuban newscaster Reyes hosted the late-night and early-morning "News en Espanol" telecast on WTVJ from 1960 to 1977.[51] When it premiered, the station's switchboard lit up with complaints from English-speaking viewers. In addition, public-affairs programs were rebroadcast in Spanish. WTVJ's documentary about a Cuban refugee's adjustment to Miami life, "The Plight of Pepito," was aired by seven other stations and by the United States Information Agency throughout Latin America.[52]

WTVJ Firsts

WTVJ boasts of presenting the nation's first racially integrated pro-gram—a local children's show in 1956 called Skipper Chuck's "Popeye Playhouse"—and apparently lost an advertiser because of it.[53] One national hamburger chain, no longer in business, protested WTVJ's decision by pulling its advertisements. However, the fledgling Miami-based Burger King stepped in to fill the void.[54] The "Playhouse," later called "The Skipper

48. See Metro-Dade County Planning Department, Research Division, "Dade County Facts," April 1990, p. 3.

49. Metro-Dade County Planning Department, Research Division, "Hispanic Profile," 1986, p. 4.

50. Kathryn Johnson, "Miami: New Hispanic Power Base in U.S.," *U.S. News and World Report*, 19 February 1979, pp. 66, 69.

51. See Coto, p. 18A; Nyne, p. 7; PR Newswire, "Reyes Joins International Hospital," 29 June 1983.

52. Nyne, p. 7.

53. See Nyne, p. 8; Jicha, p. 3D.

54. Jicha, p. 3D.

Chuck Show," aired on WTVJ for the next decade with Chuck Zink at the helm of the live program. It is estimated that more than 7,000 children filled its in-studio audience each year. Zink was a spokesman and station personality well into the 1970s, hosting the annual Orange Bowl parade and other WTVJ community events.

WTVJ engineers designed, modified, and constructed equipment to meet their technical needs. When outsized telephoto lenses impaired the flexibility of remote cameras, engineers crafted a prismatic folded 40-inch lens optically ground locally. The lens allowed WTVJ's first televised coverage of an eclipse and rocket launches at Cape Canaveral.[55] Other innovations attributed to WTVJ include the first local Miami documentaries and the first aerial shots from the Goodyear blimp, which aided in the stations's coverage of sporting events, including games of the University of Miami Hurricanes and the Miami Dolphins, as well as several Super Bowl games. Footage from hurricanes Donna, Cleo, Betsy, and David were all captured by WTVJ cameras and served oftentimes as the first visual reporting of a hurricane's destruction. Bob Weaver (Weaver the Weatherman), the station's weatherperson for more than three decades, is credited by many local historians for introducing the concept of entertainment weather.[56]

WTVJ has also served as fertile training ground for several award-winning network anchors and correspondents: NBC's Katie Couric, Fred Francis, Ike Seamans, David Bloom and Robin Lloyd, and CBS's Martha Teichner and Bernard Goldberg.[57] It was the place where Larry King honed his on-camera interviewing techniques.[58] King's one-on-one interviews, on radio and television, made him a local celebrity two decades before he emerged on the national scene. It was also the place where "NBC Nightly News" anchor Tom Brokaw was turned down for a job in the early 1960s.[59]

55. Nyne, p. 6.

56. Jicha, p. 3D.

57. See Coto, p18A; Inside NBC News releases, David Bloom and Katie Couric, National Broadcasting Company, 1995.

58. See Larry King, *Larry King* (New York: Simon and Schuster, 1982), p. 30; "Mutual's Larry King: Five Years of Questions and He's Still Curious," *Broadcasting* 104 (7 February 1983): 103; Jeanie Kasindorf, "King Maker," *New York* 25 (42) (26 October 1992): 56–59.

59. Coto, p. 1A.

WTVJ's War on Crime

In August 1966 WTVJ's investigative news reports made headlines
again when Renick led a campaign to rid the city of corruption. The
campaign, called "The Price of Corruption," was composed of 65 consecutive weekday editorials, surveillance by hidden cameras, on-air interviews
with informants, and speeches. According to one scholar, the series may well
have been television's first and most significant editorial crusade.[60] Dade
County was ranked as the third-most crime-ridden community in the nation
in FBI statistics released in July 1966.[61] Renick reported that the Justice
Department had said in 1964 that Miami was "totally corrupt."[62] A grand
jury also concluded that "the public reports of systematic and regular
collection of money from gamblers, prostitution operators and operators of
other forms of vice were in fact more widespread ... than had been indicated."[63] WTVJ newsmen, acting on a tip from an informant, hid in a green
panel truck for 12 hours on September 26 and filmed a sheriff's captain
meeting with five known racketeers.[64] Renick aired the film on his October
3 program.[65] The crusade coincided with Florida's 1966 governor's race.
Republican Claude Kirk blamed his opponent Robert King High for the
"cesspool of crime."[66] As a result, Kirk was elected governor and Sheriff
Talmadge Buchanan and top officials were indicted.[67] WTVJ claimed its
crusade had "proved the overall effectiveness of the television editorial,"
which in turn "provided the impetus for individual and community action

60. Ashdown, p. 427.

61. United States Department of Justice, *Uniform Crime Reports for the United States* (1966),
pp. 78–90. The figures are used as a general indicator of the security of a community.

62. See Karl Wickstrom, "Buchanan Waives Immunity" and "Sheriff, Top Command Quizzed
by Grand Jury," *Miami Herald*, 14 September 1966, p. 1A; Ashdown, p. 429.

63. Final Report of the Grand Jury, Circuit Court of the 11th Judicial Circuit of Florida for Dade
County, Spring Term 1966.

64. See Jim Savage, "Sheriff's Aide Filmed at Racketeer Hangout" and photo caption "WTVJ
Picture of Richard Gladwell at Warehouse," *Miami Herald,* 4 October 1966, p. 1A; Ashdown,
p. 433.

65. See transcript of WTVJ editorial, "Ralph Renick Reporting," 3 October 1966, WTVJ
Collection, Louis Wolfson II Media History Center, Miami-Dade County Public Library System,
Metro Cultural Center. Requests must be submitted in writing to the Wolfson Center so that material
can be identified and located. The center's holdings consist primarily of kinescope, film, and video
footage; Ashdown, p. 433.

66. See Martin Waldron, "Victor in Florida Vows Crime Fight," *New York Times*, 10 November
1966, Late City Edition, p. 52A; Ashdown, p. 433.

67. Paul Einstein, "Cameras on Corruption," *The Quill* (May 1967): 12–13.

during a critical community crisis."[68] *Time* magazine concluded that the uproar leading to the indictments was more likely "sufficient to allow reformers to win a referendum" and had not driven criminals from Miami.[69] Whatever the outcome, ratings clearly showed that viewership increased dramatically during the three-month period of the 6 p.m. broadcasts.[70] As was the case in the early 1950s during WTVJ's televised Kefauver hearings, the public fascination with evil-doings had been cited as the reason for public interest in the war on crime.[71]

WTVJ's First Anchor

To viewers and fellow broadcasters the name Renick is synonymous with WTVJ history. He was a WTVJ and south-Florida icon and as such nearly inseparable from the development of the station. "Very early on, he was a model for the local television news anchorman. And, my God, 'bigger than life' is an inadequate description of him in the Miami television market," said NBC's Tom Brokaw.[72]

Ralph Apperson Renick was born in New York City on August 9, 1928, and was raised in Westchester County. He moved to Miami from New York with his family in 1939 at age 11. Renick graduated from the University of Miami in 1949 with a major in radio and television and a minor in journalism. While at UM, he specialized in radio news and worked as a commercial-radio announcer. Following his graduation, Sydney Head, Renick's mentor at UM and a broadcast journalism scholar, helped him obtain an H.V. Kaltenborn Foundation Fellowship to study "the theory and practices of communicating ideas through broadcasting media or the press." The study fostered Renick's admiration for Kaltenborn, and this admiration, combined with Sidney Head's mentorship and Renick's employment at WTVJ, had a lasting effect on the fledgling broadcaster. Renick's 1950 report, "News on Television,"

---

68. See "News Is Not a By-Product at WTVJ" (Miami 1969), pamphlet, WTVJ Collection, Louis Wolfson II Media History Center, Miami-Dade County Public Library System, Metro Cultural Center.

69. "Messiah in Open Town," *Time*, 28 April 1967, p. 24.

70. American Research Bureau Reports, Miami (June/July 1966), January 1967; Ashdown, p. 433.

71. Bernard Rubin, *Political Television* (Belmont, Calif.: Wadsworth, 1967), p. 11.

72. Coto, p. 1A.

surveyed the then 98 stations on the air and found that 75 percent had no employees devoted exclusively to the news.[73] Based in part on Renick's findings, WTVJ offered him a job as its news editor. Head recommended that Renick take the job: "I was gung-ho. It was an absolutely unique opportunity to get in on the ground floor at WTVJ."[74] By 1953 Renick was WTVJ's news director. In 1958 he became Channel 4's vice president for news. Renick served as national president of the Associated Press Broadcasters and the Radio and Television News Directors Association and was also the 1984 recipient of its Paul White Award. He was the first television member of the National News Council.

In 1975 Renick endeared himself to the nation's 1,500 news directors by blasting the emerging power of the media consultant in his response to the Alfred I. Du Pont–Columbia University survey conducted by its director, Marvin Barrett. After Renick had convinced his station in 1974 to end its contract with Frank Magid and Associates, the industry's largest news consultant, he told the Du Pont survey, "They are really a Trojan horse. They roll it in and suddenly the enemy troops are in your camp. Too often the service is put to political use to permit management to get control of the news when the news director is in conflict with management.... Too often stations with consultants end up trying to present news only as the research results suggest the people want. But lost in this concept is that a professional journalist should have the ability and news judgment to determine what is important and significant."[75]

No doubt he was sincere in his comments, but it also must be remembered that Renick spent most of his career in charge of WTVJ's newsroom, where his word was final. Renick reported directly to Wolfson, chairman of the board of the station's parent company, Wometco. His was a rare consolidation of power as anchor, news director, and editorialist. Renick himself would not have allowed that in a station of his own: "You've got an awful lot of eggs in one basket."[76] In 1977 Wometco made him a corporate vice president with complete control over the news budget. However, Renick's role in the operation of WTVJ was about to change. The station's founder, Mitchell Wolfson, died in 1983, and the station was sold the following year. Renick's undisputed decision-making power ended.

---

73. See Earley, p. 7; Alexander, p. 58; Renick, pp. 1, 4.

74. Alexander, p. 58.

75. See Ron Powers, *The Newscasters* (New York: St. Martin's Press, 1977), pp. 87–91; "Putting the 6 p.m. News into Neat, Small Packages," *Washington Post,* 10 February 1977, p. D1.

76. See Earley, pp. 6, 10.

On April 10, 1985, Renick, then 56, resigned as vice president for news at WTVJ to launch what would become an unsuccessful bid for governor. He more than likely sensed that the change in ownership and the death of Wolfson meant that the carte blanche to hire and fire he had once enjoyed was at an end. "I've been not just an anchorman," he said. "I started the [TV] editorial in this country and essentially wrote 28 books in all those years, compiling editorials on all sorts of issues—many of which are still with us today in Florida." By October he gave up his campaign.[77] He returned to television as a commentator for WCIX-TV in 1988, where he earned that year's James Madison First Amendment Award from the National Broadcast Editorial Association. "Who would have ever thunk it?" was Renick's opening remark of his commentary the evening of August 8, 1988, on Miami's WCIX/Channel 6. His commentary that summer night focused on the irony of his new broadcast home, announcing the switch of CBS affiliation from WTVJ to WCIX. With the planned schedule change on January 1, 1989, Renick was again at CBS.[78]

Renick retired from WCIX in September 1990.[79] He died July 11, 1991, from the effects of hepatitis and liver cancer. More than 1,000 people mourned the local TV legend at St. Mary's Cathedral.[80] The *Miami Herald* editorial on that day read: "Ralph Renick delivered the news, he made the news, he was the news."[81]

On August 10, 1992, WTVJ honored him by renaming Fourth Street outside the TV station Ralph Renick Way.[82]

Wolfson Dies, Wometco Sold

WTVJ made television history again in the late 1980s following the death of Mitchell Wolfson on January 28, 1983. By then Wolfson's Wometco Enterprises had grown into a billion-dollar corporation that included five

77. See Coto, p. 18A; Cotterell, 30 April 1985; "Renick Endorses Smith," United Press International, 6 August 1986, BC cycle.
78. Alexander, pp. 57–61.
79. Coto, pp. 1A, 18A.
80. Alexander, p. 62.
81. "He Had Sand in His Shoes," *Miami Herald*, 13 July 1991, p. 25A.
82. "WTVJ-Channel 4 Dedicates Street in Ralph Renick's Name," PR Newswire, 6 August 1992.

television stations, more than 100 movie theaters, cable-television systems, a Coca-Cola bottling plant, and the Miami Seaquarium.[83]

Wometco's diverse and profitable holdings made it attractive to "corporate raiders" skilled at dividing companies and selling them off, thus creating huge windfall profits. A writer for *Forbes* suggested that "at Wometco Enterprises, the pieces may be worth more than the pie."[84] Wolfson, known as The Colonel, had maintained control of the business for 58 years. He vowed that Wometco would never be sold, not even after his death. "I have taken care of all that," he said.[85] However, his heirs didn't share his dream. They sold the company for $1 billion in 1984 to Kohlberg, Kravis, Roberts and Company, a New York investment-banking firm. "Wolfson associates concluded ... that 'his [The Colonel's] secret plan was never to leave.' He never designated a successor as corporate chairman."[86] The Wometco holdings were divided and sold.

NBC Buys WTVJ

The dismantling of Wometco led to the sale of its crown jewel, WTVJ. The fireworks came in 1987 when Kohlberg, Kravis, Roberts sold WTVJ, which had been a CBS affiliate since 1952, to NBC for $270 million. It was the first network-affiliated station in history to be purchased by a rival network.[87] "The fact that one network had never bought another's affiliate in a hundred years was just a function of, well, not doing it," says NBC head Bob Wright, noting that there was nothing illegal about the sale. Why were NBC and its parent company, General Electric, willing to break precedent and buy WTVJ? The FCC had changed the rules and was now allowing networks to own more local stations. Ownership is preferable because owning a station makes a network millions of dollars more than simply affiliating with it. The deal may not have been illegal, but it certainly was confusing. As one television critic described, "The Big Switch is the

---

83. See United Press International, 29 January 1983, BC cycle; Steve Sonsky, "Behind the Scenes of Miami TV's Big Switch," *Electronic Media*, 23 January 1989, p. 80; Steve Behrens, "Miami Braces for a Jolt," *Channels* 8 (6) (June 1988): 26–27.

84. Curtis, p. 122.

85. United Press International, 22 September 1983, AM cycle, Domestic News.

86. See United Press International, 22 September 1983; Sonsky, p. 80.

87. Sonsky, p. 80; Behrens, p. 26.

messiest, most contentious, most complicated network swap in broadcast history."[88] The sale occurred because NBC defied tradition and, according to one observer, because CBS was looking for a bargain.

In May 1986, in the midst of a bull market for TV stations, the investment bankers had first attempted to sell WTVJ to Lorimar Telepictures for $405 million, a price 21 times the station's cash flow.[89] Wall Street's reaction was that Lorimar had overpaid for the station, and within six months the deal collapsed. Although some critics point to a softening national advertising market, timid investors, and deterioration of CBS's prime-time schedule, others believe that WCIX, a Miami independent that was for sale, was used as leverage to lower WTVJ's price tag.[90] CBS offered the investment group's Wometco representative $175 million for the station. "They [CBS] didn't want to buy the station, they wanted to steal it," claimed Kohlberg, Kravis, Roberts. "They felt that they would show us, and the rest of the affiliates, that particularly in a market with a VHF independent [like WCIX] they could have a drastic effect on a station by threatening to pull the affiliation and leave us as an independent."[91] CBS's president, Peter Lund, said the interest in WCIX was legitimate; however, eventually the issue of the station's weak signal doomed the deal. Kohlberg, Kravis, and Roberts still held WTVJ, but the deal making and breaking had made buyers too nervous to venture into the fray. KKR's alternative was to identify a buyer unafraid of pulling the CBS affiliation. The answer? Another network. Capital Cities/ABC was not interested; that left NBC. Wright, NBC's chief, said, "We had a sign out on our front lawn saying, 'We'd like to purchase a TV station in a top 20 market. Please call this number if you have such a station to sell.'"[92] The sale of WTVJ to NBC in January 1987 also meant that WSVN/Channel 7 would lose its 25-year affiliation with NBC and become an independent.

WSVN's owner, Edmund Ansin, did everything to stop the deal. He sued in the courts and protested to the Federal Communications Commission and to Congress, charging that the move was "anticompetitive." He also accused NBC and CBS of a conspiracy to influence the Miami marketplace

---

88. Sonsky, p. 80.

89. Sonsky, p. 80.

90. See Fred E. Fogarty, "Wometco Breakup Pays Big Profit," *South Florida Business Journal* 7 (28) (30 March 1987): 1A; Sonsky, p. 80.

91. Sonsky, p. 80. The quote is from Tony Cassara, described by Sonsky as "KKR's man in charge of the Wometco group."

92. Sonsky, p. 80.

and force down station values. None of Ansin's countermeasures were successful. Not only that, but Ansin's actions to recoup NBC's affiliation, caused the suddenly available CBS to back off a plan to fill in the void by associating with WSVN. CBS ended up buying longtime Miami independent WCIX, leaving WSVN permanently an independent.[93] Meanwhile, WTVJ became part of a stronger network—at the time, NBC was consistently outperforming CBS in prime time ratings—and remained steeped in controversy involving the ever-changing face of television.

Summary

For nearly half a century WTVJ has been entertaining its viewers and educating them with local, national, and international news. WTVJ was the first television station in Florida and one of about 20 commercial stations in the nation when it went on the air March 21, 1949. News presentation was a major part of the station's early history, relying on local events, homemade slides, and kinescopes from New York. On July 16, 1950, WTVJ aired its first live news report in the form of "The Ralph Renick Report." The 10-minute program, featuring the station's first anchor, served as an update of the unfolding events of the Korean War and offered segments on local and international news. Renick was the program's anchorman, camera operator, news producer, and writer. Over the next 35 years his name would become synonymous with WTVJ/Channel 4. In 1952 WTVJ became a CBS network affiliate and in 1957 was the first local television station to institute a daily editorial.

In the late 1950s WTVJ served as the key station feeding CBS most of its news footage of the political upheaval in Cuba, the island nation 90 miles from U.S. shores. It was the beginning of events that would change the population landscape of Miami forever. Fueled by the exodus of refugees from Fidel Castro's regime, Miami became home to more than 300,000 Cubans by 1973. Recognizing this shift in viewership, WTVJ hired Manolo Reyes as the first Spanish-language news anchor in south Florida and aired news and public-affairs programs in Spanish from 1960 to 1977.

---

93. "WSVN Miami Files Antitrust Suit; Asks Info Over Affil 'Confusion,'" *Variety* 331 (3) (11 May 1988): 116; Gregg Fields, "Channel 7's Owner Attacks NBC's Plans," *New York Times*, 12 March 1987, sec. 4, 9.

In addition to its groundbreaking editorials, WTVJ's firsts include one of the first racially integrated children's programs; specially ground camera lenses to cover launches at Cape Canaveral; and aerial shots from the Goodyear blimp of sporting events. It was also the training ground of award-winning network anchors and correspondents, among them NBC's Katie Couric, Fred Francis, Ike Seamans, David Bloom, and Robin Lloyd, as well as CBS's Martha Teichner and Bernard Goldberg. It was the station where Larry King perfected his on-camera one-on-one interviewing techniques decades before he emerged on the national scene with "Larry King Live."

WTVJ garnered attention for its locally produced documentaries, its coverage of the Kefauver Committee hearing on organized crime in 1950, and its own war on crime to rid Miami of corrupt officials. Its 1966 campaign, "The Price of Corruption," was regarded as one of television's first and most significant editorial crusades. Attention was also focused on WTVJ following the death of its founder, Mitchell Wolfson, in 1983. At the time of his death Wolfson's Wometco Enterprises had grown into a billion-dollar corporation ripe for a corporate takeover. Wometco was sold to New York investment bankers Kohlberg, Kravis, Roberts and Company in 1984. In 1987 WTVJ made history as the first network-affiliated station to be purchased by a rival network. WTVJ's sale to NBC resulted in a complicated network swap that stripped Miami's WSVN/Channel 7 of its network ties and left it an independent. WCIX/Channel 6, formerly an independent, became the new CBS affiliate.

8 A TV Pioneer's Crusade for Civil Rights in the Segregated South: WFTV, Orlando, Florida

Linda M. Perry

WFTV Channel 9 in Orlando, Florida, led the southern press as an early and outspoken advocate for civil rights, lending its name, prestige, and human and financial resources to help Orlando shake off the remnants of slavery that lingered in rigorously enforced Jim Crow laws. WFTV news-casts, public-service programs, and editorials covered the movement and promoted public discussion and understanding. Broadcast editorial pioneer Joseph Brechner led the crusade at a time when most of the southern press "responded miserably" to the rising call for civil rights[1] and "behaved irresponsibly."[2] Many even promoted states' rights to continue segregation and defended the myth of white superiority.[3] Orlando's main newspaper, the *Orlando Sentinel Star,* was cautious in its coverage of civil rights, whereas WLOF-TV—later WFTV, when the call letters were changed in 1963—was "outspoken in its support of the civil rights movement."[4] After only two months of editorializing, Brechner commented that the station had been labeled "conservative and liberal, obnoxious and public-spirited," but it would continue to "look at the world from our end of the telescope here in

---

1. Hodding Carter, *Their Words Were Bullets* (Athens: University of Georgia, 1969), p. 64.

2. Alex Leidholdt, *Standing Before the Shouting Mob: Lenoir Chambers and Virginia's Massive Resistance to Public School Integration* (Tuscaloosa: University of Alabama Press, in press).

3. Paul Fisher and Ralph Lowenstein, *Race and the News Media* (New York: Praeger, 1967), p. 63.

4. Sigman Splichal, "'The time is at hand': The Orlando business community reacts to the coming storm of the civil-rights movement," unpublished manuscript, University of Florida College of Journalism and Communications, 1990, p. 6.

Mid-Florida and sound off."[5] Sounding off included taking on the Ku Klux Klan, which threatened to blow up the station's transmission tower.

This chapter looks at the history of WFTV and its contribution to the civil-rights movement in Orlando.

The Early Years

The story of WFTV begins, like many of the early television stations, with a radio station. Soon after the Federal Communications Commission lifted the freeze on television broadcast licenses, Brechner and John Kluge, who together owned radio station WGAY in Silver Spring, Maryland, bought Orlando radio station WLOF in 1953. Their intent, according to Donn Colee, who was WLOF radio and WLOF-TV vice president and general manager, was to acquire the television license. Colee said the partners formed Mid-Florida Television Corporation and took a huge gamble that they would obtain the operating license.[6]

The owners set a target start-up date of February 1, 1958. "We didn't really expect to be on the air [on time] because I flew the application up [to FCC offices in Washington, D.C.] on the last day of January, and then flew right back down," Colee said.[7] The *Orlando Sentinel Star's* regular column on television programming indicated on January 31 that WLOF-TV would start on "a modified basis in order to live up to its promised target date." Programming was to be curtailed for two days because the network schedule would not be "in full swing" for two weeks.[8] On Saturday, February 1, 1958, the column promised "a fine TV weekend" because central Floridians would have a choice made possible by the new station.[9] WLOF-TV would be the second television station in Orlando and the only ABC affiliate in its central-Florida coverage area. WDBO Channel 6, a CBS affiliate and the only station at the time in Orlando, had been on the air about two years.

---

5. "Editors and editorials," WLOF-TV editorial, Dec. 5, 1960, Brechner Papers Archives, Brechner Center for Freedom of Information library, University of Florida, Gainesville. Hereafter referred to as WLOF-TV editorial.

6. Donn Colee, telephone interview conducted by Linda M. Perry, Jan. 10, 1996.

7. Colee.

8. "TV news and views," *Orlando Sentinel Star*, Jan. 31, 1958, p. 9A.

9. Charlie Wadsworth, "TV news and views," *Orlando Sentinel Star*, Feb. 1, 1958, p. 7A.

The FCC granted Mid-Florida Television Corporation[10] a 90-day operating permit. Colee brought over staff from the radio station to get WLOF-
TV on the air. "We were bound and determined, hell-bent to get on the air
on time," Colee said.[11] WLOF-TV started broadcasting at 6 p.m. on February
1, 1958, in a renovated downtown furniture store at 639 West Central
Avenue.[12] The station missed its target start-up time of 5:30 p.m. by only
minutes. It was common, Colee said, for stations not to make their target
start-up dates. "After our sign-on, we got a telegram from ABC saying,
'Please advise of your new target date.' We framed that telegram," Colee
said.

The set for the sign-on event consisted of three chairs, where Brechner,
Colee, and sales manager Lee Hall sat. Brechner introduced Colee and Hall,
who had stopped calling potential advertisers only long enough for the
sign-on. Brechner promised to introduce the rest of the staff later. "Then we
went into the movie *Johnny Belinda,* which was a classic of its day," Colee
said. Hall in a letter to potential advertisers had boasted a lineup of ABC
shows, "a first-run movie every night" and 571 cartoons.[13]

"We got off to what we called a wobbly start. It was just a matter of
getting that shaky start stabilized," Colee explained. "Most of the reaction to
that first broadcast day unfortunately was about poor reception."[14] WLOF-
TV broadcast a 316,000-watt signal,[15] but sets sold in the area had been
calibrated for the only local station, at Channel 6. Because of the spectrum
gap between Channels 6 and 9, sets already in homes, especially in coastal
areas, could not receive the high-band Channel 9. "We flooded the radio
station [WLOF] with ads and put ads on other radio stations. We were urging
people to get antennas. We called television dealers to get sets calibrated.
They did, so they could sell more sets. Sets [already] in the homes were the
problem."[16]

The sign-on received little coverage in the *Sentinel Star,* other than a
note in "TV News and Views" that it signaled the sixth station, but the only
ABC affiliate, in all of central Florida. The column said ABC programming

10. Joseph and Marion Brechner owned 62 percent of Mid-Florida stock.
11. Donn Colee, telephone interview conducted by Linda M. Perry, Jan. 13, 1996.
12. WFTV continued to operate there until 1986.
13. Lee Hall, letter to potential advertisers, Dec. 23, 1957. In Brechner Papers Archives,
Brechner Management Company, Orlando, Florida.
14. Colee, telephone interview, January 13, 1996.
15. WLOF-TV advertisement in *Florida Magazine,* insert of the *Orlando Sentinel Star,* February
2, 1958, p. 14E.
16. Colee, Jan. 13, 1996.

carried by other network affiliates would shift to the new ABC affiliate. It also announced "the return of 'Voice of Firestone,'" winner of the *Sentinel Star*'s first poll on viewer favorites.[17]

There was little hint in those early days of the station's coming activism. "We were struggling the first two years, trying to reach an audience. We were in a crisis-management situation at all times, trying to sell advertising to sustain ourselves. We were a struggling station in a small town,"[18] Colee said.[19]

WFTV and the Community

In its first year of operation WLOF-TV "attempted to serve the viewers in their drives, campaigns and civic endeavors."[20] Its daytime programming practically rendered the station a public-access channel. A first-year report lists 126 public, civic, and private organizations with which WLOF-TV worked to produce live studio productions in the public interest. For example, each Monday, Fran Conklin's "Florida Room" featured fine-art demonstrations and presentations by members of the Orlando Art Association. The Orange County Medical Society worked with Lee Hall, who wrote the script, to present "With These Hands," a series of 13 live half-hour dramatic shows. On Thanksgiving Day the sixth-grade class of Park Avenue Elementary School from nearby Winter Park performed a half-hour drama on the first Thanksgiving. Danny Thomas appeared on "Florida Room" to promote a fund-raising drive by the American Lebanese Syrian Associated Charities for the construction of St. Jude's Hospital. On election night the combined staffs of WLOF-TV, WLOF radio, and the *Sentinel Star* presented election-returns coverage, which was broadcast from the Channel 9 studios and aired simultaneously on WLOF radio 950 AM. Other live public-service programming involved, for example, the Orlando Air Force Base, the McCoy Air

17. Charlie Wadsworth, "TV news and views," *Florida Magazine*, insert of the *Orlando Sentinel Star*, Feb. 2, 1958, p. 18E.

18. With a population of nearly 60,000, Orlando was the largest inland city in the Florida peninsula. It was the heart of the citrus belt, but not nearly the scene it is today as the heart of Florida's tourist industry and a metropolitan population of 1 million.

19. Colee, Jan. 10, 1996.

20. Hartwell Conklin, WLOF-TV public service director, in "In the public interest: 1st year report, WLOF-TV—Channel 9, ABC, Orlando, Florida." In personal possession of Donn Colee, Orlando, Florida.

Force Base, the Orlando Fire Department, the President's Committee to Employ the Physically Handicapped, the Rollins College Drama Department, the Red Cross, the Florida Hurricane Report, and the League of Women Voters of Orlando–Winter Park. However, WLOF-TV's most significant community involvement was its work to help gain civil rights for blacks.

WLOF-TV/WFTV Civil-Rights Activism

The sleepy Orlando that greeted Brechner in 1953 when he and his partners purchased radio station WLOF-AM was a city of the Deep South on the verge of a revolution. The U.S. Supreme Court paved the way for the revolution in 1954 when it struck down its own separate-but-equal doctrine.[21] When the partners set up Mid-Florida Television Corporation, segregated travel and public facilities—buses, water fountains, rest rooms, seating, service—were the law throughout the south. Churches and businesses were mostly segregated. Brechner soon realized that Orlando was about to go through a cultural revolution. The civil-rights movement was gaining momentum, and southern cities like Orlando were facing federal court-ordered desegregation of schools and public facilities.

The fact that Orlando in the 1950s was very different from Orlando today was noted in a 1988 ceremony to honor Brechner. Bob Billingslea, a black leader who served as president of the Human Relations Commission,[22] said, "It is difficult for many of us to picture what Orlando was like back in the mid-50s and early 60s. Blacks seldom crossed the railroad tracks into downtown Orlando after sundown. Blacks shared in few of the services provided by the city and their economic opportunities were few or nonexistent.... Bolita kings controlled the street gambling; and little was done to protect blacks from street crime. Black churches offered only moral sanctuary. Little was done to improve these conditions."[23]

---

21. The Supreme Court established the "separate but equal" doctrine in *Plessy v. Ferguson,* 163 U.S. 537 (1896), upholding segregation laws. The court nearly 60 years later ruled in *Brown v. Board of Education,* 347 U.S. 483 (1954), that segregation laws violated the equal-protection clause of the 14th Amendment.

22. Until 1967 the commission was the Human Relations Committee, previously known as the Mayor's Interracial Advisory Committee. *See* Bob Billingslea, Script, Orlando Chamber of Commerce's Joe Brechner Day, Mar. 8, 1988, pp. 14–15.

The station's involvement in civil rights began when Brechner joined the chamber of commerce and began working with its interracial committee, which had been established in 1934.[24] Brechner prodded the city to action when he met privately with Orlando mayor Robert Carr. He told Carr that the situation in the black community was "unfair and dishonest" and would "explode in our faces unless we do something about it—and soon."[25] Carr agreed and in the fall of 1956 formed the first Orlando Human Relations Committee, known at that time as the Mayor's Interracial Advisory Committee.[26] Carr and Brechner brought together like-minded businessmen who saw that desegregation efforts in Little Rock in 1957 had erupted into violent confrontations, costing those cities severe economic setbacks. Brechner and Martin Andersen, publisher of the *Sentinel Star,* worked together on the committee, appealing to black and white businessmen and city leaders to begin peaceful desegregation efforts.[27]

The members of that first interracial committee agreed on one crucial point: Peaceful desegregation was in their economic self-interests. Brechner commented later that he constructed his arguments carefully to the mayor and business leaders: "I tried to show them that integration was not only right, but that it was also good business. They began to view events from this perspective."[28] Hartwell Conklin, WLOF-TV production director, recalled, "Bob Carr decided that this was going to be an open city before the Civil Rights Act passed. He broke down [racial] barriers and took down the [segregation] signs."[29]

Ray Ruester, who was hired in 1961 as news director and on-air commentator, said the committee—largely Carr, Brechner and business owner George Stuart, Sr.—understood that the only way to have peaceful, orderly desegregation was to plan for it. The committee would, for example,

---

23. Billingslea, p. 11. Black activist Reverend Nelson Pinder said police and courts not only did little to protect blacks, they were often openly antagonistic and abusive (Splichal, p. 5).

24. The problems in 1934, as in Joseph Brechner's day, were "employment, sub-standard housing, crime and economic opportunities" (Billingslea, pp. 10–11).

25. Billingslea, p. 12.

26. Billingslea, p. 13. The Human Relations Committee became the Human Relations Commission in 1967 when Carr died and Carl Langford took over as mayor. In 1972 this commission urged passage of the Human Rights Ordinance, establishing the Human Relations Department and setting the stage for single-member district voting.

27. Marion Brechner, oral-history interview conducted by Linda M. Perry, June 28, 1991, videotape transcript, p. 1, Brechner Papers Archives, Brechner Center for Freedom of Information, University of Florida, Gainesville.

28. Splichal, pp. 7–8.

29. Hartwell Conklin, telephone interview conducted by Linda M. Perry, Jan. 14, 1996.

get local theater managers to agree to a plan to integrate theaters. "On a certain day at a certain time there would be four blacks who would go in, and then maybe two hours later there would be six blacks that would go in, and they would sit anyplace in the theater, instead of up in the balcony where the blacks had been forced to sit for years."[30] Brechner also asked business leaders to hire blacks and to increase on-the-job training for black employees. WLOF-TV had already trained and hired blacks as technicians and news personnel.[31]

Carr expanded the Mayor's Interracial Advisory Committee in 1963 from 10 members to 24, dividing the positions equally between black and white members.[32] In June the expanded committee issued a resolution to desegregate business, which the Associated Press called "the first action of this type taken in the Deep South." The chamber of commerce adopted the resolution on the following day,[33] June 11, 1963, the day that NAACP field secretary Medgar Evers was murdered in front of his home in Jackson.

The committee members' work helped Orlando avoid racial riots that were exploding in other parts of the country. In an article in *Television Quarterly,* the journal of the National Academy of Television Arts and Sciences, Brechner explained, "In my own community, the business and civic leaders and media representatives heeded the economic disasters of Little Rock and Birmingham resulting from racial difficulties. Regardless of their past conformity to so-called Southern traditions, they readily lent their names and prestige for broadcasts and publications at the first call by our intelligent and courageous mayor for the development of effective interracial policies in the community. And they did not do so under the gun of local demonstrations or in order to bargain for time."[34] Brechner emphasized, "It is essential that newscasts, special-events and public-service programs, and editorials continue to cover all these conflicts and discussions in the interest of wider public understanding." It is the duty of broadcasters not to take their lead "from the local power structure or from frightened, irresponsible sponsors or nervous advertising agencies," but instead to expose and oppose "racial injustice" wherever they found it.[35]

---

30. Ruester, personal interview, p. 1.
31. Billingslea, p. 13.
32. "Major merchants will integrate sales force," *Orlando Sentinel,* June 11, 1963, p. 1A.
33. Splichal, p. 12.
34. J. Brechner, "Were broadcasters color blind?" *Television Quarterly,* June 1966, pp. 98, 101–102.
35. J. Brechner, "Were broadcasters color blind?" p. 101.

Brechner used his station to broadcast documentaries, public-affairs programming, and editorials that supported the work of the interracial committee, and he sent copies of those editorials to civic and business leaders.[36] One such editorial on July 1, 1963, reported on the activities of the committee and offered ten "basic facts and sound opinions." Number one among them was, "Segregation is morally wrong." Also on the list was Brechner's maxim, "Most business people don't want to become involved in racial problems, but cannot avoid involvement because they trade with all races or find themselves involved whether they like it or not due to changing social patterns."[37] Many of WFTV's and Brechner's contributions to civil rights in central Florida were ideas advanced in editorials from 1960 to 1968, examined later in this chapter.

WFTV News and Public Affairs

Colee put together the first news department at WLOF-TV, hiring writers and reporters from WLOF radio, which had "an extremely success-ful" news show "with hard-hitting news. We were the only [radio] station in Florida with a news show that was not 'rip and read,'" Colee said. The news staff in the beginning worked for the radio station in the morning, then for WLOF-TV in the afternoon and evening. The station did not editorialize at that time. "Joe [Brechner] really got into it because of his background and philosophy," Colee said.[38] Brechner's personal philosophy came to be the station's editorial philosophy in 1960 after Colee left the station for WTTG, one of Kluge's stations, in Washington, D.C., and Brechner took over the daily operations. Also in 1960, the year the lunch-counter sit-in movement began in Greensboro, North Carolina,[39] the news department began editori-alizing for action to avoid problems in race relations in Orlando.

---

36. Billingslea, p. 14.

37. "Reason and intelligence in race relations," WFTV editorial, July 1, 1963.

38. Colee, Jan. 13, 1996.

39. The first sit-in was on February 1, 1960, when four North Carolina Agricultural and Technical students sat down at a segregated counter at Woolworth's in Greensboro, North Carolina. Within two weeks sit-ins had spread to 11 cities in five southern states. Arrests totaled 3,000 by 1961. Clayborne Carson, David J. Garrow, Vincent Harding, Darlene Clark Hine, eds., *Eyes on the Prize: America's Civil Rights Years* (New York: Penguin Books, 1987), p. 78. See also Taylor Branch, *Parting the Waters: America in the King Years 1954–63* (New York: Simon & Schuster, 1988), for a history of the civil-rights movement.

WLOF-TV was one of the few news outlets in the south to take a stand for civil rights for blacks. Media scholars have characterized the *Sentinel Star*'s editorial stance on civil rights during this period as "restrained," although news accounts of the movement received prominent play.[40] Under Brechner's guidance the WLOF-TV news department covered the civil-rights movement in 1961 and 1962 before it became major, national news in 1963.[41] Brechner and Ruester backed up the news coverage with award-winning and sometimes controversial commentary: editorials, discussion shows, and documentaries.

The WLOF-TV/WFTV Editorials

Brechner wrote most of the editorials at his home.[42] After 1961 Ruester delivered the editorials on air, but they reflected Brechner's philosophy. According to Ruester, "The station has a simple philosophy. Seek the truth and give the public information as accurately and objectively as humanly possible."[43] Ruester and Brechner together "were the editorial board." Viewers came to associate Ruester with the editorials, with which, he later said, he was "always in complete agreement."[44] In an editorial representing his own viewpoint, Ruester said he believed in what he was saying in the station's editorials.[45]

From 1960 to 1968 WFTV aired at least 87 television editorials reflecting Brechner's philosophy on human rights. Brechner believed that

---

40. Splichal, p. 6.

41. See Branch, pp. 758–766, for a review of the increase in national press coverage after the May 3, 1963, demonstration in Birmingham, Alabama, where city officials turned dogs and fire hoses on children and other demonstrators.

42. M. Brechner, p. 4.

43. R. Ruester, "Farewell statement," WFTV personal viewpoint editorial, Apr. 10, 1964. This statement announced Ruester's intention to leave WFTV and return to Illinois. Ruester advised viewers that the "face may change, but that policy will remain the same." He returned to WFTV as vice president for news in 1965, then left WFTV when the FCC revoked the sole ownership of Mid-Florida in 1969. He joined the *Daytona Beach News Journal* in September 1969, retiring in 1992 as associate editor.

44. Ray Ruester, oral-history interview conducted by Linda M. Perry, Mar. 12, 1992, videotape transcript, p. 5, Brechner Papers Archives, Brechner Center for Freedom of Information, University of Florida, Gainesville.

45. R. Ruester, "Whose editorial opinion?" WFTV personal viewpoint editorial, Jan. 10, 1963.

civil rights and freedom of information are "intertwined," that the rights of the First Amendment are an essential part of the fabric of human rights.[46] He was an early and outspoken advocate for cameras in the courtroom and other government proceedings, and a frequent critic of the courts' and the legal profession's lack of regard for press freedom.[47] He often commented on specific cases in which civil rights were at stake.[48] He was an early critic of the Fairness Doctrine,[49] although the FCC had found WFTV a model of fairness in its portrayal of civil rights and other community issues.

Brechner's Background and Philosophy

Brechner undoubtedly was influenced by the experiences of his parents in Eastern Europe at the close of the 19th century—his mother, Dora, in Romania; his father, Barney, in Odessa, Russia.[50] Both immigrated as young adults to escape "from the cruel Eastern European pogroms" and other oppression of Jews.[51]

Brechner married Marion Brody, whom he met just prior to World War II when they both worked in the U.S. War Department, in 1941. That same year Brechner wrote and produced the first national "Negro Soldier in the American Army" broadcast.[52] With their advertising and broadcasting backgrounds in common, Marion and Joseph entered broadcast ownership soon after the war, in December 1946.[53] The Brechners and John Kluge together gambled on a 1,000-watt station in Silver Spring, Maryland, and were finally granted the license in 1946 as WGAY 1050 AM, with Brechner

---

46. M. Brechner, p. 4.

47. See, for example, "Discrimination in the news," WFTV editorial, Sept. 11, 1962; "An open letter to a federal court," WFTV editorial, Dec. 19, 1962; "Justice on TV," WFTV editorial, Feb. 7, 1963; "Seeing is believing," WFTV editorial, Jan. 1, 1964; "The public's right to know," WFTV editorial, Sept. 16, 1964; "How to control the press," WFTV editorial, Apr. 19, 1965; "Closing the courts," WFTV editorial, June 11, 1965; "Suppression of news," WFTV editorial, Sept. 16, 1965; and "Another secret trial," WFTV editorial, July 27, 1967.

48. See, for example, "Suppression of news," WFTV editorial, Sept. 25, 1962.

49. "A statement on fairness," WFTV editorial, Aug. 10, 1965. See also "A statement on the Fairness Doctrine," *Journal of Broadcasting,* March 1965.

50. M. Brechner, p. 1.

51. Joseph Brechner, "Her zest for living strong at 95," *Orlando Sentinel,* Jan. 8, 1977.

52. M. Brechner, p. 6.

53. Brechner told the story of his foray into broadcasting in "You, too, can own a radio station," *Saturday Evening Post,* Jan. 25, 1947, p. 26.

as general manager and Kluge as operations manager. The *Saturday Evening Post* published an article by Brechner on the station's first year, which included the discovery of on-air talent in the secretarial pool and the beginning of reporting on community public affairs, controversial commentary, and editorializing.[54] *Broadcasting* magazine described WGAY as "a community minded station," and its "Community Reporter" program won national recognition in its first year of broadcast.[55]

A Safety Valve for a Simmering Conflict

Brechner's first WLOF-TV editorial on civil rights was broadcast on October 20, 1960, on the occasion of the 21st annual conference of the NAACP in Orlando. Noting that more than a month earlier some national dime stores in Orlando had voluntarily opened their lunch counters, the editorial saluted the "growing influence and increasing political power" of the black community and called for "peaceful progress."[56] The sit-in movement had reached Jacksonville in August of that year. After 10 days of peaceful demonstrations, race riots broke out and 50 were injured. Orlando stayed calm. When extremist groups on the left and on the right began to sound off about civil-rights activities, Brechner cautioned viewers to "beware the bigot who would destroy America in the guise of false patriotism." Brechner's philosophy of American civil liberties was clear in a WLOF-TV editorial of 1960: "Freedom is a personal responsibility. To protect it for ourselves we must protect it for others as well. The bomb blast of bigotry can be the end of American liberty."[57]

WFTV reminded viewers that the new nations that had risen sovereign from African colonies would be looking to America "as the free world's leader" and "to this nation's example in matters of equality, opportunity, and all the ideals of liberty."[58] America should live up to that responsibility, and "local officials and leaders should give careful consideration to race relations and prepare in advance for problems we might have to face in the future."[59]

54. J. Brechner, "Radio—What a business!" *Saturday Evening Post*, Feb. 21, 1948, p. 24.
55. 37 *Broadcasting*, July 11, 1949.
56. "The Negro's new role," WLOF-TV editorial, Oct. 20, 1960.
57. "The anti-bigotry crusade," WLOF-TV editorial, Nov. 4, 1960.
58. "Which way America?" WLOF-TV editorial, Nov. 15, 1960.
59. "Common sense in race relations," WLOF-TV editorial, Nov. 30, 1960.

On September 19, 1961, WLOF-TV was the only affiliate in Florida[60] to carry ABC's documentary, "Walk in my Shoes," which chronicled social problems in America from the perspective of African-Americans. While WLOF-TV was one of more than 100 stations across the nation to carry the documentary, stations in many parts of the south blacked it out. A WLOF-TV editorial a week later called the program "an honest, tough-talking, graphic study of a minority group in America as seen through their own eyes." [61]Brechner later commented that a white lawyer in New Orleans had blamed that city's developing racial crisis on such program blackouts in Louisiana. Brechner said that not reporting racial issues had resulted in "no safety valve or warning device" in many parts of the country, so that Americans were shocked when the "boiler" of neglected "simmering conflicts" exploded. To media critics who blamed the media for escalating violence, Brechner replied, "The problem is not too much coverage, but belated coverage."[62] Brechner's station would not be guilty of shrinking from this great social movement as it swept over central Florida. Brechner wanted to make certain the ideas of the civil-rights movement were out on the public agenda so people would "be able to form conclusions."[63] Brechner in station editorials would comment many more times on the responsibility of the news media to lead public discussion on the movement.

In September 1961 an editorial reported that two people had phoned the station to protest the editorial "The Failure of the Rabble Rousers," which hailed the successful desegregation of schools in Atlanta and Daytona.[64] One viewer threatened to "phone all your advertisers and tell them I won't patronize them." Brechner responded that he intended to "keep talking, editorially, in the public interest."[65] One viewer wrote that he believed WLOF-TV was "telecasting propaganda" for the federal government because it held the station's license. Brechner responded that the FCC encouraged editorializing, but added, "We express our own ideas freely and unequivocally based upon our belief and faith in democracy.... Nothing is more important for ourselves, our families, our friends, and our Nation than

---

60. Brechner estimated there were only five or six ABC affiliates in Florida at that time.

61. "A sponsor speaks," WLOF-TV editorial, Sept. 27, 1961.

62. J. Brechner, "Were broadcasters colorblind?" pp. 99–100. Brechner's remarks, reprinted in *Television Quarterly*, had been given first in an address at a freedom-of-information meeting in 1966 at the University of Missouri School of Journalism.

63. Ruester, personal interview, p. 1.

64. "The failure of the rabble rousers," WLOF-TV editorial, Sept. 7, 1961.

65. "Letters to the editorials," WLOF-TV editorial, Sept. 13, 1961.

the protection of our liberty and our right to act and speak as free men."[66] For the most part, viewers approved the station's activism, even if they didn't always agree with its point of view."[67]

A Voice in the Wilderness

The activism of the civil-rights movement struck Orlando in 1962. Young African-Americans, mostly high-school students, began demonstrations under the leadership of the Reverend Nelson Pinder—a black activist who came to Orlando from Wisconsin in 1959—to desegregate playgrounds, Little Leagues, schools, and parks. The students began sit-ins at the dime-store lunch counters where they had been denied seating, resuming their passive protest "every day after school." At first the stores reacted by closing the counters in front of the students.[68] The committee's strategy of negotiating a plan with managers was used to desegregate the lunch counters. Billingslea said the activists "were welcomed without incident. No riots. No protests."[69]

WLOF-TV in 1962 increased coverage of civil rights.[70] The station editorials called on viewers to "overcome prejudices and misunderstandings which threaten our democracy and hurt our business, social and political relationships." One said the whole world was "in revolt against bigotry, fear and prejudice."[71] Another cautioned parents to follow Dr. Benjamin Spock's latest advice on how to avoid teaching prejudice.[72] One editorial called the civil-rights movement "another Civil War," both "passive and legal," that "will end only after years of effort on the part of all races."[73]

---

66. "Editorial criticism," WLOF-TV editorial, Dec. 12, 1961.

67. "Editorial reaction," WLOF-TV editorial, Nov. 2, 1961.

68. S. Barbieri, "With sit-ins, they took their stand," *Orlando Sentinel,* Feb. 25, 1992, pp. E1–2.

69. Billingslea, pp. 15–16.

70. Mayor Carr appointed Brechner to the Citizens Advisory Committee for Community Improvement, which advised on urban renewal. Local press noted WFTV's "vigorous editorial positions on area problems, including urban renewal." "WLOF-TV's Brechner on Orlando civic group," *Radio-TV,* May 3, 1962.

71. "A space age job for you," WLOF-TV editorial, Feb. 16, 1962.

72. "Do parents teach prejudice?" WLOF-TV editorial, Mar. 26, 1962.

73. "Sacred cows and good citizens," WLOF-TV editorial, Sept. 14, 1962.

In October 1962 WLOF-TV took an unnamed local newspaper to task for its emotional handling of the James Meredith story.[74] The issues involved—integration, federal authority over the states, and executive-branch responsibility to enforce judicial orders—were complex "problems of Constitutional government." Not to enforce the court order "would have made a mockery of our courts and destroyed our civil rights." The editors of the local paper, not named in the WLOF-TV editorial, had shirked their journalistic duty and shown "journalistic contempt for law and order." The editorial continued:

> To react to such complex matters with simple emotional tantrums, to cartoon and distort to ridiculous simplicity these serious questions of human rights ... is, in the opinion of Channel 9, a travesty of journalistic responsibility. The newspaper has a right to disagree with any government action. But to serve its readers, its opposition should be based clearly on facts and logical persuasion....
>
> To support and condone violence and to debase the President's responsibility to execute the orders of our established courts in the face of open threats of physical resistance to such orders is, in our opinion, a demonstration of journalistic contempt for law and order.
>
> It is easy to assume the position and views of the loud vocal groups who have no sensitivity about human rights. It is easy to cater to the misguided prejudices of rabble rousers and neurotics. It is easy to exploit an outmoded regional tradition into a space-age spectacular.[75]

WLOF-TV received mail from viewers on the Meredith story well into November, the largest mail response until that time, with "at least 80% favorable" to the station's position. One viewer said the station was "a voice in the wilderness when so many newspapers are playing into the hands of the mob."[76]

Criticism of WLOF-TV spilled over into Orlando's main newspaper. The *Sentinel Star* ran several letters referring to a WLOF-TV editorial of April 26, 1962, entitled "Nut Gathering," which was based on a Channel 9 news report of a speaker at the American Legion. Critics called the editorial

74. The U.S. Supreme Court ruled in September 1962 that the University of Mississippi Law School must admit James Meredith. Governor Ross Barnett blocked Meredith's entry three times before President Kennedy sent a large force of federal marshals to enforce the court's order. The ensuing riot on Sept. 30 resulted in two deaths.

75. "Responsibility and the news," WLOF-TV editorial, Oct. 4, 1962.

76. "Mississippi reaction," WLOF-TV editorial, Oct. 9, 1962. See also "From the editorial mailbag," WLOF-TV editorial, Nov. 19, 1962.

"slander" and a "distortion of the events." Some letters were supportive. Brechner stood by his reporters and responded in a WLOF-TV editorial on May 14: "Those who would deny the existence of the two rabble rousing, race-hating and race-baiting uniformed storm troopers who distributed the most serious hate literature we've ever seen, either were not present or were blind." Brechner added that the "so-called anti-communists are really anti-American in their ... generalized attacks on responsible citizens and organizations," inciting "emotional reactions, rather than intelligent consideration."[77]

Whose Voices Will Rise?

The year 1963 brought images on national television of police abuse against passive demonstrators and had come to be seen as a pivotal point in the civil-rights movement. WLOF-TV became WFTV in 1963 and increased its commentary on civil rights, including 16 editorials. Editorials applauded progress in central Florida and other parts of the nation and helped bring the events in other southern communities to the consciousness of viewers.

In August WFTV aired the five-part ABC News production, "Crucial Summer: The 1963 Civil Rights Crisis." The station urged viewers to watch a segment "to understand better the issues involved in the Civil Rights march [on Washington August 28] which climaxes this crucial summer."[78] But the long, hot summer exploded in tragedy in Birmingham on September 15, 1963, with the bombing of a black-community church, resulting in the deaths of six children and the injury of many others. WFTV called on local officials and law-enforcement officers to prevent such tragedy in Orlando with "firm and fair leadership and the strict respect and enforcement of laws." This was essential "if race problems are to be solved fairly and satisfactorily."[79]

Brechner kept up the pressure on local leaders to lead Orlando into the new era of race relations. The WFTV news department focused on the Washington Senators baseball team, which had held spring training in Orlando for decades. "After blacks started playing in the major leagues and the major leagues were desegregated, the black players had to find someplace

---

77. "Letters to the editor," WLOF-TV editorial, May 14, 1962.
78. "Crucial summer," WFTV editorial, Aug. 23, 1963.
79. "The Birmingham tragedy," WFTV editorial, Sept. 16, 1963.

to stay whenever they came to Orlando for spring training," Ruester said. "They couldn't stay with their team." Not only was this treatment of players offensive, it presented practical problems because there was only one motel in the black community. "Our news department would do editorials, saying this is one of the things showing segregation was wrong," Ruester said. "This was before the 1964 Civil Rights Act. But all of these things were leading up to the Civil Rights Act, which dealt mainly with ... freedom of travel from state to state."[80]

WFTV closed the year with editorials on recent racial unrest in the nation's oldest city, nearby St. Augustine on Florida's northeast coast. A St. Augustine grand jury had blamed "two militant Negro leaders and the Ku Klux Klan" for the upheaval there. But a WFTV editorial attributed the disturbances to human nature, closing with a maxim: "One ounce of common sense in race relations is worth a thousand rulings from every court in the land."[81]

An ugly incident at a sit-in at Jackson, Mississippi, seemed to awaken the slumbering conscience of central Florida. The *Sentinel,* like many newspapers in the nation, had run a photograph of a former Jackson police officer stomping a black man who had been pushed to the floor in a lunch-counter sit-in. White onlookers mocked and assaulted the passive demonstrators, while "local police looked on indifferently." A WFTV editorial asked, "Whose voices will rise to protest? Where [is] the courage to resist and overcome human injustice? Do we *dare* sit by quietly, leaving law and order to the battering fists and stomping feet of Benny Oliver, a former Jackson lawman?" The editorial compared the silence of America then to the silence of the world "when Nazis and storm troopers murdered 6-million souls, when lynchers in pure white mocked justice." Calling silence to racial injustice "the greatest threat to our liberty," WFTV implored viewers to speak out—to let the station know "that at least one other American felt as we did: sick at heart—dismayed—ashamed that this should happen here, in the land of the free."[82]

The station soon had its answer. "A heavy batch of mail with no prize give-away—with no popular star. Eight to one you support us—angry, sick, ashamed, resenting the mistreatment of any human being. What you wrote made sense, was heartfelt."[83] The editorial said the positive response from

---

80. Ruester, personal interview, p. 3.
81. "Human nature," WFTV editorial, Dec. 19, 1963.
82. "The shame of Jackson," WFTV editorial, May 29, 1963.
83. "Mail reaction—Jackson disgrace," WLOF-TV editorial, June 3, 1963.

viewers reflected Orlando's progress in race relations. "While other areas have had violent upsets, Orlando and most of Central Florida have moved forward sensibly into the difficult and sensitive areas of race relations." Cities suffered "serious economic setbacks" wherever leaders "carelessly let matters get out of hand." But leaders in Orlando "backed intelligent efforts to eliminate the cause of racial dissension which led to disturbances in other cities. As in all such cases, firm leadership, knowledge, understanding, fair and firm law enforcement, and above all a desire to apply the rules of fair play and justice determine the success of local efforts."[84]

WFTV advocated proactive business involvement in democratic affairs. On June 11, 1963, shortly after President Kennedy's appeal to business leaders to lead the fight for integration,[85] and on the same day that Kennedy told the nation segregation was morally wrong,[86] Brechner challenged businesspeople to get behind the movement. In a WFTV editorial he wrote, "In the past weeks and months an era has passed. Until recently national companies were committed to meet the requirements of disagreeable local customs. They paid lower salaries in low pay areas and conformed to morally degrading racial practices to avoid stirring up local issues. Like the violation of any moral principle, a two-faced policy could not be sustained. How could an enlightened management practice and support Democratic principles on a national level and then practice a bigoted, backward policy in the treatment of American citizens in some of the local outlets?" Brechner approved of the emerging idea, evoked by Kennedy, of the inherent social responsibility of business in a free society:

> This is the way free enterprise should assert itself in a Democratic society. It cannot maintain high business standards in a society of low social and bigoted human standards.
>
> In the opinion of Channel 9 these companies will earn for themselves the respect and appreciation of most Americans. We needed and appreciate their leadership and good sense in advancing race relations in our precious country and in our community now striving to pass through a difficult era and to get on with our economic progress.[87]

---

84. "Race relations improve," WLOF-TV editorial, June 6, 1963.
85. "JFK pushes for faster mixing," *Orlando Sentinel*, June 5, 1963, p. 3A.
86. Carson et al., p. 320.
87. "Which way progress?" WFTV editorial, June 11, 1963.

WFTV also promoted equal opportunity in hiring. A WFTV editorial said businesses who had hired qualified employees without regard to race or color were "pleased with the results."[88]

The Ku Klux Klan reacted to WFTV's programming with intimidation and threats, beginning with a calling card left on the station's doorway in April 1963.[89] In July 1963 WFTV took on the Klan. One editorial scoffed at the Klan's claimed new policy of nonviolence and warned viewers that the Klan's threats to march and rally in eight southern states, including Florida, "revealed their old zest to stir up violence." The editorial compared the Klan to Hitler's Gestapo and storm troopers. Klan members were "cowards hiding under hoods and robes preaching hatred and committing violence."[90] In October WFTV spoke out against activities by both the KKK and the White Citizens Council of Georgia in nearby Marion County.[91]

When the Klan had begun night cross-burning rallies in the fields of central Florida in 1965, WFTV showed pictures of one of the rallies and a KKK sticker during an editorial endorsing the elimination of the Klan:

> The KKK sticker is believed to be a warning to those who may disagree with the Klan's bigoted views. WFTV once had such a sticker pasted on our front door which read: "A Ku Klux Klansman was here."
>
> The time has come to eliminate this vicious and dangerous organization which rides in the night to frighten, beat, bomb and murder without fear of apprehension and punishment.... We must rid ourselves of these shrouded examples of lawlessness from a better-to-be-forgotten past. The Klan's philosophies and activities have not only delayed progress in the South—but where they exist they have been a costly economic and social cancer.
>
> The investigation to expose the Ku Klux Klan nationally will be lengthy and tedious. Local and state officials should begin now to put our house in order; to expose and discharge the die-hard Klansmen in Florida who have infiltrated into positions of public trust.
>
> There should be no place in any public office or law enforcement agency for members of an organization that condones crime, including violence and murder.[92]

---

88. "Does DeSegregation hurt business?" WFTV editorial, Aug. 9, 1963.
89. "Editorial mailbag," WFTV editorial, May 2, 1963.
90. "A Klan warning," WFTV editorial, July 15, 1963.
91. "Rabble in Marion," WFTV editorial, Oct. 24, 1963.
92. "Klan investigation," WFTV editorial, Apr. 2, 1965.

In June 1965 a United Press International survey indicated southern senators believed the Klan of the day "is very small, is politically impotent, and feeds on publicity." However, Brechner admitted, "We may never completely rid our communities of the vicious, irresponsible troublemakers and crackpots, but we must continually resist." He took the opportunity to fine-tune the WFTV position on the Klan in American democracy: "WFTV has said many times that a well-informed, responsible citizenry is the main deterrent to those forces which would divide, spread hate and fear and have turned some communities into living nightmares."[93]

WFTV aired a series on the Klan in 1966, including a discussion on "Viewpoint 9" with Robert Shelton, imperial wizard of the United Klans of America. To critics of this appearance Brechner said, "We did not invite Mr. Shelton to appear on the program because we wanted to give a platform to the Ku Klux Klan," but because "the public has an interest in this secret society" and "should know as much as possible about the Ku Klux Klan and its leaders."[94]

The KKK surfaced again in October 1967, this time seeking new members and real estate in central Florida for a "concentration center." WFTV denounced the Klan as an enemy of democracy and rejected arguments that the First Amendment protects Klan activities:

> While the issue of freedom of speech and assembly is basic in the land, the issue of Klan activity here represents a renewed menace to the progress and tranquillity of Central Florida.
>
> The very history of the Klan in the South, its violence, its vigilantism, its use of terror and force to impose its malicious will upon citizens, constitutes an undesirable and repulsive intrusion in our state and community affairs.
>
> Those who confuse the Klan with legitimate political organizations overlook the long history of graft, financial exploitation of dupes and their violations of the laws and decency involving murder, mutilation and destruction.[95]

Citing increased Klan activity in the area, the city prosecutor in November 1967 asked the Mayor's Interracial Advisory Committee to call

---

93. "Southern senators speak," WFTV editorial, June 21, 1965.
94. "A conversation with a KKK imperial wizard," WFTV editorial, Dec. 2, 1966.
95. "Renewed menace," WFTV editorial, Oct. 17, 1967.

for police surveillance of the Klan.[96] The day after that story hit, a WFTV editorial, "Clear and Present Danger," promoted a "Viewpoint 9" program produced in South Florida on the KKK. The Klan threatened to blow up the WFTV transmitter if the program was aired. "Our newsroom has also received threats of bodily harm if we continue to criticize the klan," the editorial said.[97]

Hope for Brotherhood

WFTV often editorialized on the responsibilities of public officials in the civil rights movement. In April 1964 nonviolent demonstrators in St. Augustine had been met with violence. WFTV blamed the rising violence on "poor leadership and negligent police control." ABC News had shown "uniformed police officers standing by as violence rages before their eyes in our neighbor city." WFTV called on law-enforcement officials to follow their "oath to maintain law and order while protecting the rights of citizens." The station supported the passive tactics of civil disobedience to change unjust laws. An editorial admonished the critics of the growing demonstrations to "ask themselves about the alternatives. Non-violent mass demonstrations, properly directed and controlled, represent a legitimate, legal, democratic method of protest. The alternative is secret, and often violent, protest." The editorial continued: "The Rev. Martin Luther King was thrown in jail only this afternoon for daring to insist on service at an all-white restaurant. This drastic crime, according to St. Augustine officials, is enough to warrant a period behind bars." WFTV blamed the "civic and business leadership" for the St. Augustine upheaval. "They have ignored their responsibilities to liberty in these changing times, and have betrayed the glory of St. Augustine's past."[98]

---

96. "Racial unit asks klan clampdown," *Orlando Sentinel*, Nov. 16, 1967. The committee had become very active by this time. In September the committee urged public housing and more jobs ("Interracial committee urges public housing," *Orlando Sentinel*, Aug. 17, 1967, p. 1B) and repair of streets serving public schools ("Interracial unit urges repair of school streets," *Orlando Sentinel*, Sept. 21, 1967).

97. "Clear and present danger," WFTV editorial, Nov. 17, 1967.

98. "The tragedy of St. Augustine," WFTV editorial, June 11, 1964. Orlando police chief Stoney Johnson, a loyal supporter of Mayor Carr, is credited with much of the success of Orlando's peaceful integration.

Orlando's record of solid progress in race relations seemed threatened in July 1964 when rising crime and gang violence swept over central Florida. Brechner noted that police said the crimes and violence were not related to racial unrest.[99] In late July, Brechner produced a statement on violence—that violence is incompatible with democracy—in the editorial "Violence is Color Blind." Citizens must take a stand against violence, he argued, because "extremist groups, white, colored and mixed, ranging from the Ku Klux Klan to the Black Muslims, the American Nazi party and so-called gun clubs, presumed a right to use violence and force in solving political and social problems of the day." The editorial chided the media who have been "equally careless or indifferent." A statement on violence followed:

> Violence can never be justified in a civilized society which purports to operate as a democracy under a constitution and due process of law. Violence is generally a reminder of the deep, dark core of evil madness that remains in some human hearts. Perhaps the affairs of the world in this century of great atrocities have hardened us to indifference. We weep poetically for the fallen sparrow, but close our eyes and minds to human slaughter on a major scale.
>
> Violence is not a matter of race or creed. Black or white suffer equally in pain, and are equally guilty when they afflict it on others. We still have much to learn in our pursuit of the wise precept "Peace on earth, good will to men." We still have a long way to go, not only on earth, but within each community and within each person's heart, to eliminate indifference, false standards, violence and injustice in meeting the problems of human relations.[100]

In a 1964 editorial entitled "Danger—Cowards at Work," WFTV took on St. Augustine public officials again. Weekend reports of gang terrorism revealed "a frighteningly sad case of advanced cowardice," the station argued. "The cowardice of St. Augustine's leaders does little to lend encouragement to those hoping for the enforcement of law in that troubled city. When police and city officials are more afraid of the opinions of a noisy few than they are of eroding rights and freedoms, everyone suffers."[101]

In several 1966 editorials WFTV called for action by Orlando public officials, especially the utilization of federal Economic Opportunity Act

---

99. "Gangs, hoodlums and mobs," WFTV editorial, July 14, 1964.
100. "Violence is color blind," WFTV editorial, July 24, 1964.
101. "Danger—cowards at work," WFTV editorial, June 22, 1964.

antipoverty funds for urban renewal.[102] Editorials criticized Orlando leaders' slow progress in slum clearance,[103] and fear of "federal entanglement" with the city's independence. Opposition to the use of these federal funds came at a time when "Orlando has not been able to solve the problem of providing low rent housing."[104]

Calling attention to the needs of Orlando's underprivileged—better housing, job opportunities, and health, educational, and recreational facilities—a WFTV editorial said it was an "inevitable necessity to correct the mistakes, the inequalities and the indifferences of the past." It cautioned viewers not to ignore "disturbing conditions" that could touch off the kind of unrest erupting in other cities, including Jacksonville, Chicago, Los Angeles, Omaha, and New York. To those who feared inciting such anarchy by exposing and discussing it, WFTV replied:

> Silence in racial matters or in serious community problems of human relations has never been a successful solution or effective prevention of outbreaks. Silence has only led to misunderstanding, to a failure to realize deep felt needs and feelings, and has only resulted in surprise and confusion when an outbreak occurred. By then talk is difficult and the harm has been done.
>
> Our purpose today is only to remind local citizens, officials and police and social workers not to misinterpret silence and inaction as the calm of satisfaction with conditions and circumstances in our area. The greatest danger to human relations—as it is in marriage—is complacency and indifference to the thoughts, feelings and the needs of the other person.[105]

In late July 1967 WFTV endorsed a petition by the Florida NAACP for a select committee to study racial unrest in the state. The editorial predicted the committee would find that a main source of frustration for minorities "is their exclusion from serving in some capacity and having a

---

102. "War on poverty struggle," WFTV editorial, Jan. 13, 1966. The Economic Opportunity Act created in August 1964 the Office of Economic Opportunity to develop and administer antipoverty programs. Brechner also approved use of federal funds to correct school systems that had wasted years and millions of tax dollars duplicating schools and facilities to preserve segregation. "What's wrong with our schools?" WFTV editorial, Nov. 30, 1966.

103. "Favorable slum clearance publicity," WFTV editorial, Jan. 24, 1966.

104. "Federal slum aid—no but yes," WFTV editorial, Apr. 6, 1966.

105. "How to prevent racial unrest," WFTV editorial, July 25, 1966.

voice, even a minority voice, in the affairs of the state and their local communities."[106]

Common themes in the WFTV editorials were the ideas that minorities must have a voice and that the media must put the concerns of minorities on the public agenda. A November editorial acknowledged that some people would prefer to ignore the concerns of the black community. But the people of this community had "real ideas. And ideas are often more powerful than bullets or tyranny." The danger was not in airing the concerns of the black community, but in ignoring them. "What would be even more dangerous to our society is to leave this fuse smoldering unnoticed. Then in the event of an explosion, to bewail the surprise like the lawyer who complained during the [Louisiana] crisis that the news media kept most of the facts about race problems from the people."[107]

WFTV continued to criticize irresponsible journalism. One editorial told viewers in April 1964 about a book by Warren Leslie, a former *Dallas News* reporter who accused the *Dallas News* of "helping to generate a climate of hate." *Dallas News* editorials "found even President Eisenhower too far to the left" and took no stand against the radical right's censoring textbooks. A WFTV editorial hailed Leslie's book as a wake-up call, and a

> warning for all of us. A climate of hate is distilled from many poisons, not the least of which is the closed mind. Book banning and any suppression of freedom of thought can occur in any community without a clear, reasonable voice to cry out in opposition.
>
> Responsible news media, courageous public officials and enlightened citizens must remain constantly on guard—and seek out and demand free discussion, based on honesty and accuracy.[108]

WFTV urged broadcasters to "face the test of their conscience" and "no longer permit themselves the false comfort of hiding behind the protection of local prejudices."[109] The station endorsed the consensus of a conference

---

106. "Who represents the minority?" WFTV editorial, July 28, 1967.

107. "Freedom now," WFTV editorial, Nov. 8, 1963. The original editorial referred to a Mississippi crisis. In an article for *Television Quarterly,* Brechner later referred to this lawyer as commenting on events in New Orleans.

108. "A climate of hate," WFTV editorial, Apr. 30, 1964.

109. "All broadcasters are not color blind," WFTV editorial, Nov. 18, 1965. Brechner took his view of the role of the media in the civil-rights movement to a national audience of journalists in November 1965 when he addressed the Freedom of Information Conference at the University of Missouri. The eighth annual conference explored the relationship of the racial crisis and the news media and identified a new civil-rights beat in journalism.

of journalists: "News media should report accurate information exactly as it happens and as soon as possible. They should neither exaggerate nor minimize reports. Law enforcement officers should set up an information headquarters so that news media can doublecheck their own information to present accurate reports."[110] A follow-up editorial added that "responsible news media *should* report the outstanding news of the day—both good and bad—fairly, without regard for race, creed, age or other factors."[111]

Waiting for the Dream

As Brechner began his last year in control of WFTV, a free-speech issue arose in 1968 in Gainesville, Florida, when two civil-rights workers were charged with contempt of court for criticizing a judge and the grand jury investigating racial and gender discrimination in Gainesville jails. WFTV reported that the paper *Black Voices* had accused the judge and grand jury of racial bias. WFTV raised the issues of "the right to criticize a judge outside the courtroom" guaranteed by the First Amendment, and the right to bail when charged with contempt.[112]

Following the report in January of a national survey of employment agencies, WFTV conducted a survey of private agencies in Orlando, finding 10 out of 11 were "willing to accept a job order calling for employment discrimination based on race and religion. Only one of the agencies refused." This reflected the findings of the national survey of "widespread employment discrimination in violation of federal, state and local laws."[113]

When Dr. Martin Luther King was assassinated on April 4, 1968, in Memphis, WFTV declared that the murder had "shocked a nation of black and white people into an open, uncensored dialogue of self-analysis"[114] and had fostered rededication to liberty and "the proposition that all men are created equal."[115] In "A Sense of Outrage," Brechner wrote that King

---

110. "Race riots and broadcasting," WFTV editorial, Aug. 16, 1967.

111. "Viewers comment on racial discrimination," WFTV editorial, Aug. 23, 1967.

112. "Contempt and freedom," WFTV editorial, Jan. 12, 1968. In addition to civil rights, WFTV in 1968 focused on other issues pressing the nation, including growing unrest over the Vietnam War. Marion and Joe Brechner traveled as ABC correspondents to Vietnam and Cambodia for two weeks in 1968 to interview Florida soldiers for WFTV News.

113. "Employment discrimination," WFTV editorial, Jan. 23, 1968.

114. "After Dr. Martin Luther King," WFTV editorial, Apr. 5, 1968.

115. "A moment for rededication," WFTV editorial, Apr. 9, 1968.

had a dream and now has bequeathed it to us, his survivors, along with his repressed outrage.

How long can we endure the enemies of truth, justice and democracy? How much longer must we tolerate indifference? How long must we hope for a change of spirit? When will all Americans accept and support the promise of full freedom....

As we wait for the consummation of these great truths, this American dream, too often we seem very alone with our impatience and sense of outrage.[116]

Soon after King's assassination WFTV renewed its call for blacks and whites to understand their common goals, and for equal protection from law-enforcement officers.[117]

WFTV was widely recognized for its activism in civil rights. In April 1964 WFTV was cited in *Broadcasting* as one of the two television stations in the country selected by the Federal Communications Commission for an "in-depth study" of aggressive editorializing.[118] In December, after a year of investigation, the FCC declared WFTV a model of fairness in its editorials.[119] In May 1964 WFTV won the U.S. Conference of Mayors' national award for excellence in community-service programming, including public debates on community issues and daily editorials. Brechner remarked that second place went to "a little station known as WCBS-TV of New York City."[120] The award "was a salute to those stations which recognize their obligation to the public ... and who tried to keep their audience alert to public issues and informed and knowledgeable about local situations." The award specifically cited "locally initiated, locally produced features" and "its forthright daily editorials on public issues, its 'Project 9' documentaries exploring serious community problems in depth, [and] its 'Pro and Con' debates on pressing questions of the day."[121]

In March 1965 WFTV won the Du Pont Foundation Award for service in the public interest in 1964. The award recognized WFTV for "exposing its viewers to a generous range of viewpoints and attitudes through such programs as WFTV's Project 9 documentaries, Moral Issues of Our Times, Pro and Con debates and the Discussion 64 panels." Du Pont Foundation

---

116. "A sense of outrage," WFTV editorial, Apr. 8, 1968.
117. "Rumors and violence," WFTV editorial, Apr. 12, 1968.
118. 66 *Broadcasting,* Apr. 6, 1964, p. 141.
119. "The dilemmas of broadcast news," WFTV editorial, Dec. 9, 1964.
120. "Local station captures award," *Corner Cupboard,* May 28, 1964.
121. "An award to WFTV," WFTV editorial, May 25, 1964.

cited WFTV editorials as "appealing ... for intelligence, moderation and good will in the solution of social problems that have only too often, in other communities, been met with mindless violence."[122] A 1965 editorial brought the station national recognition in February 1966 when the Freedoms Foundation at Valley Forge honored the station for the editorial "Inspiration for Progress."[123]

Despite his award-winning broadcasts and contributions to improve racial relations in Orlando, Brechner lost control of WFTV in 1969, ironically because of an FCC ruling concerning minority ownership. When the FCC had granted Mid-Florida Television the construction permit for Channel 9, it had denied the application of WORZ, owner of a local radio station.[124] WORZ filed suit claiming one of the members of the FCC had had an ex parte conversation with an Orlando banker about Mid-Florida's application for the license. On remand from the U.S. Supreme Court and the U.S. Court of Appeals for the District of Columbia,[125] the FCC reopened the licensing process for operation of Channel 9 in 1965.[126] Five groups, including Mid-Florida, applied for the license. The FCC granted Mid-Florida the interim authority to continue operating Channel 9, but the Court of Appeals in 1968 again reversed the FCC on the grounds that as long as Mid-Florida Television occupied and ran the station, it had an "unfair advantage" in the competition for the license. Ultimately, the FCC approved a settlement in which Mid-Florida would vacate the station and lease its facilities to a joint venture of all five applicants, Channel 9 of Orlando, which took over operation on April 1, 1969.[127] Mid-Florida retained 28.33 percent ownership of Channel 9 of Orlando until 1984.[128]

Channel 9 of Orlando was awarded the operating license on the strength of minority ownership—two black shareholders held 14 percent of the stock of Comint Corporation, one of the applying groups.[129] "The points made for minority ownership made the difference," Ruester said. "There's something of an irony there. He [Brechner] was the one who actually went out front for

122. "Du Pont Foundation Award," WFTV editorial, Mar. 22, 1965.
123. "Seven from area win freedom awards," *Orlando Sentinel,* Feb. 22, 1966, p. 18A.
124. 22 FCC 1254, 12 R.R. 1157 (1957).
125. WORZ Inc. v. FCC, 268 F.2d 889 (D.C. Cir. 1959), 323 F.2d 618 (D.C. Circuit 1963).
126. FCC 65-1020, 1 FCC 2d 1377 (1965).
127. Memorandum Opinion and Order, FCC 81-311 (1981).
128. WFTV was embroiled in license-dispute litigation for 25 years, operating on temporary permits. WFTV today is licensed to Cox Communications. It is still an ABC affiliate and is rated number one in viewer share in its coverage area.
129. Initial Decision, FCC 70D-20 (1970).

blacks.... The corporation that took over did none of what Joe Brechner had been doing for the black community."[130]

Epilogue

When Brechner was removed from active management of WFTV, a voice of reason over the airwaves was silenced. Brechner continued to speak out on issues of the day as an opinion columnist in the *Orlando Sentinel* from 1970 to 1977. In 1981 Brechner established an endowment at the University of Florida for scholarship in freedom of information. In 1985 he donated $1 million to endow an Eminent Scholar Chair in Freedom of Information and to establish a freedom-of-information center at the University of Florida. The Brechner Center for Freedom of Information publishes *The Brechner Report,* a newsletter summarizing and indexing critical freedom-of-information and other media-law issues for journalists and media lawyers in Florida. Brechner died on February 26, 1990, bequeathing his vision to the Brechner Center to keep vigilant and to alert the press of critical issues involving the American birthrights of civil liberties and freedom of information.

130. Ruester, personal interview, pp. 4–5.

9

The Nation's Station: WLWT-TV, Cincinnati

Russell A. Jenisch and Yasue Kuwahara

To understand the pioneering programming efforts of WLWT, one must understand the influence and philosophy of engineer, inventor, and entrepreneur Powel Crosley, Jr., who began broadcasting via radio station WLW in Cincinnati in the early 1920s. Powel Crosley, Jr., began his radio activities in 1921 when his son asked him for a "radio toy." Crosley, upset that the radio receivers of the day cost upward of $130, decided that he would make his own receiver as a gift to his son. The resulting crystal radio receiver was built for about $20, and Crosley called it the Harko. Crosley began mass-producing these radio receivers and eventually sold them for as little as $9 each, making the Harko an immediate success among people eager to listen to this new mass medium.[1] Crosley's success with the Harko and other radio receivers, including the Roamio, the first production car radio, earned him the title of the Henry Ford of Radio and propelled the Crosley Manufacturing Company into the position of "world's largest producer of sets and parts."[2]

The cheaply made Harko did not receive distant signals very well, thereby limiting the number of stations available to Harko owners. Powel Crosley, Jr., had a way to overcome this problem. He decided that he would simply operate his own radio transmitting station. In September 1921 Crosley was granted a license to operate station 8CR. Six months later he

---

1. William Diehl, Jr., "Crosley's Clear Channel Colossus," *Cincinnati Magazine,* March 1968, p. 28.

2. Lawrence W. Lichty and Malachi C. Topping, *American Broadcasting: A Source Book on the History of Radio and Television* (New York: Hastings House, 1975), p. 448.

obtained permission to use the call letters WLW, and the station officially went on the air on March 2, 1922. Although WLW used a 50-watt transmitter, Crosley wanted to operate a station at the highest possible power.[3]

Between 1923 and 1928 WLW gradually increased its power and its reach. In 1923 the transmitter was increased to 500 watts. In 1924 the power doubled to 1,000 watts, and in 1925 the station became a 5,000-watt station. Later that year Crosley announced his intention to seek permission to broadcast at 50,000 watts. After settling issues concerning the chaos in the ether, the Federal Radio Commission approved Crosley's request to broadcast at 50,000 watts in 1928, and WLW joined KDKA in Pittsburgh, WEAF in New York City, and WENR in Chicago as the most powerful radio stations in the United States.

Crosley, never one to be fully satisfied with his work, was still not fully satisfied with the limitation placed on the power of his station, and its subsequent reach. So early in 1934 he began experimental broadcast transmissions at 500,000 watts on WLW. The Federal Radio Commission allowed such a dramatic increase in power in order to gauge the response from audiences and advertisers, and to measure daytime and nighttime interference.[4] On May 2, 1934, President Franklin D. Roosevelt officially ushered in WLW's superpower days, by throwing the switch to activate the broadcast.

This station reigned as a true superstation of its time, becoming a one-station network whose reach included listeners (as legend would have it) from as far away as Hawaii and Europe. "Peter Grant and the News," which had begun in the days prior to the superstation status, became the most widely heard news show in the country. "Listener surveys showed WLW as 'first' in preference polls in 13 states and 'second' in six additional states—all of the Midwest and a chunk of the South and the East."[5] The station's program guide was carried by 76 newspapers in the United States and its promotion aimed at 345 U.S. cities. Throughout the 1930s, and even to this day, WLW lays claim indeed to the title of the "nation's station."

In 1939, responding to requests from other stations desiring to broadcast at 500,000 watts, the FCC limited WLW's power once again to 50,000 watts, except for the hours of 1–6 a.m., when it was allowed to power back up to 500,000 watts. In 1942 wartime restrictions on radio stations kept

3. Diehl, p. 28.

4. "WLW/VOA Radio Field Day" (a complimentary program by Allied Broadcast Equipment), 1981, pp. 3, 8.

5. Christopher H. Sterling and John M. Kittross, *Stay Tuned: A Concise History of American Broadcasting,* 2nd ed. (Belmont, Calif.: Wadsworth, 1990), p. 155.

WLW from exceeding 50,000 watts, a restriction that continues to present day.

Besides WLW, Crosley Broadcasting owned and operated several other radio stations, including W8XAL, which began broadcasting Spanish-language programs from Cincinnati to South America via shortwave radio. In 1943 Crosley built the Bethany Relay Station just north of Cincinnati and established what would become the first radio relay station in the U.S. government's "Voice of America" operation.

The Cradle of Stars

Having an audience and advertising base throughout the country, WLW contributed greatly to early radio programming. "It introduced the world to the soap opera (Procter and Gamble has its world headquarters in Cincinnati), quiz shows, mystery programs, and religious broadcasting."[6] "The first play especially written and produced for radio was broadcast by WLW."[7] Crosley conceived radio's longest-running soap opera, "Ma Perkins"; first quiz show, "Dr. I.Q."; first mystery, "Dr. Konrad's Unsolved Mysteries"; and first religious program, "The Church by the Side of the Road." In addition to its superstation status, WLW benefited from program distribution via NBC Blue and NBC Red networks and, along with WGN Chicago, WOR Newark, and WXYZ Detroit, was a founding station of the Mutual Broadcasting System.

Known as the Cradle of Stars, WLW introduced to the world numerous people who would go on to become internationally known artists, writers, and performers. WLW helped launch the careers of Red Skelton (who is credited with saying WLW stood for "world's lowest wages"), Doris Day, Rosemary Clooney, Frank Lovejoy, Paul Stewart, Eddie Albert, the Ink Spots, the Mills Brothers, and Fats Domino. Rod Serling and Norman Corwin began their careers by writing scripts for WLW dramas. WLW radio received the first ever Golden Microphone Award from the Broadcast Pioneer Foundation in 1961.[8]

---

6. Diehl, p. 26.
7. Lichty and Topping, p. 317.
8. Diehl, p. 29.

Radio with Pictures

Powel Crosley, Jr., began research and experimentation in April 1937 to make television broadcasting in Cincinnati a reality. By the end of that year all of the equipment needed to put experimental station W8XCT on the air, including a transmitter and three cameras, was developed. R.J. Rockwell led a group of engineers, most of whom had previous experience in AM broadcasting, in making television transmission possible in Cincinnati. One of the early iconoscope cameras developed by the station ultimately was shipped to Du Mont Television for early use in television broadcasting.

Television made its official public debut at the World's Fair in New York on April 30, 1939, with NBC demonstrating its television broadcasting system. Powel Crosley, Jr., was at the fair, but not as a broadcasting mogul. There Crosley introduced his "compact" automobile, the Crosley, to a public looking for a more affordable and economical mode of transportation. The activities of Crosley Broadcasting, however, had not subsided. Rather, four days before that first public demonstration of television in New York, on April 26, 1939, the Crosley Broadcasting Corporation produced a closed-circuit television exhibition for the press, marking the first demonstration of television in Ohio. Two years later, in April 1941, air transmission and reception were realized. However, Crosley's experiments with television were halted, partly because of World War II and partly because of the costs. Crosley later recalled that he was not really an early believer in television. "I did not see how stations would be able to pay the immense cost of producing programs. I did not realize that sponsors would be willing to pay as much money for programs as they pay now."[9]

Authority to construct an experimental television station was granted to the Crosley Corporation by the FCC in August 1940. While waiting the approval for station construction, Crosley leased the 48th floor of the Carew Tower in downtown Cincinnati to serve as the site for the first television broadcast in Ohio. The facility would house a temporary studio and have transmission capabilities. In 1942 Crosley leased the Elks Temple at 9th and Elm streets, for one dollar per year, as the home for WLW and WSAI radio. WLWT remained in the building for over 50 years, announcing in 1995 plans to move.

---

9. "Mr. Crosley Recalls WLW's Start in '21," *Cincinnati Post,* 27 September 1960, p. 21.

Crosley, the "man with the Midas touch,"[10] had other interests outside radio and television. He was the inventor or developer of many home appliances, including the Shelvador refrigerator, which utilized storage space on shelves recessed into the door. He invented a mechanical scalp massager and a replacement for the traditional baby carriage. In 1936 Crosley purchased the Cincinnati Reds baseball team in order to "guarantee that the team would remain in Cincinnati." "He renamed Redland Field 'Crosley Field' and introduced night baseball to the major leagues."[11] Crosley was a man of ideas and was truly a working man's man. His inventions were aimed at making life better for the common person. As such, Crosley, from an early age, was most interested in manufacturing automobiles for the average American. In 1945 Crosley sold his Crosley Corporation to his wartime partners, the Aviation Corporation (which later became the Avco Manufacturing Corporation and, ultimately, Avco Broadcasting) in order to devote his time and energy to developing small, efficient, and inexpensive cars. But Crosley's tradition, philosophy, and inventiveness for programming continued under Avco's direction.

W8XCT

On August 8, 1940, the Crosley Corporation received an experimental license to operate W8XCT at 1,000 watts on Channel 1 in Cincinnati. Four years later the *Columbus Citizen* newspaper printed this brief announcement: "The Crosley Corporation, operator of radio station WLW in Cincinnati and other stations all over the country, yesterday asked the Federal Communications Commission for authority to construct a new television station in Cincinnati."[12] Shortly thereafter, when the war ended, experimental station W8XCT resumed operation. On March 1, 1946, the license for W8XCT was changed to assign the experimental station to Channel 4. Subsequently, the station's frequency was changed to its present channel, 5. On June 4, 1946, the station, with special permission from the FCC, "sent out the first television pictures to be broadcast and received in Cincinnati."[13]

10. Daniel Hurley, *Cincinnati: The Queen City* (with histories of corporate sponsors by Leo Hirth) (Cincinnati: Cincinnati Historical Society, 1982), p. 134.
11. Hurley, p. 134.
12. Ed Dooley, "History of WLWT," unpublished paper, WLWT, 1987, p. 2.
13. Dooley, p. 2.

Two days after the first experiment "the first live pictures were broadcast and received in Cincinnati at the WLW studios and at the Crosley factory engineering department. A box of Borax powder was used to demonstrate advertising."[14] These and other early experimental broadcasts were of pictures only and did not have audio. Pictures and sound were first telecast on W8XCT on February 25, 1947. Night broadcasts began in April 1947, and on July 31, 1947, "W8XCT took to the air on a 'regular' one-hour-per-week schedule. By the end of the year the station was averaging 20 hours of programming a week, furnishing a wealth of varied entertainment for the fewer than 100 TV sets then in the Cincinnati area."[15]

The first regular program was a variety show originating at the Carew Tower studio from 8:30 to 9:30 p.m. "Every phase of public life became a target for TV cameras as religion, popular parlor games, quizzes, swimming exhibitions, baseball, football and other sports, and musical programs using WLW (radio) were televised."[16] Live remote productions became a staple, as well, for Cincinnati television viewers. The first remote television equipment arrived in Cincinnati on September 14, 1947. The next day W8XCT engineers experimented with the cameras, shooting various scenes around the city, making it the first remote broadcast in Ohio. A week later a doubleheader between the Cincinnati Reds and the Philadelphia Phillies became the first major-league baseball game televised in Ohio. With little time to rest, the experimental station broadcast wrestling, football, an ice show, boxing, church services, political forums, professional and college basketball, all before the year was out.

In January 1948 Crosley Broadcasting was granted a commercial license, and W8XCT became WLW-T, the first television station in Cincinnati and one of the first commercial stations in the country. Three months later WLW-T signed the first affiliate contract with the NBC network.[17] The formal birth of WLW-T was on February 9, 1948, although this was a mere technicality.

The first sponsored program, the "Golden Gloves" boxing show, was telecast a week earlier and sponsored by the Wiedemann Brewing Company. "The first sponsored program was both a command performance and one night stand"[18] recounts Ed Dooley in his unpublished account of the "History

14. Dooley, p. 2.
15. Dooley, p. 3.
16. Dooley, p. 3.
17. Dooley, p. 5.
18. Dooley, p. 4.

of WLW-T." "The bouts of this date were not scheduled [for broadcast], but the Cincinnati TV audience, and the barside ticket holders in particular, were not to be denied. Wiedemann Brewing Company stepped into the breach. Via WLW-T, the bouts were televised. The next morning, the station became W8XCT again. The first station break using the WLW-T call letters aired at 7:30 p.m."[19] Because television sets were still too expensive for many, the residents of Cincinnati and northern Kentucky watched at neighborhood bars, including Saratoga's and Duke's Tavern. It is therefore appropriate that the first commercial television program was a boxing match sponsored by a brewery. Of course, the bar owners enjoyed the benefits of increased customers, who packed the room to watch television.

The popularity of television is attested to by the notice issued by the Kentucky Department of Revenue in the fall of 1948. The notice read, "operators of amusement and entertainment establishments who were using television to draw crowds and were charging an admission fee were subject to state admission taxes."[20] Local appliance stores heralded the advent of television in Cincinnati and cosponsored many television events. Peppers Radio and Television in Newport, Kentucky, marked the birth of WLW-T with an open house announcing that "this is a day we have been looking forward to for many months ... truly this is an epic event and we feel proud and happy to have you as our guest at this time."[21]

With the remote equipment and sponsors, sports programming was extremely popular. Sports announcer Vernon "Red" Thornburg began his tenure at WLW-T in the days of W8XCT and remembers that "the early—VERY early—days of WLW-T were a melange of movies, game shows, cooking classes, and sports. Lots and lots of sports—like college and high school football, bowling, boxing, baseball, softball, and, of course, the staple item, wrestling."[22] Indeed, WLW-T was known for the first broadcasts of various sporting events, including wrestling (September 26, 1947), football (October 11, 1947), professional boxing (October 27, 1947), team bowling (November 15, 1947), an aquacade (January 12, 1948), and the first televised baseball game in the Midwest (September 23, 1947).

Thornburg was an announcer for many of these events. "During those early days, much, if not all of the athletic attractions were strange to the audience. And there were no instant replays or stop-action cameras. I'd

19. Dooley, p. 4.
20. Jim Reis, "The TV Era Ushered in by Advertising," *Kentucky Post,* 21 June 1993, p. 4K.
21. Reis, p. 4K.
22. Martin Bogan, Jr., "In the Beginning...," *Cincinnati Enquirer,* 4 April 1967, p. 31.

diagram basketball plays. Then we'd have wrestlers demonstrate their holds and fighters show their different punches. That way the television audience could get closer to the action, they knew what was going on."[23] Thornburg's early efforts and experience in Cincinnati elevated televised sports, and his own popularity, nationally. Thornburg even wrote an article for *Broadcasting* about how to televise a baseball game.

Network Television

But local programming at WLW-T was much more than sporting events. On August 10, 1949, "Boston Blackie" became the first locally produced dramatic show. The script for this half-hour production was loaned by Ziv Television Programs to WLW-T for a one-time experimental broadcast. Frederic Ziv said the experiment "might possibly lead to filming of a 'Blackie' series for the use of television stations over the country."[24] Of course, it was, and "Boston Blackie" became the first syndicated program.

WLW-T became the first NBC television network affiliate in the country, signing an affiliate's contract in April 1948. "Kukla, Fran and Ollie," "The Gulf Road Show," and the "Texaco Star Theatre" made their way to Cincinnati. These programs were recorded and played back through a kinescope until September 5, 1949, when Cincinnati was connected to the network's coaxial-cable delivery system. Also connecting to the coaxial system by 1950 were Avco's television stations WLW-D in Dayton, Ohio, and WLW-C in Columbus, Ohio. NBC celebrated the hook-up with a television-network special production called "NBC Salutes WLW-Television," featuring special performances and messages from New York NBC stars and network officials. A year later "Kukla, Fran and Ollie" traveled to Cincinnati for a special production celebrating the station's second year of commercial operation. The program was the first originating from Cincinnati to be fed to the NBC network.

The network affiliation, while providing live programming and national talent to the Cincinnati market, did little to diminish WLW-T's local efforts. Crosley believed that WLW-T should develop talent locally and should produce original programming. WLW-T programmed an average of

---

23. Bogan, p. 31.
24. Dooley, p. 6.

40 hours of live studio features each week, many of which were fed over the Avco television network of stations. By 1950 more than 65 percent of WLW-T programming was locally originated.[25] Avco created its own regional microwave network of television stations, which included Avco-owned WLW-D in Dayton, Ohio, WLW-C in Columbus, Ohio, and later WLW-I in Indianapolis, Indiana. (Avco also owned station WLWA in Atlanta, Georgia, from 1953 to 1962.) The network relied on WLW-T for the production and distribution of television programming to its other stations across the Midwest. After acquiring 68 films from the J. Arthur Rankin Company in 1950, the local television schedule at WLW-T averaged 117 hours per week.

WLW-T produced the first live performance of a symphony orchestra ever seen on American television, featuring the Cincinnati Symphony Orchestra. Horse racing from River Downs and Cincinnati Reds baseball were added to the station's sports repertoire. Several programs originating from WLW-T rose to national fame, beginning in 1950 with "Cincinnati at Sunset" and "Dude Ranch Holiday." Most popular and successful among these was the program "Midwestern Hayride." Originally called "Boone County Jamboree," this country-music show moved from radio to television in 1948. WLW-T, in keeping with the trend nationally, expanded several of its most popular radio programs and developed them into television programs. "Midwestern Hayride" featured a regular cast and guest musicians, comedy routines by Zeke and Bill, and square dancing by the Midwesterners, who were considered the best in the country.[26]

"Midwestern Hayride" rode a wave of popularity all the way to the network when, in 1951, NBC chose it as a summer replacement for Sid Ceasar's "Show of Shows." The program remained on NBC as a regularly scheduled program, averaging a 25 rating during the summer of 1953,[27] and later aired on the ABC network. Although the cast changed over the years, "Midwestern Hayride," a "country-music institution," demonstrated remarkable staying power for 20 years through syndication in over 40 markets.

WLW-T was one of NBC's most important affiliates. On January 1, 1954, the station became the first color affiliate, telecasting the Tournament of Roses parade in color.

---

25. Untitled manuscript. Don Smith, WLWT Engineering Files, pp. vii-55. The manuscript is in the personal possession of Don Smith. Hereafter referred to as Smith manuscript.

26. "Avco Broadcasting Corporation Souvenir Program Midwestern Hayride," Cincinnati Historical Society Library, p. 17.

27. Smith manuscript, pp. viii–32.

Something to Talk About

Talk was king, or maybe queen, at WLW-T long before the development of the "Phil Donahue Show." Ruth Lyons's "50-50 Club" outperformed
all WLW-T programs. Lyons began her career in Cincinnati as a piano player
at WKRC radio in 1929. She was called upon to fill in for an ill talk-show
host and was embraced instantly by her Cincinnati audience. Lyons moved
to WLW's sister station, WSAI, and in 1942 started doing her show, "The
50 Club," from the Gibson Hotel in front of a live audience. The name was
representative of the number of persons able to be seated at the hotel for the
program. In addition to the radio program, each audience member was served
lunch. As with so many other radio programs, "The 50 Club" was thrust
before the television cameras as Lyons teamed up with Paul Jones to host
the program on WLW-T. However, the new television studio could now seat
an audience of 100, so the show was renamed—not the "100 Club"—but the
"50-50 Club." The luncheons continued for some time, with audience
members being served lunch on one floor before moving into the television
studio for the show.

Ruth Lyons became something of a "television phenomenon,"[28] and
from 1949 until her retirement in 1967, she sustained her considerable
reputation.[29] The 90-minute talk/variety show aired five days a week and
attracted industry's top performers, including Bob Hope and others. The
audience, who referred to Lyons as "mother," lined up to spend time with
her daily, causing a three-year wait for tickets.[30] Sponsorship for the program
was sold out for an incredible decade in advance. In 1952 the "50-50 Club"
joined other WLW-T-originated programs, like "Straw Hat Matinee,"
"Breakfast Party," "Cincinnati at Sunset," "Dude Ranch Holiday," and
"Midwestern Hayride" on the NBC network. WLW-T became the network's
top independent program supplier in all of the country.[31] Because of its
programming, production, and distribution philosophy—not because of
power or the reach of its signal—WLW-T lived up to the moniker of its radio
father as also being the "nation's station."

Ruth Lyons, still a singer-songwriter, wrote many original songs for
her broadcasts, but none more successful than "Wasn't the Summer Short,"

---

28. Diehl, p. 32.
29. Diehl, p. 32.
30. Diehl, p. 32.
31. Dooley, p. 7.

later recorded and popularized by Johnny Mathis and Peter Nero. Among its other accomplishments, the "50-50 Club" became the first locally originated program produced in color, in August 1957. A month earlier Ruth Lyons had taken her black-and-white cameras outside the Crosley studios to show off WLW-T's new color mobile unit. This color mobile unit was the first of its kind among nonowned-and-operated stations and would be used extensively for both studio and remote productions. The mobile unit was parked outside of Crosley Square and served as the control room for the many local, studio-based productions.

Personal tragedy—the loss of her own daughter to cancer—led to Ruth Lyons's retirement in 1967. The years did nothing to diminish her talent or popularity. Perhaps the greatest tribute to Cincinnati's first lady of television is the continuing Ruth Lyons Children's Christmas Fund, which was established by Lyons in 1939 to provide toys to children at Cincinnati's Children's Hospital. Over the years the fund has contributed millions of dollars to the hospital and to the Barrett Cancer Center for the purchase of equipment and treatment for children with various diseases and illnesses.

WLW-T had a knack for creating or developing successful local shows, especially talk shows, and over the years supplied several more shows to a national audience. John Murphy, an Avco vice president, was convinced that "local shows could be profitable because they created tremendous audience loyalty."[32] Having experienced the phenomenal success of the Ruth Lyons show, Murphy suggested an extension of it: "informal, ad lib programs with a strong personality as a star, live music, one or two singers, a live audience and guest stars when available."[33] The successful formula led to the redevelopment of the "Paul Dixon Show."

Paul Dixon arrived in Cincinnati in 1946 to be a newscaster on WCPO radio. He was best known as the reporter who crawled into a collapsed building to interview a person who was trapped in the rubble. Dixon became a popular personality and moved from being a newscaster to a disc-jockey on radio, eventually becoming the popular talk-show host on start-up station WCPO television. WCPO-TV went on the air in 1948. WCPO's daily broadcast of the "Paul Dixon Show" was fed to the fledgling Du Mont Television Network in August 1950 and later that year had a command performance on Du Mont every Tuesday night and on ABC for a half hour every Thursday night. In the early 1950s Dixon moved to New York to

---

32. Diehl, p. 32.
33. Diehl, p. 32.

originate his "Pantomime Hit Parade" for Du Mont until the network folded in 1955. His show was carried on WLW-T.

After the Du Mont Network demise John Murphy summoned Paul Dixon back to Cincinnati as host of "Midwestern Hayride." But Murphy really wanted Dixon for his new morning show. Dixon recalled, "Everybody thought John was nuts.... A live audience show at nine in the morning with me at the helm. He had to be kidding!"[34] But the "Paul Dixon Show" became equally as popular among female viewers as Ruth Lyons proved to be.

The "Paul Dixon Show" opened each week with Dixon looking at the female audience's knees through a set of binoculars, for which he was the self-proclaimed "Mayor of Kneesville."[35] Murphy attributed the success of the "Paul Dixon Show" to its heretofore unique format and Dixon's phenomenal appeal to young women. When Dixon broadcast from Dayton, Ohio, one morning in 1967, "all available seats were gone and he announced that he would dip into the mailbag, select one more request, and visit the woman personally. When he arrived at her home after the show, he found 400 women standing in her yard in the rain waiting for him."[36] In 1973 Dixon ventured back into syndication as his "plays and games" segment was distributed nationally. For 19 years, from 1955 until Dixon's untimely death in 1974, the "Paul Dixon Show" remained a Cincinnati institution.

Another institution that originated at WLW-T was the "Bob Braun Show," which went on the air in January 1967. Braun was a Ludlow, Kentucky native who grew up in the shadows of Cincinnati. He began his broadcasting career in the television industry at WCPO-TV by appearing on the "Bride-to-Be" program when he was 19 years old. While at WCPO, Braun "sang, worked props, ran camera, including the *Paul Dixon Show,* and swept the studios. He later became staff announcer."[37] Braun moved to WLW-T, where his career drifted somewhat.[38] He did a teenage "bandstand"-type morning show from a department store (receiving an offer from Dick Clark to host a similar show in Honolulu), and hosted "Your Zoo." More important, Braun was Ruth Lyons's side kick on the "50-50 Club" for 11 years before Lyons retired in 1967.

Upon Lyons's retirement John Murphy was not ready just to let the "50-50 Club" go. He believed, though it was a gamble, that Braun had earned

34. Diehl, p. 33.
35. Diehl, p. 33.
36. Diehl, p. 33.
37. Dooley, pp. 9–10.
38. Diehl, p. 33.

the audience's approval and that he could carry the show by himself. After 27 years somebody other than Ruth Lyons was driving the "50-50 Club." Braun likened his work to an extended coffee break for his audience. "The average woman gets up, feeds her husband and kids and gets them off, cleans house, does the shopping, watches the budget, and then at four, they start coming back. The kids are yelling, hubby comes in and flops on the couch to watch television. She cooks dinner and washes the dishes and everybody goes to bed. We talk to them, not at them. It brightens their day."[39] In 1968, one year after he replaced Lyons, the "Bob Braun Show" reached over 3.5 million homes with an average daily combined listening and viewing audience of 500,000. Now called "Braun and Company," the Bob Braun show remained on the air until 1985, when a new management team decided to focus all efforts on improving the station's news ratings.

WLW-T and parent company Avco Broadcasting also parlayed their successful formula of television talk into what would become the model of all talk shows in the future. In 1967 WLW-T's sister station in Dayton, Ohio, WLW-D, decided to create another local talk show. Station manager Don Dahlman chose Phil Donahue as host. The "Phil Donahue Show" entered syndication in the fall of 1969. Of course, Donahue became the dean of talk-show hosts, creating some controversy along the way. His style and the show's format are probably the most copied in television history.

Early Effects

Television expanded in Cincinnati to include WCPO-TV (June 1948), WKRC-TV (July 1948), and WCET, the first licensed educational television station in the country (July 1954). (Although WCET was the first educational station licensed by the FCC, KHUT-TV was the first educational station on air.) As the number of homes with televisions increased, some expressed concern, of course, about the potentially negative influence of television programming on its audience, especially children. In 1951 Crosley Broadcasting funded an Xavier University study surveying the effects of television on schoolchildren. The results of the survey concluded that "among those students surveyed, those with television in their homes watched about 30

---

39. Diehl, p. 33.

hours of television per week."[40] Compared to students without television, "there was no noticeable difference in school grades."[41] The study further stated that "the main difference between good and poor students was the influence parents exercised over all aspects of their child's life."[42]

Avco Broadcasting was concerned about television's impact on the community. Early productions at WLW-T included a Saturday-morning children's show, "The Big Wheels Club," which was one of the most popular programs on television in the early 1950s. The program was created and hosted by Red Thornburg and had 12,000 children, ages six through 14, among its members. WLW-T was also instrumental in getting WCET, Cincinnati's noncommercial station, on the air. WLW-T offered $150,000 to the fledgling station but, more important, leased its tower and building to WCET for one dollar annually until the 1970s. WLW-T also began airing membership and promotional spots for WCET in the 1960s, while many members of the on-air talent participated in other fund-raising activities for the educational station.

By the mid-1950s Avco Broadcasting established the first weather station designed expressly for a radio-television operation.[43] Included in this technological wonder was a radar storm-warning system that served stations throughout the Midwest. WLW-T was also viewed as a public servant when, in 1966, Ohio governor James Rhodes "appealed to Avco Broadcasting to help promote the [Ohio State] Fair with live broadcasts" from Columbus, Ohio.[44] The station obliged the governor with live productions in 1967, which not only required the use of the mobile production unit, but required "an airplane, a caravan of buses, cars, a semi-trailer, small trucks, and motorized carts. Some 300 people were involved in the production, as was every piece of portable equipment owned by the station."[45] The effort paid off. Attendance at the fair increased fourfold, from 400,000 in 1966 to 1.6 million in 1967, making it the second-largest state fair in the country.

---

40. Reis, p. 4K.
41. Reis, p. 4K.
42. Reis, p. 4K.
43. Dooley, p. 8.
44. Diehl, p. 63.
45. Diehl, p. 63.

Ownership Change

Through its programming Avco Broadcasting kept the spirit and philosophy of Powel Crosley, Jr., alive at WLW-T. Crosley once said, "If you
want a good show, sell it yourself."[46] In 1975, however, Avco Broadcasting
decided to sell its television and radio stations in Cincinnati. WLW radio was
sold to Queen City Communications. (In 1995 WLW is owned by Jacor
Communications.) WLW-T, the "Phil Donahue Show," and the station's
mobile production units were sold to Multimedia. Gone was the informally
recognized hyphen from the television station's call letters. WLW-T, became
WLWT in Cincinnati. The breakup of the Crosley radio and television
stations was marked with sadness by many. "The breakup of this truly great
Midwest television and radio combination marks the end of 53 years of
broadcasting history, over a half century in which radio and TV have become
so much of our lives.... I don't know what changes will come about now that
this era has ended, but I salute the men and women who contributed so much
over the years to Crosley-Avco Broadcasting."[47] In making these remarks, a
local journalist, Mary Wood, was expressing concern about the continuation
of local programming, which often distinguished WLWT from other stations.

Multimedia purchased a station, WLWT, steeped in local programming excellence and continued the tradition Crosley initiated through the
new general manager, Walter Bartlett, a 23-year veteran of Crosley-Avco
Broadcasting. Besides the "Phil Donahue Show" and the "Bob Braun Show,"
which they acquired from Avco, Multimedia Productions syndicated numerous country-music programs including "Pop! Goes the Country," "Nashville
on the Road," and the very popular daily radio program, "The Ralph Emery
Show." By the end of the 1970s WLWT could call itself "the Originator"
since "outside of Los Angeles and New York—and excepting the three TV
networks—Multimedia Program Productions is the major producer and
supplier of TV shows in the land."[48]

---

46. P. J. Bednarski, "Bob Braun the Overlooked Institution," *Cincinnati Post,* 11 August 1981,
p. 1B.

47. Mary Wood, "Sale of WLW Marks End to Broadcasting Era," *Cincinnati Post,* 11 June 1975,
p. 23.

48. Scott Aiken, "Cincinnati 'Originator' Catches Nation's Eye," *Cincinnati Enquirer,* 8 April
1979, p. D-1.

In the early 1980s public service continued to be a priority. WLWT produced "Newsign," the only local news program in Cincinnati translated into sign. The station in the late 1980s offered "Take Five for News" (WLWT broadcasts on Channel 5) to all high schools in the Warner Cable–franchised area in and around Cincinnati, as an alternative to the widely criticized and commercialized Channel 1 news-program service. The program was hosted by former Cincinnati mayor, and then current WLWT anchor, Jerry Springer. Springer posed a discussion question following each story.

The 1980s were difficult times for local broadcasters, with increased operating costs and a depressed advertising market. WLWT and Multimedia experienced the downturn with the rest of the country. Additionally, WLWT's newscasts fell from their number-one ranking to third place. Between January and July of 1983 the station changed anchors on its newscasts an incredible five times, but none resulted in improved ratings. A change in station management brought Anthony Kiernan to Cincinnati. Kiernan expanded Jerry Springer's role on the evening newscasts. Springer had been reading nightly commentaries for the station when Kiernan named him as the station's prime anchor. WLWT returned to its position atop all other news stations in town until Springer left the news for good in 1993 as the production of his nationally syndicated talk show moved. Interestingly, WLWT brought in another former Cincinnati mayor and U.S. representative, Charlie Luken, to replace Springer.

Kiernan, who, as most general managers in the '80s, had a keen interest in the bottom line, canceled the "Braun and Company Show" in 1985. He expanded the early-evening news to one hour. Unfortunately, regular local programming all but disappeared from the station. With the exception of Cincinnati Reds baseball, no longer could WLWT be classified as "the Originator." Most local productions took the form of specials, and few were seen outside the Cincinnati market. Parent Multimedia continued the talk formula in the 1990s through Phil Donahue, Sally Jesse Raphael, and Rush Limbaugh, among others. In 1994 the company launched an all-talk cable-television network. WLWT did, however, originate the "Jerry Springer Show" when it went into production in 1991. Once into syndication, Multimedia moved the program to Chicago in hopes of attracting more notable guests and perhaps a higher visibility.

The relaxing of ownership rules in the mid-1990s contributed to Multimedia's decision to sell its media properties, including WLWT. In 1995 Gannett, the nation's largest newspaper publisher (including *USA Today* and

Cincinnati Enquirer) with significant broadcast holdings, won the bidding war for Multimedia with a $1.7 billion offer, continuing the trend of larger broadcast companies buying smaller ones.

One could argue that the legacy of Powel Crosley, Jr., is no longer evidenced at Crosley Square, home of WLWT. As WLWT leaves the former Elks Temple, it leaves behind many ghosts of television past. Although WLWT has in recent years offered many local specials, including a look at riverboats on the Ohio River from another bygone era, several zoo specials from the world-renowned Cincinnati Zoo, and a Catholic priest's ordination, the emphasis placed on local programs that gained a distinct identity has diminished significantly and will probably never again match the effort put forth in the Golden Age of Broadcasting by Powel Crosley, Jr., and WLW-T.

10

A West Texan
Fulfills His Dream:
KDUB-TV, Lubbock

Jay A. R. Warren

Nineteen fifty-two was a historic year for the television industry. It was the year the FCC announced its new allotment system for the nation's television markets and channels, ending its four-year license freeze. People were lining up to submit their applications for licenses.[1] "I Love Lucy," "Texaco Star Theatre," and "Arthur Godfrey and Friends" ruled the airwaves in 1952; but from television's first introduction until the FCC announced its new allotment system, the medium had been for those who lived in the big, metropolitan areas of the country.[2]

Thanks to the FCC's new allocation system, the residents of the smaller markets would begin to have the opportunity to see these popular programs.[3] Of course, it would take someone to prove that television could be profitable in these locales—markets that, for the most part, had few television sets in the households of their residents, a quality not appealing to advertisers.

One television pioneer who proved the small market's profitability was Dub Rogers. On November 13, 1952, Rogers's station KDUB-TV went on the air in Lubbock, Texas, just five weeks after the license had been awarded. KDUB was the first "postfreeze" television station to go on the air in Texas, beating stations in other cities like El Paso, Atlantic City, Little Rock, and Columbia, South Carolina. More important, KDUB was the first station in

---

1. *19th Annual Report of the Federal Communications Commission*, 1953.
2. See *Broadcasting and Telecasting*, Oct.–Dec. 1952.
3. *Sixth Report and Order*, FCC, 11 Apr. 1952, reprinted in *Broadcasting and Telecasting*, 14 Apr. 1952, p. 8.

the short history of television to go on the air in a small market.[4] Rogers succeeded when few people believed that small markets would be able to support television.

Background

At the time the television freeze was put in place, 37 stations were in operation, 86 construction permits had been issued, and 303 applications for new licenses had been filed with the FCC.[5] The resolution of the issues involved in the freeze took almost four years, and during that time the nation was served by no more than 108 television stations.[6] A "Weekly Television Summary" in *Broadcasting and Telecasting* showed that three other cities in Texas had television stations during the freeze: Dallas/Fort Worth, with WBAP, KRLD, and WFAA; Houston, with KPRC; and San Antonio, with KEYL and WOAI. Matamoras, Mexico, also had one station, KXLD, that was connected with Brownsville, Texas. In neighboring Oklahoma, Oklahoma City and Tulsa both had one station each; and in New Mexico, Albuquerque had one station. The total number of television sets in Texas, according to this August 1952 estimate, was more than 420,000.[7]

During the four-year freeze the public's interest in television increased dramatically. The "Sixth Report and Order," the document that lifted the freeze, reported that the commission had "endeavored … to provide television service, as far as possible to all people of the United States and to provide a fair, efficient and equitable distribution of television broadcast stations to the several states and communities."[8] In order to accommodate this number of channels, both the stronger VHF band and the weaker UHF (ultrahigh

    4. See *Broadcasting and Telecasting*, Oct.–Dec. 1952. Also, W.D. "Dub" Rogers, oral-history interview conducted by John R. Sparks, Apr. 1992, videotape recording, W.D. "Dub" Rogers Television Collection at the Mass Communications Building, South Plains College, Levelland, Texas. Hereafter referred to as the Rogers Television Collection.

    5. Henry L. Ewbank and Sherman P. Lawton, *Broadcasting: Radio and Television* (New York: Harper and Brothers, 1952), p. 84.

    6. Christopher H. Sterling, *Electronic Media: A Guide to Trends in Broadcasting and Newer Technologies 1920–1983* (New York: Praeger, 1984), p. 18.

    7. "Weekly Television Summary," *Broadcasting and Telecasting*, 4 Aug. 1952, p. 67. Matamoras, Mexico, was listed as the city for station KXLD.

    8. "Sixth Report and Order," Federal Communications Commission, 11 Apr. 1952, reprinted in *Broadcasting and Telecasting*, 14 Apr. 1952, p. 8.

frequency) band were used. The VHF stations were numbered 2 to 13, the UHF stations 14 to 83.[9] Most of the VHF stations were distributed to the larger cities; however, the commission "emphasized that it did not believe large cities should receive an 'undue share' of the 'relatively scarce' VHF channels." In accordance, a share of the VHF channels were given to smaller communities, but none were allotted for cities with populations of less than 30,000.[10]

The report listed all the communities that had been selected to receive at least one channel and gave the channel numbers. Lubbock, which was grouped with Amarillo and Monahans (all three located in west Texas), was allotted VHF Channels 5, 11, and 13, and UHF Channels 20 and 26. This section of the report stated that the "standard metropolitan area of Lubbock has a population of 101,000 with the city of Lubbock having a population of 72,000."[11]

The Innovator

Wesley DeWilde Rogers, Jr., who was nicknamed "Dub" by his father, was born in Waco, Texas, in 1920. Music, which had been a hobby since his childhood clarinet lessons, helped him to work his way through Baylor University, where he was the leader of a dance orchestra. Rogers's first job was in the music industry as a musical-instrument salesperson for the C.G. Conn Company. In 1942 Rogers joined the Air Force and was stationed in Dallas, Texas. The *Saturday Evening Post* reported that "Rogers decided at the end of the war that the best opportunity for an ambitious young man was in radio and television." But instead of finding a job in broadcasting, he moved his wife and two children to Lubbock, Texas, where he took a job as a salesman for a soft-drink bottling company. Rogers said, "I knew that West Texas was the place for me."[12]

Rogers and his family moved to San Antonio in 1949, where he helped launch a new television station. The owners of the station, which was given

---

9. *18th Annual Report of the Federal Communications Commission*, 1952, p. 110.

10. "Thaw July 1," *Broadcasting and Telecasting*, 14 Apr. 1952, p. 63.

11. "Sixth Report and Order," Federal Communications Commission, 11 Apr. 1952, reprinted in *Broadcasting and Telecasting*, 14 Apr. 1952, pp. 78, 134.

12. Joe Alex Morris, "Home-Town TV Makes a Hit," *Saturday Evening Post*, 3 Sept. 1955, p. 50. Rogers graduated from Baylor University in 1941.

the call letters KEYL, had received the license prior to the enactment of the 1948 freeze. It was the nation's 89th station.

Rogers served as vice president of KEYL-TV until it was sold in 1952. This was good timing for Rogers, as the licensing freeze was being lifted, thus allowing him to move back to Lubbock and try to bring this new medium to a small market.[13] Rogers said that it had been one of his long-time goals to help pioneer the small/medium-size television market. In speeches he made during the FCC freeze period he would continually tell audiences, "Somebody has got to pioneer the medium of television into the small/medium market. Currently television is running in the top 40 markets in the U.S., but as far as I am concerned, if we don't expand television past those select markets, then the stations in the first 40 are going to die and we are going to lose this industry. Also, if we don't expand this industry past the top 40, we are never going to have a truly national television service."[14]

Why Lubbock?

Of all the small- to medium-sized communities in which Rogers could have chosen to build a station, he chose the west-Texas community of Lubbock. One of KDUB's early promotional brochures donned a sprawling headline that read "3rd in Growth in the Nation."[15] Certainly the ability of the Lubbock residents to spend, and therefore to attract advertisers to the new television market, was a ranking criterion in Rogers's decision to develop a television market in Lubbock.[16]

Rogers has said that one of the determining factors in his decision was what he called Lubbock's "progressive" nature: "There were a lot of people in Lubbock that I felt were extremely progressive. In Lubbock in those days, there was very little self-seeking interest. Everyone was trying to pull together to do something in the community."[17] Lubbock business owner Kline Nall, who owned an electronics store during the 1940s and 1950s, agreed with Rogers's assessment. He said, "The business owners and citizens

---

13. Morris, p. 50.
14. Rogers, Apr. 1992.
15. KDUB brochure, Lubbock Chamber of Commerce Files, Southwest Collection, Texas Tech University, Lubbock, Texas.
16. Rogers, Apr. 1992.
17. Rogers, Apr. 1992.

were willing to take on extra taxation or whatever in order for the city to grow or progress."[18]

A *Variety* article also described Lubbock's attitude: "Along with this growth, has come a fierce regional pride, a 'let's put Lubbock on the map' attitude that's resulted in a city promotional operation that would put many a high-powered New York public relations operation to shame."[19] This progressive environment was important, because Rogers would be asking the business community to take a risk advertising in an unproved medium.

The final reason Rogers selected Lubbock was its flat terrain and its location. He planned not only to pioneer a station in a medium-size market, but to develop a chain of medium-size stations. "I had the dream of pulling together medium and small market stations into a package and tie them together into a mother station," Rogers said. The flatland in the Texas Panhandle provided a perfect location for this dream, as the signals could be transmitted over large distances with little interference. Rogers said, "I knew we could transmit this signal out here with fewer towers and units," but to reaffirm his gut feeling, Rogers had an engineer do a topographical study of the area. The engineer's results confirmed Rogers's assumptions.[20]

Lubbock's location was perfect, as there were no other major cities near it. Lubbock was the largest metropolitan area between Dallas/Fort Worth and Albuquerque (650 miles), San Antonio and Denver (961 miles), and Oklahoma City and El Paso (725 miles).[21] This meant that the station's reach would include the 21 counties, called the South Plains, that surrounded Lubbock. Lubbock functioned as "the Hub" for these 21 counties. A 1952 promotional brochure for KDUB estimated that the population in this area was more than 200,000 and that the buying income in these 21 counties was more than $237 million.[22]

---

18. Kline Nall, oral-history interview conducted by Jay A.R. Warren, 16 Feb. 1995, Lubbock, Texas.

19. Bob Chandler, "TV in Lubbock Keeps Pace With Growth of Texas 'Wonder Town,'" *Variety*, 15 Apr. 1953, p. 25.

20. Rogers, Apr. 1992. Rogers built a television chain with Lubbock as the mother station. He had other stations in Abilene/Sweetwater, Big Spring and Clovis, New Mexico. These four stations made up the West Texas Television Company.

21. Speech made by Rogers at a 1953 district meeting of the National Association of Radio and Television Broadcasters, Rogers Television Collection. Rogers served as the chair of the Small Market Television Panel during the 28 Apr.–1 May 1953, NARTB Conference in Los Angeles, California.

22. 1952 KDUB promotional brochure, Lubbock Chamber of Commerce files, Southwest Collection, Texas Tech University, Lubbock, Texas.

Also, the wide-open space of the South Plains meant that there would be little to no interference from other television stations. "Lubbock is unusually located from a geographical standpoint," Rogers has explained, "in that it does not have any other metropolitan areas anywhere near it with a television station casting its magic lantern signal into our coverage area."[23]

Getting the License

Having decided on Lubbock, Rogers and his company, Texas Telecasting, went about the business of applying for a license. On October 9, 1952, Rogers was awarded a license for VHF Channel 13. *Broadcasting and Telecasting* described Rogers's station, to be designated KDUB-TV and affiliated with CBS and Du Mont, and estimated the cost for construction of the station at $469,676, with another $180,000 to be spent on first-year operating expenses. An estimate for the first year's revenue was not given. The description also listed the principal partners in Texas Telecasting, including President W.D. Rogers, Jr. (22.2 percent); Vice President Vernice Ford (23 percent); Secretary-Treasurer W.W. Conley (11 percent); Roger L. Kuykendall (23 percent); and A.L. Lott (11 percent). All of the partners were involved in other Lubbock businesses.[24]

Joe H. Bryant, of Bryant Radio and Television, also received a license for a station in Lubbock. Byrant's channel, which went by the call letters KCBD, was assigned VHF Channel 11 and was affiliated with NBC. The estimated construction costs for KCBD were $342,100, and first-year operating expenses were estimated at $312,000. Bryant officials estimated that first-year revenue would exceed $340,000.[25] A *Lubbock Morning Avalanche* article reported that both stations were to go on the air in the spring of 1953.[26]

Dirk West, a Rogers colleague and former employee, recalled that U.S. senator Lyndon B. Johnson of Texas, who became Senate minority leader in

---

23. Speech made by Rogers at a 1953 district meeting of the National Association of Radio and Television Broadcasters, Rogers Television Collection.

24. *Broadcasting and Telecasting*, 13 Oct. 1952, p. 72.

25. *Broadcasting and Telecasting*, 13 Oct. 1952, p. 72. I believe that the estimates for the construction costs and first-year operating expenses and revenues were taken from the two stations' FCC applications. This would explain the wide difference in estimates given by the two stations.

26. "Two TV Stations in City Get Final Okay," *Lubbock Morning Avalanche*, 10 Oct. 1952, p. 1.

late 1952, was instrumental in securing the license for Rogers: "Dub was close friends with Lyndon Johnson, and this of course was a big help in getting the FCC license as quickly as he did. All Dub had to do was make one phone call to LBJ, and LBJ would put the pressure on the FCC to hurriedly grant the license to Rogers. This was a big help, because after the war people were lining up to get licenses. We got ours before Cincinnati and St. Louis."[27]

Johnson did have contact with the FCC during the first few months following the freeze. Johnson himself applied for and was awarded a license for a television station in Austin, Texas. William B. Ray in his book *The Ups and Downs of Radio-TV Regulations* explained why there were no competing applications filed for the VHF channel in Lubbock. "No one submitted a competing application," he wrote. "One observer later remarked, this was not surprising in view of Johnson's political clout. Filing a competing application would have been a waste of money." Johnson's station went on the air on November 27, 1952, just three weeks after KDUB's debut.[28]

Rogers may not have needed any help from Senator Johnson, as he was already well established in the television industry. His experience in San Antonio with station KEYL-TV and the contacts within the television industry while he was there were no doubt helpful in securing the license and building KDUB.[29]

After receiving the license, Rogers wasted no time putting the Lubbock station on the air. A deep desire to be the first station to go on the air in Lubbock or in west Texas motivated Rogers. He also believed that the publicity and attention surrounding the early debut would help him attract local and national advertisers. In addition, Rogers believed that the temporary operating site would help him build a television viewing base. He said, "The interim operation ... could keep television in front of the people. It would encourage the purchase of sets. Without sets I don't have a market.

---

27. Dirk West, oral-history interview conducted by Jay A.R. Warren, 22 Feb. 1995, Lubbock, Texas. There were no records in Rogers's files, and no one else was able to verify that Senator Johnson used his connections and influence to help Rogers. However, there was one file in the Rogers Television Collection devoted to correspondence between Rogers and Johnson. The only letters in the file pertained to a monthly filmed message by Senator Johnson that Johnson wanted aired on KDUB. In two of the letters Rogers addressed Johnson as "Lyndon," indicating that the relationship was friendlier than just a working relationship. Memos from the Rogers Television Collection.

28. William R. Ray, *The Ups and Downs of Radio-TV Regulations* (Ames: Iowa State University Press, 1990), p. 38.

29. Morris, p. 50. Also, "Dub Rogers Fulfills Lubbock Ambition," *South-Plains Farm Review,* 9 Apr. 1953, p. 1.

This way we would have a base market of home sets when we got out here to the [permanent] station."[30]

Rogers secretly started making arrangements to set up a temporary operating site that could be used until the permanent station was finished. He believed that the bigger the surprise of the opening, the more publicity and interest the station and Lubbock would receive. The tallest building in downtown Lubbock, then known as the Lubbock National Bank Building, was selected. The building's size gave that much more height to the antenna. He worked with the bank's chairman and president, C.E. Magin and Charlie Magin, Jr., respectively, to rent two floors of the building. Rogers said all that was needed was space for a few offices, a small studio, an elevator large enough to accommodate the transmitter, and, of course, space on the roof for the tower.[31]

Rogers stressed that the temporary operating site and the plans to go on the air before the spring of 1953 were confidential. He said, "It had to be a tightly held secret. Only a couple of bank officials and my small staff knew what was going on." He even went so far as to erect the tower on the roof at night using large spotlights. A hole in the roof for the tower was cut from the underside so that the work would be undetected by passersby.[32]

In late October, Rogers had to end the secrecy because the lack of television sets in the community. A 1955 *Saturday Evening Post* article about Rogers and KDUB reported that Rogers made the announcement about the early opening of the station at a dinner he hosted for representatives of television-set distributors.[33] On October 22, 1952, the *Lubbock Morning Avalanche* reported that KDUB would be on the air within three weeks. Rogers said that the station would be able to broadcast about 25 miles from a 202-foot-tall tower at the temporary operating site. The *Morning Avalanche* also reported that ground had been broken for KDUB's permanent home on 74th Street and College Avenue.[34]

---

30. Rogers, Apr. 1992.

31. Rogers, Apr. 1992.

32. Rogers, Apr. 1992. The Du Mont transmitter and other broadcast equipment arrived in Lubbock on 16 Oct. 1952; see "Interest in TV Showing Sharp Upturn Over Lubbock Section," *Lubbock Avalanche Journal*, 26 Oct. 1952, p. 1.

33. Morris, p. 50.

34. "TV Station Here to Go on Air Within Next Three Weeks," *Lubbock Morning Avalanche*, 22 Oct. 1952, p. 1.

During these early days and throughout KDUB's time at the temporary site, the staff consisted of about 17 employees, including two engineers, two announcers, and three sales representatives.[35]

The Opening

On November 13, 1952, Dub Rogers announced to a downtown Lubbock crowd of about 1,500, "You are waiting on us to turn on your television station. But you are going to do it. You're going to pull the switch." Rogers had a strong belief that KDUB was Lubbock's station, and he could think of no better way than to allow Lubbock's people to turn on their own station.[36] For a little more than two weeks the Lubbock community had known that KDUB would be debuting four months early, but there was still some uncertainty about the specific date that the station would go on the air.[37] And just as Rogers had been secretive in the beginning stages of building the temporary operating site, he was also secretive about the date and the plans surrounding the premier. Again, Rogers believed that the bigger the surprise, the more publicity the station and Lubbock would receive.[38]

Rogers and his small staff planned an extravagant premier. The evening was to start with a dinner for invited guests. Four days before the debut Rogers started inviting to the dinner city and area leaders, CBS and Du Mont officials, and other leaders of the television industry. He told them only that "this will be an important event that you will long remember." Following the dinner, the invited guests were to join the residents of Lubbock outside the bank building for the official "turning on" of the station.[39]

Rogers planned more than a speech and a flip of a switch. He planned a ceremony in which the people of Lubbock would actually pull the switch to turn on "their television station." Outside the bank building Rogers had parked a 48-foot flatbed trailer, which was decorated and used as the stage

---

35. Personnel Directory, Nov. 1952, Rogers Television Collection.

36. Rogers, Apr. 1992.

37. A test pattern was broadcast seven days prior to the station's debut. In a KDUB press release Rogers explained that the test pattern, which reportedly resembled a target, would help the television service representatives install the sets. Rogers Television Collection. Also see, "TV Test Patterns on Air Here," *Lubbock Morning Avalanche*, 6 Nov. 1952, sec. 2, p. 1.

38. Rogers, Apr. 1992.

39. Rogers, Apr. 1992.

for the event. Next to the stage two of Rogers's engineers had constructed a massive electrical switch, which was connected to a 500-foot rope that the people of Lubbock and Rogers's guests would pull to turn on KDUB.[40]

On the day of the premier Rogers ran newspaper and radio ads announcing that the station would debut at 8 p.m. and inviting all the residents to come to the bank building to be a part of the ceremony.[41] The half-page ad in the *Lubbock Morning Avalanche* had a sprawling headline that read, "DON'T MISS The Great Premier of West Texas' First TV Station." The ad touted the following features of the new station: top CBS and Du Mont shows, Paramount Film Network shows, wrestling from Chicago and Hollywood, daily "Telenews," and weekly sports. Lubbock's mayor, Murrell Tripp, proclaimed November 13 "Television Day," in honor of the "new entertainment medium" that was making its debut in Lubbock.[42]

After an elaborate dinner party at the mezzanine of the Hilton Hotel, which was across the street from the bank building, the invited guests joined the more than 1,200 Lubbock residents who had shown up to participate in the ceremony outside the bank building.[43] Entertainment during the outdoor segment of the program was provided by the Texas Tech band, the Shelton Brothers western comedy team, the TV Trio, and vocalist Jackie Bishop. Bobby Peterson, of WBAP-TV in Fort Worth, served as master of ceremonies. Speeches were made by Rogers, Mayor Tripp, and Edward Scoville, station-relations manager for CBS.[44]

After the speech-and-entertainment portion of the program, the 500-foot rope was stretched down Texas Avenue, and Rogers invited all of the guests and participants to grab hold "tug-of-war style" to turn on the station.[45] The *Lubbock Morning Avalanche* reported that Rogers, Mayor Tripp, 1952 Miss Texas Connie Hopping, Texas Tech president Dr. E.N. Jones, and leaders of Lubbock community organizations and the television industry

40. Rogers, Apr. 1992.

41. Rogers, Apr. 1992.

42. See the *Lubbock Morning Avalanche*, 13 Nov. 1952. The news story, "TV to Make Debut in Lubbock Tonight," appeared on p. 1, and the ad appeared in sec. 3, p. 2.

43. Rogers, Apr. 1992. There is some discrepancy as to the number of people at the opening ceremony. The *Lubbock Morning Avalanche* estimated the number to be between 1,200 and 1,500. Rogers said that there were between 3,000 and 5,000 people in attendance.

44. Kenneth May, "TV Has Debut for Lubbock," *Lubbock Morning Avalanche*, 14 Nov. 1952, p. 1.

45. Rogers, Apr. 1992. Also, "KDUB-TV's Start: Switch Thrown Thursday," *Broadcasting and Telecasting*, 17 Nov. 1952, p. 70.

were at the head of the rope.[46] After the ceremony Rogers said that now "some 3,000 persons can say, 'I put West Texas's first TV station on the air.'"[47]

The entire ceremony was broadcast on KDUB, making the dedication ceremony the first program to be broadcast on television in Lubbock. The lead for the *Lubbock Morning Avalanche's* story on the premier was, "Lubbock's first television station, KDUB-TV began broadcasting as scores of area residents tripped the master switch which sent the opening ceremonies direct from Main [Street] and Texas Avenue into the living rooms of many South Plains homes."[48] Bill Dean, a Lubbock resident, remembered watching the ceremonies with his family from their living room. "It was quite a ceremony they had down there before they went on the air and while they were going on the air. The crowd was incredible."[49]

Rogers received a great deal of correspondence congratulating him on the success of KDUB's premier. Letters and telegrams came from Allen Du Mont of Du Mont Laboratories; Justin Miller, president of the National Association of Radio and Television Broadcasters; and Dr. Frank Stanton, president of CBS. An excerpt of Stanton's letter, which was sent to Rogers to inform him that Stanton could not attend the ceremony, read, "Warmest congratulations to you and all of your associates when KDUB-TV is activated. It will be a great event and service for Lubbock and West Texas and also for CBS Television."[50]

Promoting KDUB

Reports on the premier of KDUB indicated that the television signal had reached as far as Amarillo, Texas, 120 miles north of Lubbock.[51] Stories of the event appeared in the *Wall Street Journal*, the *New York Times*, the *Dallas Morning News*, the *Fort Worth Star-Telegram*, *Broadcasting and Telecasting,* and many of the newspapers in the Lubbock area. The *Wall*

46. May, p. 1.
47. "KDUB-TV's Start: Switch Thrown Thursday," p. 70.
48. May, p. 1
49. Bill Dean, oral-history interview conducted by Jay A.R. Warren, 23 Feb. 1995, Lubbock, Texas. Dean has been a Lubbock resident for more than 55 years. He attended high school in Lubbock.
50. See letters from Frank Stanton, Allen Du Mont, and Justin Miller, Rogers Television Collection.
51. May, p. 1.

Street Journal reported that "the immediate delivery of transmitter equipment and a temporary transmitter site in downtown Lubbock has enabled the station's owners to make KDUB-TV the fourth new television operation in the United States since the end of the freeze."[52] The Associated Press also reported that KDUB was the "fourth post 'freeze' unit" to open as well as the first station to open in Texas since the lifting of the freeze. The three postfreeze stations to go on the air before KDUB were Denver, Colorado, stations KFEL and KBTV and Portland, Oregon, station KPTV."[53] *Broadcasting and Telecasting* wrote that KDUB was the 112th television station to go on the air in the nation and the 68th city in the nation to have television coverage.[54]

Rogers traveled extensively to New York, Chicago, and Los Angeles, where he would promote KDUB to potential advertisers and members of the television industry. Bill Maddox, a former KDUB-FM disc jockey and KLBK (KDUB's successor) news anchor, recalled that during these trips Rogers would take along gifts that symbolized west Texas, such as squaw dresses[55] and Stetson hats, and he would give them away to important people he met with. "Most of this was pure public relations," he said.[56]

Apparently Rogers gave gifts on a regular basis. He maintained an extensive Christmas gift and card list. Rogers liked to entertain potential advertisers and clients. Maddox said that the designs for the permanent station included a kitchen and a dining room that would accommodate 20 people.[57] In addition, Rogers had a private dining room off his office at the station. Maddox explained that Rogers would use these facilities during business meetings. "Dub had the idea that the best way to get new clients was to bring them out and feed them a good meal at the station," he said. "They used to bring clients out, and they would watch television while they

---

52. See *Wall Street Journal*, 12 Nov. 1952. Also see, *Fort Worth Star-Telegram*, 7 and 14 Nov. 1952, *New York Times*, 3 Nov. 1952, and *Dallas Morning News*, 10, 11 Nov. 1952.

53. See *Fort Worth Star-Telegram*, 2 Nov. 1952, sec. 2, p. 19, and 14 Nov. 1952, sec. 2, p. 18. KRTV in Portland, Oregon, was the first UHF station in the nation to go on the air.

54. Larry Christopher, "FCC's Pace Quickens," *Broadcasting and Telecasting*, 17 Nov. 1952, p. 67.

55. Squaw dresses were elaborately decorated skirts and were stylish in the early 1950s.

56. Bill Maddox, oral-history interview conducted by Jay A.R. Warren, 22 Feb. 1995, Lubbock, Texas. Bill Maddox is a life-long resident of the Texas/New Mexico plains. He worked for KDUB radio in the early 1960s and became one of KLBK's anchors in the mid-1960s. He was hired as the first anchor for Lubbock's ABC affiliate in 1968, where he has been ever since.

57. "Formal Opening of KDUB-TV Set for Friday Through Tuesday," *Lubbock Evening Journal*, 9 Apr. 1953, sec. 3, p. 22.

ate a meal and the sales presentations were made. Everyone loved to go get a meal at the KDUB dining room."[58]

The permanent station was also equipped with an observation booth that overlooked the main studio. The booth had 200 theater-type seats and was open to the general public. According to Maddox, in the beginning many people were curious about the station, and "the observation booth was primarily for people who didn't have a television set. Of course, there were some people who just wanted to see a live show. There were a lot of people making their way to KDUB."[59]

A January 1953 Report of Service form from the Lubbock Poster Company reports that Rogers had 12 billboards advertising KDUB. The signs were located all over Lubbock and varied in size.[60] Bill Blann, a friend of Rogers and a 25-year employee of the station, said that Rogers was always sponsoring events and promotions that would involve the community. According to Blann, when the station began, Rogers started a club for all children born on November 13, the opening day of the station. Rogers named the club the KDUB Kubs and had a birthday party at the station each year for the group. Blann said that Rogers hosted the event for at least 10 years.[61] Dirk West added, "We were constantly doing something that would promote the station. We would do remote transmissions from different places in the city. We were always prominent in all of the city's parades."[62]

An Audience Frenzy

Establishing a viewing audience was one of the many obstacles Rogers overcame. In order to do this people had to own televisions, something that

58. Maddox, 22 Feb. 1995. Maddox said the cost for a meal for employees was 50 cents. There were no records kept of the exact cost of the cafeteria and kitchen to the station; however, one receipt did show a cost of $1,724.05 for utensils, glasses, dishes, a sink, a range, and an ice-cube machine. Also, it is known that there were two full-time cooks and one part-time dishwasher. See the Rogers Television Collection.

59. Maddox, 22 Feb. 1995. Maddox said that by 1960 the observation booth was no longer in use.

60. Report of Service, Lubbock Poster Company, 1953, Rogers Television Collection. There were no prices listed for the signs.

61. Bill Blann, oral-history interview conducted by Jay A.R. Warren, 17 Feb. 1995, Lubbock, Texas.

62. West, 22 Feb. 1995.

few Lubbock residents had before KDUB went on the air. However, all indications are that getting people to buy a television was not a problem. By the time the station went on the air, *Broadcasting and Telecasting* estimated that 7,000 television sets had been sold in Lubbock and the surrounding area.[63] By January 1953 the number of sets had increased to 12,000, and by the time the station had moved to its permanent location, the number was 22,104.[64]

Kline Nall, the co-owner of Radio Lab, one of Lubbock's electronics/appliances stores during the early 1950s, said business picked up once people heard that Lubbock was getting a television station, and especially after Rogers made the announcement that KDUB would be on the air four months earlier than expected. "We were selling televisions months before KDUB actually went on the air. People were buying them in anticipation of the big opening."[65] Bill Dean, who was a freshman in high school when KDUB went on the air, indicated that his father bought his family's first television set about three months prior to KDUB's first transmission. According to Dean, "Before KDUB went on the air, we used to just sit around and watch the test pattern. Occasionally we would flip it around and we could get random stations. Once we picked up a football game by accident."[66]

Rogers described the frenzy to purchase a television set during the first few weeks after his station went on the air as "unbelievable." "We had been on the air for about two or three hours when we got the word that people were going to the stores, which had stayed open late to sell the sets, to buy televisions just like they would go to the store to buy a dozen eggs. It was unreal," he said.[67]

Rogers explained that he and a couple of the CBS executives who were in town for the opening went down to one of the stores to watch the buying frenzy. "One would stay in the car, while the other went in to buy the television. He would come back with the television still in the crate and just put it in the trunk and drive off, one car after another. This went on for days."[68]

---

63. "Weekly Television Summary," *Broadcasting and Telecasting*, 24 Nov. 1952, p. 86. "Sources of set estimates are based on data from dealers, distributors, TV circulation committees, electric companies and manufacturers. Total sets in all areas are necessarily approximate."

64. *Broadcasting and Telecasting*, 5 Jan. 1953, p. 62; and 14 Apr. 1953, p. 35.

65. Nall, 16 Feb. 1995. Nall owned Radio Lab with two of his brothers-in-law, Herbert Griffin and Doc Griffin. Nall's wife, Leona Griffin Nall, served as the store's business manager.

66. Dean, 23 Feb. 1995.

67. Rogers, Apr. 1992.

68. Rogers, Apr. 1992.

According to Nall, apprehension and speculation about the new medium kept some people from buying a television set. "There was general doubt that Lubbock would be able to support one television station, much less two."[69]

Television manufacturers invested heavily in getting the market saturated with their sets. Nearly 100 dealers from the region attended a Bendix Television Company meeting in early November 1952, to hear the district manager describe a new incentive program whereby Bendix dealers who sold a certain amount of television sets would win a trip to Paris.[70] Other companies also held training sessions in Lubbock to inform their dealers and representatives about service and installation procedures. Philco conducted a training seminar on the campus of Texas Technological College during the early part of November 1952.[71]

Programming

Initial programming on KDUB was limited to just a few hours a day. During the first months normal programming ran between the hours of 5:30 p.m. and 10 p.m.[72] By January 1953 the station had extended its airtime to begin at 4:15 p.m. and sign off at 11:15 p.m.[73] In March 1953 the station moved into its permanent facilities, allowing the KDUB staff to expand local programming and extend airtime hours again. By April the station was on the air between 2:55 and 11:30 p.m.[74]

The first day on the air, programs included dedication ceremonies for the new station at 8 p.m., various advertising from 9 to 9:16, wrestling from Chicago at 9:16, "Hollywood Half Hour" at 10:15, "This Week in Sports" at 10:45, "Telenews" at 11, "Strike it Rich" at 11:15, and sign-off at 11:45 p.m.[75] In the beginning KDUB programming consisted of a mixture of feature films, network programs sent by kinescope (films previously aired

---

69. Nall, 16 Feb. 1995.
70. *Lubbock Morning Avalanche*, 7 Nov. 1952, sec. 1, p. 15.
71. *Lubbock Morning Avalanche*, 6 Nov. 1952, sec. 1, p. 14.
72. See *Lubbock Morning Avalanche*, Nov.–Dec. 1952.
73. KDUB Program Schedule for the days of 14–18 Jan. 1953, Rogers Television Collection.
74. See *Lubbock Evening Journal*, Apr. 1953.
75. KDUB Program Log and Daily Work Sheet, 13 Nov. 1952, Rogers Television Collection.

as network shows, because there was no coaxial cable) and locally originated shows.

For the first three years CBS was the primary source of network programming, with Du Mont supplementing the programming schedule.[76] A *Lubbock Morning Avalanche* story reported that "at present there are no immediate plans for the bringing in of live network programming to the city. Such an arrangement will require either a coaxial cable or booster towers serving the Lubbock area." Rogers explained that network programs would be delayed about one week after they originally aired elsewhere,[77] and that the networks would "bicycle" the films from stations to station. "The film would arrive from New York; we would show it and ... ship it on to Los Angeles and, after they aired it, they would ship it to Portland, Oregon, and then it would go back to New York."[78]

Rogers also bought an extensive film library, which gave him flexibility in programming—something he advised all medium-market station owners to do.[79]

KDUB's programming was "informal." According to the *Saturday Evening Post*, "Many local programs are played by ear rather than by script. Open-neck sport shirts are popular with announcers, and a comic weather bird enlivens the daily forecast. A firecracker is likely to explode during a hillbilly song program, and the president is frequently in the act."[80] Bill Dean, a longtime Lubbock resident, agreed with this assessment. "KDUB was a lot more laid back. They ran a telethon [in 1953] that was almost slap-stick," he said.[81] Much of this informality can be attributed to the amount of local programming the station ran. Dean believed that KDUB built its image by covering the community. He said, "They established their identity by doing local programs. They had a lot of locally oriented shows."[82] One of KDUB's most successful shows was the March of Dimes Telethon. The telethon, which was in its third year nationally, ran on January 31, 1953, and the station

---

76. Chandler, 15 Apr. 1953. A memo dated 11 Aug. 1955, from Du Mont Television, informed Rogers that Du Mont would be terminating its contract with KDUB. Robert L. Coe wrote, "Please understand this action is taken simply because of the lack of network business to justify the maintenance of an affiliation in your market." Rogers Television Collection.

77. "TV Station Here to Go on Air Within Next Three Weeks," p. 1.

78. Rogers, Apr. 1992.

79. Speech made by Rogers at a 1953 district meeting of the National Association of Radio and Television Broadcasters, Rogers Television Collection.

80. Morris, p. 50.

81. Dean, 23 Feb. 1995.

82. Dean, 23 Feb. 1995.

raised more than $16,000 during the 12-hour broadcast. Rogers said that an additional $8,000 was donated the week after the telethon.[83] *Variety* reported that the telethon "kept the entire countryside up all night."[84]

Dirk West, who served as host of a children's show after KDUB had moved to its permanent facilities, said there was not enough studio space at the temporary operating site for the production of many live, local shows, but this changed once the station got settled into its new home.[85] By June 1953, just three months after the new facilities had opened, KDUB aired 64 locally produced shows. Eighty percent of those shows had local (and some national) sponsorship, accounting for the majority of the station's revenues.[86] Each week, 12 hours of the station's airtime was spent with network shows, the advertising during these shows accounting for less than 5 percent of the station's revenues.[87]

"There was no precedent for a medium-size television market, so basically we were just winging it in those first few days. It was a no-holds-barred environment, where we would simply put shows on the air that we thought the people would enjoy. If they didn't, we yanked them off and tried something new," Dirk West said, adding that the early productions were "homey, a natural fit for West Texas."[88]

Rogers believed that the local shows worked because of "human interest." "In our size city you either know practically everyone, or know of them—but large or small, live programming is a necessity so that you can give to your programming the flavor of the community or the area that you are servicing," he said.[89]

One of the first locally produced live shows was Dirk West's "The Studio Children's Theatre." During the show West would draw cartoons and have the studio audience, full of children, draw along with him. "I would draw until it felt like my arm was going to fall off," West said, noting that a

83. "Dub Rogers Fulfills Lubbock Ambition," *South-Plains Farm Review*, 9 Apr. 1953, p. 1.

84. Chandler, 15 April 1953. Rogers Television Collection. Also see Blann, 17 Feb. 1995.

85. West, 22 Feb. 1995.

86. Speech made by Rogers at a 1953 district meeting of the National Association of Radio and Television Broadcasters, Rogers Television Collection.

87. Chandler, 15 April 1953. Rogers Television Collection.

88. West, 22 Feb. 1995.

89. Speech made by Rogers at a 1953 district meeting of the National Association of Radio and Television Broadcasters, Rogers Television Collection. Bill Dean participated in one of these locally produced shows. He appeared on a regular local panel-discussion show on Sundays in which local-area high-school students expressed their concerns and thoughts about the trials of being teenagers. Dean was one of three regular student panelists, and other students were guests. A Lubbock minister served as the show's moderator.

two-hour block of time was sometimes difficult to fill. They invited special guests to the show periodically and added a clown and cowboy to the show's regular cast. "Dub was very well connected in New York and Los Angeles," West said. "This helped us to get some pretty big stars to come on our show."[90]

Bill Dean vividly remembered West's show. "He was gang-busters funny. Dirk was very, very popular."[91] The show's popularity overwhelmed West at times. Once the show sponsored a contest in which West asked all of the children to draw a picture of their bicycles. The child who had the best drawing would receive a new bicycle, donated by one of the local bicycle shops. West said that within two to three days after the contest announcement, he had received more than 4,000 drawings. "The response to that contest was unbelievable. Needless to say, we were unable to run any more contests after that."[92]

Selling Time

Rogers spent much of his time promoting KDUB and Lubbock to potential advertisers, locally and nationally. Advertising rates for KDUB averaged about $20 for a one-minute spot. In 1953 the local advertising accounted for 84 percent of KDUB's revenues.[93] In 1952–53 KDUB reported that the net sales for December totaled $21,860, with $15,602 coming from local advertisers. Net sales in January 1953 totaled $29,841, with $19,168

---

90. West, 22 Feb. 1995. Examples of some of the first shows produced at KDUB included cooking shows, farm shows, and even a game show. The name for the cooking show was decided by a contest in which women were asked to send in their suggestions for the title. Rogers said that with 32,000 television sets in the area, they received 6,000 suggestions in a four-week period.

91. Dean, 23 Feb. 1995.

92. West, 22 Feb. 1995. "The Studio Children's Theatre" was sponsored by Bell Dairy. West said that about every 15 minutes he would break away and do a "plug" for Bell Dairy. He said that many times the children in the audience would receive free ice cream or milk during the show. West said the show made him an overnight local celebrity. "The kids all knew you. It was kind of like being an instant celebrity. Television had ten times the impact then than it does today. We did personal appearances like opening a super market and the turn-out would be fantastic." The show stayed on the air for three years. West said that the schedule was too demanding to keep up for much longer than three years.

93. Speech made by Rogers at a 1953 district meeting of the National Association of Radio and Television Broadcasters, Rogers Television Collection.

coming from local advertisers.[94] All of the local ads were live, and they usually were voiced by a KDUB staff member. "We had to memorize the script because there were no TelePrompTers back then," Dirk West said. "Sometimes we would write it out on cards and lean them against the wall, but usually we just memorized it."[95]

Some could say that Rogers had it easy, since television took such a hold in Lubbock. In 1952 the only activities in Lubbock and the surrounding area were either to go to the movies or, after KDUB's debut, to watch television. *Variety* described, "The Lubbock area is dry (no alcohol may be sold within the city limits), night clubs are at a minimum, and film houses provide about the only means of entertainment." *Variety* also reported that theater revenues decreased as much as 50 percent after the debut of KDUB. He wrote that television's power was so strong in Lubbock, it became a matter of pride to buy products advertised on the new medium. "Kent cigarettes were introduced to the area via [the] CBS [program] 'The Web,' and stores were sold out of all initial stocks within two weeks." Of course, since Lubbock was dry, this meant that Rogers could not depend on any alcohol advertising, a big mainstay even in those days.[96]

Dirk West, one of KDUB's first on-air employees, told a similar story. He said that one advertiser ran an evening commercial announcing a sale on Polaroid cameras, of which, the ad claimed, there were only 120 in stock. Within one day of the airing of the commercial the store owner had sold all 120 cameras. "People had seen it on television and they had to have it," he said.[97] The *Variety* story reported that KDUB was "completely sold out of its Class A time" slots, which included the $20 one-minute ad and the $200-per-hour sponsorship. The story said, "Sponsors report excellent results from their TV campaigns and TV advertising has taken hold more quickly and with more permanency than in most other markets."[98]

94. "Recap of Sales for the Month of January, 1953 and Increase over December 1953," KDUB financial document. No documents were located that showed the sales for other months. Rogers Television Collection.

95. West, 22 Feb. 1995.

96. Chandler, 15 Apr. 1953. Rogers Television Collection.

97. West, 22 Feb. 1995.

98. Chandler, 15 Apr. 1953. Rogers Television Collection.

The Permanent Station

The permanent station, which opened April 9, 1953, started with just as much fanfare as the temporary operating site. Rogers and his staff organized a four-day open house for the public. Rogers said, "We invite everyone to come for a guided inspection tour of the new plant." Rogers also had a guest list of people he had invited to attend the opening. The *Lubbock Evening Journal* reported that even Alan Du Mont attended the opening.[99]

Rogers also described the permanent facility as state-of-the-art. He said, "We profited from previous experience and as a result, our new building is designed to incorporate all the improvements and advances found lacking in the earlier stations." The *Lubbock Evening Journal* reported that television-film salesmen who attended the opening found the facility to be "one of the most functional designs" they had seen.[100]

The new building had 2,280 square feet, complete with two studios, dressing rooms, offices, a cafeteria, an observation booth, and the "tallest tower in the south." The *South-Plains Farm Review* reported that the tower was 78 stories tall, making it taller than New York's Chrysler and Woolworth buildings. The 852-foot tower was pieced together in 30-foot sections and held together with more than 2,500 bolts. It was reported that the tower could withstand wind gusts of 150 miles per hour.[101] By the time KDUB had moved to its new facility, the staff consisted of 32 full-time and five part-time employees, double the number Rogers had had at the temporary site. There were six full-time engineers, six sales representatives/employees, one full-time promotion/publicity coordinator, three announcers, and eight programming employees.[102]

---

99. "Formal Opening of KDUB-TV Set for Friday Through Tuesday," p. 22. All of the KDUB staff were present at the opening to mingle with the guests and answer any questions. Guests were also able to watch the station produce live television shows from the observation booth.

100. "Formal Opening of KDUB-TV Set for Friday Through Tuesday," p. 22.

101. See "Formal Opening of KDUB-TV Set for Friday Through Tuesday," p. 22; and "KDUB-TV Holding Open House April 10 Through 14," *South-Plains Farm Review*, 9 Apr. 1952, p. 1. All of the station's original equipment came from the Du Mont Laboratories. Bill Blann said the Du Mont equipment was later replaced with GE equipment.

102. Speech made by Rogers at a 1953 district meeting of the National Association of Radio and Television Broadcasters. Also see the Nov. 1952 Personnel Directory, Rogers Television Collection. The majority of the part-time employees were students in Texas Tech's engineering or radio/television programs.

In interviews conducted for this article, a few key words were used over and over to describe Dub Rogers. He was called a pioneer, an innovator, flamboyant, and a promoter. All of these terms help to define who Dub Rogers was, and they help explain how he was able to accomplish all that he did. Rogers not only brought television to Lubbock, Texas, he brought television to small markets all over the nation. His courage and foresight led the way for others. Bill Maddox said, "It took somebody like Dub, with his capabilities, to not only get television started in this market, but also to help the television industry to develop, even from little old Lubbock."[103] By the following spring stations were opening in other small markets, like Amarillo, Texas; Lynchburg, Virginia; and Fort Smith, Arkansas. Television was becoming a permanent facet in the lives of Americans, no matter the size of their communities.[104]

---

103. Maddox, 22 Feb. 1995.
104. *Broadcasting and Telecasting*, 13 Apr. 1953, p. 35.

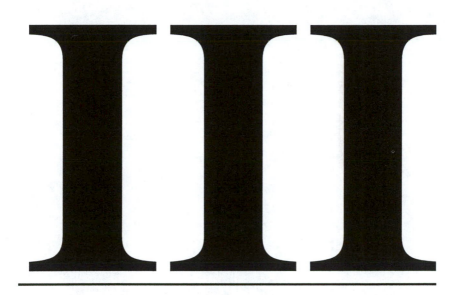

The Central Heartland

11

First in Education:
WOI-TV, Ames, Iowa

Dom Caristi

WOI-TV was the 100th television station on the air in the United States, and the first television station on the air owned and operated by an educational institution. In fact, Iowa State College, now Iowa State University, first applied for permission to build the station seven years before the Federal Communications Commission had even reserved channels for educational stations.

Iowa State was founded as a land-grant institution, whose mission included bringing education to the people of the state of Iowa. Electrical engineering was one of the early offerings, so it was only natural that the college would become involved in using broadcasting as a means of supporting its educational outreach. In 1914 an electrical-engineering professor began operating 9YI, an amateur radio station. In 1921 that station began to transmit music and voice programs over a 100-watt transmitter, and in the following year WOI was licensed by the Department of Commerce. Despite many frequency, power, and transmitter changes in its first decade, it quickly established a program schedule that included agricultural programs, weather forecasts, market reports, classical music, and news. For 20 years station management was the responsibility of Professor D. C. Faber, the director of Engineering Extension Services. Faber saw the college's mission and the station's mission as one and the same. WOI radio had firmly established two goals: It would serve the college mission of educational extension, and it would become a laboratory for electrical engineers.[1]

In 1941 the college began making inquiries into the paperwork that would be necessary for a television application. A letter from the FCC in May 1941 provided basic rules, including the requirement that stations operate a minimum of 15 hours per week.[2] Perhaps due to World War II, or perhaps because of financial reasons, nothing was done formally for three years. It was in 1944 that Iowa State College president Dr. Charles Friley appointed a committee to study the prospects for a television station. The composition of the committee demonstrated the institution's view that broadcasting was important to the engineering department. The head of the committee was the head of electrical engineering, one of five of the 12 committee members who were from the electrical-engineering department. In addition, two other members were the radio station's director and chief engineer. Only one other faculty member (from architecture) served on the committee. The remaining participants came from the college's central administration: an assistant to the president, the information-services director, the college business manager, and the physical-plant supervisor.

The following year Iowa State filed an application for a construction permit with the Federal Communications Commission. The committee still had not issued a final report on the college's involvement in television but applied for the permit nonetheless. President Friley expressed his concern that channel assignments for experimental stations were going fast, and that an application ought to be filed as early as possible. His sense of urgency was demonstrated in his not waiting for the board-of-education meeting for approval but filing the application two weeks prior (at which time the board gave its approval). Friley knew that the FCC would require several months of review before taking action and believed the timing would coincide with the college's own deliberations.

In a memo the year earlier President Friley went so far as to say that the application for a television station could go forward and "that we need not be concerned about the problem of purchasing expensive equipment for the next eight or ten years."[3] When the construction permit was issued in

---

1. W.I. Griffith, "Report on Radio Activities of Iowa Colleges and Universities," Iowa State College (mimeographed report), 1935, Iowa State University Archives.

2. Letter from T.J. Slowie, secretary of the FCC, to M.S. Coover, electrical-engineering department head, May 24, 1941, Iowa State University Archives.

3. Letter from C.E. Friley, Iowa State College president, to M.S. Coover, July 28, 1944, President Friley File 2/9 Box 1, Iowa State University Archives.

1947, the college was prepared to move ahead. It is somewhat unclear as to whether the construction permit (CP) approval was the cause of the committee's decision to forge ahead with a station, but given the predisposition of most of the committee members, the CP was merely a formality—most had concluded that Iowa State would have a station. President Friley urged the state's board of education, later called the board of regents, to develop a station at Iowa State.

Although the will to construct a station was there, the means were still lacking. In a 1948 letter to the Philco Corporation, WOI radio director Richard Hull speculated on whether the college would actually have to drop the television project due to lack of money and equipment.[4] The college had been given an extension on the original construction permit. Surprisingly, the college would receive a second extension, to 1949. With assistance from General Electric, the college was able to secure much of the transmission equipment it needed at little or no cost.

In spite of assistance from General Electric, there were still substantial costs associated with construction of the new television station (approximately $135,000).[5] During his tenure President Friley always liked to brag that not a single dollar of state funds was used to construct or maintain WOI-TV. How the station was financed, however, is still a source of much speculation in Iowa.[6]

In 1942 Iowa State became involved in the Manhattan Project, the supersecret exploration of atomic power and weaponry. Between 1942 and 1946 Iowa State produced over 2 million pounds of purified uranium for use in the various projects and experiments. For its efforts the university received a 5 percent overhead payment. Due in part to the secrecy of the project, and in part to the nature of the college's accounting in that era, it is difficult to trace exactly where the overhead was deposited, or for what purposes it was withdrawn. Although no conclusive evidence has ever been presented, many people have speculated that the overhead money from the Manhattan Project served as seed money for the construction of WOI-TV.[7] The *Des Moines*

---

4. Letter from R.B. Hull, director of WOI Radio, to the Philco Corporation, September 30, 1948, VP Information and Development, WOI Radio and TV File 5/6/1 Box 1, Iowa State University Archives.

5. *Television Management Seminar* (Urbana, Ill.: National Association of Educational Broadcasters, 1955), Iowa State University Archives.

6. Jim Pollock, "WOI Has Lively, Controversial History," *Des Moines Register,* March 2, 1994, Metro sec., p. 1.

7. E. Nusbaum, "ISU's Secret Past: From Radio-activity to Television Activity," *Des Moines Register,* September 20, 1993, Today sec., p. 1.

Register in 1984 interviewed several surviving WOI founders, none of whom could provide evidence to prove or disprove the possible link between the Manhattan Project and WOI-TV.[8]

At the time the construction permit was approved, no one at Iowa State could foresee the freeze that the FCC would impose on television station licenses in 1948. Had the college taken much longer to make a decision on whether to pursue a station, the possibility would have been stalled until the freeze was lifted in 1952. Instead, the college received its approval the year before the freeze and was able to sign on the air at 6:30 p.m., February 21, 1950. WOI-TV was licensed as a commercial station, despite being owned by a not-for-profit educational institution.[9] The next two stations owned by educational institutions did not begin operation until 1953, but growth came rapidly after that. By 1955, 10 institutions had television stations. The fact that WOI-TV went on the air during the freeze would significantly impact its reach, audience, programming, and mission philosophy for years to come.

Nonlocal-Advertising Precedent

The college had added an FM station in 1949, and both WOI radio stations were noncommercial from their inception. No advertising had run on the stations, whether sold locally or contained in programs produced elsewhere. Before 1952 no frequencies had been reserved for noncommercial television stations, and the station was able to forego advertising without a requirement from the FCC. It chose not to sell local advertising in its early years; however, it did carry advertising already contained in network programs. The fact that Iowa State College had a commercial television license made it not only the first television station owned by an educational institution, but one of only three stations on unreserved commercial channels owned by colleges in the 1950s. WOI would continue its policy of not selling local advertising time until 1955.

In addition, because WOI had beaten the freeze, it was the only station licensed to the Des Moines market. Although it was not the only television station in Iowa (the state's other stations were in Davenport, on the eastern

---

8. "ISU's Role in Atomic Bomb Helped Spawn WOI-TV," *Des Moines Register,* June 10, 1984, p. 3B.

9. John C. Schwarzwalder, *ETV in Controversy* (Minneapolis: Dillon Press, 1970), p. 44.

border, and Council Bluffs–Omaha, on the western border), WOI-TV would remain the only television station in central Iowa throughout the years of the freeze. Only in 1954 did a second station appear in the Des Moines market.

Because it was the only available station in the area, all four existing television networks approached WOI-TV hoping it would carry their programs. This made it possible for WOI-TV to select what it considered the best programs from the schedules of the American Broadcasting Company, Columbia Broadcasting System, Du Mont, and the National Broadcasting Company. Because WOI was the only channel the majority of Iowans had to see network programs, the station considered carrying the programs both a means of attracting an audience and a form of public service.[10] The state board of regents approved the station's affiliation with the networks.

From the very beginning WOI-TV tried to make the most of its dual role in programming. The month prior to the station's first telecast, the state board of education approved a policy statement that enunciated the state's interest in operating with a noncommercial approach in a commercial environment. The statement included the following tenets:

1. While WOI has always operated non-commercially [referring to the radio operations], this has been a matter of choice on the part of the college and not a requirement by the FCC. A major factor in determining this choice was the existence of commercial stations in the state with which the College did not wish to compete. Likewise, WOI-TV may operate non-commercially or commercially, as College policy may direct. The factor of competition is now absent, however, in the case of television in the WOI-TV area. Furthermore, this affords an opportunity to cooperate with industry in the growth and development of a new medium and to make available some types and kinds of programs which education does not presently have available. With this back-log, WOI-TV can then pioneer educationally.

   a. There are and will be no other TV stations in the area for a two-year period; hence, there is no competition for commercial accounts.

   b. The policy of "alternative programming" followed by WOI and WOI-FM does not prevail with WOI-TV. There is no alternative. The College TV station is "all things to all people."

   c. Commercial network programming on WOI-TV will totally help, not hinder, the growth of television in Des Moines and adjacent

10. Daniel F. Wozniak, "Education's First Television Station," master's thesis, Iowa State College, 1958, p. 62.

areas and will provide future TV stations with ready-made audiences and familiar programs. It will be the chief element in the sale of TV receivers, a matter of great concern to Iowa State if there is to be a satisfactorily large TV audience.

2. By following a semi-commercial policy, reserving selected portions of the broadcast day for school broadcasts and accepting payment in return to maintain a considerable portion for network features carried WOI-TV could acquire a fund which would aid greatly in securing the additional equipment necessary for a full-scale television operation.

3. Any and all network arrangements which might be made should be based on four principles:

   a. Any WOI-TV network affiliation should be written in such a manner as to protect the right of each Des Moines station presently affiliated with a network to secure that network's television broadcasts in the event the station commences television operation. The agreement with any network should be written to expire in two years. There should also be an option for WOI-TV renewal of network contracts in the event a given station in Des Moines is not prepared to use the network in question.

   b. No exclusive contracts should be written with any network, and desirable arrangements would include WOI-TV affiliation with at least two of the networks existent, and as many more as feasible.

   c. Contracts should be made only with networks, not with Des Moines affiliates of networks.

   d. WOI-TV should retain complete rights of program control and ability to cancel, discard, or censor network programs at will for good and sufficient reason.

The Committee feels this is a logical, practical, and entirely justifiable method of meeting a new and difficult problem and which would discharge the television responsibilities of the College over WOI-TV to a larger public in a more satisfactory manner over the initial two-year period of operation than would any other arrangement.

By virtue of making all arrangements directly with New York headquarters of the several networks, the onus of local commercial criticism would be removed. At the same time, the general public will receive more programs of better quality than WOI-TV could initially produce; and the several Des Moines stations benefit not only from the television promotion of their particular networks but ultimately from the larger number of TV sets which will be available when they commence operation.

Finally, and most importantly, not only will the financial return insure a complete equipping of WOI-TV at no expense to the State, but will allow the WOI-TV staff to devote all of its time and energies to producing a two-year program of creating and developing educational programs for a full-scale independent operation.[11]

From this policy statement several station philosophies were established that were consistent with the institution's educational mission. The station founders provided a rationale for having a state institution operating a commercial television station. They discounted possible criticism by demonstrating that the station would not be in competition with any existing TV station, and that it would surrender network affiliations as stations came on line.

The policy statement also underscores the national thinking at the time that television stations were extensions of existing radio facilities. The statement speaks quite specifically to the institution's desire to "protect the right of each Des Moines station presently affiliated with a network to secure that network's television broadcasts."[12]

The policy also touted the fact that the station would be good for future commercial broadcasters because it provided a sizable base of homes with TV sets. As radio had demonstrated decades earlier, sets would not sell until there was programming available to be heard. By providing "high quality" network programs, WOI-TV would encourage Iowans to purchase television receivers and increase the potential audience available to new stations entering the market. There must have been at least a grain of truth to this. When WOI-TV signed on, there were an estimated 3,500 TV sets in service in central Iowa. After just one week of broadcasting, 5,600 more sets had been sold. By the end of 1950 there were 30,000 sets in WOI's viewing area, which the Iowa Electric League claimed made WOI the fastest growing station in the United States.[13] According to research by WOI, there were 248,000 sets in the viewing area by the time WHO-TV, the second station in central Iowa, signed on the air in 1954.

---

11. Minutes of the State Board of Education, January 17, 1950. Call number L148 B5 1949/50, Iowa State University Archives.
12. Minutes of the State Board of Education, January 17, 1950.
13. Wozniak, p. 84.

Early Facilities

When WOI-TV signed on the air in 1950, the station's facilities consisted essentially of a small transmitter building. One year later the station still had the transmitter building but had added a 20-by-30-foot studio in the radio station. The "studio" was equipped with two cameras and all the requisite control-room support.

Perhaps because of the college's engineering program, WOI-TV had one of the early kinescope recorders. In October 1951 the station installed its first kinescope and began testing. Before 1951 ended, WOI-TV was producing kinescope prints that were suitable for airing. By March of the following year the station had shortened the time between recording and airing with the use of a "hot processor." In less than one year the station had recorded more than 100,000 feet of kinescope film.

After two years of operation WOI-TV moved into what was to be its home for two decades. A spacious area was remodeled in Exhibit Hall, so named because it had earlier served for livestock exhibits. Although the building's previous use was not terribly glamorous, the total area available to the station must have seemed palatial. WOI-TV needed a larger studio, in particular to accommodate Ford Foundation–funded programs, some of which involved as many as 40 people. The station now had over 7,000 square feet of space, providing room not only for a studio, but for set construction and storage, engineering and production. Having experience with lobby conversions, the station changed its new lobby to a second studio in its first year of operation, to meet the need for rehearsal space while the main studio was in production.

Moving to Exhibit Hall also meant the facilities would be more centrally located on campus. At the old transmitter site, three miles from the central campus, it was less likely that anyone would "drop by" to see the operations. Exhibit Hall was only a few hundred yards from the administration building and made the station's presence much more visible.

The station was also able to increase the power of its signal. WOI-TV signed on the air on Channel 4, but in June 1953 the station switched to Channel 5. From its original 5,000-watt transmission, the station incrementally increased power until it reached its allowed maximum, 100,000 watts, in early 1954.

WOI would also be creating an audience for network programs, so that as stations went on the air, thus acquiring one of WOI's network affiliations and its corresponding programs, viewers would likely migrate to the new stations to see programs they had become interested in. This expectation was proven correct in the first bit of research conducted by WOI after WHO signed on. In May 1954 WOI's telephone survey determined that stations won viewership during time slots in which a network program was carried opposite a local program. Later that year audience surveys again indicated that local programming on WOI ("Teachers' Telecourse" and "Farm Facts") lost to network offerings on WHO ("Pinky Lee" and "Robert Montgomery"). Unfortunately for WOI, during time slots wherein network programs went head-to-head, ABC's offerings were often not as popular. The 1954 survey showed WHO (carrying NBC programs) had ratings between 41 and 69 for "Dragnet," "Ford Theater," "Martin Kane," and "Superman," whereas WOI's ratings were between 8 and 38 for "Lux Video Theater," "Kraft Television Theater," and "Place the Face."[14]

The network programs would also provide a larger audience for educational programs that WOI planned to run as part of its educational mission. Although a cooking program by a home economist might not attract much attention on its own, the audience might be considerably larger if the program was preceded or followed (or both) by the sort of popular entertainment shown by the networks. That mix of education and entertainment was evident from the outset. On its first day of broadcasting the station's three-hour-and-ten-minute programming day was primarily made up of three educational films from the college's film library and three kinescopes of network programs. The station also recognized the necessity of justifying its existence through a commitment to noncommercial activity. A brochure produced by the station in 1953 indicated that 93 percent of the station's labor and 73 percent of its budget were devoted to noncommercial activities. The station conducted a survey in December 1953 and found that 95 percent of all television households within the viewing area had watched "Challenge," an educational program on enzymes. With all due respect to the producers, the show was not particularly compelling but was literally the only program available. In its first decade the station signed on and off with the following statement: "WOI-TV, the first educationally owned television station in the nation, is dedicated to bringing the best the College has to offer to the schools, cities and farms of Iowa, with programs of education, entertainment, and

14. Wozniak, pp. 193–195.

public service."[15] One of the earliest local programs was "Your Home Hour," produced by the college's extension service. On the assumption that the educational offering would not necessarily draw the largest possible audience on its own, the program was sandwiched between two network offerings.

Perhaps because it was central Iowa's only television station, WOI seemed to have a reach far beyond what engineers had originally expected. The first broadcasts were over a 5,000-watt transmitter—quite small by today's standards. The station considered its viewing area to be a 55-mile radius of the transmitter, but towns double that distance reported receiving the station's signal. As a matter of fact, during the month prior to signing on officially, viewers in Missouri, Kansas, South Dakota, Minnesota, and even Illinois reported receiving test transmissions from WOI-TV.[16]

As the freeze was lifted and WOI faced competition from new television stations, a number of changes were forced upon it. In 1954 the station lost its NBC affiliation. In 1955 another new Des Moines television station acquired the CBS affiliation. Although this situation had been anticipated when the station policy had first been created, few people had probably recognized the financial impact of the loss of network affiliations on the station. Until 1955 the station had not accepted local advertising. This policy was consistent with the operation of its two radio stations, neither of which had ever accepted advertising, though the AM station had never been legally required to remain noncommercial.

Challenges

At this time WOI-TV was faced with a critical question: If the station maintained its refusal to accept local advertising, the state of Iowa would have to provide funds to keep the operation going. The college was quite proud of the fact that no state funds had been used to construct, operate, or maintain WOI-TV. If the station accepted advertising to keep itself self-sufficient, however, it countermanded a founding principle that it not be competitive with other available commercial-television service.

15. James H. Davis, "Credit and Non-credit Telecourses," Iowa State College (dittoed report), July 3, 1956, Iowa State University Archives.

16. "Reports of Reception Are Highly Pleasing to Those in Charge of Station WOI," *Ames Daily Tribune,* February 20, 1950, p. 1.

Another critical change had occurred in the college's leadership. Dr. Friley was no longer Iowa State president. His successor, James H. Hilton, assumed the presidency in 1953 and lacked the context of WOI-TV's dual role. In a 1954 speech Dr. Hilton reiterated three goals of WOI-TV: to serve as a branch of the college's extension mission, as a laboratory for students, and as an environment in which new television programs and techniques could be developed.[17]

With the loss of network affiliations and increasing costs of operations, Dr. Hilton saw the television station as costing money rather than generating income. In May 1954, the month following the loss of the station's NBC affiliation, station revenue dropped from almost $90,000 to just less than $65,000. In the month following the loss of WOI's CBS affiliation in August 1955, the month's revenue dropped to $52,000. With increased local programming, station staff had grown from only 24 at the start of 1951 to a record 159 (full- and part-time) in April 1954. In 1955 Dr. Hilton put forth a proposal to the state board of education that WOI-TV begin selling advertising. The proposal specifically stated the choice before the board: either increase revenue by the sale of advertising, or receive state support (i.e., tax money) for operation. The proposal added that the station would still reject advertising for alcoholic beverages and any other advertising it deemed "unsuitable for telecasting." Needless to say, the board approved the recommendation, and WOI-TV began selling advertising, slowly at first, but more aggressively by the late 1950s.

Early Programming

When WOI-TV signed on the air in February 1950, its only equipment was a transmitter, a sync generator, one iconoscope-film pickup camera, two 16-millimeter film projectors, one three-by-four-inch opaque projector, two microphones, two turntables, and an audio console. Needless to say, the station operated strictly a film-and-slide operation for most of its first year. With one exception the only "live" programming was the announcer's voice over slide material.

---

17. "Voices of Experience," Washington, D.C., Joint Committee on Educational Television, November 17, 1954, p. 7.

One notable exception occurred three months after sign-on, when the Du Mont Network brought a group of engineers and a remote truck to Ames to cover Iowa State's annual VEISHEA celebration. VEISHEA, an acronym for the college's programs of study, was (and still is) a week of activities each spring celebrating the school's educational heritage. Parades, plays and musical performances, carnival rides, and appearances by major celebrities are all a part of the festivities. During VEISHEA Week 1951, WOI aired more than 11 hours of local programming, which amounted to almost half of the week's programs.

News and information were essential to WOI's radio operations, so it was only natural that WOI-TV would assume a similar role. When it came time for the 1950 general elections in November, the station telecast its first live studio programming using its own cameras. Six different reporters worked to provide local and state results to central-Iowa viewers between 10:45 p.m. and 1:30 a.m. The local results were interspersed with network coverage of national results and other material (such as film and slides).

Given the station's connection to the college's extension mission, it should come as no surprise that WOI-TV's first regularly scheduled, locally produced live programming was an informational program. "Farm Facts" went on the air in March 1951. Later that month WOI-TV entered the daily live, local news business with a newscaster underwritten by International Harvester. The programs originated from a "studio" on the Iowa State campus that had previously served as the radio station's lobby.

Nineteen fifty-one was also the year that WOI-TV created "The House with the Magic Window." When the program debuted, it was produced in cooperation with the college's child-development department as an educational and entertaining program for preteens. The program has the distinction of having been the longest continually running, locally produced children's television program in the nation. The program length was changed, it was scheduled in several different time slots, and it ceased to be a cooperative venture with the child-development department, but "Magic Window" aired on WOI-TV from 1951 until the station was finally sold in 1994. Equally incredible is the distinction earned by Betty Lou McVay (later Varnum). Betty Lou took over as the show's host in 1953 and served in that capacity until the program was canceled in 1994. She had taught craft projects and introduced cartoons to hundreds of thousands of central-Iowa children over five decades.

In 1951 WOI-TV received one of the first grants ever from the Ford Foundation. The station received $180,000 to produce local programs through the Fund for Adult Education, which the Ford Foundation created. One of the 16 series produced with the grant money was "The Whole Town's Talking," consisting of a filmed segment followed by a live, in-studio discussion addressing community issues. The station even hired a guest director to handle the first seven programs. The FAE grant brought quite a bit of attention to the young station, as well as over 300 observers from 37 states and 18 foreign countries to learn from the program's operation.[18]

WOI's first week of broadcasting totaled 17 hours and 40 minutes. Before the year was out, the station was averaging more than 60 hours of broadcasting weekly. Most of those hours were on weeknights: The station did not begin regular weekend broadcasts until October 1950. For the first year broadcast time was primarily filled with network programs and educational films from the college's library; during the first couple of months educational films represented over half the on-air hours. But before the end of 1950 network programming had assumed the role of major program source.

As one might expect, the amount of time devoted to local programs increased as the station matured. Except for VEISHEA Week, the station averaged fewer than two hours of locally originated programming each week in its first year of operation. The greatest proportion of those local programs were agricultural, and news and public affairs. The amount of local programming more than doubled as the station moved into its new facilities. Also as might be expected, the percentage of the broadcast day devoted to network programming grew smaller as local production increased. As was the case with most television stations in the 1950s, the number of hours broadcast each week was also seasonal: Much more network product was available in winter than in summer.

Because the station was located within an educational institution, the level of activity closely matched that of the college. As network minutes waned during the summer, so, too, local production decreased as the size of the campus shrank. Similarly, local programs were not often produced on weekends, as the majority of college offices operated on a weekday schedule (and thus so did their employees).

---

18. Ruth Wagner, "The Whole Town's Talking," *Midland Schools,* April 1952, VP Information and Development, WOI Radio and TV File 5/6/4 Box 5, Iowa State University Archives.

Because of the college's mission a small percentage of programming time, in-school telecasting, and noncredit college courses were an important part of WOI's schedule. The station started producing and airing its "systematic" educational programs in 1952. Each year WOI devoted 10 to 20 percent of its schedule to such programs. Obviously, in-school programs were less likely to draw the large audiences that evening telecasts drew, so the fact that these programs were broadcast during the school day fit nicely with the station's dual mission of entertainment and education.

By 1954 the station had become a full-time television operation. The average broadcast day lasted 17.5 hours, as much as a week's worth of broadcasts just four years earlier. WOI produced as many as 60 local live programs each week, a figure, it claimed, that made it not only the most productive television station in the country, but that exceeded the output of CBS's Television City.

Nineteen fifty-four also brought the first competitor to the Des Moines market, and a loss of WOI's NBC affiliation. This loss of programming was not too difficult to overcome; the station simply increased its use of ABC and CBS programs to fill the void. The loss of the CBS affiliation the following year, however, hit the station much harder. At that time ABC was still a "part-time" network, providing programming only in the late afternoons and evenings. Even increased local production was unable to keep up with the hundreds of hours of programming lost each month, and the station showed a decline in on-air hours, whereas it had shown a steady increase in broadcast hours during its first five years of operation. From fewer than three hours each weekday, the station was averaging over 16 hours per day by March 1954. That level of activity continued until the final affiliation switch took place in July 1955. By August the station had eliminated morning broadcasts and was averaging fewer than 12 hours per weekday. This was a gigantic step backward, as WOI had not averaged so little airtime since September 1952. It would be many years before the station would return to 16-hour broadcast days.

Not only did the station lose programs, it lost large shares of its audience. Obviously, all viewers were tuned in to the station when it was the only channel in central Iowa. But by August 1955 only one of the 15 top-rated programs was aired on WOI-TV.[19] The CBS network programming, which aired on KRNT, accounted for 13 of the top 15 programs. Losses of network

19. "Special Television Audience Report, the WOI-TV Des Moines Grade B Coverage Area," New York, American Research Bureau, 1956.

programs and their corresponding audiences were understandable, but the station also lost head-to-head local news battles. In August 1955 WOI's 10 p.m. newscast had a rating of only 8.3, while WHO had a 12.3 rating, and KRNT, the CBS affiliate that had been on the air the least often of all three stations, won the time slot with a 24.2 rating. As an early employee of WOI news wrote, "It was clear that WOI-TV's 'monopoly honeymoon' was over."

Epilogue

Without a doubt WOI-TV's Golden Age was its first decade of operation. The number of "firsts" established by the station in the 1950s is indeed impressive. But as the station faced increased competition, loss of revenues, and a changing mission, its status declined. As early as 1958 questions were being raised as to whether the state should own such a commercial venture. By the 1960s the state legislature was reconsidering the station's role. Questions continued within the board of regents, the Iowa legislature, and the governor's office. After a protracted legal battle the Iowa board of regents sold WOI-TV to Citadel Communications in 1994. The nation's first "educational" station had finally been sold.

12 Pulitzer's Prize: KSD-TV, St. Louis

Michael D. Murray

The first broadcast day in St. Louis television, February 8, 1947, was both a reflection of what had gone before and a clear vision of the future. Because of its ties to the *St. Louis Post-Dispatch* and Pulitzer radio station KSD, newspaper and radio staffers were directly involved in the programming that day.[1] Internationally known editorial cartoonist Daniel Fitzpatrick was on hand, for example, to make on-camera sketches of the event. Frank Eschen, who had already established himself as KSD radio news director, reported on the inauguration of the station, and St. Louis Cardinals sports figure, Joe Garagiola, was interviewed by the *Post-Dispatch* sports editor, Roy Stockton. The programming also included an exhibition by professional wrestlers and ballroom dancing. Obviously, station management had some clue regarding the potential of this new medium to appeal to the public, based on their experience in other media.[2] At the same time, some new and specialized television staff helped lead the charge into the future.

The station recruited Keith Gunther from the NBC network in New York to help lay the groundwork for the development of television programming and the recruitment of personnel. Although he was a native of St. Louis, his East Coast exposure included working with national talent, such as famed NBC symphony orchestra conductor, Arturo Toscanini. Gunther spent a great deal of time identifying and developing program sources that would

---

1. Irving Litvig, "Golden Age of St. Louis Radio," *St. Louis Post-Dispatch,* March 12, 1969, p. 3F.
2. John Roedel, personal interview, February 21, 1985. See also Michael D. Murray, "KSD Veteran Roedel Retires," *St. Louis Journalism Review,* February 1986, p. 23.

encourage the purchase of television sets, including live sporting events. The first such program, originating from Kiel Auditorium, was offered just one week after programming began and consisted of the play-by-play telecast of a college basketball game.[3] Within two months St. Louis Cardinals baseball was also being offered to viewers, an opportunity the team gave the station in exchange for the purchase of two seats.[4]

Gunther was assisted by a very able cast of radio professionals who made the transition to television while maintaining their commitment to KSD radio. They included Harold Grams, a key player in the sports department; Frank Eschen, host of numerous news and entertainment programs; Russ Severin, who was recruited to develop programming for the fledgling operation; and George Burbach, who managed the station.[5] Burbach's contribution was key because it was he who first sold Joseph Pulitzer on the importance and potential of television. Burbach was advertising director, first for the *Post-Dispatch*, then for KSD radio, and had also served as a director of the company since 1922.[6] He first saw television displayed while on a visit to London in 1936 and promptly set about on an internal campaign to sell its potential from his base of operation in the advertising department, which had unique, nationally recognized standards. In fact, a Pulitzer policy banning advertisements from the middle of radio newscasts in which war-related news was being reported created a national stir.[7]

Most of the news standards in both radio and television were set locally by Francis "Frank" Eschen, a University of Missouri Journalism School graduate, who reported on a mine explosion with over 100 trapped just one month after television's first broadcast in St. Louis. Eschen balanced his hard-news reporting with his role as host of the Laclede "Little Symphony." He also conducted interviews with visiting actors and actresses as part of a continuing entertainment program from the cities' Municipal, or Muny, Opera in Forest Park. On one occasion he appeared in a cameo role, playing the part of a reporter in a Muny Opera production. Earlier Eschen had traveled to Europe with the Catholic archbishop of St. Louis, John Glennon,

---

3. Harold Grams, personal interview, July 19, 1985.
4. Keith Gunther, personal interview, May 15, 1985. See also Michael D. Murray, "Audiences Were in His Hands in TV's 'Diaper Days,'" *St. Louis Journalism Review,* July 1985, p. 14.
5. Russ Severin, personal interview, August 12, 1985.
6. "Twenty Years at Channel 5," *St. Louis,* May 1982, p. 19.
7. Michael D. Murray, "The *St. Louis Post-Dispatch* Campaigns against Radio Middle Commercials," *American Journalism,* vol. 5, no. 1, 1989, p. 30, and see Michael D. Murray, "Frank Eschen Gave for Twenty Years: A Profile of a Pioneer Newsman," *St. Louis Journalism Review,* January 1987, p. 8.

when the prelate was being made a cardinal in Rome. Before they returned to the states, Glennon died on a stopover in his birthplace in Ireland, and Eschen functioned briefly in a press-relations role before reporting the event to the heavily Catholic population of St. Louis.

In its first few months on the air a number of "special event" type programs were presented over Channel 5, but few could compare in scope to the 1947 Veiled Prophet Ball telecast. The community social pageant, which had been cloaked in an atmosphere of mystery and was open only to St. Louis's so-called elite or "upper crust," was suddenly being brought into the homes of anyone willing to buy a television receiver. The event was promoted vigorously by the station, and television dealers invited friends and prospective buyers into their showrooms for an "open house" on those occasions.

Channel 5's Veiled Prophet coverage became a ritual. Announcers and technical crew would outfit themselves in white tie and tails and take off in the station's remote truck or a newspaper delivery truck to catch the action, thereby giving all of St. Louis the chance to eavesdrop on the social set. A columnist for an early publication, *TV Review,* once described Keith Gunther's status at the ball as chief decision maker with respect to which debutante would get favored video treatment. According to one writer, a number of the participants paid almost as much attention to the television cameras and technicians as they did to the regal festivities of his Mysterious Majesty from Khorassan. Some young ladies were even caught mugging for the cameras until a parent moved in to express stern disapproval.

When one father caught himself staring at a television monitor, he exclaimed in embarrassment how foolish he had been to watch the program on a small black-and-white monitor in the back of the auditorium, thoroughly taken in by all this new visual gadgetry, when he had paid so dearly to observe his daughter's participation firsthand. The attraction went beyond the confines of Kiel Auditorium, and by 1951 the two-hour telecast of the ball attracted an audience estimated at close to a million, due to the station's feed to 47 NBC-TV affiliate stations. The event demonstrated well the potential of television to draw a crowd.

Just five years after television debuted in St. Louis, Senator Estes Kefauver brought his Special Crime Subcommittee to town. Reportedly more than a million people were able to see the hearings, either in their homes or in local taverns. The then conservative competitor of the *Post-Dispatch,* the *St. Louis Globe Democrat,* estimated that local drinking establishments

contributed greatly to the television audience, attracting many more customers than usual during the hearing. The issue of television's impact on the
outcome of the hearing was raised, with one potential witness commenting
to the press on the effect of the extra lighting required for the cameras.
Another report suggested that Frank Eschen, who at this time was in charge
of coverage for the station, take the stand and submit to questions on this
potential problem, while his associate Harold Grams fought local radio
stations' attempts to place microphones with their station call letters directly
in front of the cameras.[8]

Grams's career in broadcasting began early. He started at WOC radio,
where he first auditioned for Ronald Reagan's brother Neal, then a representative of the station's parent organization. Grams was shortly promoted
to the company's larger-market station in Des Moines, WHO, where future
President Reagan was a sports announcer. Grams auditioned at KSD radio
to do sports and news in the later '30s. By the time the first television
broadcast was under way, he already had close to 10 years' radio experience
under his belt, as well as contacts with national broadcast figures like Bill
Stern and Ted Husing. Most of the early sports telecasts at KSD-TV bore his
imprint—if not in front of the camera, then behind the scenes. He worked
closely with Keith Gunther, the station's technical supervisor, on all assignments. Gunther was often perched with a walkie-talkie aloft a Channel 5
truck handling sports assignments from the field. The station had, for
example, a specially designed RCA mobile unit for the United States Golf
Association 47th Open Championship, June 12–15, 1947, played at the St.
Louis Country Club. In perhaps Channel 5's most ambitious undertaking to
that time, the station provided the NBC Television Network with this
nationally broadcast program. Two Image-Orthicon cameras and telephoto
lenses were employed to produce close-up shots of the contestants from the
green. Station representatives pointed out that only a participant making a
putt could have gotten a closer look at the action. Frank Eschen supplemented
the program with interviews conducted in an area across from the official
scorers' tent near the 18th hole. Harold Grams provided audio commentary
in instances when viewing was impaired or when action momentarily
slowed.

---

8. "Crime Inquiry Attracts Crowds Like World Series," *St. Louis Globe-Democrat*, February
24, 1951, p. 1; "TV Gives Front-Seat View of Crime Inquiry," *St. Louis Post-Dispatch*, February
24, 1951, p. 2A; and also, William M. Blair, "'Outraged' Over Video at Hearing, Carroll, Bet Expert,
Defies Senators," *New York Times*, February 25, 1951, p. 1.

Gunther directed a technical staff of 12, unprecedented for that time, and Eschen conducted interviews with prominent guests and dignitaries, including USGA president Charles Littlefield and golf legend Byron Nelson, an earlier Open Champion. Frank Eschen hosted musical programs, as well, the most popular being "The Laclede Little Symphony," which attracted national attention and gave its sponsor, Laclede Gas, and its partner, D'Arch Advertising, recognition as leaders in the field of quality programming in the Midwest.

Popular Programming

The station's symphony program was born when officers from St. Louis's Laclede Gas Company decided to develop a program tied to community activities, and civic campaigns, and one they could sustain over time. The network had already proved its interest in concerts, with Arturo Toscanini and the NBC Symphony on radio and television. The fact that St. Louisans loved good music was the premise on which Laclede based the series. And, after all, when George Burbach had erected a television tower on the *Post-Dispatch* building, it had seemed only logical that Laclede would extend its efforts in that direction. As Laclede officials pointed out, the KSD tower was within viewing range of company president Judge R. W. Otto's office window.

Right from the start Laclede officials were convinced they had a winner. A telephone survey once indicated that 78 percent of those called could identify some elements of the program. These findings compared favorably with the ever-popular "I Love Lucy," of which only 45 percent could recall details. Laclede was also aware, along with partners Channel 5 and D'Arcy Advertising, that it was providing a unique and valuable cultural service to the community.

The "Laclede Little Symphony" was first telecast on Channel 5 October 7, 1950. Concertmaster Harry Farbman was joined by a group of musicians from the St. Louis Symphony. The time slot for the show, 9:30 to 10 p.m., eventually established the program as the oldest uninterrupted local spot and St. Louis's first regularly scheduled live telecast of fine music. The popularity of the program was due in large measure to the quality of the musical performances. Viewers were treated, for example, to celebrated soloist Van Cliburn and many others. For a good number of these performers, the Laclede program represented their first television appearance anywhere, and it was often a very productive and positive experience.

The success of the "Little Symphony" encouraged Laclede to take another chance in yet-untested television waters with another musical program, but with a different format and orientation. "Sunday with Sorkin," hosted by disc jockey Dan Sorkin, was first introduced on October 4, 1956, at 9:30 p.m. Guests for the first show included Roger Williams, Betty Martin, and Len Dressler—a recent winner in Arthur Godfrey's "Talent Scouts." The Laclede Showroom at 11th and Olive streets was often converted into a gigantic television studio, with nine musicians and KSD's technical director, Elmer Peters, providing the technical broadcast expertise.

Each week Dan Sorkin traveled from his home in Chicago to host the series. For this first show Betty Martin did a rendition of "Happiness Street," and Len Dressler and his orchestra followed. Roger Williams played "Tumbleweed" and "I Got Rhythm." The series was definitely off to a good start. In the weeks that followed Sorkin introduced some of America's premier performers in live concerts telecast over Channel 5. They included Bill Hayes from the original Sid Ceasar's "Your Show of Shows," Cab Calloway, George Shearing and the Shearing Sextet, Billy William's Quartet, and Singleton Palmer's Dixieland Six. Both the February 25, 1956, and March 3, 1957, programs featured Andy Williams. He sang "Canadian Sunset" and also a title song written by Steve Allen especially for the motion picture *Picnic.*

On a couple of telecasts the host's humor was overshadowed by his guests. One such occasion took place during April 1957. Sorkin introduced the country music/comedy act of Homer and Jethro by admitting that he could not find a better way to bring them before the camera than to quote from the press release they had prepared about themselves. It was cornball stuff of the first order and an obvious carryover from radio, but the audience, no doubt, ate it up: "Our names are HOMER and JETHRO. All our lives we have lived music, talked music, breathed music but so far haven't learned to sing or play music. How do we select our songs? If someone wants to hear a song badly, that's the way we sing it.... Our first records were received with mixed emotions, like watching your mother-in-law drive your new Cadillac over a cliff."

Laclede continued to sponsor many musical programs, including important contributions by the St. Louis Symphony's Vladimir Golshmann and

"Muny Opera Preview" telecasts, also with Frank Eschen. Laclede began presenting the "Preview" radio-television program simulcast in stereophonic sound from the St. Louis Municipal Opera. In its second season it presented native St. Louisan Virginia Gibson, who appeared on Broadway and on the network-television program "Your Hit Parade."

In what would become known as the Golden Age of Television, Laclede's local contributions were unparalleled. They included celebrity-specialists from a variety of areas, such as Wilma Sim, St. Louis's best-known television home economist. She was selected to represent Laclede on many of its cooking programs. Sim, a graduate of the University of Minnesota, worked for KUOM in Minneapolis while she was completing her schooling. After graduation she conducted cooking schools for Swift and Company before joining the staff of KSD. The program was extremely popular.

Another popular program, and the first consistently sponsored show on Channel 5, was "Tele-quiz-Calls," put forth by Union Electric, one of the station's first program sponsors. Broadcast from the station's main studios at the old 12th and Olive location, with hosts Dottye Bennet and Harry Gibbs, the program revolved around appliance dealers who would sponsor parties from their dealerships in the area. People attending these parties would serve as contestants and would compete for electric toasters and, of course, television sets. The hosts, Gibbs and Bennet, used charades as their vehicle and quizzed contestants, making sure that everyone was a winner of sorts. According to Gibbs, the purpose of the show, in addition to providing local entertainment, was to demonstrate the medium to potential buyers—"to show that you could actually get something on that set beside a test pattern."[9]

Gibbs's partner on the program, Dottye Bennet, began her involvement in television conducting interviews, or what we now call "person on the street" type programs, and every variety of musical show. These included the Charade/Pantomime show for Union Electric, and a musical program for RCA Victor. The "Dottye Bennet Show" helped establish her as one of St. Louis's best-known broadcast personalities. Her popular television show made use of musical selections from the Snade Film Library Service, an early music-video resource for television stations.

Another show, "It's a Hit," premiered on May 13, 1948, and featured Al Chotin and, for a time, John Roedel as hosts. The program gave the television audience, as well as a studio audience, a chance to compete for

---

9. Harry Gibbs, personal interview, July 8, 1985.

prizes using a form of "baseball." Ray Hoffstetter, who ran the time clock for the show, described the premise as one whereby contestants would try to answer a question in a specified length of time in order to score a home run. As the clock ran down, scoring opportunities diminished until the "batter" struck out. The games were often held in conjunction with "television parties" in dealer's showrooms. Calls were made from the store to the program. This was, of course, a prime opportunity for appliance dealers to impress their guests with the entertainment fare television had to offer—not to mention the prizes!

For the staff of these shows, working conditions were quite demanding. Early television required a lot of lighting, and these programs routinely employed five banks of spotlights, each with 1,000 650-watt bulbs—all encased in netting, as on occasion the lights would explode. The early studio was part of a converted printing-press room, walled off with insulation to deaden the noise, but with the effect of retaining heat.

Work outside the studio was often a welcome relief. Even the well-known violinist and professional musician, Ernie Heldman, is remembered by some viewers as much for his magic performances during breaks in the action at the ball park as he is for his "The Ernie Heldman Show," a disc-jockey-type program. Also popular on both KSD radio and television was Ed Wilson, who frequently referred to himself as St. Louis's "biggest" disc jockey but was well-known for his work as a weatherman at the station.

Beginning in the fall of 1950 Channel 5 introduced a half-hour quiz program entitled "What Would You Do?" with former baseball Cardinal infielder "Buddy" Blattner and Carl McIntire. The premise of this program, sponsored by So-Good Potato Chips, was to have four prominent St. Louisans explain how they would respond to certain situations and compare their answers to those of experts. Blattner went on, of course, to become a network sportscaster and frequently worked with Dizzy Dean.

One of the other big areas of developing interest was the nature program, particularly animal shows. NBC-TV picked up Marlin Perkins's "Zoo Parade" in the middle '50s and by the start of the next decade was running "Mutual of Omaha's Wild Kingdom," with Perkins as host. Perkins was a native Missourian and well-known as director emeritus of the St. Louis Zoo. The show, filmed mainly on location, was later syndicated and is still offered to viewers on KSD-TV. The program was a viewer favorite and was endorsed by the National PTA for television recommended for family viewing. It was also recipient of 41 major awards, including four Emmys from the National Academy of Television Arts and Sciences. Perkins himself was honored with the Governor's Award from the academy's St. Louis chapter shortly before his death.

Gradually, as the station found its niche in the social life of the community, more sophisticated programming strategies began to develop. Children of the "baby boom" generation were fascinated with television. The success of "Howdy Doody" and "Kukla, Fran and Ollie" proved their attraction to the new visual medium.

Even in the early 1950s successful regional children's shows were beginning throughout the country. These were not syndicated shows per se, but early attempts to offer quality programming for kids in a particular region—cartoons, or series such as the highly successful "Little Rascals." One such effort was a Chicago-based television series featuring Bruce Roberts, or "Texas Bruce," a namesake developed and sponsored by Dean's Dairy. When Dean's started marketing a chocolate-drink product after World War II, the company hoped to branch out from Chicago and succeed in St. Louis. It sought a local talent to fill the boots of its Chicago namesake, as all of its promotional efforts, including point-of-purchase displays, had been developed around the "Texas Bruce" theme.

Harry Gibbs was selected to play the part in St. Louis because of his previous experience and an early effort he had made to sell a western radio program. The radio series was unsuccessful, but a KSD salesman remembered the series, and Gibbs's background, when it came time to cast a local television cowboy. Gibbs was born in New Mexico. He began riding horses as a youngster and speaking Spanish as a second language. After graduation from high school in New Mexico he worked as a ranch hand. Later he became an expert in the use of firearms while serving in the U.S. Marine Corps. He had the qualities of a bona fide cowboy. He could ride and shoot with the best of them. The Chicago-based "Texan" went on to become a sportscaster of some renown.

Within a year after "The Wrangler's Club" went on the air, E. C. Adams Dairy in St. Louis acquired the property and formed an agreement with Harry Gibbs that would take full advantage of his skill as horseman and cowboy. Working with the show's advertising agency, Adams Dairy promoted the program through hundreds of personal appearances by Gibbs and his horse "Trusty," visiting grocery stores, PTA benefits, scouting events, fairs, and every conceivable type of charity function. Each appearance resulted in a mob scene. Hundreds of kids and their parents would descend on a converted van prepared by the Adams company to receive a postcard-sized likeness of Gibbs. There were also a number of opportunities to see Gibbs at rodeos and watch him perform rope and gun tricks astride his mount. Such events were often complemented with the appearance of Adams's "Six Pony Hitch," frequently with Mr. Adams himself at the reins.

"The Wrangler's Club" show began as a 15-minute program airing five days a week, Monday through Friday, on Channel 5. Like many shows of its kind, it consisted of segments from Hollywood western series featuring such well-known figures as Duncan "Cisco Kid" Reynaldo. Using cartoons and "Little Rascal" film features, it evolved to a half-hour format. Eventually it was broadcast six days a week and once was expanded to 90 minutes in length.

"Little Wranglers" visited the studio and were interviewed by Gibbs. He often integrated Spanish into the show and encouraged kids to have an appreciation for the language. Asked about their likes and dislikes, they were also given an opportunity to say hello to their friends and relatives. The format led to an alleged incident in which a wrangler was supposed to have made an obscene gesture after having said, "Hi, Mom. Hi, Dad. Hi, everybody. And this is for you, Herbie!" *Post-Dispatch* columnist Elaine Viets devoted a 1983 article to this event in which Gibbs confided that the story was folklore—a city legend.

By 1963 Harry Gibbs was ready to leave the limelight of local television and pursue advertising interests. Gibbs's commitment and dedication to the show and its followers was reflected in his sign-off from the last "Wrangler's Club" broadcast, in February 1963, during which he nearly lost his composure: "We better go now…. If we don't get out of here pretty soon, the fields'll be too wet to plow." It was an emotional parting, and Gibbs confessed that he still experiences guilt when he runs into people among those on a three-year waiting list to visit the program. They never made it to the Channel 5 studios to visit St. Louis's best-known cowboy—a premier performer.

Viewer Favorite

On the entertainment side of the ledger, KSD-TV relied very heavily on an import from St. Paul, Minnesota—Russ Severin, a singer who became an entrepreneur in television production and programming. Severin developed programs especially for children and housewives, including quiz shows, amateur hours, and specials such as the "Mrs. America Show." On those occasions when performers did not appear or meet his standards, he would simply wheel out the piano and perform himself. His most successful program, a viewer favorite, was started just one year after the founding of the station—a daily afternoon program, "To the Ladies."[10] The program lasted eight years, and its studio audience consisted of over 100 housewives every week.

One particular housewife evolved from part-time contributor to host of the program and gained a tremendous level of popularity in the process. Charlotte Peters became St. Louis's premier female personality and host of the "To the Ladies" program, which not only attracted many viewers but became the base of operations for visiting national entertainers. When Russ Severin left to pursue broadcast interests in California, Peters took over as host of the program and acquired a female producer, Frankie Helms. They helped build the city's most popular locally originated early program. A technical staff of 10 supported the effort, and Peters sometimes went outside the studio and the community to broadcast the show from a statewide event, such as the state fair in rural Sedalia, Missouri. Similarly, when the circus came to town, entertainers would be invited to perform. Each production followed an agenda, though some of the promotional staff maintained the program was mostly ad-lib and 90 percent spontaneous.[11]

The host was a dynamic and talented performer who associated herself directly with sponsors' products, explaining how she employed a particular brand name in household chores while making fun of the process of keeping her own home neat and tidy. As a take-off on network actress Loretta Young, Peters would sometimes dress in a flowing gown of graceful, elegant fashion; then one of her sidekicks would run onstage and hit her in the face with a pie in true slapstick tradition. As the show progressed in stature, Peters often went out of her way to poke fun at her own lack of interest in household chores, taking advantage of the growing sophistication of her audience. A key ingredient in the success of the show was the extent to which it tapped into local women's organizations. The show frequently focused on an issue

10. "Anything Goes ... on Charlotte Peter's Show," *TV Guide,* April 28–May 4, 1956, p. A37. Glen Goellner, "Charlotte Peters Discloses Her Secret of Success," *St. Louis Review,* January 20, 1961, p. 1.

11. Robert E. Hannon, "Putting Together the Charlotte Peters Show...," *Pictures Magazine, St. Louis Post-Dispatch,* January 28, 1962, pp. 2–5.

related to the activity of a particular visiting group among the 100 participants welcomed as the weekly studio audience.

As a means of providing contrast to her mostly female audience, she
would sometimes invite members of male-dominated professions, such as
local policemen and firemen, to discuss their work. This was often accompanied by her direct involvement in activities such as scaling a hook-and-
ladder truck in fire fighter's gear. On one occasion, when a multistory
building adjacent to the studios caught fire, she left her studio audience and
reported on the event herself, interviewing firemen and observers on the
scene. As a result, the program frequently made news in St. Louis and
sometimes garnered national attention.

Studio guests were showered with sponsors' gifts, usually consisting
of bags of groceries, canned goods, cosmetics, or cleaning products. A
particular product would become the host's theme endorsement for the
program. Peters invited her audience to participate in singing contests and in
games, which would always result in special prizes for anyone willing to take
a chance on the vagaries of this new medium.

The entertainment segment of the program was followed by a short
news update and an audience-participation segment in which Peters would
honor a "Birthday Child" and ask quiz questions about the city's history. She
took great pride in promoting city-sponsored events. The station once
reported receiving 40,000 responses to a contest Peters introduced in the late
1950s, and she later wrote in *McCall's* magazine about her pride in her
hometown.[12] Members of her staff became well-known local figures for
years to come. A singer featured on the program, Marty Bronson, became a
much-sought-after local entertainer.

The program's news segment was covered by John Roedel, who
remained a reporter at the station until the 1990s. Two of Peters's on-air
assistants, George Abel and Stan Kann, also remained active on the local
entertainment scene for many years. Abel hosted a popular children's program, and Stan Kann performed regularly at the keyboard in St. Louis's
premier theater, the Fox. On one occasion he mounted a casket on top of his
theater organ on Halloween, and as the music started, Charlotte Peters
emerged from below the casket to the howls of the audience. Stan Kann later
became a regular visitor of NBC's "Tonight Show" with Johnny Carson. As
one might expect, the Peters program welcomed many network performers

---

12. Charlotte Peters, "This Is My St. Louis," *McCall's,* May 1964. See also, "Charlotte's World,"
Key Magazine, March 16–31, 1954, pp. 34–35.

as well. Comedian Jonathan Winters said it was the "fastest moving" program he had ever seen.[13]

Peters set the standard for women in broadcasting in Missouri. When she left KSD-TV to join a competing station, KTVI-TV, the move made the front page of both newspapers in St. Louis. Because she had been embroiled in a dispute with the station's management, her decision set a new tone for women broadcasters and demonstrated a level of confidence and independence rarely seen in 1964. Other local women who made inroads early in St. Louis television included Eleanor Donahue Werner, a producer/director; Dottye Bennet, a singer who had her own program; and Lee Shepard in news. Much later Dianne White, the first female African-American broadcaster in town, and weatherperson Mary Frances Luecke—subsequently known as Mary Frann on the network's "Newhart" program—made additional significant inroads in the largely male-dominated culture of television news.

Teen Scene

Mary Frann was initially employed to read commercials during a teenage program, "St. Louis Hop," which, at least for a time, surpassed the Peters program in viewership. Saturday-morning studio audiences of as many as 500 13- and 14-year-olds attended the production in the ballrooms of local hotels, skating rinks, and arenas.

Initiated by the station's music director, Russ David, the teenage music program began with a popular local disc jockey, Ed Wilson, at the helm. He was quickly replaced by a youthful associate producer, Russ Carter, who sang with a local orchestra to supplement his work with the station. At one point, with the advent of videotape, three one-hour programs were being taped on Saturdays before three separate audiences—usually of a hundred or more. This strategy eventually allowed the production schedule to accommodate a taping every other week, with some junior high schools designated for special-audience occasions. During that era guest performers were invited to each of the three program tapings. The success of the program was aided by the fact that by the 1960s rock-and-roll acts were proliferating to take advantage of the baby-boom market. The introduction of videotape

---

13. Harry Honig, personal interview, April 2, 1986.

allowed teens to attend a program, then tune into the station to observe the event with friends.[14]

Newsbeat

By October 1955 the station was ready to attempt a network feed for "Wide, Wide World," a live news program, from the confluence of the Missouri and Mississippi rivers. Earlier broadcasts of police-board hearings had created a sense of expectation that more and more live opportunities would be presented. Other live news telecasts the station had been credited with included a number of major stories, one involving the kidnapping and murder of a six-year-old child, covered by both Kansas City and St. Louis stations as well as by the NBC network. The case had everything, including very wealthy parents, a $600,000 ransom, and the death of the boy, which sadly contributed to the story's sensationalism, but was further indication that St. Louis television news could cover an important story well.

KSD-TV also provided the network with another story of national import in 1953, the looting of a major financial institution, Southwest Bank, surrounded by 100 city police officers, and the resulting shoot-out, which was later depicted in a Hollywood motion picture, *The Great Bank Robbery*.[15] Reports on riots in Missouri prisons in the middle '50s and live coverage of natural disasters such as floods and tornadoes toward the end of that decade gave further credibility to the station's news operation. On one occasion in 1959 the community was designated a disaster area by Dwight Eisenhower, and field crews from the station reported how 21 people had died and 300 had been injured by the twister. The station also engaged in relief-fund efforts with the American Red Cross. Clearly, KSD-TV was establishing that it could be more than a headline service, with its capacity to take viewers to the scene of events even if time and technology worked against it.

During this period the newsroom expanded and evolved. The value of writing and reporting became central. News personnel were removed from the responsibilities of reading commercials, and the "anchor" concept began

---

14. Russ David, personal interview, March 4, 1986.
15. Dickson Terry, "Even Strangers Believe They Know Him," *St. Louis Post-Dispatch,* October 3, 1953, p. 1G.

to catch on. To take advantage of its position, which it holds to this day, as market leader, the station frequently welcomed NBC-network reporters to town. For example, United Nations correspondent Pauline Frederick was invited to give speeches more than once, and in the middle '60s she received an award for Outstanding Working Woman in the Nation at a conference in St. Louis at the Statler-Hilton Hotel. At least a decade before broadcast-news opportunities really opened up for women, Frederick was also honored for her work with a Distinguished Service Award from the University of Missouri School of Journalism.

As a result of its efforts, by the 1960s the station was honored many times with awards and recognition, including a National Emmy Award for a documentary entitled "Operation Challenge," which targeted an under-privileged black community. That program was produced by the coordinator of the documentary unit, the first female member of station management, Mary Spencer. She instigated additional efforts to address community problems. Spencer also produced "No Room at the Bottom," a careful look at vocational education, which included an interview with then labor secretary Willard Wirtz, and "Performing Arts in Missouri," which was honored by the state commission on art.

The Pulitzer tradition of arts coverage carried over to KSD-TV as well as emphasis on breaking news and the big events of the day. The new lightweight remote equipment introduced during this era helped the cause considerably. In October 1965 when the Gateway Arch was topped off and, three years later, when it was dedicated by the National Park Service, the station included interviews with Hubert Humphrey, then vice president of the United States. When the city hosted national sporting events, such as the U.S. Professional Hardcourt Tennis exhibitions and Cardinal baseball championships, the station responded with full coverage and even produced a documentary entitled "3623 Dodier," the location of the old baseball park, when the town's premier sports team relocated to downtown and Busch Stadium.

During this period the station hired its first minority reporter, Julius Hunter, who currently anchors the evening news for competing St. Louis station, KMOV-TV, a CBS affiliate. Many changes have occurred in the interim. By the time Pulitzer Broadcasting sold the station to Multimedia to make it KSDK-TV, the anchor team of Dick Ford and Karen Foss was established as a local institution and a ratings phenomenon. Market dominance continued even after Ford left to join the local ABC affiliate, KTVI, a station that only recently—as of August 1995—changed affiliation to Fox due to the new network purchase, while KSDK and Multimedia courted takeover overtures from Gannett. Not surprisingly, KSDK continues to dominate the St. Louis television-news market as the NBC network's highest-rated local affiliate. Old viewing habits die hard.[16]

16. See, for example, Pete Rahn, "KSDK Sweeps the May Ratings," *St. Louis Globe-Democrat,* June 27, 1986, p. 10C, and "NBC Is Leading in Emmy Race," *St. Louis Post-Dispatch,* August 1, 1986, p. 2A.

13 News in the Heartland: WBBM-TV, Chicago

Marjorie Fox

WBBM-TV, Channel 2, is the CBS-owned-and-operated station in the nation's second- and more recently third-largest market, Chicago. Both WBBM and the ABC-owned WLS claim a parental tie to Chicago's first commercial television station, WBKB. The organization that became WBKB was one of several operations in Chicago that experimented with television from 1928 through World War II. Owned by the Balaban and Katz Theatre Corporation, it began transmitting test signals in 1939. In 1940 the Federal Communications Commission gave the organization an experimental license. So far as the station knew, only 12 receivers existed in the Chicago area at that time, and engineers would contact the owners frequently to assess the quality of reception.[1]

Later there were an estimated 200 to 300 television receivers in Chicago, and the experimental station, W9XBK, was broadcasting twice a day, mostly test patterns and films. In 1944 the FCC "granted the station a construction permit for commercial operation with a change in call letters to WBKB. By 1944 WBKB was producing 25 hours of programming a month."[2] Around this time WBKB began using "on-camera news performers." One of the experiments involved two announcers in shirtsleeves in a noisy newsroom setting, which would be the look WBBM would adopt 30 years later, to great success. The format was explained by general manager

---

1. Theodore Lynn Nielsen, "A History of Chicago Television News Presentation (1948–1968)." Ph.D. diss., University of Wisconsin, 1971, p. 56.
2. Nielsen, pp. 58–60.

William Eddy: "The double feature allows one anchor to consider his lines as well as the picture. While his colleague is talking, there is an opportunity for him to develop well thought out questions and answers to sustain the interest of the audience."[3]

The promotion manager at WBKB in those days was Sterling "Red" Quinlan. He remembered the general manager as "a renaissance man" who was "the real father of television in Chicago."[4] Quinlan himself would go on to have an important career in television; he would head WBKB/WLS in the early 1960s and write a book on network television, *Inside ABC.*

Programming on WBKB consisted largely of daytime women's shows, amateur-talent showcases, and sports. In 1946 the station broadcast the first baseball games from Wrigley Field. WBKB was initially an ABC affiliate but in 1949 became the carrier of the CBS network in Chicago, which heretofore had been carried on WGN-TV. However, WBKB aired few CBS programs, and the network was seeking an opportunity to buy a station in Chicago. The other networks were ahead of CBS in Chicago. ABC-owned WENR went on the air in September 1948; NBC's owned-and-operated station, WNBQ, began operating in January 1949.[5]

One of WBBM's dominant television personalities emerged on WBKB's early women's programming. Lee Phillip was going to college and working in her father's flower shop when she made her first television appearance in the early 1950s. She arranged flowers in a florist-sponsored segment, and Red Quinlan quickly offered her a regular job. Phillip's television roles ran the gamut—from weather, to a children's show, to anchoring news, to traditional homemaker shows. At one point Phillip did five shows a day, seven days a week. During the polio epidemic of 1956 Phillip was lauded for her efforts to promote the polio vaccine for children. In 1972 she won a top honor in journalism, the Du Pont Award, for a documentary, "The Rape of Paulette."[6]

The amateur program was a staple on at least three Chicago television stations in the early days. Red Quinlan recalled a quartet that came in to audition for the live programming. "I put them on at night before wrestling.

---

3. Nielsen, p. 44.
4. *Legends of Chicago Television,* videocassette #TV-02748, production of the Chicago Television Academy and Chicago Museum of Broadcast Communications, 1991.
5. Nielsen, pp. 59–69.
6. *Lee Phillip: Salute to Lee,* videocassette #TV-0025.1, production of WBBM-TV, circa 1985, Chicago Museum of Broadcast Communications, 15 min.

Got a call from the Chicago police—'keep those guys on. The one on the left is wanted for burglary.'"[7]

Amid the talent shows and the sports there was a bit of news programming on WBKB in the earliest days. The schedule for news, however, was rather erratic. "Today's World Picture," for example, was aired at different times Mondays, Tuesdays, and Thursdays. After 1950 WBKB started carrying the CBS News at 6:30, preceded by a 15-minute local newscast. The station was the first in Chicago to have regular news programming.[8]

In 1951 WBKB's parent company, United Artists–Paramount Theatres, merged with ABC. This resulted in the merger of WBKB with the ABC-owned station WENR-TV, whose broadcast assignment was Channel 7. The ABC station continued to use the WBKB call letters until 1968. CBS got permission to buy a Chicago station, the former WBKB (Channel 4), and was given permission to switch to Channel 2. Channel 2's call letters became WBBM-TV to match the CBS radio station.[9] So by the mid-1950s Chicago had three network-owned-and-operated stations and a strong independent, WGN-TV.

A Fast Start in News

In 1953 the new WBBM-TV, under the leadership of General Manager H. Leslie Atlass, established a competitive news organization, airing two 15-minute newscasts each day. Through most of the decade the early-evening news aired at 6:15 p.m. with the CBS news following. WBBM's late-night news effort started with two separate programs. At 10 p.m. WBBM aired the "Standard Oil News Roundup," which was followed by a 15-minute variety program. And then at 10:30 p.m., the "John Harrington News," a feature-oriented program, aired. The two late newscasts merged in 1959, though late-night news programming did not extend to 30 minutes until the mid-1960s.[10]

The leading newscaster in Chicago in the '50s, was WBBM's Fahey Flynn. Flynn's radio career started in 1934 in Fondulac, Wisconsin. He moved on to Madison, then Milwaukee, where he did baseball broadcasts.

---

7. See *Legends of Chicago Television,* videocassette.
8. Nielsen, p. 90.
9. Nielsen, pp. 76–77.
10. Nielsen, pp. 91–104.

In 1941 Flynn won an audition for a job at WBBM radio. He served in the Navy during the war, then returned to WBBM, where his radio news career included a Peabody Award for documentary.[11] When WBBM television started, management brought Flynn on board. His television debut was March 3, 1953. Flynn's popularity grew, and his 10 p.m. news became the top-rated program in Chicago. Flynn's opening line remained consistent through the years: "How do you do, ladies and gentlemen? I'm Fahey Flynn, and here's what's happening." And through most of Flynn's long career, his attire remained distinctive—he wore a bow tie.

In the late 1950s Flynn had a three-to-two edge over his competitors in viewership. His 10 o'clock news was dominant until 1965. As one report said: "Facing Flynn five nights a week is likely to leave rival program men with spots before the eyes and a lingering debility in the night time ratings."[12] Flynn, at WBBM and more so in his later career at WLS, is linked with aspects of "showbiz" journalism. WBBM general manager Les Atlass is credited with embracing that approach with the decision to bring weather forecaster P. J. Hoff onto the news set to interact with Flynn. Dick Goldberg, a producer at WBBM, recalled early on-camera exchanges between Flynn and Hoff. Flynn would ask P. J. about the weather outlook; Hoff would give a short response. Because Flynn and Hoff were warm personalities, people responded favorably. WBBM then added John Drury to create Chicago's first dual-anchor team. "It became more important for the guys to relate to one another," producer Dick Goldberg remembered. It didn't work, because Flynn, according to Goldberg, was reluctant to share the spotlight with a second anchor.[13]

The news director during WBBM-TV's first 10 years was William Garry. With a comparatively large staff, Garry's news department was able to come through on the important stories. A tragic event in 1958 gave WBBM the opportunity to show its dominance over its competition in Chicago. Ninety-five people, mostly children, were killed in a fire at Our Lady of the Angels School. Producer John Gibbs remembered the coverage: "I think we had three or four crews and they were all on the story with Frank Reynolds

---

11. *Fahey Flynn: May the Wind Be at Your Back,* videocassette #TV-0009, production of WLS-TV, 11 Aug. 1983, Chicago Museum of Broadcast Communications, 30 min.

12. Nielsen, p. 325. From *Chicago Tribune,* 7 Aug. 1962.

13. Ralph Whitehead, Jr., "There's No Biz Like News Biz," *Chicagoan,* March 1974, p. 63.

and Hugh Hill, and we really scooped the town on that big fire because we had the horses to go."[14]

Gibbs was one of the first newswriters hired by WBBM in the early 1950s. He started as vacation-relief newswriter at WMAQ but soon made the switch. Most of the other WBBM writers were radio veterans, and Gibbs said some of them had trouble writing for film. He said Fahey Flynn was concerned about the tendency by some writers to use film that didn't work well with the copy. Gibbs also recalled how difficult it was to get film from out of town for the news programs—a story from Washington had to occur in the morning to have any chance at all of getting film processed and shipped to Chicago in time to make the late news.

In the '50s, the news operations used four- or five-man film crews to carry and operate the cumbersome 35-millimeter equipment. In the '60s, when the switch was made to the more portable 16-millimeter cameras, three-man crews, comprising the cameraman, the soundman, and the light man, were still the norm in Chicago. Cover footage was generally shot with handheld silent-film cameras. The sound-on-film cameras had to be mounted on a tripod. WBBM employed two sound-effects people to add background sound to news stories shot with silent film.

Gibbs said the practice of using sound effects stopped in the early 1960s. Supporters of both candidates in the 1960 presidential race were watching television news closely and would call to complain that there wasn't enough applause in the background for their candidate, or that there was too much applause for their opponent. WBBM then started using sound cameras to shoot crowd actuality.

By the late 1950s the drawing power of news was apparent in Chicago, and the Standard Oil Company paid $10,000 each week as sponsor of the WBBM-TV late news. At the same time WBBM's success showed that a station needs to spend money in order to make money. WBBM had larger staff and, in Fahey Flynn, an anchor with great viewer appeal.

---

14. John Gibbs, oral-history interview conducted by Bob Conway, audiocassette #OH-003, Chicago Museum of Broadcast Communications, 29 Jan. 1987.

Tough Competition

The 1960s saw the expansion of news programming, the emergence of new talent in Chicago (some of whom would have stellar careers stretching into the 1990s), and WBBM's decline as the dominant news force in Chicago television. The end of the decade featured rumblings of change in news formats as the traditional anchorman was supplanted by friendlier news teams. And one can't discuss '60s television in Chicago without attention to the 1968 Democratic Convention and the presidential debate at the start of the decade.

The 1960 presidential campaign put the WBBM studio in the national spotlight—and in the history books. It was there, on the evening of September 26, 1960, that the first televised debate between John F. Kennedy and Richard Nixon took place. As every student of campaign history knows, Kennedy won the televised debate that night, though most who heard it on radio gave the edge to Vice President Nixon. Kennedy was well rested and well prepared when he arrived at WBBM. Nixon came to Chicago late in the evening before the debate, exhausted and ill. He ignored advice to arrive in Chicago early and to rest. On the day of the debate, campaign chronicler Theodore H. White said Nixon was "incommunicado" with staffers who wanted to prepare him for the debate. The vice president had spent most of the day alone in his hotel, except for one ill-considered appearance before a hostile union audience. Then, upon arrival at WBBM, Nixon winced as he struck his already-injured knee on a car door.

Nixon arrived at the studio about an hour before airtime. His light suit blended into the studio backdrop. A camera test showed that Nixon looked pale; but he declined the WBBM makeup artist's offer of assistance and, instead, had an aide apply a light coat of pancake makeup. Kennedy was naturally tanned and wore a dark suit that contrasted nicely with the light background. However, in his predebate studio check technicians and aides noticed that his white shirt glared under the lights. An aide had time to return to Kennedy's hotel and get a blue shirt for him.[15]

White described chaos in the studio due to a horde of still photographers permitted on the set. The technical director for WBBM the night of the debate, Roger Santschi, said later that the descriptions of confusion and chaos

---

15. Theodore H. White, *The Making of the President 1960,* paperback ed. (New York: Atheneum, 1967), pp. 321–329.

are exaggerated. Santschi said campaign aides were not crowding and yelling at the director, Don Hewitt, who went on to become the executive producer of "60 Minutes." Santschi did agree with other accounts that say CBS board chairman William Paley and news president Dr. Frank Stanton were in and out of the control room before and during the debate.[16]

Though the debate put WBBM in the history books, and its news ratings continued strong through 1965, the '60s overall were troubled years for the station.

By 1963 poor health forced the popular Bill Garry to resign as news director, and station manager Clark George appointed John Madigan as his successor. Madigan had been city editor for the Chicago *American*. Critics attacked Madigan's personality and his desire to run his television news shop like a newspaper. Supporters praised his background as a Chicago newsman and his vast network of sources.[17]

Among those who couldn't stomach Madigan was WBBM anchor and star reporter Frank Reynolds. Reynolds later became an anchor for ABC, but his new boss in Chicago didn't seem to like anything about him. Reynolds heretofore was able to do pretty much what he wanted at WBBM. But Madigan waded into Reynolds on several fronts, including his feeling that Reynolds concentrated too heavily on racial news. Reynolds responded heatedly: "I kept hearing that the man on the street was sick of the integration story. My answer to that was 'so what'."[18]

Most agreed that Reynolds had made WBBM's 6 o'clock news a high-caliber local-news program. Madigan changed the format, which was covering a few stories in depth, to a broader approach, without the "editorializing" he saw in Reynolds's work. Critics believed this approach was not likely to improve WBBM's position in the audience-ratings race, in which WMAQ-TV was making gains.

Reynolds wanted out. CBS offered him a correspondent's position in Washington, but he instead accepted a lucrative two-year contract with WBKB in Chicago, which was, for the first time, starting to build a competitive news operation. (In 1968 WBKB changed its call letters to WLS.) Several other key WBBM employees left in the early '60s. Hugh Hill, one of WBBM's important reporters for 10 years, also clashed with Madigan and

16. *Lee Phillip Show: 25th Anniversary of Kennedy-Nixon Debate,* videocassette #TV-0025.1, production of WBBM-TV, 1985, Chicago Museum of Broadcast Communications, 30 min.

17. John D. Calloway, "Chicago's TV News: Testing," *Chicago Scene,* vol. 5, no. 2, 1964, pp. 15–16.

18. Calloway, p.16.

went to WBKB/WLS. Upon Hill's resignation WBBM's business manager gave him only a few minutes to clean his desk and escorted him out the door. Within a year of Madigan's appointment as news director, however, the dust settled and morale improved. Among his hires were several people from the Chicago *American,* including 26-year-old Walter Jacobson. Jacobson, a Chicago native, had worked for UPI before joining the *American.* Madigan hired Jacobson as a newswriter in 1963. He went on to become one of Chicago TV's most successful journalists.[19]

In 1963 and 1964 WBBM and WMAQ expanded the 6 o'clock program from 15 to 30 minutes. Further expansion of the early-evening news occurred in 1965 when WMAQ began programming an hour of news starting at 5 p.m. By the end of 1968 WLS was running an hour-long news program at 5 p.m. That year also saw the emergence of station promotions and demographic information in ratings books. WLS boasted that its early-evening news was watched by more young women than was WBBM's.[20]

The late-news block, 10 p.m. in Chicago and the rest of the Central Time Zone, was expanded and became a competitive arena in the 1960s. Independent station WGN was the first to expand its 10 o'clock news to 30 minutes and for about a year challenged WMAQ for the number-two spot. But WGN's ratings success was short-lived, and its 10 o'clock news was dropped. But the "horserace" atmosphere in the 10 p.m. ratings race started at this time, though the 30-minute late-news blocks did not begin until 1965 for WMAQ and 1968 for WLS and WBBM.[21]

Upon the resignation of Frank Reynolds, Fahey Flynn, who for years had dominated the 10 p.m. news ratings, took over WBBM's 6 p.m. news as well. His 10 o'clock news was still far ahead in the ratings; but WMAQ, with an impressive new anchorman named Floyd Kalber, now had the edge at 6 o'clock.

WMAQ, the NBC-owned station, eventually supplanted WBBM as the dominant news station in Chicago. Station manager Bob Lemon hired Bill Corley as news director and expanded the station's staff and equipment. In 1960 Lemon brought Kalber to Chicago from Omaha, Nebraska. Within a couple of years WMAQ had a versatile and loyal team of proven news broadcasters.

19. Calloway, pp. 20–22.
20. Nielsen, p. 334.
21. Nielsen, pp. 101–105, 327–330.

Kalber's audience grew steadily through the '60s. By 1967 WMAQ had succeeded in the task of winning the news race; Floyd Kalber had 63 percent of the audience.[22] In the mid-1960s, as WMAQ was gaining on them, WBBM bosses started worrying about Fahey Flynn. He had long worn a bow tie. In 1966 management "ruled bow ties 'old', therefore out. Flynn started wearing a four-in-hand."[23] By 1968, with Kalber clearly on top, Flynn went to WBKB, which was now known as WLS.

WBKB/WLS had not made a serious news effort in Chicago until 1963. But it was the 1968 pairing of Fahey Flynn with Joel Daly, new to Chicago from Cleveland, that would eventually give WLS the ratings lead in Chicago. WLS allowed Flynn to put the bow tie back on.

Television in Chicago was thrust again into the national spotlight in August 1968 when the Democratic party held its national convention in Chicago. The party was fractured over the anti-war candidacy of Senator Eugene McCarthy, the decision by President Johnson not to seek re-election, the emergence of Vice President Hubert Humphrey as the candidate of party regulars, and the ill-fated candidacy of Senator Robert Kennedy—all of this on top of disturbances in many American cities, including Chicago, in the wake of the assassination of Dr. Martin Luther King. Tens of thousands of protestors had announced plans to come to Chicago for the convention.

The intention of some of the protestors to cause trouble was widely reported. Until the summer of 1968 the Chicago media and the Chicago police had relatively little trouble. In the wake of riots in the Watts area of Los Angeles in 1965, and in Detroit and Newark in 1967, a great deal of attention was paid to how the media, television specifically, should cover civil disorder. Task forces repeatedly called for responsibility by the media and cooperation from the police. The need to assist the media was made policy by the Chicago Police Department. And the need to behave responsibly and cooperate with police was made policy by many news organizations, including CBS.

But as the convention approached, relations between the media and the police became strained in disputes over convention-coverage credentials. Also, a strike by electrical workers against the telephone company delayed the installation of equipment for live broadcast of the convention. A moratorium on the dispute was called a month before the convention, allowing

---

22. *Chicago Daily News Panorama,* 21 Mar. 1970, Chicago Historical Society, clipping file: Chicago, Television, Newscasting.

23. Joanna Steinmetz, *Chicago Today,* 11 Nov. 1969, Chicago Historical Society, clipping file: Chicago, Television, Newsmen.

installation of broadcast equipment at the International Amphitheatre. But live coverage from the hotels was impossible. Labor troubles also hit WBBM in early August when the film editors went on strike. Union workers at the other stations supported the action, so film as well as live coverage was threatened. The strike was settled before the convention, but this, along with an overloaded telephone system in downtown hotels and a taxi drivers' strike, compounded the tension.[24]

By the weekend before the convention, more than 2,000 demonstrators had arrived in Chicago, most of them gathering in Lincoln Park on the city's north side. At the same time, more than 6,000 news personnel were in Chicago, 4,000 of them from out of town. Monday, August 26, is described in the official record, the Walker Report, as one of the most hazardous for newsmen. That afternoon a TV reporter was warned by two police detectives to be careful, "the word is out to get newsmen." That night at least 20 journalists covering demonstrators on the north side were hurt in confrontations with police.[25]

The night the world remembers from the Chicago convention was Wednesday night, August 28, when police and demonstrators clashed in front of the Conrad Hilton Hotel. The networks showed 30 to 40 minutes of film of the clash on Michigan Avenue. At least one network juxtaposed the film of the disturbance with live shots of Mayor Daley laughing and smiling on the convention floor. CBS commentator Eric Severeid called that night "the most disgraceful night in the history of American political conventions."[26]

The next morning Daley blamed the news media, especially television, for the disorders, arguing that they gave the demonstrators too much preconvention coverage. Thursday night on CBS, Daley complained that television did not show the provocation by demonstrators nor discuss the number of policemen who were injured. And Daley charged that many reporters were part of the protest movement, claiming "some of them are revolutionaries and they want these things to happen."[27]

Though many of the antipolice comments that provoked Daley came from network sources, the fallout from the convention left its mark in

24. Walker Report to the National Commission on the Causes and Prevention of Violence, *Rights in Conflict: The Violent Confrontation of Demonstrators and Police in the Parks and Streets of Chicago During the Week of the Democratic National Convention* (New York: Bantam, 1968), pp. 85, 86.

25. Walker Report, pp. 301, 312.

26. Dean Gysel, "TV Showed Chicago Like It Is." *Chicago Daily News,* 30 Aug. 1968, p. 37.

27. Walker Report, p. 330.

relations between city officials, police, and the Chicago media. Mayor Daley was scorned by several local reporters and commentators for the rest of his life. Years later Frank Sullivan, press officer for the Chicago police in 1968, recalled that WMAQ-TV had "a three year vendetta with the Chicago police as a result of the convention." He characterized a 1971 WMAQ report about declining crime rates as historic: "That was the first night in a thousand nights Floyd Kalber had not sneered at the camera when he mentioned Daley or the Chicago police."[28]

The late '60s also saw "staging" controversies in Chicago television news. Charges were leveled in connection with the coverage of the convention protestors. An assistant U.S. attorney told the Walker Commission that he had witnessed a film crew focusing on two men in white coats kneeling over a young man who was lying on the ground. The witness said the young man and the medics walked away after the film crew left, and the young man did not appear to be injured. Senator Gale McGee of Wyoming reported seeing a TV crew lead two young demonstrators to a spot near National Guard troops. "When the cameras started to roll one of the girls cried, 'Don't beat me! Don't beat me!'"[29]

Even before the convention, controversy over staging news footage was on the minds of many in Chicago news, because WBBM was under investigation by the FCC for staging a "pot party" at Northwestern University. Reporter Jack Missett said he had been invited to film the students as they smoked marijuana. But critics charged that WBBM bought the "pot" and arranged the party. The documentary, "Pot Party at a University," was aired in two parts in November 1967. CBS conducted its own investigation of the charges and found that WBBM staffers had not staged the party. But in January 1969 FCC examiner James D. Cunningham ruled that the party had been "pre-arranged for the benefit of CBS, and that this particular party would never have taken place but for Missett's request." CBS urged that the inquiry be dropped and said 25 pot parties had taken place in the student apartment in the previous year and WBBM didn't arrange anything that would not have happened without the news crew. "It's impossible, given the nature of the medium, to conduct interviews without some prior arrangement between the broadcaster and the interviewee," CBS argued.[30]

---

28. *MBC Seminar: 20 Years Later, the '68 Democratic Convention,* videocassette #TV-02334, production of the Chicago Museum Broadcast Communications, 1988.

29. Walker Report, p. 303.

30. *New York Times,* 19 Feb. 1969, p. 95.

A few months later the House Commerce Committee found that WBBM had "contrived and staged the filming of 'Pot Party' so as to enhance its news ratings for the time periods involved and thereby increase its advertising revenues."[31] The FCC later upheld the examiner's finding that the party was staged but placed the blame on the shoulders of an assistant assignment editor and "absolved WBBM and CBS of major responsibility." In response CBS set up guidelines to involve top management in the supervision of investigative projects.[32]

Hard News versus Happy Talk

In the '70s, all three network-owned stations had their years on top of the news ratings. WBBM's recapture of the news-leadership position didn't happen until the end of the decade. The 1970s opened with WMAQ-TV's Floyd Kalber firmly entrenched at the top of the ratings in Chicago. As the '70s unfolded, however, Kalber was losing younger viewers to the pair WLS had teamed in 1968, Fahey Flynn and Joel Daly, and by 1972 WLS reached the top of the ratings. The WLS formula, which news consultant Frank Magid brought to the ABC-owned-and-operated stations, stressed a friendly news team, a high story count, slick packaging, and an entertaining approach that came to be known as "happy talk."

In Chicago and elsewhere viewers liked the change from the harder "gloom and doom" style, personified in Chicago by Floyd Kalber. Flynn and Daly, joined by weatherman John Coleman and sportscaster Bill Frink, were heavily promoted in amusing spots that showed the team having a great time together. Years later Joel Daly, rejecting the "happy talk" label, remembered that critics would "confuse what we did in the commercials with what we attempted to do on the air."[33]

WBBM, meanwhile, was far behind in the ratings, sometimes finishing fourth behind independent WGN. The team and approach that would take WBBM to the top of the ratings by the end of the decade was put together by general manager Bob Wussler in 1973. His choice for news director was

---

31. Associated Press, "House Commerce Panel Finds 'Pot Party' on TV Was Staged," *New York Times,* 14 Mar. 1969, p. 83.
32. Fred Ferretti, "CBS Memo Sets TV Reporting Rules," *New York Times,* 31 Oct. 1969, p. 89.
33. *Fahey Flynn,* videocassette.

Van Gordon Sauter, a CBS-radio executive who had worked as a reporter for the *Chicago Daily News* some years before.[34]

Wussler's anchor team would be Bill Kurtis and Walter Jacobson. Kurtis was a young CBS correspondent based on the West Coast. A midwesterner with a law degree from Kansas, Kurtis had been lured to Chicago to anchor for WBBM once before, during the station's difficult period in the late 1960s. Kurtis, then only 27 years old, replaced Fahey Flynn, who had been jettisoned because he seemed too old. Kurtis didn't do well in the ratings in the late '60s, so it took some talking and a lucrative contract to get him to come back to Chicago in 1973. "I really didn't want to come back," Kurtis said. "I was very happy as a network correspondent. I figured that returning to local television was a step backward. But CBS really gave me the hot-box treatment. They twisted my arm to come back here and in the end I felt that I really had no choice in the matter."[35]

The other anchor for WBBM would be 35-year-old Walter Jacobson, a political reporter and commentator for WMAQ. Wussler said he had watched many hours of Chicago television since he had taken over WBBM and "the only time the screen came alive was when Jacobson gave that commentary."[36] (Jacobson got his television news start at WBBM in the '60s. He had gone to WMAQ a few years later as a reporter and commentator.) Chicago's television observers perceived the pairing of Kurtis and Jacobson as a good move. One described the team as "the good cop–bad cop combination of solid citizen Bill Kurtis and upstart-pest Walter Jacobson." Kurtis called Jacobson "the perfect partner for me."[37] And Wussler believed that creating the team of Bill and Walter was the best of his strategic moves in building Channel 2 news.[38]

The team was heavily promoted, with the slogan "It's not pretty but it's real," when it went on the air in March 1973. But the anchors weren't the whole story. Several strong producers and reporters were hired, including Mike Wallace's son Chris. Channel 2's new set was in its newsroom, which helped sell the idea that Bill and Walter were "working reporters." And CBS bought Chicago's first minicams for the launching of the new Channel 2

34. Peter J. Boyer, *Who Killed CBS? The Undoing of America's Number One News Network,* paperback ed. (New York: St. Martin's, 1989), p. 73.
35. Gary Deeb, "Bill Kurtis: Everybody's Friend Moves on to New York and the Challenge of Befriending a Nation," *Chicago Sun-Times,* 28 Feb. 1982, Show sec., p. 8.
36. Scott Jacobs, "The Channel Two Chronicles," *Chicago,* Sept. 1978, p. 186.
37. Deeb, p. 9.
38. Jacobs, p. 187.

news. Kurtis said the team was anxious to take on WLS: "From the very beginning [we] were determined to crush the 'happy talk' newscast which was then so popular. We saw this lightweight approach to news as something that was diminishing the status of TV news."[39] Kurtis also claimed that WLS was using advertising people for story advice. He may not have known it, but news director Sauter was also turning to an advertising agency for help.[40]

Despite the journalistic and self-promotional skills of the Channel 2 team, it took two years for WBBM to make significant gains in the market and six years to pull ahead of WLS. There was plenty of hard work by the troops at WBBM, but they also had the advantage of facing a floundering competitor in the contest for the number-two spot. WMAQ went through a string of anchors to complement and then replace the once all-powerful Floyd Kalber. Kurtis said "We got lucky" when Channel 5 hired young Jane Pauley as Kalber's coanchor in 1975. "For some reason, they positioned her as the dominant anchor, and so every night she seemed to be upstaging the guy who had been kingpin anchorman in this town for more than ten years."[41]

By mid-1974 Wussler had become head of CBS Sports, and Sauter decided to put himself on the air in Chicago as an anchor on Channel 2's 5 o'clock report. It was not successful, and the new Channel 2 boss, Neil Derrough, took Sauter off the air.

It was under general manager Derrough and his news director Jay Feldman that WBBM rose steadily in the ratings. Scott Jacobs, writing in *Chicago* magazine, said they encouraged competitiveness and creative tension in a Harvard Business School approach to the newsroom: "They viewed its internal workings as a series of component parts that manufactured a product."[42]

Among the strengths at WBBM in the late '70s was a "Focus Unit," which produced in-depth reports on significant stories for the late-evening program, now promoted as "THE 10 o'clock News." Kurtis also had produced several excellent prime-time documentaries, including a "one-hour bombshell" called "Watching the Watchdog," which criticized the investigative techniques of ABC's "20-20." Channel 2 could also be counted on for pulling out all the stops in its coverage of the big local stories of the late '70s, such as the death of Mayor Daley, the crash of a DC-10 just after takeoff from O'Hare Airport, the mass murders by John Wayne Gacy, and the visit

---

39. Deeb, p. 9.
40. Boyer, pp. 78–79.
41. Deeb, p. 9.
42. Jacobs, p. 188.

of the newly chosen pope to heavily Catholic Chicago. "[The] unending string of top stories by Kurtis, the often tough nightly commentaries by partner Jacobson and the popularity of both men—coupled with the usually accurate image of Channel 2 as the place to go for news … culminated in the topping of Channel 7 in early 1979."[43]

But those years were not without their turmoil. In 1978 Kurtis and his team were outraged when Derrough hired Mort Crim from Philadelphia as a backup anchor. The move apparently was made as insurance in case Kurtis, whose contract was coming up for renewal, bolted. Kurtis was offered the anchor job at WMAQ, and a contract that included network exposure on NBC. He was ready to move. But CBS counteroffered with a deal involving comparable network exposure and, according to Kurtis, hints that he would be in line to succeed Walter Cronkite.[44] So Kurtis stayed at CBS, and their ratings climb continued. By 1979 the station's top spot in the ratings was undisputed.

Ambition and Libel

Despite the fact that WBBM's news dominance continued through the mid-1980s, the decade, all told, had more downs than ups. Bill Kurtis won top awards for his reporting and, with Walter Jacobson, achieved the goal of "killing happy talk." So no one was surprised when Kurtis got the network break he had been hoping for. In the spring of 1982 he joined Diane Sawyer as coanchor of the "CBS Morning News." Seven hundred people gathered at his farewell party "and on his last day scores of WBBM employees lined up with pictures for him to autograph."[45] His move to the network produced a column from critic Gary Deeb, with the headline "Everybody's friend moves on to New York and the challenge of befriending a nation."[46]

But, despite an initial climb in the ratings when Kurtis and Sawyer took over, the "CBS Morning News" continued behind "Good Morning America" and the "Today Show" in the networks' morning news competition. Sawyer soon left for "60 Minutes," and Kurtis was paired with Phyllis George, a

43. Deeb, p. 19.

44. Jacobs, p. 322.

45. Sally Bedell, "Can Minor League Anchorman Make It in Majors?" *New York Times,* 12 July 1982, late ed., sec. C, p. 15.

46. Deeb, p. 8.

former Miss America who was a CBS commentator for NFL broadcasts. Kurtis was unhappy with George and with CBS management and returned to WBBM in 1985.[47]

Meanwhile, Walter Jacobson had gotten into a far different sort of difficulty. Whereas Kurtis won fame for his documentaries and special reports, Jacobson was known for his "Perspectives." On November 11, 1981, Jacobson said Viceroy cigarettes (a Brown and Williamson brand) had an advertising strategy to attract young people to smoking by equating it with "wine, beer, shaving, or wearing a bra. A declaration of independence and striving for self-identity ... a basic symbol of the growing-up maturity process."[48] Brown and Williamson sued for libel. The first judge who heard the suit dismissed it. That decision was reversed, and the case finally went to trial in Chicago in late 1985. The court proceedings lasted nine days, and an eight-member federal jury took less than three hours to find Jacobson guilty and awarded the tobacco company $5 million.[49]

CBS appealed the verdict, arguing that the broadcast was an opinion and therefore not libelous. Ruling that Jacobson acted with "actual malice," the appeals court rejected that argument and "CBS's claim that the broadcast was truthful."[50]

The appeals court reduced the judgment against CBS to $3 million and upheld a $50,000 award against Jacobson. The Supreme Court upheld the appeals-court ruling in 1988. It was the largest libel verdict ever upheld on appeal, and the first major judgment to be upheld against a mainstream news organization. Afterward Jacobson said he was "obviously disappointed ... I know now and I knew then that I did not with malice or forethought tell a lie about the cigarette company."[51]

The 1980s saw the death of Fahey Flynn, the early WBBM anchor who had a second life at the top of the anchor world at WLS in the 1970s. Flynn died in 1983, just one year before he would have observed his 50th anniversary in broadcasting. His coanchor, Joel Daly, praised Flynn as a gentleman, "a competitor who wanted to win but never at the expense of someone else," and said Flynn's long tenure in Chicago belies "the unfortunate myths that

---

47. Boyer, pp. 257–271.

48. "CBS Will Appeal Jacobson Decision; Walter Jacobson Libel Suit," *Broadcasting,* 16 Dec. 1985, p. 108.

49. "CBS Will Appeal," p. 108; "Award Against Jacobson Upheld, Supreme Court Lets Stand $3 Million Libel Decision," *Chicago Tribune,* 5 Apr. 1988, Sports Final, p. 5.

50. "Award Against Jacobson," p. 5.

51. "Award Against Jacobson," p. 5.

cloud our profession, that it is cosmetic and that it is shallow, that it is slick and superficial. For Fahey, the most successful of us all, was none of these things."[52]

In early 1984 another leading man from the past, Floyd Kalber, was lured out of retirement for an anchor job at WLS. By the end of 1985, with Kalber anchoring the 6 p.m. block, WLS had caught up with WBBM in the ratings on the early news and was gaining fast in the ratings at 10 p.m. WMAQ-TV, meanwhile, finally settled on a leading anchor team in late 1985, after a decade of turmoil. WMAQ's Ron Magers and Carol Marin would take the NBC station to ratings dominance by the end of the decade.

When Kurtis decided to return to WBBM in 1985, someone else had to go at the WBBM anchor desk. That someone turned out to be Harry Porterfield, "Chicago's longest-tenured black anchor, the first to be pro-moted from the 'ghetto shift,' the industry cynics term for the disproportion-ately black and female weekend news shows."[53] Porterfield was a gentleman about the situation, but his treatment brought about a 10-month boycott of WBBM by Chicago-based Operation PUSH. The boycott lead to improve-ments in minority hiring at WBBM.[54] The reinstated Kurtis-Jacobson team, however, never regained the dominant position it had held in the late-'70s, early-'80s. In 1989 WBBM broke up the team when Linda MacLennan was named Kurtis's coanchor at 10. Jacobson continued doing his "Perspectives" on the late show and anchoring with Kurtis at 5 p.m.

Tabloid Time

By 1990 WBBM was "a distant third" in the ratings and a new vice president and general manager, Bill Applegate, was brought in to rescue it. Applegate had a reputation as "the savior of troubled news operations and the ravager of journalistic purity."[55] Critics charged that Applegate turned WBBM into a tabloid news operation. Walter Jacobson had been removed

---

52. *Fahey Flynn*, videocassette.

53. Clarence Page, "Harry's Channel 2 Blues," *Chicago Tribune*, 15 Sept. 1985, final ed., Perspective, p. 11.

54. Robert Feder, "PUSH Clergy End Channel 2 Boycott," *Chicago Sun-Times*, 26 May 1993, Sports Final, sec. 2, p. 43.

55. Robert Feder, "More Viewers Staying Tuned," *Chicago Sun-Times*, 7 Mar. 1993, final ed., p. 18.

as coanchor in 1989, but Applegate diminished his role further by taking his "Perspectives" off the 10 o'clock news. When Applegate left WBBM in 1993, Jacobson said he had turned WBBM into a "purveyor of garbage."[56]

Jacobson himself left WBBM a few months earlier. He took a pay cut to join the newly revamped Fox station, WFLD, coanchoring an hour-long newscast at 9 p.m. Jacobson's last few years at WBBM had been rough. In addition to losing the coanchor slot and the 10 p.m. exposure for his commentaries, he was blasted by critics for stooping to tabloid news himself, and engaging in stunts such as posing as a homeless person in a sweeps series. One critic said: "Toward the end, if the once-respected Jacobson wanted air time at all, he had to interview a serial killer or play disabled for a day."[57]

A year later WBBM continued to lag behind. There had been brief surges in its ratings when it had broadcast the Illinois lottery numbers and when CBS had broadcast the 1994 Winter Olympics. The president of the CBS Television Stations Group, Johnathan Rodgers, who managed WBBM in the late 1980s, said he was "embarrassed by the ratings" of WBBM and the CBS-owned stations in New York and Los Angeles. He said the situation in Chicago was frustrating because "theirs is among the best news broadcasts in the country."[58]

By early 1995 WBBM had a new news director, John Lansing, who had become well-known for developing "family-sensitive news" at WCCO in Minneapolis. With much fanfare, including a self-critical four-part series, WBBM discarded its tabloid style. TV critic Robert Feder said WBBM was airing more responsible newscasts under the new format but had possibly "alienated so much of the audience that it could take a generation for them to make a comeback."[59] Veteran anchor Bill Kurtis, however, stepped down from the 10 o'clock news, saying he'd leave rebuilding the late news to someone else.[60] Kurtis continued to do the 6 p.m. news but would devote the bulk of his energies to producing documentaries for the Arts and Entertainment network.

---

56. T.J. Howard, "Channel 2 Manager Leaving; Architect of Tabloid Format Moving to L.A. Station," *Chicago Tribune,* 19 June 1993, Sports Final, Business, p. 1.

57. Ginny Hobert, "A New Perspective: After 25 Years at Channel 2, Jacobson Skips to Fox," *Chicago Sun-Times,* 3 May 1993, Sports Final, sec. 2, p. 27.

58. Jon LaFayette, "CBS Eyes the Prize, Network Focuses on O&Os' Lagging News Ratings," *Electronic Media,* 1 Aug. 1994, p. 20.

59. Jon LaFayette, "WBBM Goes Less Sensational," *Electronic Media,* 9 Jan. 1995, p. 63.

60. Jon LaFayette, "Chicago's Bill Kurtis Cuts Back on Anchor Duties," *Electronic Media,* 17 Apr. 1995, p. 4.

Work in a Chicago television newsroom, especially WBBM's, has long been part of the career path of many people who go on to leading roles at the networks. The CBS-network experience of Bill Kurtis has been noted. Among the many other WBBM alumni who have made it to the top of network news are Johnathan Rodgers, president of the CBS television stations, Bob Wussler, who headed the CBS Television Network in the 1980s, Van Sauter, who headed CBS News under Wussler, John Lane, an executive vice president of NBC, Eric Ober, president of CBS News, Eric Sorensen, recently producer of the "CBS Evening News," and Rick Kaplan, producer of "ABC News with Peter Jennings," after stints producing "Nightline" and "Prime Time Live." "More people passed through Chicago on the way to important network positions than any city you can name," according to Kaplan.[61] Some of the network correspondents who once reported for WBBM are Jacqueline Adams, Bob Jamieson, Rene Pouissant, and Chris Wallace.

WBBM's importance in the history of television journalism is secure, given its early commitment to news coverage and programming, its role as the scene of the first 1960 presidential debate, its successful hard-news approach to the happy-talk competition in the '70s and '80s, its legacy of notable alumni, and, indeed, its struggle in the '90s with the temptations of tabloid journalism.

---

61. Marilyn Preston, "Chicago Connection: If You Want to Make It in TV, Get a Windy City Resume," *Chicago Tribune Magazine,* 21 July 1985, p. 48.

14 News Leader: WCCO-TV, Minneapolis

Mark Neuzil and David Nimmer

There was no dramatic beginning in the history of WCCO television. Instead, it started with a slow walk through the bureaucracy of the Federal Communications Commission, which in July 1946 received an application for a television license from a Minnesota newspaper scion named Bill McNally and a Minneapolis radio-station employee named F. Van Konynenburg. A half century later the continuing FCC licensing requirement was one of the few remaining links to the founding of one of the upper Midwest's most powerful media outlets.

The history of news broadcasting at WCCO-TV, Channel 4, Minneapolis, is examined in this chapter. WCCO-TV was selected because, although it was not the first television station in the upper Midwest (KSTP, St. Paul, was first), the station's newscast became nationally known for innovative and controversial ideas, such as an extended 45-minute newscast, the establishment of one of the first documentary units, a "family sensitive" 5 p.m. newscast (which attempts to leave out some violent content at that hour), and the cutting away from parent network's "CBS Evening News."

The Influence of Radio

In addition to radiolike government licensing requirements, the influence of radio on early television news was apparent in the format of the first news broadcasts and the use of ex-radio personnel as on-air talent, management, and staff. In Minnesota one person who recognized the possibilities of television was the general manager of WTCN radio in Minneapolis, F. Van Konynenburg. WTCN's story began in 1934 when the families who owned the *Minnesota Tribune* and the *St. Paul Pioneer Press* newspapers purchased a local radio station, WRHM, for $140,000. Leo Owens, who ran the St. Paul paper, was a nephew of *Tribune* publisher F. E. Murphy, and Owens convinced "Uncle Fred" to form a company to buy the radio station, which they renamed WTCN (after Twin Cities newspapers).[1] After World War II, many of the newspapermen who ran the company, called Mid-Continent Radio, were convinced that FM radio was the wave of the future; they wanted to pour resources into the station's FM outlet.

Sold on the idea that television was more marketable than radio, Konynenburg contacted Twin Cities businesses, asking for commitments for advertising dollars for a hypothetical TV station. He received commitments for about $100,000 in advertising for the first year. The radio station's board of directors was not enthusiastic, but Bill McNally, who was running the *Tribune* after the death of Murphy, convinced the board to apply for a license, which was granted in October 1946.[2] The FCC gave the license holders until July 1, 1949, to get the station up and running, a deadline they beat by six hours. Channel 4, known as WTCN-TV, went on the air with one studio camera, one film camera, a projector, and two mobile-unit cameras. WTCN's owners were the Ridder newspaper family, which ran the St. Paul newspaper; the Murphy-McNally family; and John Cowles, who had merged the *Tribune* and *Star-Journal* into one newspaper company in Minneapolis in 1942.[3] Its competition—broadcasting since April 1948—was KSTP-TV, an NBC affiliate operating on Channel 5 across the river in St. Paul.

WTCN, which was not affiliated with a national network, used programs wherever it could find them—from ABC, Mutual, and CBS, in addition to kinescopes from Fox and other outlets that supplied motion-picture houses. WTCN's own programming was limited to sportscasts and barn dances. In all about 35 hours of programming per week were on the air in 1949.[4] The local station was also able to put together a newscast—one per week, broadcast on Friday nights. The newscast began with International

1. Tom Doar, oral-history interview conducted by Mark Neuzil and David Nimmer, July 15, 1994, Minneapolis, Minnesota. Transcript in possession of University of St. Thomas Library.

2. Will Jones, "WTCN to Begin TV Shows Today," *Minneapolis Tribune*, July 1, 1949, p. 18.

3. Doar, July 15, 1994.

4. WCCO-TV internal memo, 1949, WCCO-TV, Minneapolis.

News Service newsreels, similar to those in movie houses, except that a local announcer would read the script. Sometimes the script matched the film, sometimes it did not. Konynenburg also found creative ways to provide visual images when moving pictures were not available. For stories on the national pastime, for example, baseball cards of newsworthy players were placed in front of the camera.

In the spring of 1950 Channel 4 added a new piece of technology to its studio—a leased wire-photo machine—and hired an announcer named John Ford to read a five-minute newscast every weekday at 6:40 p.m. The show, modeled after radio-news updates, was called "Close-Ups in the News," and its sponsors included the Twin Cities Milk Federation and Midland Bank. After six weeks interest from advertisers and viewers was enough to convince management to expand the program to 10 minutes. By September 1950 separate 10-minute shows on weather and sports were in WTCN's lineup, also modeled after radio programs. It would be more than a year before management decided to package all three into one half-hour program. The most significant test of the new operation came in January 1951 when the Minneapolis teachers went on strike for a month and the station suspended its regular programming to provide classroom instruction on the air.[5]

The influence of radio was apparent in the design of the early TV newscasts, both in length and presentation. Essentially, the first broadcasts were radio scripts read on television. Sometimes still pictures or kinescopes matched the copy, but just as often there were no visuals. The Associated Press and other wire services provided national and international copy. "Our newsroom was three wire machines in a closet," said one employee.[6] Television newscasters also read commercials live—the same way radio newscasters presented advertisements. In one regular spot WTCN's Ford—who was sponsored by the milk federation—drank a glass of milk on the air each night. On one memorable occasion he toasted the camera with his glass but managed only a sip and a grimace before setting the glass down, saying, "Well, I'll have to finish this after the show." The audience did not know that the stage crew couldn't find any milk and had replaced Ford's usual drink with chalk water just before airtime. Ford arrived late for the newscast, and in the confusion no one had told him not to drink the "milk."[7]

---

5. WCCO internal memo, 1949.

6. Dave Moore, oral-history interview conducted by Mark Neuzil and David Nimmer, July 14, 1994, Minneapolis, Minnesota. Transcript in possession of University of St. Thomas Library.

7. Don Betzold, "Racing Toward Tonight: The History of a TV Newsroom," University of Minnesota summa cum laude thesis, 1972, p. 11.

In addition to programming similarities, another influence of radio on early television news was personnel. Besides Konynenburg, Channel 4's early roster included radio veterans like Charles "Chick" McCuen, Bob Ball, Arlie Haeberle, and Ford. By the early 1950s radio broadcasters were perhaps the most recognized journalists of the era, and many of them were recruited to television on the basis of their star power. In Minneapolis the dominant radio newscaster of the day was Cedric Adams of WCCO-AM, Minneapolis. An oft-repeated story about Adams's popularity told of airline pilots flying over the upper Midwest knowing it was 10:15 p.m. without checking a clock because lights in the homes below were switching off after Adams's newscast was over. WTCN-TV executives were aware of Adams's popularity; in deference they did not begin a nightly summary of the news until 10:30 p.m. Adams, who also wrote a popular newspaper column for the *Star* and broadcast a daily five-minute CBS Radio Network feature, was an obvious hiring target for the fledgling industry.

The influx of radio talent increased after CBS purchased a percentage of WTCN-TV in 1952 and renamed it WCCO-TV.[8] McNally decided to sell 47 percent of the station to CBS because he wanted a network affiliation. CBS already held the maximum allowable five stations under FCC rules but could acquire a minority interest in two stations. In order to buy a minority interest in WTCN-TV, CBS was forced to sell a majority interest in WCCO radio to comply with FCC regulations. After the sale many WCCO-AM newscasters and producers had to choose between radio and television. Among the few employees to work for WCCO radio and TV at the same time was Cedric Adams, who was paid $110 per newscast at the television station.[9] Adams had experimented with television in 1950 and 1951 as a summer replacement host for Arthur Godfrey's "Talent Scout" program, although his wife recalled he was "extremely nervous" about appearing on television.[10]

Adams, with his large radio following, gave the young, renamed WCCO-TV Channel 4 news instant legitimacy. On the night of January 5, 1953, Adams did his first television newscast at 6 o'clock. A neighborly, warm, courteous man, Adams closed the 15-minute newscast with a quote from Winston Churchill: "TV has taken its place in the world. It's amazing

---

8. The call letters stood for Washburn Crosby Company, a grain-milling firm that became General Mills.

9. Moore, July 14, 1994.

10. Benedict E. Hardman, *Everybody Called Him Cedric* (Minneapolis: Serendipity Press, 1970), p.139.

to think that every expression on my face is viewed by so many. And I hope the raw material is as good as the method of distribution."[11]

The next day Adams's secretary walked through the WCCO-TV newsroom, handing white envelopes to the staff. Inside each envelope was a note from Adams, thanking people for making his first newscast a success. Attached to the note was a check for $50.[12]

Ironically, Cedric Adams did not succeed as a television newscaster. After almost six years on the air, his 6 o'clock show still ran second to KSTP in the ratings. Adams had difficulty ad-libbing and looking at the camera while keeping his place in the script. The bright lights made him perspire, and his makeup, which covered a heavy beard, ran. His glasses would slide down his nose, causing him to squint.[13] "There were absolutely no standards then," said one of his successors, Dave Moore. "Cedric had no TelePromp-Ter. He bumbled his way along just as all of us did." The ability to ad-lib, a television requirement, was not part of Adams's makeup. At the top of each night's script Adams would write, "Good evening, I'm Cedric Adams."[14]

Adams's radio following never came with him to television. He was uncomfortable, and it showed. "In a radio broadcast you have nothing more than the copy in front of you to think about, plus your voice inflections," Adams said. "When I read the 678 letters which came in after my first television show, I realized I had such things as eyebrows, hands, mouth, nostrils, necktie, shoulders, facial expressions, coat creases, shadows and a blood pressure of 265 to concern me."[15]

The Modern Newscast

If the "modern" local-television newscast is defined as half-hour programs broadcast at least twice per evening—those including segments on news, weather, and sports—it began to take shape in Minneapolis and St. Paul in the mid-1950s. Borrowing from the radio model, WTCN had broadcast separate sports, news, news analysis, and weather programs in the 6–6:30 p.m. time slot as early as 1950. By late 1951, with former Iowa-radio

11. Betzold, p. 19.
12. Betzold, p. 19.
13. Hardman, p. 141.
14. Moore, July 14, 1994.
15. Hardman, p. 152.

newsman Chick McCuen as anchor, a 15-minute news show was followed by separate shows on sports and weather. Cedric Adams replaced McCuen in 1953 at 6 p.m., and McCuen moved to a 10-minute newscast beginning at 10:30 p.m.

At WCCO-TV management worried about competing with Cedric Adams's 10 o'clock radio program with a TV news show. In addition, KSTP's 10 p.m. news was ranked first among local programs in the audience ratings. Eventually, McCuen decided to anchor a 10 p.m. newscast himself in late 1954, challenging KSTP and Adams. It was a period of rapid change in the local broadcasting industry. Two new stations—WTCN-WMIN-TV, Channel 11 (which elected not to do a news show), and KEYD-TV, Channel 9 (with a newsman named Harry Reasoner) were on the air by January 1955. In November 1954 the FCC ordered CBS to sell its stock in Channel 4, as the networks were told to rid themselves of minority properties. CBS's 47 percent was sold to Cowles and the Star Tribune Company. The WCCO-TV board of directors consisted of four members of the Murphy-McNally family, four members of the Ridder family, and Cowles.[16] It was an odd ownership arrangement that worked for 22 years before collapsing under economic and political pressures.

Amid the industry flux in the mid-1950s the competition was too much for McCuen at 10 p.m. In three months the show slipped from second to 10th place in the ratings (among all locally broadcast shows), and reports were that news was the only department at WCCO-TV losing money.[17] In June 1955 McCuen was relieved of his duties as news director and the show was moved back to 10:30, with Rollie Johnson, the station's sportscaster, serving as the new anchor and news director.

Johnson did not plan to sit in the anchor chair for long. He approached Walter Cronkite, who was unhappy with his role at CBS-TV in New York. When CBS executives learned of Cronkite's negotiations with the Minnesota station, they persuaded him to stay with a more attractive contract. Johnson's second choice for the anchor job was highly successful University of Oklahoma football coach Bud Wilkinson, a Minnesota native and a popular figure in the area. The handsome, clean-cut Wilkinson auditioned for the job and impressed WCCO's management with his on-air presence, but said he wanted to coach for one more year: His son had another year of school, and Wilkinson had just been elected president of a coaches' association. He was

16. Doar, July 15, 1994.
17. Betzold, p. 31.

also concerned that Oklahoma would have difficulty replacing him as coach with only a couple of months remaining before the season began. But Johnson was unwilling to wait a year for Wilkinson.[18] KSTP's news show, with Bill Ingram as anchor, was still first in the ratings.

Johnson decided to hire from within. The man he turned to was a booth announcer named Dave Moore, who did a variety show, hosted "Bowlerama," and served as a voice and face on several commercials. Moore was a transitional figure in WCCO's history because he did not have a radio-news background—he was an actor who studied drama at the University of Minnesota before joining the station as a part-time announcer in 1950 at the age of 26.[19] But Moore was pleasant, intelligent, and had an actor's ability to improvise. Johnson and Konynenburg were confident he could learn the newscaster's role. "I was on my way over to St. Paul to audition for 'Dial M For Murder' when Sherm Headley, the general manager, called and asked me to read for the evening newscast," Moore said. "I said I was going to read for a part in the play, and Headley said he was a member of the theater board and something could be worked out." Moore got both jobs: "Dial M For Murder" ran for three weeks in St. Paul; Moore kept the anchor chair until 1991, more than 34 years.[20]

The modern newscast at WCCO-TV debuted in March 1957. From 10 to 10:15 p.m. Moore reported the day's news. Weatherman Bud Kraehling received a five-minute segment followed by 10 minutes of sports from Dick Enroth. Crime news was important to the telecast—the newsroom used police and county-sheriff radios with tape recorders attached to them for audio. A dispatcher was hired to direct photographers to crime and fire scenes. Footage was shot and often sent back to the station by taxicab while the photographer went off to the next story. Automobile accidents were a favorite topic: "It was visual, it was accessible, and it had all the elements of urgent journalism," Moore recalled. Two-way radios were installed in the company's cars, and competitors at KSTP occasionally eavesdropped. On slow news nights the radio setup led WCCO dispatchers and photographers to "send" a car to a nonexistent crime scene.[21]

Crime news was the primary emphasis of local television news, and it led to a more general pattern of covering urban social issues—including

18. Moore, July 14, 1994.

19. Noel Holston, "Dave Moore Nearing Final 6 p.m. Sign-Off," *Minneapolis Star Tribune*, November 16, 1991, p. 1A.

20. Moore, July 14, 1994.

21. Moore, July 14, 1994.

education and politics. By the late 1950s the WCCO newsroom staff was expanded to 19 people as a personnel shift was under way from ex–radio newscasters to writers and producers hired from other television stations. Reporters were assigned beats as in the newspaper tradition, and "stand-ups"—reporters filmed at the scene—were shot. The creation of a workable videotape machine in 1958 allowed commercials to be done in advance; the technology was paid for by increasing advertising rates. The videotape machines worked for newsreels as well as for commercials. By 1964 the station traded its two monochrome recorders for three color machines.

None of the local stations had what in the next decade would be considered a "set"—a backdrop, a desk, a screen, and other images for the viewer. WCCO's first set—84 feet long, with a nine-by-12 screen and a huge globe—did not fit into the studio door, so it had to be cut into sections before it was ever seen on television. There were other problems with the big set—Moore was dominated by the background, his head blocked part of the screen, and the projector motor was loud enough to be heard on the air. Eventually, it was reduced to a small screen to the side of the newscaster, a desk, and some curtains.[22] One of the functions of the desk, besides the air of authority it gave the newscaster, was to hide the reams of copy from the viewer.

The man instrumental in developing WCCO's modern news format and taking it to national recognition was Joe Bartelme. He was among the new generation of television journalists who were trained at universities (he had a master's degree in journalism from the University of Iowa). Hired as a reporter in 1957, Bartelme worked his way up to news director.[23] It was Bartelme's idea to adopt the beat system and allow reporters to do stand-ups. He emphasized good writing and reporting: The station won a Peabody Award in 1961 for its reporting on the misuse of funds at the Sister Kenny Institute, a hospital that cared for polio patients.[24]

Bartelme created a Sunday program called "WCCO Reports," which was modeled after "CBS Reports," the network's successful news show. Among the stories it covered were unadopted children in Minnesota, how small towns treated senior citizens, and the effects of a steel strike on mining towns in the state. A program on unwed mothers won another Peabody

22. Betzold, p. 44.
23. "Joe Bartelme, Newschief of Channel 4, Dies," *Minneapolis Star Tribune,* September 6, 1991, p. 4B.
24. WCCO internal documents. Memo to file from Nancy Mate, 1-17-85. Subject: Completion of Awards, p. 4.

Award and helped convince station management to move the show from Sunday afternoon to a Thursday-night prime-time slot in 1961. In 1962 Johnson hired late-night radio-talk-show host George Rice to do television editorials. The format for the modern newscast of the 1960s was in place. The decade would end with WCCO positioned among the nationally prominent local TV news operations.

Nationalization of News

The emergence of WCCO-TV news as an important player in the television industry in the 1960s cannot be told without putting it in context with what was happening in Minnesota in that decade. In politics Vice President Hubert Humphrey and Senator Eugene McCarthy made national headlines. Riots in Minneapolis in 1966 and 1967 received national attention. In sports the baseball Twins and the football Vikings were successful. Much of the Minnesota economy—buoyed by firms like 3M, Dayton-Hudson, Honeywell, General Mills, and Pillsbury—was growing, and the Twin Cities' population was growing along with it. What was happening in Minnesota often made national news, and many of the stories were first done on local television. For example, WCCO did a live field broadcast of President Lyndon Johnson's visit to flood-ravaged southern Minnesota in 1965.

Local television stations also began doing their own versions of national stories. For the first time reporters and photographers ventured far outside Minnesota to get stories. Among the best reporters at WCCO was Phil Jones, who later left for CBS. Jones came from Terre Haute, Indiana, where he was news director, in August 1962. In 1965 WCCO sent Jones to Vietnam with photographer Les Solin and 1,200 feet of color film. The two spent a month overseas, reporting on the war, but the station did not have the equipment to process the film, so it was sent to a lab in Chicago before arriving in Minnesota. Nonetheless, Jones's Vietnam reporting was an important step in the nationalization of local television news. Later that year reporter Ron Handberg went to Sweden for a series of reports geared to Minnesota's large Scandinavian population. Rice traveled to the Soviet Union in 1966, and Jones returned to Vietnam in 1967.

The station also served as a training ground for reporters and others who would be promoted to the networks. In addition to Jones, Skip Loescher, who later won a wide audience at CNN, joined WCCO in the mid-1960s. Lead photographer Stan Zieve became NBC's West Coast photo chief, Tom Pettit and Ann Rubenstein became NBC reporters, and Ned Judge was promoted to the network as a producer. In 1971 Bartelme left for the NBC affiliate in Los Angeles. He eventually became NBC vice president for news programs, executive producer for the "Today" show, and the network's chief political editor.

CBS often drew from WCCO's talent pool. Among the WCCO alumni at CBS in the 1960s and 1970s were Thomas H. Dawson, president of the network in the 1960s; reporters Susan Peterson, Bob McNamara, Susan Spencer, Jerry Bowen, Don Kladstrup, Barry Petersen, and Sam Ford; and producers Jim Anderson, Les Edwards, Marc Koslow, and Quent Neufeld. Bill Stewart, who was killed on assignment in Nicaragua in 1979, joined ABC in New York, as did photographer Les Solin.

Rival KSTP went to a color broadcast in December 1963 and managed to hold on to the ratings lead for much of the decade. Channel 4 converted to full color on election night in 1966. On November 20, 1967, Bartelme and his staff assembled a pilot for a 45-minute news program, which, in addition to being 50 percent longer than before, was noted for its transitions.[25] Dave Moore would turn to Bud Kraehling for a look at the weather and chat with Hal Scott on the day's sports news.

The rigid segmentation of news-weather-sports as essentially separate broadcasts packaged in a 30-minute spot became one 45-minute show with transitions between segments. The extra 15 minutes often were devoted to a spot called "Action News," when Skip Loescher answered viewers' mail (they wrote him with problems they thought he could solve). The staff did seven pilots before putting the show on the air at 10 p.m., January 8, 1968. The show was called "The Scene Tonight," a title supplied by the Martin-Williams Advertising Agency.[26] When it established itself as the clear ratings leader at 10 p.m., the station added a "Scene at Six" in a 30-minute version. Stations around the country took notice, and soon versions of "The Scene Tonight" were broadcast elsewhere, eventually copied by more than 50 stations in the United States.[27]

25. Ron Handberg, oral-history interview conducted by David Nimmer, July 11, 1994, Minneapolis, Minnesota. Transcript in possession of University of St. Thomas Library.
26. Betzold, p. 84.
27. "Joe Bartelme, Newschief of Channel 4, Dies,"p. 4B.

One of the factors that made "The Scene Tonight" so successful in Minneapolis–St. Paul was the work of producer Ron Handberg. He was a veteran journalist who came to the station from WCCO radio in 1963. Handberg was a first-rate writer who liked the idea of a longer format. "It was a journalist's show," Handberg recalled, "with more time, more stories and more perspective."[28] The 10 p.m. show featured regular editorials by Al Austin, a successor to George Rice, who had quit the station to run unsuccessfully for Congress in Minnesota's third district. Austin's editorials usually had a biting edge; he was not reluctant to take after the Minneapolis and St. Paul police departments following news reports of brutality complaints against officers. In fact, it wasn't unusual for WCCO police reporters to hear complaints from detectives and department administrators about Austin's editorials—two or three years after they were broadcast. "The Scene Tonight" also featured in-depth reports by station veterans like Bill Stewart. He did a five-part series on flimsy screening procedures by private Twin Cities security firms, four of which had hired an ex-felon. The series generated a lot of attention and a request from two companies for an injunction to prohibit WCCO from airing the last two segments; a judge denied the request, and the station broadcast the stories amid a flurry of newspaper publicity.

By the end of 1968 Handberg was appointed assistant news director to Bartelme, and the two were a formidable pair. Bartelme had good news instincts, and Handberg had the people skills to interpret the ideas and directives from the low-key news director to his staff.[29] They insisted on sparkling writing and critiques of their news product. While WCCO's nightly television news was doing well in the ratings—some nights with more than half of the Twin Cities' viewing audience—the station's documentary unit was attracting attention. Established in the late 1950s, the documentary unit grew and, by 1970, was producing a weekly newsmagazine called "Moore on Sunday." The half-hour program combined profiles, features, and investigative reporting. "What we had were some very intense film-makers sitting in a basement bunker doing whatever their instincts dictated," said former producer Mike Sullivan, who later joined PBS's "Frontline." "They were doing what '60 Minutes' did, only on a local level."[30]

28. Handberg, July 11, 1994.
29. Handberg, July 11, 1994.
30. Mike Sullivan, oral-history interview conducted by David Nimmer, July 13, 1994, St. Paul, Minnesota. Transcript in possession of University of St. Thomas Library.

With Dave Moore as host, the program examined people, politics, pressure groups, and public expenditures. None generated more heat on the politicians than a program called "Towering Infuriation," an exposé of the expensive furnishings the Hennepin County Board of Supervisors used to decorate the new government center, including rosewood paneling for the commissioners' offices. The documentary unit also probed social issues, including reports of prejudice against the Twin Cities gay community. In a program broadcast October 3, 1977, called "Fair Game Faggot," the producers interviewed local gays about the troubles they encountered. And they showed film of Anita Bryant, an outspoken gay-rights opponent, taking a pie in the face at a community meeting in Iowa. The station's critics accused WCCO of staging the pie episode, which the producers denied. What they couldn't deny was the fervor of Dave Moore's editorial comment at the end of the show. Speaking to those intolerant of gays, Moore said: "You ought to be ashamed. You simply ought to be ashamed."[31] The show gained national recognition, including the Edward R. Murrow Documentary Award from the Radio and Television News Directors Association.

From the debut of "The Scene Tonight" through the early 1970s, WCCO television news was riding high. Its only real competition was KSTP; national awards rolled in; and when Handberg and Bartelme lost a reporter to the networks, they always managed to find a quality replacement. But the local news scene kept changing, and the rate of change was increasing.

Transition

The 1970s and early 1980s were an era of transition for WCCO. The station's longtime ownership group was restructured; management changed, ratings fell, its technology lagged, and journalistic content was affected. For five years "The Scene Tonight" dominated the ratings. By 1973 change was foretold in a newspaper column by Forrest Powers: "Channel 5, the former dominant news station here, was overtaken by Channel 4 a few years ago and has been fighting to reclaim its audience. The station is beaming over January Nielsen and American Research Bureau ratings reports which, in

---

31. Nancy Mate, oral-history interview conducted by Mark Neuzil and David Nimmer, July 14, 1994, Minneapolis, Minnesota. Transcript in possession of University of St. Thomas Library.

one section, contain figures indicating Channel 5 has gained a good deal of ground on its rival."[32]

By now Handberg was WCCO's news director, and he countered KSTP's ratings gains by taking "The Scene Tonight" from 45 minutes to an hour. The show featured a fancy, neon-sign effect and a new chrome-edged set with a see-through Plexiglas tabletop. The additions to the show included "Dear Dave," a segment in which Moore responded to letter writers with serious-to-whimsical retorts; "Shoestring Living," a guide to coping with rising costs; "Case Unsolved," a second look at unsolved crimes; profiles on unusual personalities; and a helping-hand feature. It was a move to counter ratings slips with more content, more stories, more special features. This time it failed.

KSTP had hired a new anchorman, Ron Magers, who proved to be one of the most popular personalities in the Twin Cities. Magers, combined with aggressive coverage of breaking news by KSTP reporters and photographers, lifted the station into first place for more than five years. While WCCO struggled to catch up, the station's ownership structure—essentially unchanged since 1954—was about to undergo a significant shift. Almost from its inception WCCO television had been run by its news managers, with little interference from the owners. The Murphy and McNally families did not take an active role in station management; and the newspaper owners, the Cowles and Ridder families, had been advised by their lawyers to keep their hands off management—lest they offend the U.S. Justice Department.

In 1974 Tom Doar, a lawyer from New Richmond, Wisconsin, succeeded Bill McNally as the leader of the Murphy-McNally interests. One of the first problems he encountered was a decision by the Ridders to sell their interest in WCCO. Robert Ridder told Doar that his family's newspapers were about to merge with the Knight newspaper chain, and lawyers advised getting rid of the broadcast interests. Ridder preferred to sell to the Murphy-McNally family; the problem was the family was not an operating company and had no cash on hand. And few potential buyers were interested in getting involved in such a complicated ownership arrangement. Finally, Robert Ridder came up with a potential buyer—Donald Pels of Lin Broadcasting in New York. Pels offered $12 million for the Ridder family's half of the 53 percent interest in Midwest Radio and Television. But Doar was frightened: "It scared me to think of some New York hotshot coming in here and being

---

32. Forrest Powers, "News Scrap Continues—It Figures," *Minneapolis Star,* March 9, 1973, p. 23A.

our partner."[33] Doar also had the right of first refusal, so he began to look for ways for his family to buy out the Ridder interest.

Among the first contacts Doar made was with Nebraska financier Warren Buffet. Over lunch one day Buffet told Doar to get rid of the family stock in the *Star and Tribune* newspaper, buy out Cowles's 47 percent of the broadcast property, and borrow money to purchase the Ridder interest. Doar's first task was to persuade John Cowles, Jr., to trade his 47 percent interest in Midwest Radio and Television for Midwest's 15 percent interest in the *Star and Tribune.* Cowles asked for $20 million cash in the deal, which Doar negotiated down to $1 million. The Murphy-McNally families now owned 53 percent of the broadcast property and were ready to buy out the Ridders.

"With the *Star and Tribune* deal completed," Doar said, "Midwest moved from a personal holding operation that dispersed dividends to a real operating company that can borrow money." The firm was lent $12 million from the Prudential Life Insurance Company and bought out the Ridder interest. By the end of 1976 WCCO radio and WCCO television belonged solely to the Murphy and McNally families, their sons, daughters, nieces, and nephews. "Now we are out of the newspaper business. We are the operators of radio and television stations and we had a $12 million debt. We either had to put up or shut up," Doar said.[34]

Doar decided that the family needed a new chief executive to run the properties. He remembered meeting James Rupp, a young executive formerly with Cox Broadcasting, when Rupp showed up unannounced at the New Richmond law office one day, looking to buy out the Ridders. Doar had been impressed with Rupp's presentation, complete with pie charts, graphs, and income analyses, which Rupp said showed the station could be more smartly run and more profitable. In 1976 Rupp was hired as the vice president in charge of station operations. Rupp, in turn, brought in Paul Hughes to replace Sherm Headley as general manager of WCCO television.

Hughes, who had managed stations in Albany, New York, and Flint, Michigan, did not take long to shake up the newsroom. An aggressive manager, Hughes quickly hired a coanchor to work with Dave Moore, commissioned a new set, cut the late news back to 30 minutes, and replaced veteran weathercaster Kraehling with a younger man. But nothing upset the newsroom staff more than the day Hughes tried (and failed) to kill a news

---

33. Doar, July 15, 1994.
34. Doar, July 15, 1994.

story. "News staff members accused Hughes of going beyond the proper role of management in supervising news operations, restricting travel and the amount of film cameramen could shoot and reviewing Moore on Sunday scripts. A reporter said the long-stable staff was 'to the point of mass looking for work.'"[35]

For eight months news director Handberg struggled to hold the newsroom together, trying in interviews with local newspaper reporters to put the best face on the management changes. But a story in the University of Minnesota *Daily* publicly blew the lid off the newsroom's discontent. The story, written by Karl Vick, covered four pages of the tabloid, complete with pictures of Handberg, Kraehling, and Hughes. The story said, in part:

> WCCO-TV News is headed for the toilet and Paul Hughes has his hand on the chain.
> Since taking over as station manager, Hughes has tarnished from within the once-sterling news department and might at any time send the entire operation into the dregs where other local newscasts operate.[36]

Handberg took this opportunity to issue an ultimatum to his bosses, Rupp and Doar, that the newsroom wasn't big enough for him and Hughes. Handberg expected he'd be the one who had to go. But two weeks after the *Daily* article, Hughes announced his resignation. Tom Doar asked for it, over the objections of Rupp, who then took on double duty as chief executive and station manager. Hughes left the station believing he had simply tried to bring discipline and budget principles to a news operation that had known neither. But reporters, editors, and photographers in the newsroom celebrated, believing good journalism had triumphed over corporate greed.[37]

For the next six years traditional journalistic values prevailed in the WCCO newsroom.[38] The station won more national journalism awards, produced critically acclaimed documentaries, and occasionally beat archrival KSTP in the ratings. In 1980, at the urging of reporter Don Shelby, Handberg launched an investigative-reporting team, one of the first such broadcast units in the country. The I-Team featured three of the station's best

---

35. Neal Gendler, "WCCO's Hughes Resigns," *Minneapolis Tribune,* November 18, 1977, p. 12A.

36. Karl Vick, "WCCO," *University of Minnesota Daily,* November 4, 1977, pp. 9–10.

37. Handberg, July 11, 1994.

38. For a thorough discussion of the development of standards of journalism, see Hazel Dicken-Garcia, *Journalistic Standards in Nineteenth-Century America* (Madison: University of Wisconsin Press, 1989).

reporters—Shelby, Austin, and Larry Schmidt. There also was a full-time producer and supervisor, public-affairs director Mike Sullivan.

In the next decade the I-Team would produce and report dozens of stories, two of which won national Emmys from the Academy of Television Arts and Sciences. The first, however, could hardly have been more memorable. The I-Team followed 10 Minneapolis housing inspectors around for five weeks.

> The I-Team's sleuthing paid off. One work day they followed inspector Martin Thompson (salary: $24,000) traveling from a one-hour morning coffee break to a bakery, friends and his home. Thompson reported making 13 inspections on a day when the I-Team cameras proved he hadn't driven within 12 blocks of his inspection sites.
>
> And inspector Karl Wade spent one day working for 30 minutes and goofing off for five hours. He then overbilled the city for mileage he had not driven. The I-Team concluded that the Minneapolis housing inspectors spent only one-quarter of their workday on the job. The citizens of Minneapolis were paying them $68,000 in salary for their morning coffee breaks alone.[39]

Within days of the first episode, some city-council members were blaming each other, some were blaming the city administrator, and all agreed to form their own I-Team to investigate charges made by WCCO. The two worst offenders were fired and eight others were suspended. More often than not WCCO's 10 p.m. newscast was a ratings winner on the nights the I-Team broadcast. "We had to develop a great storytelling technique," said executive producer Sullivan. "I always said it doesn't matter whether it was visual. If it's a good story, we'll make it work on television."[40]

Under Sullivan's direction the station also continued to produce five or six hour-long documentaries each year. They covered a dizzying array of topics: "You're Only Old Once," on aging; "Suffer the Children," on youngsters living in poverty; "Armies of the Right," on the moral majority; "Death of an American Girl," on victims of pornography; "On the Edge," on African-American youth and their struggles; and "The Betrayal," on sexual abuse. Many of these documentaries were followed with electronic town meetings, televised discussions involving local subjects, experts, and administrators. In the decade from 1980 to 1990 the reports won dozens of awards,

39. Paul Fishman Maccabee, "Who Are These Men, and Why Are They Following You?" *Twin Cities Reader,* January 21, 1981.
40. Sullivan, July 13, 1994.

including an Emmy, a Peabody, and an Alfred I. Du Pont–Columbia University Award. The WCCO Public Affairs Department, including the documentary unit, the public-service division, and the I-Team, involved as many as 18 people—producers, reporters, photographers, editors, and research assistants.

The award-winning, substantive journalism that had been the hallmark of WCCO held the upper hand. Handberg was named general manager in 1981. Handberg's appointment meant he and Rupp patched their differences; Rupp was confident enough in Handberg to make him his successor as general manager. One of Handberg's first moves was to appoint Reid Johnson as news director. Like Handberg, Johnson's only professional home had been WCCO; like Handberg, Johnson's star rose as producer of the 10 p.m. news show.

Even the station's building changed. In 1983 WCCO moved to a brand-new facility in downtown Minneapolis. There was a greater variety of in-studio shots, thanks to the three separate sets for anchors, sports, and weather. The building's designers described it as a state-of-the-art facility with space and equipment to adjust to the changing world of television. If the claims sounded slightly exaggerated for public consumption, they were not to those who had worked in the station's dingy and overcrowded quarters three blocks away. The old quarters had housed the broadcast operation since the station had gone on the air in 1949. Reporters, producers, and photographers worked in a basement newsroom, where as many as three persons shared a single desk. The building had only one control room for all its live broadcasts, and sometimes producers had to race up four flights of stairs when the old elevator broke down.

Most of the time in the old building the newsroom produced only two shows per day—at 6 and 10 p.m. In the new building the staff did four shows per day—at noon, 5, 6, and 10. Those shows took advantage of changing technology: live-shot vans, a satellite truck, an electronic paint-box, sprightly graphics, Beta cameras, and more versatile editing suites. Reporters were asked to do promotional "teases" for their stories. Most shows contained at least one mandatory live shot. One result was that the correspondent who could report aggressively and write well—on videotape—was not as much in demand as the one who could talk glibly—live.

Still, the station sought substance over style through most of the 1980s. In 1986 a fifth news show, called "Newsday," was added, featuring two veteran reporters as anchors. The show was a newsmagazine, a combination of hard news, live interviews, character profiles, and viewer call-ins. Critics called it a "community treasure." Within two years market forces caught up. According to the *Star Tribune,* "A viewer couldn't really ask for much more in the way of journalistic surrogates (the anchors). The problem, unfortunately, is that viewers are asking for less. For the first year it was broadcast, Newsday had modest but tolerable ratings: audience shares around 22 percent. Then last fall KSTP-Channel 5 shifted Oprah Winfrey's phenomenally successful syndicated gabfest from weekday mornings to afternoons at 4. Newsday's share plummeted."[41]

That drop meant the show was hurting the station's 5 p.m. newscast, maybe its entire early-evening lineup. In August "Newsday" went off the air. Some of its staff were reassigned; three left the newsroom, not to be replaced. The show had fallen victim to the increasingly competitive television market in the Twin Cities. By late 1988 the majority of viewers had remote control and cable television. News directors received overnight ratings reports so they could see how their shows fared against the competition—and react. And advertisers had a third station whose newscasts were gathering the younger viewers they wanted. The Gannett Company, publishers of *USA Today*, had purchased WTCN, Channel 11. With a combination of money, sparkling photography, and a popular anchor and weathercaster, Gannett had given the chronically third-place operation a makeover. Gannett ushered Twin Cities competitors into an era of marketing.

The Marketing Era

Gannett purchased WTCN in 1983. Since its inception in the 1950s, it had been the also-ran. WCCO and KSTP drew about 80 percent of the Twin Cities viewers at 10 p.m., while Channel 11 got about 10 percent. Gannett changed the call letters to WUSA, then KARE. A young anchor, Paul Magers, came from San Diego; his brother Ron had been the market's most popular anchor at KSTP. Paul Douglas, a young meteorologist with a marketing flair, was hired to do weather forecasts outside, in the station's backyard. Gannett redesigned the set and outfitted reporters and photogra-

---

41. Noel Holston, "WCCO May Have to Axe Newsday," *Minneapolis Star Tribune,* May 14, 1988, p. 1E.

phers in red, white, and blue jackets. Reporters were required to use microphone flags with the station's call letters.

At WCCO news managers scoffed at Gannett's early attempts to attract
attention to its news shows. But when Gannett launched a series of commu-
nity-promotion projects, WCCO took notice. Promotion is where KARE
made its greatest impact. The station also offered the most aggressive crime
coverage in the Twin Cities and had the highest-quality photography and the
best-looking graphics. By July 1987 KARE was first in the market at 10
o'clock, KSTP was second, and WCCO had fallen from first to third. The
story was front-page news in the metropolitan edition of the *Star Tribune*.[42]
A year later Pat Miles, WCCO's coanchor of the 5 and 10 p.m. news since
1981, defected and signed a five-year contract with KARE. Miles said she
wanted off the 10 p.m. newscasts because she was raising two small children,
and KARE was willing to let her work on its 6 p.m. show.

At the same time that KARE was outpromoting, outmarketing, and
stealing talent from WCCO, Midwest—WCCO's parent company—was
hemorrhaging financially. The go-go 1980s saw the company restructured
in 1985, in what analysts called a leveraged recapitalization. The move was
made to quiet restless stockholders, some of whom wanted to borrow against
their Midwest stock holdings but were turned down by the banks. Under
pressure from the family, now into its third and fourth generations, Tom Doar
and the Midwest board of directors borrowed $146 million—$100 million
from the First National Bank of Chicago and $46 million from a teachers'
pension fund. They used the money to buy out 92 percent of each family
member's stock; they also sold about 10 percent of the stock to key station
managers and set aside 5 percent for an employees' stock-ownership plan.
"The whole scheme is projected to work with a conservative five percent
revenue growth each year," Doar recalled. "The bankers believe it; the
teachers believe it; and our board believes it."[43]

For the first two years the restructuring went as planned; Midwest was
even paying down the debt ahead of schedule. Then came the recession of
the late 1980s. Banks merged, a large Minnesota savings and loan collapsed,
and advertising revenues fell far behind projections. All this happened just
as Midwest added another $1 million per month to its expenditures in interest
and principal payments on its loans. In the fall of 1987 the company was

---

42. Colin Covert, "KARE 10 p.m. News Takes 1st," *Minneapolis Star Tribune,* August 20, 1987,
p. 1A.
43. Doar, July 15, 1994.

looking for new partners or new owners to pay off the debts that were bleeding its bottom line.

Meanwhile, belt tightening in the newsroom was approaching strangulation, in the eyes of the newsroom managers. In two years Handberg dropped the newsmagazine show, closed the Washington bureau, eliminated the St. Paul bureau, consolidated his beloved documentary unit and the I-Team, and put a lid on overtime, travel, and new hires. On June 27, 1989, Handberg announced he was taking an early retirement. Handberg tried to be polite and upbeat in his public statements, but it was easy to read between the lines: "My pride has come from cutting edge journalism that has been represented by The Moore Report and the I-Team and some of the series over the years. As the strings have tightened, those things are not impossible, but they take on a different priority. I found myself struggling with budgets and things that weren't the source of my satisfaction. I'm much more of a broadcaster, I think, than a businessman."[44]

Midwest's CEO Rupp took over as acting general manager. Four months later Rupp named Bob McGann, whose background was in sales, as general manager. Rupp also appointed 29-year-old John Culliton as his news director. Culliton, a four-year veteran of the station, had been in charge of the 10 p.m. newscast and the executive producer of its Dimension segments, the station's effort to provide background and perspective reports for its viewers. The direction Culliton and his managers established took the newsroom toward analysis of social issues and lifestyle concerns. The 10 o'clock anchors traveled to the rain forests of Brazil and the orphanages of Rumania. There was a series about how to find day care. Culliton fired associate news director Doug Stone, a former *Star Tribune* reporter, and hired John Lansing from rival KARE. The team brightened the newscasts' graphic look and set about to upgrade photographic quality.

Culliton paid attention to marketing and promotions. When the Minnesota Twins won the American League pennant in 1991, Culliton sent his 10 p.m. anchors to Atlanta to do the news from the home of their World Series' opponent. CBS was carrying the World Series, so it represented a chance for some effortless cross-promotion from network games into local news. The coverage, however, turned out to be embarrassingly short on journalistic substance and long on boosterism. For example, the anchors complained about the inherent racism of the tomahawk chop, the rudeness

44. Noel Holston, "Midwest Communication Chief Takes Over," *Minneapolis Star Tribune,* June 28, 1989, p. 3B.

of the Atlanta fans, and the defacing of a Twins' billboard. The reaction from one Twin Cities' TV critic, Adam Platt, was swift and angry: "There was something terribly pathetic about WCCO's newscasts last week. They were unctuous, provincial, and cloyingly saccharine, as if [anchors] Don Shelby and Colleen Needles had been dipped in Karo syrup before each broadcast. The duo demeaned themselves in ways they will probably never grasp, as did the whole WCCO-TV news operation. Make no mistake, WCCO may still shoot the highest, but it now reaches the lowest."[45]

Not all of Culliton's innovations were poorly received by the critics. Earlier in 1991 the WCCO newsroom not only shot high, it succeeded in hitting the target with its coverage of the Persian Gulf War. In January, Culliton and Lansing did the unthinkable: They cut from CBS in the middle of the network's evening newscast to pick up CNN's coverage of the initial bombing of Baghdad. Local overnight ratings showed the number of people watching the station skyrocketed after it abandoned CBS and picked up CNN's compelling live reports.

Culliton's bold action, along with his staff's stellar performance, went a long way toward solidifying his position with WCCO's top management. Even CBS officials were impressed with the WCCO packages and the audience reaction to them. That turned out to be fortunate for Culliton because by the end of 1991 Midwest Communications and CBS were in the final stages of making a deal. The FCC rules on the number of network-owned-and-operated stations had changed again, and CBS wanted WCCO back. Pressure from the lenders on Midwest Communications pushed the sale along. Midwest sold the TV station and its other broadcast properties to the network for $195 million, about half of what stockholders hoped it was worth. CBS was the only bidder. "We simply had our backs against the wall," Doar recalled. "And all of this happened when broadcast properties, on the market, were a dime a dozen."[46]

CBS tinkered little with the news operation. Culliton was appointed vice president and general manager, succeeding Bob McGann, who took a similar job at WBBM in Chicago. In turn Culliton promoted his friend and confidant, Lansing, to news director. In August 1993 the pair debuted another new approach. They called it "Your News," a concept developed after station managers held five large public meetings and a dozen smaller focus groups,

45. Adam Platt, "The World Series of Shamelessness," *Twin Cities Reader*, October 30, 1991, p. 9.

46. Doar, July 15, 1994.

asking viewers what they wanted. At the meetings viewers said they wanted news that reflected their communities, news that represented "a different approach," news that noted triumphs as well as tragedies, and news that treated crime from a broader perspective.

The response was to put together news programs that featured a computer center to explore uses for the information superhighway; a U-Team to investigate consumer rip-offs; stories of courage and perseverance; and a nightly spot called "Bright Side," calling attention to the upbeat and hopeful in the day's news. WCCO also began what it called a "family sensitive" newscast for the 5 p.m. show. The concept meant leaving out violent videotape that the station thought might be unsuitable for younger viewers. The idea drew national attention, including the following observations from *Time* magazine: "The crime was sensational, the kind that local TV news operations salivate over. A 14-year-old boy had shot himself to death in a parked car beside a freeway moments after killing his mother in their suburban Minneapolis home. Like every other station, WCCO-TV gave the story prominent play on its early-evening newscast. But, astonishingly, the station showed none of the gruesome footage that was available.... Instead the story was told by old-fashioned talking heads: reporters describing the events; child therapists talking about why such tragedies occur."[47]

As important as the national attention was the reaction of local viewers. It was overwhelmingly positive, especially among families with small children. In fact, the reaction to the entire "Your News" package was paying off; in the spring 1994 ratings sweeps, WCCO led its competitors at 5, 6, and the all-important 10 o'clock broadcast. And for the first time in years the station was attracting younger viewers, those more attractive to advertisers.

Changes

Throughout the station's first 50 years political forces affected how the place was managed. The Federal Communications Commission, the overseer of television and radio in the United States, issued a license to WCCO; more important, its presence as a regulator played a major role in how the station's ownership was constituted. For example, the threat of action by the FCC, through the Justice Department, upset the initial stable ownership group by

---

47. Richard Hoglin, "All The News That's Fit," *Time*, June 20, 1994, p. 55.

suggesting the Ridder family sell its interest. FCC rules were changed three times, first to allow CBS to buy a minority interest in WCCO, then to force the network to sell it, and finally to allow the national broadcasting concern to buy the entire operation again. Economic forces were at work, as well. The rise of television as a business in the United States throughout the period kept the ownership of WCCO happy and well paid, until the third or fourth generation of family members. The station's ownership was restructured to satisfy family members not interested in the television business, but the restructuring—complete with heavy debt—came right before an economic recession made the debt nearly impossible to service.

WCCO-TV news underwent at least five evolutionary changes during its first half century. In its infancy the station was founded and operated by former radio-station employees who recognized the potential in television. As more technology became available and television grew in popularity, the "modern" nightly news schedule was developed in the mid-1950s; television professionals replaced the old radio newscasters. With the societal changes in the 1960s, local television news kept pace by going national (and international)—covering stories in Asia and Europe as well as across the United States. The networks noticed, and hired many journalists from WCCO. By the 1970s economic and political pressures on the station's once-stable ownership, as well as the rise of competition, left the station in a state of flux. WCCO responded to the changes by increasing its emphasis on in-depth television journalism in the early 1980s.[48] By the end of the decade, however, market forces took their toll on the owners, and social forces affected the viewers, who were less interested in documentaries and more interested in where to find good day care for their children. By the 1990s marketing played the central role in the development of a news product at WCCO-TV.

---

48. The term "in-depth television journalism" is somewhat problematic, since the authors are unaware of any attempts to explore differences in media when it comes to journalistic standards. Dicken-Garcia's definition, which reads, in part, that standards are "the rules of procedure governing the accomplishment of an occupational end" (*Journalistic Standards,* pp. 10–11) is used in this work.

15

In the Public Interest: WEWS-TV, Cleveland

Mary E. Beadle

Cleveland became part of the television era when WEWS began regular broadcasting December 17, 1947. Scripps-Howard, the news and broadcast service, named the station WEWS in honor of the founder of Scripps-Howard, E.W. Scripps, the legendary journalism figure. Fifty years earlier he had founded his first newspaper in Cleveland. WEWS was the first television station licensed to Scripps-Howard, the first television station in Ohio, and the 11th station in the nation. The station signed on with: "We're feeling our way. None of us professes to know how to publish news by way of sound and motion pictures. We're going to find out."[1]

As these pioneers felt their way during the first decade of operation, WEWS gave its audience many television firsts and programming that reflected a commitment to public interest. The firsts included the first college course offered for credit in the country, the first woman newscaster, and the first station to receive the George Foster Peabody Award for local service.

Scripps-Howard Broadcasting Company, originally known as the Continental Radio Company, emphasized news coverage and local service. When World War II ended, Scripps-Howard applied for and was granted a television license in Cleveland. A transmitter and a 450-foot tower were constructed in Parma, a suburb of Cleveland, and space was leased in an office building in downtown Cleveland for TV, AM, and FM offices and studios. The station guaranteed good coverage within 40 to 50 miles.[2]

---

1. "Scripps-Howard Enters Television," *Scripps-Howard News*, March 1948, p. 1.
2. V. Trimble, ed., *Scripps-Howard Handbook* (Cincinnati: E.W. Scripps), p. 328.

In the WEWS building at 1816 East 13th Street, next to the Allerton Hotel, there was one studio, 55 by 75 feet and 25 feet high. Executive offices were on the second floor, lounges and dressing rooms on the ground floor, a film lab under the first floor, and a TV truck with accompanying station wagon. Conduits under the stage piped the audio and video to the hotel roof, where they were relayed to the transmitter by microwave.

The best coverage was in Cleveland, Akron, and Sandusky, with the signal sometimes picked up in Toledo or Warren, about 110 miles away. Facilities and equipment were continually upgraded, including new equipment for remotes, three downtown studios and one audience studio seating 400, two 16-millimeter film projectors, one 35-millimeter filmstrip projector, and seven cameras, including three dual IO chains and one iconoscope-projection chain.[3] In 1952 WEWS added one telop, nine cameras, and two iconoscope-projection chains.[4] In December 1953 a new transmitter was put into service in Parma, increasing power from 16,000 watts to 93,000 watts. After the power increase the coverage included 31 Ohio counties, five Pennsylvania counties, and increased the number of sets receiving WEWS to over one million.[5] Plans to move to new facilities on East 30th Street were announced in January 1956, with the move taking place in late 1957. WEWS has remained at this location since 1957. As technology changed and the station grew, WEWS added equipment and personnel but has never changed call letters, channel assignment, or ownership from the date of sign-on.

WEWS began with a staff of 54 people: nine in news and film, 12 in programming, 19 in technical, 10 in the office, and four in management, including James Hanrahan, "a resolute, decisive man [who] ably directed television's nervous navigation through its first years here."[6] In 1935 Hanrahan became the first employee of Scripps-Howard's new Continental Radio Company and worked in both Cincinnati and Knoxville. Once Scripps-Howard decided to pursue a television station in Cleveland, Hanrahan was assigned the job to begin the first TV station in Ohio. Except for a stint in the army during World War II, he was in Cleveland from that time on.

---

3. WEWS Rate Card #2, effective September 1, 1948, Northeast Ohio Broadcast Archives, John Carroll University, Cleveland, p. 2. New Collection, uncataloged. Hereafter referred to as WEWS-TV Collection.

4. WEWS Rate Card #8, effective October 1, 1952, WEWS-TV Collection, p. 5.

5. WEWS Program Schedule for January 10, 1954 (quoted in *Television*, August 1953), p. 2.

6. George Condon, "The Day Our Lives Changed," *Cleveland Plain Dealer Sunday Magazine*, December 17, 1967, p. 4.

One area that Hanrahan continually tried to improve was local programming. For example, he had the station present a "Festival of Live
Television" in January 1958. George Condon, TV critic, wrote, "What
happened at WEWS this month to reinstate live performers on the local
television scene is not entirely clear, but the move by General Manager James
C. Hanrahan should be applauded."[7]

He was committed to hiring minorities and was the first in the nation
to hire a woman newscaster, Dorothy Fuldheim, and a woman producer and
director, Betty Cope. Cope explained that he was ahead of his time in hiring
women and blacks, but that still did not prevent some animosity from the
all-male crew.[8] Dorothy Fuldheim, a news analyst on radio, was invited by
Hanrahan to join Scripps-Howard, formulating her own show with comments and interviews.[9] About her boss Fuldheim said, "He was such a wildly
creative and wonderful man that I could never refuse him. I owed him so
much, for he was the only man in the country willing to give a woman the
chance to anchor a news show."[10] *Scripps-Howard News* reported that his
favorite epitaph was: "He was just wise enough to employ men who knew
more than he."[11]

The First Week

There were about 300 sets in Cleveland in 1947, most in taverns and
showrooms. The *Cleveland Press* noted this trend in 1947, predicting that
early television tastes would be formed in public places, and that sports would
be important programming.[12] WEWS did not have network interconnection
by coaxial cable, and kinescope programs from other stations were rare.
Cable was being laid, anticipating sports broadcasts like the Rose Bowl
game.

---

7. George Condon, "WEWS Rates Big Cheer for Trying Bold Experiment," *Cleveland Plain
Dealer*, January 18, 1958, p. 16.

8. Betty Cope, oral-history interview conducted by Mary Beadle, August 17, 1976, Cleveland,
Ohio. Tape-recorded and in possession of WEWS-TV Collection.

9. Dorothy Fuldheim, *A Thousand Friends* (New Jersey: Doubleday, 1974), p. 13.

10. William Hickey, "Dorothy Fuldheim's 25 Years With WEWS-TV Draw Acclaim," *Scripps-
Howard News*, December 1972, p. 6.

11. *Scripps-Howard News*, October 1957, WEWS-TV Collection, p. 3.

12. Stan Anderson, "Third TV Station, WXEL, Opens This Saturday," *Cleveland Press*, December 14, 1949, p. 29.

Sponsors were rare, and commercials few. In 1953 spot announcements were one minute in length, with a limit of five announcements for each
30 minutes. By 1954 that increased to six one-minute announcements every
30 minutes. WEWS also reported that its advertising code was stricter than
the NATRB Code, and at no time allowed pitchmen for mail-order accounts
to advertise.[13]

WEWS began broadcasting experimental programs a few months
before regular operation was undertaken, often showing nothing more than
a picture of a brick wall. The first public telecast on December 17, 1947, was
a remote from the Cleveland Public Auditorium of the *Cleveland Press*
Annual Christmas Show. The newspaper reported the television cameras
would be onstage in full view of the audience. The opening also included
600 people gathered in the Higbee Department Store auditorium to see this
broadcast, including out-of-town executives who claimed there was not a
better opening in any city. This first broadcast was not without mishap. The
antennas were anchored to the roof with sandbags, and a high wind knocked
an antenna over, for a few minutes killing the video portion of the show.[14]
Director of operations Ernie Sindelar solved the problem when he and a
couple of helpers sat on the antenna to steady it.

WEWS began regular broadcasting about two hours per day, five
evenings a week, Tuesday through Saturday. All programs were local and
live, using remotes and some film. Much of the programming the first week
depended on local organizations providing Christmas carols or other seasonal entertainment. The first evening of broadcast began at 7:30 p.m. with
the test pattern and music, followed at 8 p.m. by the Press Christmas Show.
Special film presentations were "Felix the Cat" and "Daffy Duck." Thursday,
Friday, and Saturday followed similar schedules, beginning with the test
pattern at 7 p.m., followed by basketball or a local variety show.

Programming Expands

Six months after the start of broadcast, in June 1948, WEWS added
Sunday and Monday to the schedule. Programming those two days averaged

---

13. "U.S. Television Stations and Market Data," *Television Yearbook-Marketbook*, 1957–1958,
p. 194.

14. Stan Anderson, "Radio," *Cleveland Press*, December 18, 1947, p. 41.

3½ hours, with the rest of the week averaging six hours per day. There was still no network service, but the use of film increased, making up 16 percent of the broadcast hours. Many programs were five, 10, 15, or 20 minutes in length, with the resultant program times at 7:25 p.m. or 8:50 p.m. The station log for this period noted: "All programs are live or remote unless otherwise specified."[15]

A big contribution to local programming was the pennant-winning Cleveland Indians baseball team. The broadcast day was expanded to cover the games with sign-on as early as 1 p.m. for afternoon games, and sign-off as late as 11 p.m. "Indians baseball ... was the first glimmer of the astounding potential of television."[16] Because network interconnection was not complete until the fall of 1948, WEWS sent a newsreel cameraman to Boston to film the American League play-offs between Boston and Cleveland. WEWS was the first to televise live Cleveland Indians home games in 1948. This included three 1948 World Series games that were fed to the CBS network because partial interconnection of the network was then completed. The pennant fight also boosted television-set sales, so that by October 1948 there were more sets in Cleveland (12,000 to 15,000) than the national average.

Station logs from 1948 indicate a special film transmission of a flashing lighthouse, the symbol of Scripps-Howard, at the beginning and the end of the broadcast day. This flashing lighthouse had special meaning. "Give light and the people will find their way" was the slogan associated with the lighthouse. WEWS explained what this meant to television: "Television—combining all the arts of sight and sound—can be the clearest brightest light to illuminate our world today."[17]

During the fall of 1948 WEWS broadcast the first network programs, which immediately accounted for 39 percent of the total broadcast hours. This decreased local programming to approximately 50 percent of the broadcast day. WEWS also faced another challenge to local programming as the first year of operation came to the end—its first competitor.

In October 1948 WNBK (Channel 4), an NBC affiliate, began operation. Although WEWS had signed a primary-station agreement with CBS, other network programming was available, and WEWS used programs from CBS, ABC, Du Mont, and even NBC newsreels. The programming logs from

---

15. WEWS Station Log, June 13–19, 1948, WEWS-TV Collection, p. 3.

16. Bill Barrett, "Memories of 25 Years Ago Stirred by 25th Anniversary of WEWS in Cleveland," *Scripps-Howard News,* January 1973, p. 18.

17. "In the Public Interest: The WEWS Story," circa 1955, WEWS-TV Collection.

that period indicate a station symbol that incorporated both ABC and CBS logos.

The broadcast day averaged almost six hours, with programs still beginning at irregular times because of 40-, 20-, or 15-minute programs. There was a pause between afternoon and evening programs when the station signed off the air for an hour or so. The evening broadcast usually began about 6:30 p.m. with the news.[18] There was a special broadcast during elections, and on Tuesday, November 2, the station provided election returns.

By June 1949 network programming still accounted for just under 50 percent of the broadcast day. However, as the total number of programming hours increased, the use of network programming also increased. Local programming remained below 50 percent. The broadcast day averaged seven hours, and programs became standard lengths of 15, 30, or 60 minutes. The test pattern was still telecast twice a day. On Saturday and Sunday the programming was almost entirely network and film.

Challenges

In December 1949, after two years of operation, WEWS faced some additional competition from WXEL (Channel 9), the third VHF station in the market, a Du Mont affiliate. WEWS lost many Du Mont programs but did carry those that WXEL rejected and also carried other network programs from ABC and CBS. Network programming remained at slightly under 50 percent of the broadcast hours. Local programming increased to 48 percent of the broadcast hours, and film use decreased. This drop in film use may be explained by the fact that WEWS wanted to insure that viewers would not switch to the new station, using network and local programs to keep them tuned to WEWS. Weekdays expanded with continuous programming through the afternoon, for a total of 9½ hours.

Another major programming problem faced by WEWS was losing the Cleveland Indians baseball contract to WXEL in June 1950. Until 1950 the use of network programming increased and local programming decreased. In 1950 WEWS expanded the broadcast day by the use of local programs. From 1950 to 1956 broadcast hours increased, with network programming

18. Linn Sheldon, oral-history interview conducted by Mary Beadle, August 16, 1976, Cleveland, Ohio. Tape-recorded and in possession of WEWS-TV Collection.

slowly replacing local programming. In 1951 WEWS was broadcasting about 15½ hours per day, signing on at 9 a.m. Network programming dominated the schedule, particularly in the evening. Local programs continued in the morning and afternoon. In January 1952 WEWS expanded the broadcast day to 16 hours by signing on one hour earlier, at 8 a.m., two hours earlier than its competitors. By January 1954 WEWS was broadcasting 17 hours per day.

Changes

In January 1956 a decrease in network programming occurred for the first time in six years when WEWS changed affiliation from a strong network (CBS) to a weaker one (ABC). This change in affiliation created programming problems for WEWS. ABC had no afternoon programming and a much weaker schedule than had CBS. WEWS, therefore, had to produce local programs. As director Jim Breslin put it, "It was sink or swim."[19]

In response to this change the broadcast day changed: Network programming decreased to its lowest use on the station in years; local programming increased to its highest use in four years. For the first time in the station's history the use of film comprised more hours than did local productions. The broadcast day decreased slightly to about 15½ hours. New local shows included "Gene's Song Shop" with Gene Carroll; "Uncle Leslie," a clown created by Linn Sheldon; and "Texas Jim," a children's show hosted by director Jim Breslin. However, the increase in local programming lasted a short time, for as ABC became stronger, network programs again replaced local ones.

By the 1957–58 television season the broadcast day increased to 16 hours. WEWS still aired the NBC "Tonight Show," because the NBC affiliate in town did not carry the program. The expansion of the broadcast day for the most part was due to the addition of local programming. However, network programs eventually replaced local programs, which were then relegated to the weekend.

Despite the commitment of WEWS to local programming, this was not an indication that the station was as commercially successful as competitors.

---

19. Jim Breslin, oral-history interview conducted by Mary Beadle, August 8, 1976, Cleveland, Ohio. Tape-recorded and in possession of WEWS-TV Collection.

Rates, as reported in *Broadcasting-Telecasting Yearbook*, were consistently lower for WEWS, indicating a smaller audience for this station than for the other two stations. The advertising rate charged by WEWS for Class A in 1948 was $300 for one hour.[20] By 1958 the highest Class A one-time hourly rate was $1,800, compared to $2,000 for each of the other two television stations.[21]

Television Firsts

In addition to the first baseball broadcasts, WEWS was responsible for many other television firsts in Cleveland, including the first broadcasts of live and film network programs from ABC, CBS, NBC, and Du Mont. The station broadcast with the use of stratovision, picking up an experimental telecast of the Louis-Wolcott heavyweight fight from a plane 33,000 feet over Pittsburgh. The first commercial sponsor of a regular television program was SOHIO, sponsoring "SOHIO's Television Talent Search." WEWS was the first to broadcast beauty contests, televising the Miss Cleveland and the Miss Ohio contests in 1948. Western Reserve University and WEWS developed the first college courses for credit in the country. Also, WEWS was the first to produce dramas for television, including the first television production of a George Bernard Shaw play.

WEWS produced many locally written and acted live television dramas in cooperation with Western Reserve University. The first broadcast of a television adaption of Shaw's comedy *The Devil's Disciple* was produced by WEWS with the Cleveland Playhouse and the Western Reserve Players. Probably the greatest contribution to local television drama made by WEWS was the production of Menotti's opera *The Medium* with Cleveland's Karamu House, the world-famous African-American cultural center. This production was still considered the finest in local programming in 1953.[22] During the period of live television drama Cleveland was considered to have the best television facilities between New York and Chicago and was predicted to become a major television center, both because of the city's

---

20. WEWS FCC Annual Reports, 1953 and 1954, WEWS-TV Collection.
21. WEWS Rate Card #8.
22. Stan Anderson, "See-Hear," *Cleveland Press*, January 27, 1953, p. 18.

position as an economic center, and because of Cleveland's rich cultural life, capable of producing programs of interest locally and around the country.[23]

Public Programming

WEWS presented the first live television course in the country to offer college credit. In the spring of 1951 WEWS executives asked Western Reserve University to consider a formal course over television for the 1951–52 academic year. Western Reserve agreed if it would not cost the university anything. The Cleveland Foundation and seven local citizens agreed to underwrite the project, with WEWS providing airtime and facilities free.

The first four courses were so successful, with more than 3,000 viewers participating, that all guarantees were called off within the first month. This interest continued throughout the year, and the project closed with a small profit, which was turned over to the university to develop academic television further. The courses were broadcast until the 1960s. At that time the station dropped the telecourses because it was out of available time. While the service lasted, it was one the audience greatly appreciated.[24]

Another joint project of Western Reserve and WEWS was the first broadcast of a college reunion. In 1955 WEWS broadcast remote, from the university gym on the campus of Western Reserve, a 90-minute reunion, estimated by university officials to have reached 30,000 alumni in the area. By 1953 the close association of WEWS with Western Reserve University resulted in the production of over 850 programs.

Other educational institutions also presented programs over WEWS. FCC reports from 1951 and 1954 indicated that the station took the initiative in all instances, gave airtime and facilities free, and gave direct financial assistance to two universities.[25] WEWS also helped the local churches develop religious programming.

In 1953 and 1954 WEWS conducted television workshops so that religious groups could learn how to use television more effectively. In 1954 WEWS arranged six Religious Television Institutes at its studios, involving

23. Patrick Crafton, "Cleveland Due to Become Focal Point of Television Industry, Official Says," *Cleveland News*, October 29, 1948, p. 21.
24. Alan Bush, telephone interview conducted by Mary Beadle, July 19, 1994, Cleveland, Ohio.
25. WEWS FCC Annual Reports, 1951 and 1954, WEWS-TV Collection.

lectures on TV-program problems by the staff members, and studio sessions to familiarize people with the practice of television production.

In 1962 WEWS won the Gold Bell Award, the Catholic Broadcasters Association's highest honor, as the best station in the country for Catholic programming and other public-service broadcasts. Highlights from the videotape entered in the competition included portions of "Inside Catholic Schools," the oldest continuous Catholic educational program in the country; Catholic Charities 50th Anniversary; the Newman Club 40th Anniversary; and John Carroll University's 75th Anniversary.

In addition to the local education and religious institutions WEWS also looked for joint program sponsorship with the local government. In 1949 the Cleveland Division of Recreation sponsored two television programs: "Book of Talent," on WXEL, and "Something for All," on WEWS. Mayor Burke explained the purpose of the city's involvement with television: "We are endeavoring to provide all the citizens of Cleveland with proper access to recreation.... Our television recreation program gives us the opportunity of bringing our recreation activity to them in their homes. It is a very worthwhile project."[26]

Public service was also contributed to the city by WEWS in November 1950 with around-the-clock coverage during the worst snowstorm in the city's history. The dedicated staff made it to the studio despite the weather. Director Betty Cope rode a horse to work because the streets were closed.

Interviews with Dorothy Fuldheim were also important contributions to public service.[27] One public-issue program listed in the 1954 FCC Annual Report was a special arrangement to broadcast the "See It Now" program with controversial Senator Joseph McCarthy because it was not regularly scheduled in the area at the time. Paid and free time was also made available to political candidates. In 1954 this included an invitation to all candidates for congressional and state offices to appear for an interview with Dorothy Fuldheim.

When changes occurred in technical aspects of broadcasting, WEWS helped inform the viewers. The 1954 FCC Annual Report listed a daily program, "Here's Looking at You," that saluted 40 towns and cities new to the coverage area after the power increase in 1953. In 1953 the station produced a 20-minute film, "Right Before Your Eyes," which traced the development of television and saluted proposed UHF television stations.

---

26. "City Sets Example in TV Broadcasts," *Cleveland Plain Dealer*, December 18, 1949, p. 11E.
27. WEWS FCC Annual Reports, 1951, p. 13, and 1954, p. 28.

This program won the AFTRA Public Service Award for Unselfish Promotion.

WEWS helped promote good community relations and interracial understanding, often through announcements during programs of organizational activity, including that of the Kiwanis Club and the American Red Cross. WEWS also aired many local variety shows that employed talent of different races and color without segregation. Participants in public discussions represented every leading nationality group. Since 1948 the station has employed blacks in management and women as producers, directors, and newscasters.

Because of WEWS's promotion of good community relations and interracial understanding, in 1953 the station was awarded the first George Foster Peabody Award for Outstanding Public Service by a local station. The citation for this award read, in part, "In 1952 [WEWS] televised more than 700 formal community service programs; it integrated public service and human relations material into many regular entertainment programs, and it drew upon a variety of religious and racial groups for talent and staff."[28] Following the Peabody Award, the city council of Cleveland and the state senate of Ohio "passed unanimous resolutions commending WEWS for the award and for its intergroup activity."[29]

Popular Programming

WEWS also provided many entertainment programs that were hosted by popular local personalities. These shows included garden shows, music shows, children's shows, and women's shows. The personalities included Dorothy Fuldheim, Bill Randall, Paul Hodges, and Linn Sheldon. Music was performed on the station by the Channel 5 Orchestra, George Duffy's Band, or Crandel Henderschott at the organ. Some of the music programs included "Take 5," a show hosted by Linn Sheldon and his wife; the "Pee Wee King Show," originated for ABC; the "Norge Block Party," a remote telecast, with host Bob Dale and the Johnny Pecon Band playing in a different neighborhood every week; and the "Old Dutch Polka Review," a music-variety show sponsored by Old Dutch Beer. This show was produced by Gene Carroll and

---

28. WEWS FCC Annual Report, 1953, pp. 7–8.
29. WEWS FCC Annual Report, 1953, p. 8.

featured guest stars and large production numbers, with a live studio audience receiving all the beer they could drink until the state of Ohio stepped in and put a stop to that particular amenity.

Not only popular music was aired. WEWS broadcast the top three winners of a violin concert sponsored by the Music School Settlement and WJW radio. Bill Randle, a nationally known rock-and-roll disc jockey, hosted a 60-minute program at 11 p.m. in 1950 that featured rock-and-roll bands in the WEWS studio. In 1958 a "Festival of Live Television" featured a special hour-long program starring Mildred Miller of the Metropolitan Opera and the Cleveland Orchestra. Other performers during the month-long festival included Beverly Sills and Cleveland Ballet dancers. When the program went beyond 9 p.m., WEWS sacrificed its network revenue for a half hour. Officials estimated that the loss was around $1,000. The production costs on the Miller program were estimated to be $5,000. Host Tom Fields explained the importance of such local programming: "While many television programs originate live from Hollywood or New York ... and many are on film, we feel that WEWS would fall far short of its obligation to Ohioans if we failed to present as many as possible of our own local shows."[30] Jim Frankel, a newspaper critic, said: "WEWS ... made the supreme sacrifice in its rededication to the highest principles of broadcast conduct. At this point it's best to simply say thank you."[31]

Many early local programs focused on women and children. One popular children's show, broadcast for nine years, was "Uncle Jake's House," with Gene Carroll. This program used a live studio audience and elaborate sets, including a living room, basement workshop, a temperamental elevator, a dining room for birthdays, an attic, and a front porch. "Captain Penny" provided afternoon entertainment for children with cartoons. A one-hour ladies' program, "Distaff," which included guests and interviews, was hosted by Alice Weston and directed by Betty Cope. This show eventually evolved into three half-hour shows broadcast about 30 minutes apart. Cooking shows included Rachel Van Cleve, who sang arias while cooking, Ethel Jackson, and Barbara Page. Exercise was provided by Paige Palmer. Later the "One O'Clock Club," with Dorothy Fuldheim and Bill Gordon, provided information and entertainment. Women paid $1.50 to attend a luncheon at the studio at noon, followed by the show.

---

30. Jim Frankel, "WEWS Gets Pat on Back for Grade-A Local Show," *Cleveland Press*, circa January 1958, WEWS-TV Collection.
   31. Frankel.

Probably the most popular ex–radio talent was Paul Hodges, who "must have seemed as if he was the only one" on television.[32] His jobs on WEWS included announcing, newscasting, weathercasting, interviewing, and entertaining. On "Dress 'n Guess" he did a reverse striptease, the clues being the clothes he put on to become a famous person. "Arriving and Leaving" was an interview show broadcast remote from the Greyhound bus station. To obtain interviews, he often woke travelers sleeping on benches. "The situation got so bad that scores of bums, resentful of television's invasion of their privacy, abandoned the old bus station and took their patronage to the railroad terminal in protest."[33] Another popular local personality was Fred Griffith, who still hosts the "Morning Exchange" after 25 years. This program gave ABC the format for "Good Morning, America."

No history of WEWS can leave out the one person who left an indelible mark on the viewers, Dorothy Fuldheim. In her biography released by the station, she is described as having more seniority on TV than Ed Sullivan. During 1952 she conducted more than 250 interviews. She won awards ranging from local newspaper popularity polls (Favorite Cleveland Newscaster in every survey from 1947 to 1957) to the Overseas Press Club Award for her coverage of the 1955 Formosa crisis. A Gallup poll circa 1956 named Fuldheim among America's Most Admired Women.

Prior to her work at WEWS she was a commentator for ABC radio. She joined the staff of WEWS in 1947. During her time there she flew all over the world to cover news stories. She would usually get a call in the early hours of the morning, when station management would get an idea, such as sending her to Formosa to interview Chiang Kai-shek. Her interviews even included one with Adolf Hitler in 1932 in Munich's Brauhaus.

For seven years she hosted the "One O'Clock Club" and often did book reviews that raised the status of book reviewing to an art.[34] National television audiences became familiar with her because of appearances on the "Tonight Show" with Johnny Carson.

"Highlights of the News," her five-night-a-week news show, featured commentary and interviews with international, national, and local guests, including Walter Reuther, president of the AFL-CIO; the Duke of Windsor; writers Tennessee Williams and Rachel Carson; Washington columnist Drew Pearson; and Senators Hubert Humphrey and Estes Kefauver. After

---

32. Condon, "The Day Our Lives Changed," p. 5.
33. Condon, "The Day Our Lives Changed," p. 5.
34. Hickey, p. 6.

serving on WEWS for 37 years Dorothy became too ill to work in 1984. On November 3, 1989, WEWS announced to its viewers that Dorothy Fuldheim had passed away.

Legacy

The legacy of WEWS is somewhat idealistic. The station pioneers firmly believed that television would change people's lives for the better by providing programs that served the local interest. General manager James Hanrahan deserves much credit because he kept focused on the public interest. His choice of words describing the audience as "neighbors" indicates a relationship that was achieved by involving many community groups in the development of programming. Emphasis on local programs and public interest resulted in many awards for WEWS, including the first George Foster Peabody Award for public service, and many programming firsts that gained national recognition. It is a legacy that would be difficult to duplicate in today's market.

16 "In the Heartland": WDAF-TV, Kansas City

William James Ryan

WDAF-TV was the progeny of WDAF, the radio station farthest west on the original AT&T chain and a charter member of the National Broadcasting Company network.[1] Like WDAF, WDAF-TV was first licensed to the Kansas City Star Company, publisher of the morning *Kansas City Times* and the evening *Kansas City Star* newspapers.[2] With the Federal Communications Commission's freeze on new construction permits September 29, 1948, shortly after Star's was authorized, WDAF-TV was the only television station in the area until 1953.

Kansas City, Missouri, is the city of license in a seven-county two-state region. Suburban sprawl gave the metro area a post–World War II population of 634,093, ranked 17th among national broadcast markets. By December 15, 1945, VHF channels 2, 4, 5, and 9 had been allocated to Kansas City.[3]

It is notable that the conservative Star Company—not KMBC's pioneering Arthur B. Church, or KCMO's Tom Evans, close friend of Harry S.

---

1. WDAF was Kansas City's fourth radio station, signing on 5 June 1922. William J. Ryan, "Which Came First?—65 Years of Kansas City Broadcasting," *Missouri Historical Review* 82 (July 1988), pp. 408–423. Re: AT&T chain, see William P. Banning, *Commercial Broadcasting Pioneer—The WEAF Experiment, 1922–1926* (Cambridge: Harvard UP, 1946), pp. 178ff.

2. Hereafter referred to as the *Times* and the *Star*; the company is sometimes referred to as Star.

3. On Kansas City's geographical significance, see Richard Rhodes, *The Inland Ground* (New York: Atheneum, 1970), ch. 7; and, Rowe Findley, "Kansas City, Heartland U.S.A.," *National Geographic,* July 1976, pp. 112ff. The seven counties are Clay, Ray, Jackson, and Cass in Missouri; Platte, Wyandotte, and Johnson in Kansas. See "TV Channel Assignments by Cities," *Broadcasting Yearbook 1946,* p. 441.

Truman—obtained the first license.[4] For 12 years the *Star* had followed television's progress with visits to East Coast TV labs.[5] Although some board members were reluctant, and longtime WDAF general manager H. Dean Fitzer was not enthused, WDAF's William A. Bates piqued the interest of Star president Roy A. Roberts. When newspapers in St. Louis, Milwaukee, and Atlanta, entered television, Roberts sent Bates to visit them.[6]

Bates argued that TV would spread the influence of the *Kansas City Star*. But he also had an altruistic motive: "So, part of my campaign was 'The *Star* can contribute to the good of our community.' And in our early days, we had some good, strong, socially oriented programming."[7] The board passed the proposal 4–3; Roberts was the swing vote.

To stimulate public interest, WDAF-TV broadcast sample programs in conjunction with a big retail exhibition, September 11–13, 1949.[8] The *Star* touted TV as a totally new medium and predicted it would help hold the family together at home.[9]

WDAF-TV was fortunate in 1948 to hire an experienced crew. Engineers James Schmidt and Harold DeGood had helped build Houston's first TV station.[10] Projectionists and film editors Charlie Ford and David McKinstry came from cinema houses, stagehands Ray Maier and Bob Taylor from legitimate theater. Returning from NBC-TV, Maier built WDAF-TV's first news set—a small desk with drapery in front and flats behind.[11]

---

4. Jerry Taylor's Central Radio and Television Schools had subcontracted with KMBC to build a TV station in 1948. "Midland's Portable Television Demonstration," *Centralian*, vol. 7, no. 1, p. 3. Central demonstrated TV at state fairs in 1948. James Schmidt, interview by William J. Ryan, 10 July 1985, Kansas City Broadcasting Oral History Project, Kansas City Broadcasting History Collection, Rockhurst College, Kansas City, Missouri. Hereafter referred to as KCBOHP.

5. "The Story of the Kansas City Star," Souvenir Booklet (Kansas City: Kansas City Star Company, May 1948), p. 37.

6. William A. Bates, interviews, 18 July 1985 and 30 July 1985, KCBOHP. Unless otherwise stated, all subsequent Bates quotes are from 18 July interview.

7. Bates, 30 July 1985, KCBOHP.

8. WDAF-TV's first test pattern was broadcast 20 Aug. 1949. John Doohan, interview, 15 July 1986, KCBOHP.

9. "Every New Epoch Has Opened to the Accompaniment of Jeers," *Star,* 11 Sept. 1949, p. 16-G.

10. Harold DeGood, interview, 1 July 1985, KCBOHP. Subsequent DeGood references are from this interview. They graduated from Central Radio and Television School, formerly National Television Institute—the city's first TV licensee (W9XAL-TV, 1932).

11. In the trade since silent movies, McKinstry was sent to WDAF by the International Alliance of Theatre and Stage Employees, as was Maier. David McKinstry, interview, 22 July 1985 KCBOHP. Ray Maier, interview, 14 July 1986, KCBOHP. All subsequent Maier references are from this interview.

Production in 1949 took place in a 20-by-20 studio, with two large floor-mounted RCA monochrome cameras on heavy dollies. Each camera had four fixed-focal-length turret-mounted lenses. Lights were so hot one performer said the studio was like "a furnace."[12] Engineers ran equipment because, said Schmidt, "They had to know enough about the camera to work on it during the middle of a show."[13]

WDAF-TV began with a five-kilowatt transmitter and a 724-foot tower next to the studio on Signal Hill (31st Street and Summit), high above the convergence of the Kansas and Missouri rivers. The mobile unit was a converted Packard hearse with a platform on top for tripod-mounted cameras and a 55-inch-diameter steel parabolic microwave antenna, which sent the video signal back to Signal Hill. The FCC then required phone lines for audio. Long camera cables snaked from the unit to cover sports, speeches, and other events.

WDAF-TV began at 6 p.m., October 16, 1949, with the national anthem. Fitzer introduced Roberts, and announcer Randall Jessee interviewed other notables.[14] Special programs followed: a live telecast from the American Royal horse and livestock show; a 10-minute film, "The National Broadcasting Company Salute to WDAF-TV"; the station's own film, "The Story of WDAF-TV"; and a special-edition film of "Arthur Godfrey and His Friends" in an hour-long salute to the new station.

The first week WDAF-TV broadcast four hours Sunday, Monday, and Thursday, and three hours, 6–9 p.m., the other days. A 15-minute newscast aired at about 7:30 each evening. Viewers' "WDAF-TV Reception Reports" from summer test signals indicated about 7,500 TV sets in the area.[15] The *Star* estimated 100,000 people watched the inaugural broadcast.[16]

Now Fitzer was general manager of both radio and TV. Verne S. Batten was his assistant manager and vice president; Bates was program director; Jessee, regionally well-known on radio, became assistant program director, news director, and chief TV news announcer. Martha Spalding, a WDAF talent since the 1930s and Fitzer's administrative assistant, was women's director. E. Mannie Russo was commercial manager. Bill Ladesh, Charles

12. Al (Vaughn) Vunovich, interview, 23 Feb. 1989, KCBOHP.
13. James Schmidt, interview, 10 July 1985, KCBOHP. Subsequent Schmidt references are from this interview.
14. Cf. Bob Taylor, interview, 10 Sept. 1985; and Bates, 18 July 1985, KCBOHP.
15. "Sales Surge On," *Star,* 18 Dec. 1954, p. 1-G.
16. "TV on Tonight," *Star,* 16 Oct. 1949.

Jones, and Norm Bernauer were early directors, and Joseph Flaherty, Sr., with WDAF since the 1920s, was chief engineer.

As the lone Kansas City station, WDAF-TV could telecast all four networks (ABC, CBS, Du Mont, and NBC), though not live at first, because Kansas City was not yet linked by coaxial cable. The key to TV network expansion, the FCC noted, "was the linking of the eastern and midwestern coaxial cable systems, bringing 14 metropolitan areas into the coaxial and microwave relay chain."[17] Before this linkage WDAF-TV relied on kine-scopes shipped after network telecasts.

Local production required more trained hands. Bates remedied this problem in 1950, hiring from the first generation of university graduates with education in television. From Northwestern came Harold Glazer, Jay Bar-rington, and Joe Bodwell;[18] from Kansas, Bill and Bob Wormington.

Live network programs began when the cable arrived September 30, 1950—when WDAF-TV officially joined the NBC-TV network. WDAF-TV promised 52 programming hours a week for its 50,000 TV households.[19] DeGood remembered that the first live East Coast network feed (via Omaha) was a Notre Dame football game; the first West Coast feed was United Nations coverage. The World Series became an annual highlight. Before the cable's arrival the station came on the air at 6 p.m. with four hours of variety. A typical Tuesday began with "Cartoon Comedy" ("Red Riding Hood," "Last Dance," and "Blue Blazers" with Buster Keaton); followed by I.N.S. Telenews Newsreel; sports spots with Jay Barrington; news with Randall Jessee; "Howdy Doody" (NBC); Dave Garroway (NBC); "Original Amateur Hour" (Du Mont); "Skyway to Romance"; "Plainclothesman" (Du Mont); and "Chance of a Lifetime" (ABC).

Early news pictures were on film—slides, monochrome prints, and motion picture. Ford shot some; the rest came from Sammie Feeback, a self-taught wire-service photographer working freelance for TV. "We'd take pictures off the telephoto machine—a facsimile machine—and set 'em up and re-shoot 'em on 35mm slides."[20] Feeback became WDAF-TV's first full-time news photographer in 1954, stayed 17 years, was a stringer for NBC and *Life*, and won numerous national awards. Although rough in speech, he

17. *15th Annual Report* (GPO, 1949), p. 42.

18. Harold Glazer, interview, 5 June 1985, KCBOHP. Subsequent Glazer references are from this interview.

19. "Busy for Years," *Star,* 13 Sept. 1950, pp. 1F, 3F.

20. Sammie Feeback, interview, 9 Aug. 1985, KCBOHP. Unless otherwise stated, subsequent Feeback references are from this interview.

became trusted by news makers and sometimes was the only photographer allowed primary access to major events. He believed TV had a public responsibility to *show* news events, "not some talkin' head up there." He once filmed ten stories for one newscast.

Projectionists were busy in early TV days, running kinescopes and editing film for movies, news, and commercials. Good movies were scarce. "Hollywood wouldn't send you one foot of it," Bates explained. "They thought [TV] was their competitor." He found films from Europe and the U.S. Army. Movies improved after Hollywood studios released pre-1948 films for TV in about 1956.[21] Internal complications at Star aggravated the situation. The employee-owned company was worried that Bates had gotten them into "some expensive toy that's just going to blow our fortunes," he recalled. He had "terrible fights" with the purchasing agent to get good films. But when WDAF-TV became profitable, Bates became a hero.

Watershed

Events from 1951 through 1955 shaped the next 40 years of Kansas City television. First, in the summer of '51, live coverage of twin disasters heightened public awareness of the broadcast journalist's role in the rapid diffusion of information, affirming the value of broadcasting "in the public interest, convenience and necessity."

On Friday, July 13, 1951, the flooding Kansas River met the Missouri at Kansas City, causing a major disaster directly below WDAF-TV—safe atop Signal Hill.[22] From the studio roof announcer Frank Feeley, news director Jessee, and camera operator Harry Thomas reported the flood's advance, prompting many volunteers to fight the flood. When a large oil-storage tank tumbled through the torrent and exploded, billowing black smoke could be seen throughout the city, and again citizens could watch close-up, safely in their homes—on TV. More than any broadcast to that date, flood coverage boosted WDAF-TV's news reputation, and Shelby Storke's

---

21. See Sydney Head and Christopher Sterling, *Broadcasting in America*, 4th ed. (Boston: Houghton Mifflin, 1982), p. 203.

22. See National Board of Fire Underwriters, *The Flood Problem in Fire Protection* (New York, 1951 edition), pp. 123–126; and "Vast Flood Cost," *Star*, 14 Sept. 1951.

weather reports gained importance. Randall Jessee became a household name, thereafter known locally as "Mr. Television."[23]

The public was further hooked when WDAF-TV fed NBC the Kansas City hearings of Estes Kefauver's Senate committee investigating organized crime. Viewers saw TV's social-responsibility dimension—it was not just for entertainment. TV-set sales boomed.

Public-affairs programming was integrated with commercial fare in the early '50s. On a rotating basis local clergy hosted the five-minute "Pulpit Portraits" daily at 5 p.m. Bill Ladesh produced "This Is Kansas City," a half-hour public-affairs show moderated by Tony Chap, with a popular segment from city manager L.P. Cookingham's office, written by Miriam Marshall.[24] With expanded local programming, a new studio was begun in 1952.

But threats to WDAF dominance were imminent. First, the independent *TV Preview* program guide emerged in February 1952, carrying news about TV and TV-set advertising—a warning that the Star conglomerate could not remain a monopoly. Two heavier gusts shook Star's media tree, the first June 10, when the U.S. Department of Justice authorized a probe of the Kansas City Star Company for alleged violations of the Sherman Anti-Trust Act. The second came July 1, when the license freeze ended and the FCC began processing new CP applications; WDAF-TV would face competition.

Still, WDAF-TV remained dominant—due to popular NBC programs and the increasing expertise of local production crews. WDAF-TV planned a power increase to 100 kilowatts that spring, expecting new, larger audiences. Second-generation broadcasters emerged at Channel 4 when the other channels were still silent. One was Joseph A. Flaherty, Jr., who began helping televise Kansas City Blues baseball. He later invented electronic news gathering (ENG), which replaced film, and became a CBS senior vice president.[25]

Early TV production at Blues Stadium was basic. WDAF bought its first zoom lens chiefly for baseball when stadium pickups used two cameras, one behind home plate, one on the first-base side. Microwave equipment was on the stadium roof. College-sports coverage was also important. In 1952

23. Frank Feeley, interview, 7 Jan. 1987, KCBOHP. Subsequent Feeley references are from this interview.

24. "Interest in City Government Fostered by a Video Series," *Star*, 14 Sept. 1952, p. 4-F. Tony Chap, telephone interview with author, 1990.

25. Joseph A. Flaherty, Jr., interview, 29 Mar. 1987, KCBOHP.

Owen Bush and Jay Barrington announced Kansas University's NBC-TV football debut from Lawrence. Games were analyzed and prognosticated by *Star* sportswriter Bob Busby every Thursday on "Pigskin Preview" at 10:30 p.m., preceded by "The Big Seven Game of the Week," a highlights film.

Ike's Campaign

Dwight D. Eisenhower's presidential campaign came to Kansas City, Friday, September 19, 1952, when he broadcast a nationwide speech from WDAF-TV's studio. Using a two-way hookup, Eisenhower answered questions from people Jessee interviewed on a downtown sidewalk.[26] Ike's standard reply to a wide range of questions was that the country should change administrations.[27] He appeared to speak impromptu to concerns of fellow midwesterners. But as the floor manager that night later explained, "The people on the street were carefully chosen and ... rehearsed. Eisenhower's answers were carefully scripted and rehearsed."[28] It was a model of strategy developed by Young and Rubicam's Frederick A. Zaghi, publication director for Citizens for Eisenhower,[29] who used all forms of mass media to sell a "cleaning house" theme, getting the Democrats out of government.[30]

That November, President Truman was in town for an election-eve speech, televised by WDAF-TV and fed to NBC. This was the first presidential election return for which WDAF-TV had a direct, live link with the network.

26. Cf. DeGood, 1 July 1985, KCBOHP.

27. "Ike Tempo Rises," *Star*, 18 Sept. 1952, p. 1; and, "The Eisenhower Radio-TV Talk," *Kansas City Times*, 20 Sept. 1952, p. 14.

28. Glazer, KCBOHP.

29. Frederick A. Zaghi, oral-history interview by Dr. John E. Wickman, 5 Nov. 1986, Dwight D. Eisenhower Presidential Library, Abilene, Kansas. Also, Young and Rubicam, Record of "Citizens for Eisenhower" 1952–1961, Y&R File, Dwight D. Eisenhower Presidential Library, Abilene, Kansas.

30. "The Eisenhower Campaign" in Young and Rubicam Record of "Citizens for Eisenhower," pp. 2–3. Dwight D. Eisenhower Presidential Library, Abilene, Kansas.

Dawning

Status quo ended in 1953. The most obvious turn of events came January 6 when a grand jury indicted the Kansas City Star Company for monopolizing both news and advertising—commencing the end of Star media dominance. Roberts called the government investigation an "inquisition" and noted: "We pioneered in this field because we felt it was an opportunity to serve our community. We took a financial beating for years."[31]

Next, the American Federation of Television and Radio Artists struck WDAF and WDAF-TV May 22. Management wanted to give announcers a base pay for anything management asked. AFTRA wanted a higher base, plus additional pay for extra work, such as late shifts and spot commercials.[32] The strike also forced those with dual roles to choose sides.[33]

Then came competition. The first of four new stations in 1953 was KCTY-TV, the city's first UHF station (Channel 25), which began June 6 planning to air CBS, ABC, and Du Mont fare. With WDAF-TV dark and school out for the summer, conditions couldn't have been better for a new station. A KCTY poll estimated there were 45,000 sets with UHF converters.[34]

But WDAF-TV returned June 19 with a new contract, in time for the nation's top story on the 9:30 newscast: the execution of Ethel and Julius Rosenberg for treason.

WDAF-TV's first serious competitors were on Channel 9. When the license freeze ended, four radio stations scrambled for Kansas City's two remaining VHF channels.[35] WHB and KMBC wanted Channel 9, so the FCC unconventionally awarded them separate licenses for the *same channel*! Carrying popular CBS programming, the Channel 9 twins signed on August

31. "The Kansas City Star Makes Answer to the Government's Anti-Trust Suit" (advertisement), *New York Times*, 9 Jan. 1953, p. 22.

32. Murray Nolte, interview, 29 May 1986, KCBOHP. Subsequent Nolte references are from this interview.

33. Martha Spalding, interview, 16 Aug. 1985, KCBOHP. See "TV Strike Talks Go On," *Kansas City Times*, 3 June 1953, p. 1.

34. KCTY-TV was owned and operated by Empire Coil Company of New Rochelle, New York. FCC, "Final Report and Order" (April 11) *Annual Report* (GPO, 30 June 1952). See "Herbert Mayer: Faith Turns Industrialist Into 'Mr. Television,'" *TV Preview*, Aug. 1953, p. 4; Fred Kiewit, "The Second Television Station Here Goes Into Action Quickly," *Star*, 14 June 1953.

35. KCMO and WIBW (Topeka) wanted Channel 5. Channel 13 was assigned to Topeka. Channel 2 had been reassigned to St. Joseph, Missouri.

1, 1953.[36] When KCMO-TV began on Channel 5, September 27, WDAF-TV's news staff now competed simultaneously with three separate news teams, including veteran radio news directors Claude Dorsey (KMBC) and Jim Monroe (KCMO), and the aggressive Charles Gray (WHB). Still, WDAF-TV's experience and the *Star*'s resources proved crucial when a major news event occurred at summer's end.

The Greenlease Kidnapping

The kidnapping of young Bobby Greenlease became nationwide news the week of September 28, 1953, reminiscent of the Lindbergh kidnapping. Police contacts, and Feeback's acquaintanceship with the family, gained WDAF-TV exclusive coverage. Feeback followed this case vigorously from the discovery of the boy's body to Bobby's funeral, and to the kidnappers' subsequent trial and execution. KCMO's Harold Mack Grove recalled this as one of the significant stories of his 21-year career: "But unfortunately, this was a case of the *Kansas City Star* and the police department and the FBI being in very close collusion."[37]

When the trial began, Thomas Hart Benton sketched scenes for TV, and Feeback sent photos to NBC's nightly news with John Cameron Swayze, former Kansas City newscaster. WHB's Gray recalled, "Channel 4 had its own filming staff. None of the rest of us did. We were too new in television."[38]

WDAF-TV remained competitive in 1953. Bates became station manager, Al Ladesich became program director, Vic Peck was assistant program director. Channel 4 was on with the "Today" show almost two hours before Channel 9 began. Neither KCTY nor KCMO-TV programmed until 4 p.m. WDAF's slogan "There's more on 4" was no exaggeration.

WDAF-TV's weather announcer for 18 years was Murray Nolte. "[Weather] was very similar to what's done now in presenting the national picture, the regional picture and then the forecast." He memorized the whole show and wrote on the map with a paint stick as he talked. His five-minute segment included a minute of extemporaneous commercials.

36. *Broadcasting Yearbook 1985*, p. C-34; Pike states it was 2 Aug. Bo Pike, interview, 1 July 1986, KCBOHP. Compare Bo Pike personal collection of WHB schedules; "Sigh at Job End," *Star*, 13 Sept. 1953, p. 3F; *TV Preview*, 14 Sept. 1953, p. 5; and *TV Preview*, Aug. 1953, p. 3.

37. Harold McGregor Grove, interview, 20 June 1986, KCBOHP.

38. Charles Gray, interview, 5 Oct. 1990, KCBOHP.

Before the freeze ended, WDAF-TV originated network shows for both CBS and NBC. Most went to NBC, but productions of the "Fred Waring Show" and Ed Sullivan's "Toast of the Town" were for CBS.[39] WDAF-TV also produced a number of local shows, like "Videosyncracies," hosted by Bob Kerr, and "Western Roundup," with "Frito Frank" Feeley—possibly the first Kansas City TV show with children on the set.

While some programs focused on social issues, television's profit-making demands steered it away from Bates's earlier ideal that "by this direct personal communication, this could be made into a much better world.... [TV] turned into a bit of that, but mainly a marketing device. And, [as] I think back on it now, that is probably what made it viable."[40] Still, believing TV could provide community service *and* be fiscally sound, he supported a strong news team throughout his tenure, appointing successively three talented news directors: Jessee, Walt Bodine, and Bill Leeds.

The age of local ownership ended in 1953 when Meredith Broadcasting Corporation took over KCMO AM-FM-TV, November 23. In December, Du Mont Laboratories bought KCTY and closed it in February.

WDAF-TV continued to roll with the first color pickup of a regular NBC-TV network program, March 5, 1954 (not a reality for many viewers because few had color sets). A lack of relay equipment had delayed color from reaching Kansas City from New York. Television normally came from Chicago through Omaha. The NBC color transmission came instead via a series of AT&T microwave relay towers from St. Louis. WDAF predicted that regular color broadcasts would begin that summer.[41]

At year's end Kansas City had nearly 338,700 TV sets in use;[42] by late summer 1955, a half million. The two-set home was becoming the norm. Screen sizes had grown from 10 and 12 inches to 21 inches.

A network affiliation switch in 1955 affected WDAF's competitors. KCMO-TV moved from ABC to CBS. WHB dropped TV. KMBC-TV switched to the weaker ABC but countered WDAF and KCMO network fare with top-quality local daytime shows.[43]

---

39. Bob Wormington interview, 25 June 1985, KCBOHP. Subsequent Wormington references are from this interview.

40. Bates, 30 July 1985, KCBOHP.

41. See "'Go' to Color TV," *Star,* 18 Dec. 1953, p. 1; and "Ready on Color," *Kansas City Times,* 19 Dec. 1953, p. 1.

42. "Big TV problem: Counting the Sets," *Sponsor,* 22 Feb. 1954, p. 27.

43. ABC-TV programming began at 5:30 p.m.

The Star Bows Out

The government's case against the Kansas City Star Company was considered the most extensive antitrust proceedings yet leveled against a daily U.S. newspaper—a landmark in mass-media antitrust history. The company was in court 12 years.[44] Although the trial focused on newspaper practices, WDAF and WDAF-TV were integrally involved.

Some thought politics played a role, that the suit was Truman's retribution for *Star* investigations of voting fraud during his 1930s senatorial campaign and the 1947 Democratic primary.[45] The indictment was handed down shortly before Truman left the White House.

There were both criminal and civil charges.[46] The criminal trial began January 17, 1955. Most testimony dealt with the newspapers, but WDAF-TV was charged with refusing to sell time to advertisers who would not also advertise on WDAF or in the papers.[47] *TV Preview* also had been denied the right to advertise on WDAF-TV. The future of WDAF and WDAF-TV rested with the outcome of the civil trial. The government asked the court to halt the company's monopolizing actions and to revoke Star's broadcast licenses.[48] Judge Richard A. Duncan could either separate the broadcasters from the newspapers or revoke the broadcasting licenses altogether.[49]

The company was found guilty on two counts and its ad manager on one February 22, 1955. Appeals were denied.[50] In the final decree, November 15, 1957, Star agreed to sell WDAF and WDAF-TV, to transfer the licenses,

44. See Lorry Elbon Rytting, "United States of America, et al. v. The Kansas City Star Company, et al.—An Antitrust Case Study," Ph.D. diss., University of Wisconsin, Aug. 1969.

45. See Randall Jessee, oral-history interview by Dr. Philip C. Brooks, Copenhagen, Denmark, 19 May 1964; Harry S. Truman Presidential Library, Independence, Missouri. Cf. Letter to Mary Jane Truman, 12 May 1948, Post Presidency File, Memoirs, box 47, set 1, Harry S. Truman Presidential Library, Independence, Missouri. And Harry S. Truman, Memorandum, 10 Jan. 1952, President's Secretary's Files, Box 334, longhand notes, n.d., Harry S. Truman Presidential Library, Independence, Missouri.

46. Criminal Action No. 18444 and Civil Action No. 7989, both filed in U.S. District Court for the Western District of Missouri.

47. The Kansas City Star Company v. U.S., Emil S. Sees v. U.S., 3 Jan. 1957. 240 F. 2d 643. AP, "Kansas City Star Indicted as Trust," *New York Times,* 7 Jan. 1953, p. 29. See also: Ronald E. Tidwell's testimony cited in Rytting, pp. 210–211.

48. The Kansas City Star Company v. U.S. 3 Jan. 1957. 240 F. 2d 643. Also, "Kansas City Star Indicted as Trust."

49. See sec. 311, Communications Act of 1934; "'Star' Station Ownership…" *Broadcasting,* 28 Feb. 1955, p. 72; and Rytting, pp. 213–214. See Civil Complaint, pp. 11–14.

50. U.S. Appeals Court, Eighth District, 3 Jan. 1957. 240 F.2d 643, p. 666.

and not to acquire any interest in commercial radio or television stations in Kansas City without court approval.[51] Fortunately for the public, broadcasting was uninterrupted.

After much speculation about likely buyers, National Theaters announced November 26 it would pay $7.6 million for the stations.[52] The deal went through in May 1958. Charles L. Glett, president, put Elmer C. Rhoden in charge of the Kansas City operation.[53]

New Era

Viewers watching Channel 4 at 5:30 p.m., May 28, 1958, witnessed the end of 36 years of broadcasting by the *Kansas City Star*. They saw the half-hour "History and Horizons—The Story of WDAF Radio and TV," then heard Roberts pledge to continue a strong newspaper presence in the city and, with emotion in his voice, announce the transfer.

NBC's Harry Bannister noted that WDAF-TV was "one of the founding stations of the NBC television network." He welcomed the new owner, which he said had "the means, the know-how, and the desire to make WDAF and WDAF-TV a source of affection and pride to all Kansas Citians."[54] This matched the *Star*'s desire to keep the stations "in the hands of people who had Kansas City interests at heart."[55]

It was a smooth transition and a time of high morale. Fitzer retired after 33 years; Bates became vice president and general manager of radio and TV. Glett gave management freedom to operate as they knew best in the market they knew best. Bodine succeeded Jessee as news director and, independent of the *Star*, "had the rare opportunity of putting together from scratch a television and radio newsroom for an ongoing station."[56]

---

51. See Rytting, p. 241. Former *Star* Librarian John Doohan recalled the company had the choice of divesting the *Times* instead of the broadcast operations but chose to stay solely in the newspaper business. KCBOHP.

52. "KC 'Star' Signs Decree to Sell Its WDAF-AM-TV," *Broadcasting,* 18 Nov. 1957, p. 9. "Star Sells Stations," *New York Times,* 26 Nov. 1957, p. 67.

53. *New York Times,* 30 May 1958, p. 41; Bates, KCBOHP, 18 July and 10 July 1985. National Theaters held title as National Missouri T.V., a Missouri subsidiary of National Theaters, with stock held by another subsidiary, National Film Investments, "WDAF Sale Is Finished," *Star,* 28 May 1958, p. 1.

54. "WDAF, TV in New Hands," *Kansas City Times,* 19 May 1958, pp. 1, 4–5.

55. Martha Spalding, interview, 16 Aug. 1985, KCBOHP.

It became arguably the most complete, experienced news operation. As Bodine recalled 30 years later, "I *did* do it well, in the sense that I hired a number of really fine people." He included Bill Leeds, "who while he was with us won the Earl Godwin Award for news coverage, served in the London bureau on NBC for six months and came back to us, then was hired by NBC—he ran the *Meet the Press* program"; John Harrington, later an anchor at Cleveland's NBC affiliate; Joe Benti, who later replaced Mike Wallace on "CBS Morning News"; and Chris Condon, who became an anchor in St. Louis.

National Theaters had hoped to expand in several cities, but Glett died and Transcontinent Television Corporation snapped up WDAF properties in 1960 for $9.75 million.[57] Bates remained general manager, and the staff basically remained intact.

Programming

Kansas City teens were dancing to Top 40 music, so TV dance programs soon emerged. Jay Barrington's "TV Teen Town" was the city's first, premiering on Channel 4 in January 1955, directed by Bill Donovan.[58] It was on every Saturday for three years.

Top network shows originated from WDAF-TV in 1955, including the "Today" show. Bob Wormington recalled: "Over the next handful of years I directed I guess 200 or more network television programs.... It was a great time to be in live television." Most memorable to Schmidt, who became chief engineer in 1956, was Dave Garroway's "Wide Wide World" series. One featured Missouri artist Thomas Hart Benton, another the famed Menninger Clinic in Topeka.

Local programming included a studio show with top Kansas City jazz artists. So much could be done locally partly because evening programs were blocked into quarter hours. "Remember," said Wormington, "the old *Tonight Show* had a 15-minute window before it started and we used to do a *Tonight*

56. Walt Bodine, interviews, 18 June 1985 and 15 Jan. 1987, KCBOHP. Subsequent Bodine references are from these sources.

57. Major stockholders in 1961 were Paul A. Schoellkopf, Jr. (chairman); J. Fred Schoellkopf IV; George F. Goodyear; Jack Wrather, Jr.; General Railway Signal Company; and Edward Petry Company. *Broadcasting Yearbook 1961.*

58. Cf. James Bray, interview, 21 July 1985, KCBOHP.

in Kansas City." "Dr. N. Ventor" (1956–59) was a popular 90-minute local children's program that required daily creativity and improvisation. Glazer created an "Idea Box," which introduced cartoons and a zany inventor "whose inventions never worked." Nolte, the inventor, ad-libbed every line, used no "inside jokes," and tried never to "talk down to children." The show had a remarkable 42 percent audience share in July 1956.[59]

News and Videotape

Videotape arrived in Kansas City about 1960. At WDAF-TV it was used first for commercials, then for news inserts, and sometimes to delay network shows. Yet with videotape, television, in Schmidt's words, "lost a lot of its punch," as talent knew they could redo the material, so "didn't put their best stuff into it." ENG was even more revolutionary.

But ENG didn't arrive in time to cover the killer tornado that slashed through suburban Ruskin Heights, Missouri, May 20, 1957.[60] Unlike the '51 flood coverage, this event could be fed to the network live. Using a National Guard generator for power, DeGood's crew waited all night with the mobile unit to send it to the "Today" show at dawn.

In 1963 DeGood designed a new mobile news unit with a microwave subcarrier for audio—the forerunner of today's microwave vans. The truck was busy, sometimes at a hectic pace. James O'Connor remembered, "We did two shows—two live feeds—in a half hour newscast one time from two different locations, just by keeping the generator going so all the equipment was hot. Do a shoot; tear down and run."[61] Between September 1963 and April 1964 the mobile news crew was on the road virtually every day.

59. A.C. Nielsen Company, cited in Phil LaCerte, "Former Merriam Mayor Recalls TV Kid Stuff," *Journal Herald* (Merriam and Shawnee, Kansas), 14 May 1986, p. 1.

60. See "It Seems Like Only Yesterday," videotape on the 20th anniversary of WDAF-TV, 1969, WDAF-TV archives.

61. James O'Connor, interview, 25 June 1985, KCBOHP.

Taft Buys WDAF

WDAF-TV changed abruptly when Cincinnati-based Taft Broadcasting Company bought the radio and television stations February 19, 1964, for $26.9 million. The mobile news operation stopped; 18 people, including the entire news staff, lost their jobs;[62] movies and syndicated shows preempted network programming. Bates left to advise Kansas City Southern Industries' cable-TV venture. Bob Wormington became general manager, but he and Bill also eventually left, each becoming a general manager of competing UHF stations. Some local programs continued, but budget cuts took their toll. WDAF-TV news ratings quickly dropped from first to third. This scenario lasted through the decade—the most serious local example of using accounting figures to rationalize layoffs.

Another strike was inevitable. One director sensed after the first employees' meeting with Taft that "as each contract came up ... they were going to be in for a battle."[63] After months of negotiations 25 on-air personnel and directors began picketing December 11, 1965.[64] The key issue was what management called "job flexibility." AFTRA's David Schnabel said, "We have to guarantee this flexibility will not cost us jobs."[65] When Taft brought in employees from other cities, AFTRA accused management of trying to break the union.[66] This became the most grueling and nonproductive strike in Kansas City broadcasting—and was never settled.

A new face appeared on Channel 4 newscasts August 5, 1967, as Lena Rivers Smith became the first African-American journalist on Kansas City television. Although copywriter Joan Plavnick was the first woman in a Kansas City TV newsroom,[67] Smith was the first on camera, as a general-

---

62. They included Leeds, Benti, Conden, Del Donahue (KYW, Cleveland), Tom Reed (NBC, news producer), Ken Robinson (Phoenix, news director), Sam Stuart (Tulsa, news director), and Don Harness (Tom Brokaw's producer). See Wormington, KCBOHP, and Bodine, KCBOHP.

63. Robert Musberger, interview, 27 Mar. 1987, KCBOHP.

64. "In Talks at WDAF," *Star,* 4 Mar. 1965; and "End Talks with WDAF," *Kansas City Times,* 7 Dec. 1965, Missouri Valley Room local history collection, Kansas City, Missouri, Public Library, main branch.

65. "Report Progress in Strike at WDAF," *Kansas City Times,* 5 Mar. 1966, Missouri Valley Room local history collection, Kansas City, Missouri, Public Library, main branch.

66. "Group Replacing Strikers at WDAF," *Kansas City Times,* 13 Dec. 1965, Missouri Valley Room local history collection, Kansas City, Missouri, Public Library, main branch.

67. WDAF-TV's Walt Bodine hired Joan Plavnick, a Missouri University Journalism School graduate, in June 1958. Joan Plavnick, interview, 10 Nov. 1993, KCBOHP.

assignment reporter. She focused on public schools and the teachers' union.[68] She also worked tirelessly for racial integration and civil rights. When her career was cut short at age 46 by a fatal heart attack on November 18, 1968, the interracial Panel of American Women established a college scholarship fund in her name for black students entering journalism.[69]

Racial Crisis and Vietnam

The biggest test yet for Kansas City broadcasters came in April 1968, following the funeral of the Reverend Dr. Martin Luther King, Jr. Long-pent-up frustration and dashed hopes burst forth in a student march to city hall. After police fired tear gas into the crowd there and again at an Episcopal church, riots began, and Kansas City joined other U.S. cities with tense days and nights of fires, shootings, and curfews. WDAF and WDAF-TV simulcast a public-affairs panel discussing the unrest to help ease tensions.[70]

In Vietnam, Leeds and Feeback covered local angles of the war and sent reports to NBC. Back home, Feeback sent film about families back to the soldiers. For this innovation he was recognized in Washington by the VFW women's auxiliary.[71]

Sales

By the end of the '60s the TV industry was on a roll, and those in sales knew it. When Gerald Uppman began at WDAF-TV in local sales in 1960, there was a local sales manager and a national (or general) sales manager and three local salesmen. Thirty years later the number had more than doubled, and he estimated that women held at least half the city's TV sales positions. In his early days, Uppman said, "it was very unsophisticated.... Nobody

68. "Lena Rivers Smith," obit., *Star,* 19 Nov. 1968, Missouri Valley Room local history collection, Kansas City, Missouri, Public Library, main branch, microfilm box 82.

69. "Establish Fund as a Memorial to Newswoman," *Star,* 19 Nov. 1968, Missouri Valley Room local history collection, Kansas City, Missouri, Public Library, main branch.

70. "Test Case Blamed in Disorder," *Kansas City Times,* 10 Apr. 1968, p. 6B. Compare Neil Poindexter, interview, 11 Jan. 1987, KCBOHP.

71. Sam Feeback interview with John Pritchett, 6 May 1985, *Town Hall,* WHB radio. Feeback, KCBOHP.

cared at all about ratings!" In those days, "You were just out selling *television*." By the mid-1960s, market research became "the only way I would have to prove to an advertiser that I could give them a better deal than the guy down the street."[72]

Although Taft was running "cost-effective," a few local shows continued. The "Betty Hayes Show" for women was replaced in 1970 by the "Beverly Breckenridge Show," aimed at young women and confronting controversial contemporary issues. On Saturday mornings in 1966 "Categories" matched wits of high-school students. It was followed by an area high-school football game. Public-affairs programs included a Sunday-morning ecumenical, issues-oriented show hosted by the Reverend Larry Thornton, a Presbyterian, and a 15-minute program hosted by Rabbi Morris Margolies. Weekdays WDAF-TV aired "Black Heritage" at 5:25 p.m. Yet viewer discontent grew as movie packages preempted NBC. When Buddy Turner arrived as operations manager in July 1973, he found less concern about ratings and local image than about profit.[73]

Renewal

A turnaround came at the end of the '70s after Earl Beall became general manager. A former sales manager, he knew the market and cared about the station's image. Mike McDonald became news director. Schmidt modernized equipment for local production. Newscasts were expanded, and Royals baseball returned to Channel 4 as WDAF-TV rediscovered the value of its traditional strong suit—serving its community.

---

72. Gerald Uppman, interview, 4 June 1991, KCBOHP.
73. Bud Turner, interview, 22 July 1991, KCBOHP.

IV

The Western Frontier

17

The West Coast's First Television Station: KCBS, Los Angeles

Steven C. Runyon

Introduction and Background

This chapter details the history, programming, and landmark achieve-ments of the first decade of experimental television station W6XAO, now KCBS television, Channel 2, in Los Angeles. The station was originally licensed to the Don Lee Broadcasting System by the Federal Radio Commis-sion in 1931 and has the distinction of being the West Coast's first television station. The efforts of the Don Lee Broadcasting System's television staff on the West Coast resulted in some of the most important technical discoveries and programming concepts affecting television's future. While television was still in its infancy throughout America, the Don Lee organization was already providing a regular programming service over its experimental station W6XAO in Los Angeles to that segment of the public possessing receiving apparatus. This is the story of that pioneering station and pioneer Harry R. Lubcke, who developed the station.

Lubcke was appointed director of television for the Don Lee Broad-casting System in Los Angeles on November 14, 1930. For a period of approximately 1½ years prior to this time, Lubcke had been employed by the Crocker Research Laboratories in San Francisco. As assistant director of research at the Crocker Labs,[1] Lubcke worked directly under Philo T.

---

1. "Abstract From Who's Who, October 1943," personal files of Harry R. Lubcke, Hollywood, California.

Farnsworth in all-electronic television experimentation and research. Lubcke was able to work with and help develop Farnsworth's image-dissector camera tube, image-display cathode-ray tube, and electronic scanning through the use of sawtooth waveshapes and magnetic deflection of the scanning beam. Lubcke, while he was with the Crocker Labs, developed the mathematical theory of admittance neutralization that made wideband television amplification practical. The results of this discovery made it possible to obtain a much better-quality television image.[2] In his apprenticeship with Farnsworth, Lubcke learned the basic television principles that he was to develop further through the support of the Don Lee organization.

Harry Lubcke married on November 1, 1930. While on his honeymoon at the Hotel St. Catherine on Santa Catalina Island, Avalon, California, Lubcke drew up a block diagram of a television-transmitter and receiver, and a proposal of estimated costs for this basic television system. This presentation material, dated November 3, 1930, and written on Hotel St. Catherine stationery, was prepared for the purpose of convincing Don Lee of the feasibility of a television-transmission facility and compatible receiving apparatus. Lubcke estimated the cost of parts for his television transmitter to be $2,003. Television-receiver parts were budgeted at $163. Labor cost for a director and assistant working for six months was projected to be $2,700. Lubcke, therefore, estimated the entire outlay for his proposed television system to be $4,866.[3] On November 14, 1930, after a number of meetings with Lee, Lubcke was made director of television of the Don Lee Broadcasting System in Los Angeles.

Regular Television Program Service

For the next year Harry Lubcke and his staff developed and built the television equipment necessary to transmit and receive visual images. On May 10, 1931, they transmitted their first television image from one side of a room to the other using all-electronic television equipment. This was the first of many such test transmissions. After slightly over one year of devel-

---

2. Harry R. Lubcke, oral-history interview conducted by Steven C. Runyon, 21 September 1974, transcribed audio recording from the personal files of S.C. Runyon, University of San Francisco.

3. Harry R. Lubcke Notes, 3 November 1930, personal files of Harry R. Lubcke, Hollywood, California.

oping, building, and testing, the Don Lee Broadcasting System's experimental visual broadcast station received test authorization from the Federal Radio Commission and began on-air testing November 29, 1931, using the call sign W6XAO. On December 23, 1931, W6XAO initiated a regular schedule of program transmissions on a one-hour-per-day, six-day-a-week basis. This program service continued and grew throughout the 1930s. These facts contradict NBC's claim that on April 30, 1939, NBC inaugurated the first regular television program service in the United States over W2XBS in New York.[4]

The FRC granted the Don Lee Broadcasting System a license to operate the station on January 15, 1932. W6XAO was one of the first television stations to operate using all-electronic equipment. It was also one of the first stations to make use of the newly available VHF band of 43–46 megahertz.[5] Motion-picture film images made up W6XAO's first programming. The motion-picture pickup equipment of W6XAO included a cathode-ray tube, motion-picture projector, and photoelectric cell.

The transmitter and television facility of the Don Lee Broadcasting System was located on the second floor of the Don Lee Building, 1076 West Seventh Street, at Bixel Street, in Los Angeles, California. A 150-foot transmission line carried the signal from the transmitter to the roof of the eight-story building, where it fed the antenna. According to a report to the FRC by Lubcke: "The maximum distance at which signals were received was thirty-nine miles."[6] In order to receive and monitor the television transmissions, Lubcke and his staff designed and manufactured an all-electronic cathode-ray tube receiver. In late 1931 and early 1932 the trans-

----

4. Niles Trammel (NBC president), address, Television Seminar of the Radio Executives Club of New York, New York City, 18 May 1944 (transcript on file in the Mass Communications History Center of the State Historical Society of Wisconsin, Madison) cited in Allan David Larson, "Integration and Attempted Integration Between the Motion Picture and Television Industries through 1956," Ph.D. diss., Ohio University, 1979, p. 33.

5. On 11 October 1929 the Federal Radio Commission issued "General Order No. 74," which allocated four 100-kilohertz-wide frequency bands between two and three megahertz for experimental visual broadcasting. By 1931 the FRC had recognized the need for experimental visual broadcasting using a much greater bandwidth in order to improve image quality. In this regard the FRC authorized experimental visual broadcasting within three VHF frequency bands: 43–46 megahertz, 48.5–50.3 megahertz, and 60–80 megahertz.

6. Harry R. Lubcke, "Report to the Federal Radio Commission on the Event of Renewal of License of Experimental Visual Broadcasting Station W6XAO" (Los Angeles: Don Lee, 1932), pp. 3–4. (The group of Lubcke's Reports to the FRC and FCC from his personal files is the third of three major sources from which information was obtained. Direct quotations and information obtained from other sources are footnoted as appropriate.)

mitted images included vertical parallel bars, a gray scale showing a gradated field of light, and triangles. During the scheduled evening transmissions, images included filmed close-up photographs of movie stars as well as motion-picture clips and film loops. From the time of its initial transmission on November 29, 1931, until license renewal on March 1, 1932, W6XAO was on the air a total of 183 hours. Approximately half of the transmissions occurred during the announced program schedule time of 6–7 p.m., Pacific Standard Time, Monday through Saturday. The balance consisted of experimental testing during other various hours.

During the last week of February 1932, Lubcke and his staff placed in operation a mechanical-disk type of scanning apparatus in order to compare it with the all-electronic scanning equipment already in service at the Don Lee television facility. They made numerous tests in order to compare and determine the interchangeability of the two scanning systems. Both mechanical and cathode-ray receivers could pick up either the mechanically or electronically scanned motion-picture images. In March 1932 W6XAO discontinued the electronic scanning of motion-picture film and began to use only the mechanical scanning apparatus that had been placed into operation the previous month. The Don Lee television engineers continued to improve the mechanical-scanning equipment, adding new components as they became available or as they were developed in the Don Lee laboratory.

First Airplane Television Reception

A major development by Lubcke and the Don Lee engineering staff was the transmission of self-synchronized images. Most early television required the same power source for both the transmission equipment and receiver in order for synchronization to occur. With Lubcke's system the synchronizing pulses were transmitted along with the coded picture information. Therefore, using the Lubcke system, the receiver could be connected to a completely separate power source, and synchronization between the transmitter and the receiver would still occur. In order to prove conclusively that synchronization did not occur because of a power source common to both the transmitting equipment and receiver, transmissions to a receiver located on a plane in flight were attempted.

On May 21, 1932, the W6XAO engineering staff under Lubcke's leadership successfully demonstrated the world's first television transmission to an airplane in flight, the first television reception aboard an airplane in flight, and the first reception of television images while traveling at air-flight speeds. Arrangements were made with Western Air Express, the predecessor of Western Airlines, and a trimotor passenger-mail plane was provided. A television receiver with a screen size approximately eight inches square, looking like one of the large radio consoles of the time, was mounted in the front of the passenger cabin centered between the seats. The front surface of the television screen faced the rear of the cabin. The self-synchronizing receiver, designed and constructed by Lubcke, was of the all-electronic type containing a cathode-ray tube. Fifteen newspapermen, invited as official observers, were present at United Airport, now Burbank Airport, in Los Angeles on Saturday, May 21, 1932, to witness the experiment and demonstration. Passengers included Lubcke, a Western Air Express radio engineer, and representatives of the *Los Angeles Examiner, Christian Science Monitor,* United Press, Associated Press, the *Pasadena Star News,* and the Central Press.

> The cabin of the plane was completely dark. Shades covered the windows so that the television screen could be seen easily. The plane taxied to the end of the runway and gently rose into the air after a short run. For the first few minutes nothing could be seen. Then as the eyes of the passengers became accustomed to the darkness they saw Mr. Lubcke twisting the dials of the cabinet. Soon flashes of light danced across the screen. Then the specks of light seemed to coagulate and black masses curled in circles. Soon this gave way to a distorted image and Mr. Lubcke pointed exultantly to the screen. Finally the image cleared and in a blue light which flickered constantly the image of a girl was plainly seen. As she talked to someone at her side the movement of her head and shoulders was discerned. The image remained on the screen for five or six minutes....
>
> "For the first time in the history of television 80 lines were transmitted in forming the image," said Mr. Lubcke. "The image was repeated 15 times per second."[7]

The airplane made a total of three flights over the Los Angeles area, reaching a height of several thousand feet and a distance of over 10 miles from the transmitter and antenna while the television receiver installed aboard the plane successfully received the W6XAO television signals.

---

7. "Television Reaches into Airplane Cabin," *Speed,* June 1932, pp. 14–15.

Transmission Across the Country

During 1932 the Don Lee television engineers built and began operation of a 1,000-watt television transmitter that operated on a frequency of 2.15 megahertz and simulcast the programming of W6XAO. The FRC licensed this station as W6XS. The engineers completed construction of the transmitter on November 17, 1932. It was decided that regularly scheduled operation of the transmitter would begin on December 23, 1932, to coincide with the first anniversary of W6XAO. Because of the frequency and transmission power, the station could be received throughout much of the United States. The transmitter was therefore dubbed "the continental frequency television transmitter." In its first 3½ months of program testing and licensed broadcasting, viewers received W6XS in various areas of California, in Oregon, Washington, Idaho, Arizona, Texas, Minnesota, and Maine. Don Lee television received 106 reception reports and 26 letters requesting information, as well as numerous telephone calls and in-person requests. The most distant reception reports came from Houlton, Maine, close to 2,700 miles from the transmission point in Los Angeles. From May 15, 1933, through May 17, 1933, W6XS broadcasts were received at the Southern California Radio Show in Los Angeles. Broadcast hours were expanded so that programming could be received from 3–5 and from 7–10 p.m. during each of the three days that the show took place. In all, over 30,000 persons witnessed the received images. This was one of the first times, if not the first time, that an audience this large was exposed to television over such a short period.

A unique long-distance test of the W6XS signals was conducted on Friday, January 5, and Saturday, January 6, of 1934. Lubcke and members of his engineering staff transported one of their custom-built receivers to the San Francisco Bay area to compare reception with that obtainable in the Los Angeles area. Using his parents' home in a residential section of Alameda as the receiving point, Lubcke attempted reception of the W6XS transmissions.[8] A number of prominent university professors and local radio engineers witnessed the tests at the Alameda residence.

---

8. "Television," *International Photographer*, February 1934, p. 10.

Commenting upon the reception, Dr. Lester E. Reukema, Professor of electrical engineering, at the University of California, Berkeley, said, regarding a close-up of a motion picture star:

"One could readily see the movement of her head, causing a slight wave of the pendant earrings she wore, and could see her lips move as she spoke. In the picture 'Madison Square Garden,' the bodies of the boxers in trunks could be clearly seen at times, also the footwork, striking of blows, the boxing gloves, dodging of blows, etc. Considering the distance covered, approximately 350 miles air-line, I was surprised that the fading was not more severe...."

The images were also witnessed by Frank C. Jones, prominent radio consultant....

"Among the scenes were those of yell leaders in a stadium leading cheers for a rooting section. The action and pictures of the yell leaders were quite good. In a Paramount short of 'Over the Jumps,' I saw some scenes of small outboard motorboat races where the boats and the waves in the wake of the boats were quite good. The pictures were much better than I expected to view over such a distance."

In commenting upon the experimental work successfully concluded in Alameda last week, Harry R. Lubcke, director of television for the Don Lee Broadcasting System, said:

"This reception, as well as reports from many short-wave listeners who chance upon the signal and listen to the voice of the announcers, establishes the fact that our television service is state-wide. It is available to anyone who will erect a good aerial and purchase or construct the necessary equipment."[9]

W6XS ceased broadcasting on October 24, 1934. Its license was allowed to expire on November 1, 1934. The total number of hours of operation was 1,856.18 during the slightly less than two years, from November 17, 1932, through October 24, 1934, that W6XS was on the air. Though W6XS was experimental in nature and on the air for only a short time, the station provided much useful information to the Don Lee engineering staff, and, like W6XAO, is a part of the heritage that eventually became KCBS Television.

---

9. "Television," *International Photographer*, February 1934, p. 10.

Transmission of a Major Disaster

At approximately 5:54 p.m., Pacific Standard Time, on Friday, March 10, 1933, a severe earthquake hit the Los Angeles area. It was an event that focused attention on Don Lee television. Known as the Long Beach Earthquake, it caused approximately 120 deaths and property losses exceeding $40 million. Long Beach, Compton, and Huntington Park were the most extensively damaged. In Compton "practically every building within a 3-block radius was demolished or badly damaged. A number of automobiles were buried beneath the debris."[10] In Long Beach "walls caved in, buildings collapsed, tanks fell through roofs, houses displaced and roads cracked, communication with city disrupted; oil derricks caught fire."[11]

Soon after the quake Don Lee television acquired motion pictures of the damage from a local film organization and transmitted the film images over W6XAO. The first film obtained was of mediocre quality due to the fact that it was shot at night using flares and temporary lights, but the shots were televised "within a few hours of the tremblor [sic]."[12] Day scenes of the disaster were obtained and televised over the Don Lee television stations, and later two full reels were televised showing the extent of the damage. A number of homes and at least two stores that were holding advertised public demonstrations of television in the Los Angeles area received the W6XAO telecasts. W6XS provided coverage to more distant areas. "Since the public was not admitted to the stricken area for some two weeks, many saw television images of the damage before they were permitted to view the actual scenes. This is believed to be the first television transmission of scenes of a major disaster, whether from film or otherwise."[13]

---

10. Frank Neumann, *United States Earthquakes 1933* (Washington, D.C.: U.S. Department of Commerce Coast and Geodetic Survey, 1935), p. 11.

11. Neumann, p. 11.

12. *Western Canada Radio News*, 2 April 1933, clipping in Harry R. Lubcke, "Report to the Federal Radio Commission on the Event of Renewal of License of Experimental Visual Broadcasting Stations W6XAO and W6XS" (Los Angeles: Don Lee, second 1933 report), p. 34.

13. Harry R. Lubcke, "Report to the Federal Radio Commission on the Event of Renewal of License of Experimental Visual Broadcasting Stations W6XAO and W6XS" (Los Angeles: Don Lee, second 1933 report), p. 7.

Motion Pictures on Television

For well over a year after the initial on-air date of W6XAO, the Don Lee television engineers had made use of a number of film loops for the purposes of testing and transmitting. Their library of loops was, however, very limited, and they had repeated each of the film loops innumerable times. To generate added publicity, and to provide, simultaneously, new film material for their viewers, arrangements were made with World Wide Pictures to televise the seven-reel feature film *The Crooked Circle.* The motion picture, an Astor Pictures Corporation production featuring Zasu Pitts, James Gleason, and Ben Lyon,[14] was televised on Thursday, March 23, and Friday, March 24, 1933, while still playing in local theaters. The telecast of this feature film was the beginning of regular showings of current films from Hollywood studios over the television facilities of the Don Lee Broadcasting System. On April 4, 1933, the daily television screening of Pathe newsreels was begun. The newsreels were changed twice a week and continued to be a regular programming feature of Don Lee television for a number of years.

Because of the success of and response to the telecasts of the feature film *The Crooked Circle* and the regular scheduling of current Pathe newsreels, the Don Lee organization attempted to acquire other feature films for television broadcast. Arrangements were made with Paramount Pictures for the regular scheduling of current and past Paramount features. The first telecast of Paramount Pictures material occurred on Thursday, August 24, 1933, when W6XAO televised the entire seven-reel feature film *The Texan,* starring Gary Cooper and Fay Wray, along with excerpts from a current Paramount feature film, Cecil B. DeMille's *This Day and Age.* A photography magazine quoted Lubcke as saying, "Although all television is as yet experimental, motion picture producers with an eye to the future are cooperating with us in the expansion of our television service.... Since the Federal Radio Commission has ruled it experimental, the transmission of featured material is prefixed with the prescribed phrase, 'these visual broadcasts are experimental.'"[15]

---

14. "The Big Four Oh, Channel 2 Birthday Party, KCBS-TV's 40th Anniversary Show," KCBS Television Broadcast, 1988.
15. "New Television Service Inaugurated," *International Photographer*, November 1933, p. 14.

During the period from September 1, 1933, through August 31, 1934, 40 Paramount features were televised, including *Blonde Venus, Love Me Tonight, A Farewell to Arms, Madison Square Garden, This Day and Age, I'm No Angel, Tillie and Gus, Duck Soup, Alice in Wonderland,* and *Melody in Spring.*[16] On the same programs with these features, 48 different Paramount short subjects were televised, including selections from the series *Paramount Pictorials,* and *Hollywood on Parade,* as well as various sports shorts. This appears to refute the claim of NBC that its telecast of Alexander Korda's *The Return of the Scarlet Pimpernel* in the spring of 1938 was "the first full-length film ever to be televised in this country."[17]

On Armistice Day, November 11, 1933, the Don Lee television stations televised scenes of the University of Southern California–Stanford football game 3½ hours after the conclusion of the game: "This is believed to be the shortest time in which football scenes have ever reached the television screen," read a contemporary account. "So far as is known, a football game has not yet been televised directly. Thus motion picture film is the only vehicle for television presentation of a scene of this nature. Paramount Newsreel made the rapid showing possible by dispatching the film to the station as soon as it came from the printing tanks."[18]

On Saturday, December 23, 1933, after two full years of regular telecasting, Don Lee television celebrated its anniversary with a special program from 5 to 10:25 p.m. The five hour and twenty-five minute anniversary program began with a historical review of the film material televised during the first two years of Don Lee television. The material that was shown included the very first image that had been televised, the images that had been sent to the Western Air Express plane in flight, and other Don Lee television firsts. At 6 p.m. a Pathe newsreel was televised, followed by a selection from Paramount's *Hollywood on Parade,* featuring Ginger Rogers, John Boles, Robert Woolsey, Johnny Mack Brown, Mary Pickford, Boots Mallory, and Dorothy Wilson, and a special edition of "Paramount News." Then at 7 p.m. the complete Paramount feature *Madame Butterfly,* starring Sylvia Sidney and Cary Grant, was televised. At 10:25 p.m. the program and

16. Harry R. Lubcke, "Report to the Federal Communications Commission on the Event of Renewal of License of Experimental Visual Broadcasting Stations W6XAO and W6XS" (Los Angeles: Don Lee, 1934), pp. 5–7.

17. "Movie Transmitted as Television Test," *New York Times,* 1 June 1938, p. 21, quoted in Allan David Larson, "Integration and Attempted Integration Between the Motion Picture and Television Industries Through 1956," Ph.D. diss., Ohio University, 1979, p. 33.

18. "New Television Service Inaugurated," *International Photographer,* November 1933, p. 14.

broadcast day concluded with the normal sign-off closing signal.[19] By 9 p.m. on Saturday, May 26, 1934, just 2½ years since its start of broadcasting, W6XAO had televised its 6 millionth foot of film.[20]

On June 28, 1934, W6XAO televised its first public-service announcement:

> For the first time in history, television was used on June 28, 1934, to advertise a forthcoming event.
>
> On that date, the Don Lee television stations ... transmitted visual announcements of the National Champion short-track Motorcycle Races, held July 2 and 3, in the Los Angeles Coliseum. The races were sponsored by the California Association of Highway Patrolmen, for the benefit of their Widows and Orphans' fund.[21]

Because television's status was still experimental, there was a question of whether or not a television-broadcast announcement of this type could be made legally. Specific permission was requested and obtained from the FRC. The spots, which ran from June 28 through July 3 of 1934, consisted of film clips of short-track motorcycle racing and a group of word titles giving specific information about the upcoming races.[22]

"High-Definition" Television Demonstration

A group of 12 reporters gathered at the Don Lee Building in Los Angeles on Thursday, June 4, 1936. There they witnessed the first public demonstration in America of what at the time was considered high-definition television transmission and reception. Standing about 10 feet from the television receiver, the dozen observers saw a Pathe newsreel that included the arrival of the *Queen Mary* in New York. This demonstration ushered in a new era of Don Lee television broadcasting.

---

19. *International Photographer* incorrectly identified the male lead of *Madame Butterfly* as Gary Cooper. "Don Lee Stations Celebrate Second Anniversary," *International Photographer*, January 1934, p. 9.

20. *International Photographer* incorrectly stated: "Transmissions have covered a period of three and one-half years." "Don Lee Television Sets New Record," *International Photographer*, June 1934, p. 6.

21. "Television," *International Photographer*, August 1934, p. 3.

22. "Television," p. 3.

Beginning the next day, Friday, June 5, 1936, W6XAO expanded its operating hours to four per day so that the demonstrations would be available to a larger audience. In order to accommodate interested viewers, a special viewing area was designed and built in the Don Lee Building at Seventh and Bixel streets in Los Angeles. This 18-foot-high room, measuring 15 by 23 feet, was located on the main floor of the Don Lee Building near one of the street entrances. The walls were built of black velvet drapes mounted on a framework, providing darkness and sound insulation. The receiver was mounted on a platform in the room so that viewers could comfortably watch while standing. During the month of June 1936 approximately 5,000 people saw the free demonstrations. Noted Larry Walters in the *Chicago Tribune:* "For more than six months (after years of experimentation) the Don Lee network has been making daily broadcasts and on June 4 made its first public demonstration of the system. Since then it has been presenting a daily four hour television schedule over station W6XAO. Thus, Mr. Lubcke pointed out, it was broadcasting publicly several weeks before RCA recently launched its experiments atop the Empire State Building in New York for a select group of privately installed receivers."[23] A number of references confirm that Don Lee television predated RCA in the public demonstration of high-definition television by close to a month. According to a 1936 annual report of the Federal Communications Commission: "On June 29 television broadcast station W2XF began operating in the Empire State Building, New York, on an experimental basis for public reception. A few receivers were distributed to selected observers. It was reported that the operation would continue as the experimental work permitted."[24] And Joseph H. Udelson, in his landmark book *The Great Television Race,* has written: "The first RCA field demonstration concerned with displaying high-definition television's program possibilities was staged on 7 July 1936, for representatives of the firm's licensees. The audience viewed the show in semidarkness on sets with 5-by-7-inch screens displaying the green hues of their pictures."[25]

---

23. Larry Walters, "Expert Explains New Television Tests on Coast," *Chicago Tribune,* 12 July 1936, clipping in Harry R. Lubcke, "Report to the Federal Communications Commission on the Event of Renewal of License of Experimental Visual Broadcasting Station W6XAO" (Los Angeles: Don Lee, 1936), p. 40.

24. "The Evolution of Television: 1927–1943," *Journal of Broadcasting* 4 (Summer 1960): 220, quoting *Second Annual Report of the Federal Communications Commission—1936,* p. 63.

25. Joseph H. Udelson, *The Great Television Race: A History of the American Television Industry 1925–1941* (Tuscaloosa: University of Alabama Press, 1982), p. 94, citing "Television Stages First Real 'Show,'" *New York Times,* 8 July 1936, p. 21.

On Tuesday, September 1, 1936, the Los Angeles sections of the Institute of Radio Engineers and the American Institute of Electrical Engineers held a special joint meeting in the second-floor auditorium of the Don Lee Building. The meeting included three talks on television by members of the Don Lee television staff. A demonstration of the new high-definition television was given, and construction information was made available at the meeting. This demonstration was especially noteworthy because, for the first time, KHJ, the Los Angeles flagship radio station of the Don Lee Broadcasting System, transmitted the audio portion of the television program, a motion-picture newsreel. This was, according to Lubcke, "another 'first time' achievement by the Television Division inasmuch as a broadcasting station and a modern high-definition television station, such as W6XAO, had never been united until the successful proving experiment" of September 1.[26]

On Wednesday evening, September 9, 1936, the Don Lee Broadcasting System began a weekly 15-minute series of television programs from 7:30 to 7:45 p.m. on W6XAO, with synchronized audio on KHJ. Bill Bird described the first in the series of regular sight-sound broadcasts in the September 14, 1936, issue of the *Pasadena Independent:*

> You probably didn't realize that you were hearing a portion of a broadcast that will, in all likelihood, be recorded as one of the important milestones in broadcasting history....
> This writer was one of the eight or nine persons to whom that broadcast will ever be a memorable event. Seated in the home of Harry R. Lubcke, director of television for the Don Lee network and a nationally recognized expert in the development of "sight-and-sound" broadcasting, we faced two receiving sets. Through one, an ordinary radio, we heard the aforementioned commentaries, which any radio tuned to KHJ at that time was receiving. Through the other, a television receiver, we saw, with discernible clarity, a reproduction of the newsreel. The synchronization of sight and sound was perfect.[27]

For a number of years W6XAO had broadcast audio announcements before and after the video signals. This was done so that persons who did not possess video receiving equipment could still receive the audio. This also

26. "Don Lee Television Passes Another Milestone," *International Photographer*, October 1936, p. 12.

27. Bill Bird, "Radio on Review," *Pasadena* (California) *Independent*, 14 September 1936, clipping in Harry R. Lubcke, "Report to the Federal Communications Commission on the Event of Renewal of License of Experimental Visual Broadcasting Station W6XAO" (Los Angeles: Don Lee, 1936), p. 51.

enabled an aural identification for those persons who could not receive the video images with enough clarity to identify the transmissions. However, due to a modification of the W6XAO license, aural transmissions were no longer allowed on the video frequency after September 29, 1936. Because of this restriction the Don Lee television engineers began to investigate the possibility of a frequency-modulated sound channel, the modulation method that is used today for television audio.

On Saturday, March 13, 1937, W6XAO televised a 25-minute preview of a soon-to-be-released feature motion picture. The preview, transmitted from 8:15 to 8:40 that evening, had synchronized audio transmitted over KHJ and nine other Don Lee radio stations. According to *The Hollywood Reporter* the feature was *Empire of the West,* starring Leo Carrillo and Sam Flint. "Never before has a Hollywood picture had its premiere by television.... Co-ordination of radio sound over KHJ with the televised motion picture was perfect."[28]

During 1937 representatives of the California Institute of Technology contacted the Don Lee organization to request a series of television demonstrations for the annual California Institute of Technology science exhibit. During the two-day exhibit, held on April 9 and 10, 1937, over 2,500 persons witnessed the reception of television during a total of 74 public demonstrations. A Don Lee experimental radio station, W10XFZ, under special authority from the FCC, separately transmitted the audio for the demonstrations. As the *Los Angeles Times* reported:

> Television demonstrations provided the major attraction yesterday when California Institute of Technology, Pasadena, opened its annual two-day public exhibition of scientific marvels. Last year's record attendance of $10,000 [*sic*] visitors is expected to be exceeded.
>
> Caltech's electrical engineering department is featuring what is asserted to be the first public demonstration of the latest developments in television reception.[29]

To provide sound with the visual transmissions on a regular basis, and to eliminate the need for the use of KHJ in this regard, the Don Lee Broadcasting System requested and received a television audio-transmitter

---

28. *Hollywood Reporter*, 16 March 1937, clipping in Harry R. Lubcke, "Report to the Federal Communications Commission on the Event of Renewal of License of Experimental Visual Broadcasting Station W6XAO" (Los Angeles: Don Lee, 1937), p. 38.

29. "Television Demonstrated at Caltech Science Show," *Los Angeles Times*, 10 April 1937, Part 2, p. 3.

construction permit from the FCC. The simultaneous aural and visual transmissions of W6XAO, beginning on May 19, 1937, stimulated an added interest in television in the Los Angeles area. The normal televising of Pathe newsreels and other film offerings were now broadcast regularly with sound instead of with the limited use of synchronized sound when KHJ was used as the sound carrier. As this era of Don Lee television, using motion-picture images exclusively, was about to end, it was reported that W6XAO had "run more than 10,496,000 feet of picture film through the Don Lee transmitter equipment during" the more than seven years that it had been on the air.[30]

Live Television

The Don Lee television engineers had not only run extensive film but had been secretly developing and testing all-electronic live television-camera equipment and, by the spring of 1938, were ready to test live television over the air. On Saturday, April 16, 1938, the Don Lee Broadcasting System telecast its first live-subject television images. Beginning on that date W6XAO broadcast live television images regularly. On Saturday and on Monday evenings motion-picture subjects were transmitted. W6XAO televised live-image television studio productions during other scheduled program times.

To provide facilities for live telecasting, a KHJ-radio studio, number two, located on the second floor of the Don Lee Building, was converted to a television studio. This studio, because of its prior use as a radio studio, was well equipped for the audio needs of the Don Lee television staff. Microphones could be hung from adjustable ceiling hangers, attached to booms, or mounted on floor or desk stands. The control-room area was equipped to mix the microphones and provide music and sound effects from transcriptions. The audio output could be connected into the Don Lee Broadcasting System's network of radio stations, or a single station such as KHJ, as well as being fed to the W6XAO aural transmitter. This television facility was in use by the W6XAO television staff until the completion of a new facility approximately 2½ years later.

A number of the early live Don Lee television programs were Mutual–Don Lee Broadcasting System network radio shows. Among the first of these

---

30. *Hollywood Reporter*, 22 March 1938, p. 8.

televised radio programs was "Frank Bull's Sports Bullseyes." It had its television premiere on June 3, 1938. This program, televised twice weekly, featured interviews with sports figures in the Los Angeles area and afforded "television receptionists a much greater enjoyment of the program than is possible with sound alone."[31] "Andy and Virginia" was a daily morning program broadcast over the Don Lee radio network, with the Monday-morning programs televised live over W6XAO. The program, which had its television premiere on June 4, 1938, featured a piano and vocal duo with added specialty acts. Another cooperative effort with the Mutual–Don Lee radio network was "Hollywood Spinsters." The June 15, 1938, episode of this serial was televised and provided viewers with the opportunity to see the radio performers in makeup and costume.

Many programs were created especially for television. Beginning on July 6, 1938, W6XAO broadcast a weekly television version of the radio series "Happy Homes." The program featured KHJ household expert Norma Young interviewing various people and demonstrating homemaking techniques. On August 12, 1938, "The Television Trio" had its premiere. This weekly series featured a group of three musicians performing on the harp, trumpet, and piano. Even Harry Lubcke became a performer. During June, July, and August of 1938, Lubcke gave a series of technical talks over W6XAO explaining the design, construction, and operation of television receivers. During this period Don Lee television inaugurated one of the first, if not the first, scheduled nightly newscasts, "World News," on W6XAO. The program featured Hugh Brundage, Bob Young, Norman Nesbitt, and James Doyle presenting news from the wires of Transradio Press and International News Service. One of W6XAO's most important and long-running programs had its premiere on November 10, 1938. This program, "USC on Parade," was produced in cooperation with the University of Southern California's Radio Division. This weekly program featured Molly Rogers, John McCallister, and the USC Men's Glee Club. A major undertaking of the Don Lee television staff in 1938 was the production of "Vine Street." Television historians consider this series, which premiered on Tuesday, November 1, 1938, to be the first serial created for television.[32] "Vine

---

31. Harry R. Lubcke, "Report to the Federal Communications Commission on the Event of Renewal of License of Experimental Visual Broadcasting Station W6XAO" (Los Angeles: Don Lee, 1938), p. 4.

32. William Hawes, *American Television Drama* (Tuscaloosa: University of Alabama Press, 1986), p. 125.

Street" was televised twice weekly on Tuesday and Friday evenings in 15-minute installments.

> In motion picture title fashion, a miniature stage starts the performance by the raising of the main curtain, the draping of a side curtain, and the retraction of side wings. This reveals a sign reading "Vine Street by W. H. Pettitt." The side wings are then moved to obscure the sign, which is immediately replaced by a second sign reading, "Starring Shirley Thomas as Sandra Bush." In the same manner her photograph is next displayed, then a sign reading, "and John Barkeley as Michael Roberts," which is followed by a photograph of Mr. Barkeley. Simultaneously with the visual action, an offstage announcer ties the forthcoming episode to the previous action and introduces the episode. A second camera then takes the scene, the action starts, and carries on to the conclusion.[33]

W6XAO received significant positive publicity due to its extensive scheduling of live programming. The Friday, November 4, 1938, issue of *Variety* that listed and described many of these W6XAO programs also noted that "program undertaking of the television department is one of the most expansive ever attempted in this country by a visible broadcast organization. It marks the first time regular feature programs have been offered in this type of airing."[34]

The Don Lee organization planned a gala premiere to inaugurate W6XAO's expanded regular program service using a new, higher-resolution scanning system of 441 lines. The premiere coincided with the opening of the 27th annual Los Angeles Motor Car Dealers' Automobile Show at the Pan Pacific Auditorium in Los Angeles. It was planned that at 8 p.m. on Saturday, October 14, 1939, Los Angeles mayor Fletcher Bowron would be seen greeting visitors to the auto show over a group of television receivers placed in the auditorium. The receivers would pick up the image and sound of the mayor, who was to be located at the W6XAO studio.[35] According to a press release distributed shortly before the event, "The teleceivers will be so placed that visiting throngs can see for themselves the practical possibili-

---

33. Harry R. Lubcke, "Television on the West Coast," in *We Present Television*, ed. John Porterfield and Kay Reynolds (New York: W. W. Norton, 1940), pp. 233–234.

34. *Variety*, 4 November 1938, p. 4.

35. Mark Finley, "Mayor to Salute Auto Show by Hollywood Television," Mutual Don Lee Television System press release, Los Angeles, October 1939, in Harry R. Lubcke, "Report to the Federal Communications Commission on the Event of Renewal of License of Experimental Visual Broadcasting Station W6XAO" (Los Angeles: Don Lee, 1939), p. 29.

ties of the world's newest art. No wires or co-axial cables will connect transmitter and teleceiver, the mayor's image and voice flashing in synchronized speed over the southland airlanes."[36] This special telecast worked according to plan, and Mayor Bowron greeted thousands of people at the auto show through television. The telecast continued with Alvino Rey, his 18-piece orchestra, and vocalists Maxine Gray and Betty Jane Rhodes. Tenor Morton Downey, who was appearing at the Coconut Grove at the time, sang three songs. Other entertainers included the King Sisters and the Brewster Twins. A comedy, "Going Up," was then presented, followed by a youthful Art Baker (of "You Asked for It" fame), who lectured on historic artwork. The telecast concluded with a presentation of "The Silver Coronet," starring Shirley Thomas, the lead in W6XAO's serial "Vine Street."[37] This program was the 2,356th telecast of W6XAO.[38] For the 10 days of the auto show it was estimated that 25,000 people witnessed the television presentations.

During the period from late 1939 through 1941, two major activities took up much of the time of the Don Lee television engineering staff. The first was the acquisition, improvement, testing, and use of a live remote unit. The second was the planning and construction of an all-new television facility to be located on Mount Lee overlooking Hollywood and the Los Angeles area.

Live Remotes

To provide live television broadcasts from locations other than the Don Lee Building television studio, arrangements were made with RCA to purchase lightweight portable television-remote pickup equipment. The total weight of the two-camera portable equipment, minus interconnecting cables, was 850 pounds. The Don Lee Broadcasting System received its suitcase-portable remote unit in 1939. The FCC licensed the unit to operate as W6XDU on a frequency of 324 megahertz. On January 1, 1940, W6XAO carried the Pasadena Tournament of Roses parade live. This date marks the

---

36. Finley, "Mayor."
37. Mark Finley, "Don Lee Opens Winter Television Season at Automobile Show," Don Lee Television System press release, Los Angeles, October 1939, in Harry R. Lubcke, "Report to the Federal Communications Commission on the Event of Renewal of License of Experimental Visual Broadcasting Station W6XAO" (Los Angeles: Don Lee, 1936), pp. 32–33.
38. Finley, "Don Lee Opens Winter Television Season."

first time that this type of RCA remote equipment was used for the relay of programming to the public.[39] Broadcast columnist Charles E. Butterfield,[40] as well as RCA and NBC engineers,[41] have noted that the first public use of the suitcase remote equipment by NBC took place on March 6, 1940. The Don Lee Broadcasting System's first public use of the suitcase remote equipment for the Tournament of Roses parade on January 1, 1940, predates the first NBC use of this type of remote equipment by over three months.

The New Year's Day remote telecast was just the first of many remote telecasts. The traditional Hollywood Bowl Easter Sunday sunrise service was fed on March 24, 1940. On Saturday, March 30, 1940, regular pickups from Gilmore Field of the Hollywood Stars Coast League baseball games began. These games were usually televised on Sunday afternoons. Besides baseball, many other sports activities were carried on a regular basis via remote telecast. Beginning April 5, 1940, boxing and wrestling matches from the American Legion Stadium were carried. Friday night quickly became known as fight night, and Monday evening became equally well-known as wrestling night, on W6XAO. These matches were carried weekly almost without fail.

On May 7, 1940, Harry Lubcke took his W6XDU equipment and crew to the RKO studios, where the first Lum and Abner picture, *Dreaming out Loud,* was being filmed. This 1¼-hour live remote television broadcast demonstrated how a motion picture is made. Other live remotes included the Young Skipper's Regatta from Echo Lake and the Junior Screen Actors Guild Bathing Beauty Parade on the lawn of the Ambassador Hotel, with the transmitting equipment located on the roof of the Coconut Grove. The remote broadcasts were among the most popular offerings of Don Lee television. Along with the many homes that now possessed television receivers in the Los Angeles area, a large number of radio dealers and stores provided public demonstrations of television. It was not unusual for as many as 50 persons to be gathered around a demonstration television receiver at this time. One broadcast wrestling match drew so many people to a radio store in Long Beach, where a television receiver was being displayed in the window, that

---

39. It is interesting to note that the assistant, a vacationing student named Dick O'Brien, whose main task was to carry and help set up the remote unit, later became director of engineering for CBS television (telephone interview by Steven C. Runyon with Dick O'Brien, CBS Television, New York, March 1976, S.C. Runyon personal notes, University of San Francisco).

40. Charles E. Butterfield, "The New Newsreel," in *We Present Television,* ed. John Porterfield and Kay Reynolds (New York: W.W. Norton, 1940), p. 216.

41. G. L. Beers, O. H. Schrade, and R. E. Shelby, "The RCA Portable Television Pickup Equipment," paper presented at the meeting of the Institute of Radio Engineers, New York, 3 April 1940.

the police had to be called to control the crowds and reopen the street to traffic.[42]

While work on the new Don Lee television facility went forward during late 1939 and 1940, W6XAO maintained a weekly broadcast schedule of from 10 to 15 hours per week. Approximately six hours per week were devoted to the televising of motion pictures. Four and a half hours per week was the average time for live studio programming. Live remote programs averaged about three hours per week. W6XAO maintained this general schedule of programming until September 15, 1940, when the station left the air temporarily to move to its new quarters on top of Mount Lee. Based on Don Lee Broadcasting System press releases, and reports to the FRC and the FCC, it can be estimated that during the period from December 23, 1931, when the first W6XAO transmission took place, until September 15, 1940, when W6XAO ceased telecasting from the Don Lee Building at Seventh and Bixel streets in Los Angeles, well over 2,600 programs totaling close to 7,000 hours and nearly 12 million feet of film had been televised.

Facility Designed for Television

During the first half of 1940 the Don Lee Broadcasting System committed over $25 million for the acquisition of real estate as a site for its new television facility and for the building of a road to the site. The location chosen was the highest of the Hollywoodland range of mountains. Christened Mount Lee, it is located approximately 2½ miles from the center of Hollywood above the now famous "Hollywood" sign that was "Hollywoodland" at the time. The location was convenient for studios, excellent for the reception of remote signals, and ideal for television transmissions. On this site a 100-by-100-by-30-foot-high studio and transmitter facility was constructed. This was the first facility to be constructed specifically for television broadcasting.[43] By February 1941 the Don Lee television engineers were

---

42. Lubcke, "Television on the West Coast," p. 238.

43. Mark Finley, "Mount Lee Highway Paving Contract Is Signed," Don Lee Television System press release, Los Angeles, 19 June 1940; and Mark Finley, "Half Way Point Reached in Construction on Mr. Lee," Don Lee Television System press release, Hollywood, 4 November 1940, in Harry R. Lubcke, "Report to the Federal Communications Commission Accompanying Renewal of License of Television Broadcasting Stations W6XAO and W6XDU" (Hollywood: Don Lee, 1940), pp. 55, 59.

ready to begin transmission tests from the new Mount Lee site,[44] and by April 1941 W6XAO had returned to the air with limited film and live remote programming. Live programming from the Mount Lee studios did not commence until April 1942.

Postscript

At the outbreak of World War II the television activities of the Don Lee Broadcasting System were greatly reduced. During the license period from November 16, 1941, through November 15, 1942, W6XAO devoted a total of 47 hours to program transmissions and 73 hours to test transmissions. W6XAO remained active throughout World War II on a limited basis. War effort and defense-oriented shows took up most of the programming time during this period.

W6XAO expanded its operations at the end of World War II. The FCC granted the Don Lee Broadcasting System a commercial television license in 1948, and W6XAO became KTSL,[45] Channel 2 in Los Angeles, in May of that year.[46] In 1951 the Columbia Broadcasting System purchased KTSL, moved the transmission sight from Mount Lee to Mount Wilson, and changed the call letters to KNXT. On April 2, 1984, the call letters were changed to KCBS.[47] Thus KCBS television in Los Angeles has the distinction of being the West Coast's first television station, and, with a long string of "firsts," a true pioneer among American television stations.

---

44. "A Mountain of Television," *Newsweek*, 10 February 1941, p. 52.
45. The call letters "KTSL" stood for Thomas S. Lee, at the time president of the Don Lee Broadcasting System.
46. "Briefly Noted," *Electronic Media*, 5 April 1984, p. 27.
47. "Briefly Noted."

18 Paramount's KTLA: The Leading Station in Early Los Angeles Television

Mark Williams

The founding of Los Angeles station KTLA reveals one the most prominent instances of the attempt of the motion-picture industry to enter the business of early television. The station's history is also central to the larger history of television in Los Angeles, which was one of the most active and successful markets of the early TV industry in this country.

Paramount Studios, under the control of mogul Adolf Zukor, had been interested in broadcasting early on, attempting in 1927 to originate a network of stations called the Keystone Chain, and subsequently offering that same year to invest in the small United Independent Broadcasters radio network.[1] These ventures never materialized, though the reasons for this are unclear. Paramount's entry into television actually began in New York, when in August 1938 the studio began to buy what would become a 29 percent interest in the Allen B. Du Mont Laboratories of Passaic, New Jersey, which it sought as an equipment source willing to undertake mutually advantageous research in video developments. Paramount engineers cooperated in establishing an experimental station in Passaic, and it was generally understood that Paramount planned to use films in television broadcasts.[2]

But the medium itself first had to be tested and developed. When the Federal Communications Commission approved Paramount's application for a Los Angeles television permit, the studio formed a company named

1. Michele Hilmes, *Hollywood and Broadcasting: From Radio to Cable* (Urbana: University of Illinois Press, 1990), pp. 38–39.

2. "Paramount Enters Television; Would Utilize Motion Pictures," *Motion Picture Herald* (13 August 1938): 17.

Television Productions in 1939. A survey of the management suggests the integration of Paramount's motion-picture and television interests. Television Productions was headed by Paul Raibourn, a Paramount vice president and the treasurer of Du Mont. Y. Frank Freeman, in addition to his duties as Paramount's vice president in charge of studio operations, was the new television company's vice president. Paramount treasurer Walter B. Cokell served in the same capacity for Television Productions. Raibourn was clearly the central figure in the studio's television efforts, becoming a leading member of the Television Broadcasters Association as well as Paramount's chief representative at the FCC hearings, which plagued for years their early ventures into television.

Paramount's license for the Los Angeles experimental station W6XYZ (tentatively assigned Channel 4) was granted in 1939. Significantly, Raibourn remained in New York with the studio's business offices, while the West Coast officers and personnel showed a condescending lack of interest. The station amounted to little more than a novelty until 1941, when Raibourn hired Klaus Landsberg, a German emigrant who was a television and electronics expert joining W6XYZ by way of Du Mont.

Klaus Landsberg and the Development of Television at Paramount

Landsberg's technical background was extensive and dramatic. Born in Berlin in 1916, he began constructing various electronic gadgetry as a youth and at age 18 was designing mechanical and cathode-ray equipment as an assistant to Professor Faerber, director of one of the first television labs in Europe. Landsberg soon lectured throughout the continent on the principles of television technology and eventually became involved in the historic 1936 television broadcast of the Berlin Olympics.[3] In 1937 he became laboratory assistant and engineer for Dr. Arthur Korn, an important German inventor of "picture telegraphy,"[4] and coauthor of the first book containing a history of television, published in 1911.[5] Later in 1937, when Landsberg's

---

3. "Klaus Landsberg Biography," Paramount Television Productions, press release, n.d., p. 3, KTLA station files, Los Angeles.

4. "Klaus Landsberg Biography," p. 4.

5. Albert Abramson, *The History of Television, 1880 to 1941* (Jefferson, North Carolina: McFarland, 1987), p. 41.

invention of an electronic navigational aid (related to radar) was suppressed as a military secret, he came to America, with his basic radar principle said to have been his passport.

In 1938, shortly after landing in the United States, Landsberg began work at Farnsworth Television in Philadelphia as a television design engineer. He moved to New York the next year to help NBC stage its 1939 World's Fair demonstration. He later moved on to Du Mont, where he helped inaugurate their New York station, WABD, and, among other duties, supervised technical operations of the television unit in use for U.S. Army maneuvers in Canton, New York.[6] At Du Mont, Landsberg designed a system called "genlock," which consisted of automatic synchronizing circuits that allow several cameras to function simultaneously on the same sync pulse.[7] After two years with Du Mont he joined Paramount in Los Angeles in the summer of 1941, carrying the parts to two video cameras in his suitcases.

The conditions for work in television were not nearly so well developed in Los Angeles, however. Even though Harry Lubcke had been producing local telecasts since 1931 on experimental station W6XAO (the subject of another chapter—a station owned by Cadillac dealer Don Lee, whose radio stations made up much of the Mutual Network on the West Coast), and despite Raiborn's enthusiasm for television in Paramount's corporate offices, Landsberg was met with little enthusiasm for his "novelty" on the Paramount studio lot. The onset of World War II meant a slowdown of even limited programming, and a military demand for materials, engineers, and technical personnel severely restricted Landsberg's progress in putting W6XYZ on the air.

In September 1942 Landsberg completed a hand-built antenna, which was placed atop the station's facilities on the Paramount lot, extending its reach and officially inaugurating its broadcasts. With limited studio facilities Landsberg accentuated mobility in the station's experimental programs, drawing on his experience with the German television system of the mid-1930s.[8] Late in 1942 the station's first "remote" telecast came from the set of the motion picture *This Gun for Hire* at Paramount, featuring glimpses of

---

6. "Klaus Landsberg Biography," p. 5.

7. Sherrie Mazingo, "Home of Programming 'Firsts'," *Television/Radio Age* (March 1987): A10.

8. The German operations are discussed in William Uricchio, "Rituals of Reception, Patterns of Neglect: Nazi Television," *Wide Angle* 11 (1) (1989): 48–66.

stars Alan Ladd and Veronica Lake.[9] As the broadcasts increased in mobility, they moved off the studio lot, and the station began to resemble and assimilate conventional broadcast strategies, emphasizing an identity as a community medium rather than a motion-picture surrogate. Remote telecasts became the station's trademark, affording both "entertainment" and "public service" programming in accordance with FCC preferences and standards.

By 1943 the station had a fully operative mobile unit, highlighting special local events, the first of which was the Sheriff's Rodeo from the Los Angeles Coliseum, an operation that required some 40 hours of preparation.[10] Regular biweekly programming began on February 1, 1943, and the operating budget for that year totaled $896,000, completely paid for by Paramount.[11]

Like many stations broadcasting part-time during the war, W6XYZ telecast public-service programs. By April 1943, for example, it was credited for having trained hundreds of air-raid wardens and auxiliary police. Every Tuesday and Friday evenings at 8:30 p.m., members of the Los Angeles Citizens Defense Corps had been gathering at various points across town that were equipped with receiving sets. Training demonstrations of civic preparedness, martial arts, and weaponry featured an interactive component, as "televiewers" could phone in to ask and respond to questions.[12] The station's reputation was enhanced when Landsberg won two awards for local television, one in 1944 from the Television Broadcasters Association, for adapting motion-picture techniques to television, and another in 1945 from the American Television Society, for continued excellence in programming.[13]

Dick Lane, a motion-picture actor who had appeared in over 250 films, developed a friendship with Landsberg on the Paramount lot in 1942 and first appeared on W6XYZ in 1943. He hosted vaudevillelike variety programs on the station, featuring gymnastics, comedy acts, and singers, and soon became one of the first "regulars" on the air. Lane was even one of the station's first newsmen before finding his niche as host, announcer, and salesman. A 1944 show called "Embarrassing Situations" reportedly some-

---

9. "KTLA's Unmatched History of Television Firsts," KTLA promotional sheet, n.d., p. 1, KTLA station files, Los Angeles.

10. John Silva, interview with author, 26 February 1990.

11. Susan K. Wilbur, "The History of Television in Los Angeles, 1931–1952: Part I," *Southern California Quarterly* 60 (1) (Spring 1978): 69.

12. "Instruction by Television," *Radio-Television Life* (4 April 1943): 10.

13. "Telefile: A Non-Network Station in Los Angeles Passes the Competitive Test With Flying Colors," *Broadcasting* 38 (20 February 1950): 70.

times featured outtakes from Paramount films. Another studio-related program was "Interview of the Stars" in 1945, which promoted Paramount talent.

The FCC resumed peacetime station licensing October 8, 1945, reserving Channel 1 for emergency use, and bumping extant channels up by one number. Landsberg resumed his bid for a commercial license for Channel 5 in 1946, by increasing programming to two nightly broadcasts per week, and winning yet another award from the Television Broadcasters Association, for best public-service program, "educating the citizens of Los Angeles by means of the television program Your Town, as to the problems of their government, as well as informing them of the growth of the community in an interesting and highly entertaining manner."[14]

The bulk of the station's 1946 programming focused on local sports coverage—boxing, horse and auto racing, basketball, ice hockey, and the two sports virtually synonymous with early television, professional wrestling and roller derby—offering the burgeoning community an abundance of this staple of early "entertainment" programming.

In addition to expanded programming, the station's regional coverage was greatly enhanced when Landsberg decided to move the broadcasting tower from the Paramount lot to Mount Wilson, nearly 6,000 feet high and located 18 miles from Hollywood, above the city's center of population. Telecasts were beamed via microwave from the station to the tower, then transmitted throughout southern California, from Santa Barbara to Bakersfield and San Diego. This increased the station's potential coverage, enhanced its future prospects to engage advertisers, and noticeably improved the resolution of its broadcast signal—the clarity of which became a station trademark.

Competition for television licenses in 1946 Los Angeles included nine applicants jockeying for seven channels.[15] In addition to Television Productions (Paramount) and Don Lee (W6XAO), Earle C. Anthony (KFI), the Times-Mirror Company (whose proposal included an exclusive contract for programming with the Pasadena Playhouse), and the Broadcasting Corporation of America (BCA, a regional radio concern centered in Riverside) were local companies with varying amounts of broadcast experience. Two national networks, ABC and NBC, were competing as well. (NBC, in fact, was

---

14. "TBA Awards Given to Nine for Notable Achievements," *Broadcasting* 31 (14 October 1946): 83.

15. "Los Angeles, New York, Philadelphia," *Television* (May 1946): 4–5.

applying for its own Los Angeles station against the wishes of Anthony, whose station KFI was the NBC-radio affiliate in town.) Hughes Tool Company had no broadcast experience but was considered a local concern; it also had an application pending in San Francisco. Dorothy Thackery, the publisher of the *New York Post,* had plenty of broadcast experience but little regional profile. She owned three radio stations nationwide and was applying for three TV stations across the country. Nevertheless, the station applications would in the next few years be awarded to all but Hughes Tool and BCA.

Commercial Television Debuts on the West Coast

In December 1946 the FCC approved Paramount's commercial television license, the first in the western United States. On Wednesday evening, January 22, 1947, the station began commercial broadcasts as KTLA, debuting with an impressive cast of Paramount talent, but following a programming paradigm that had and would continue to serve the station's best interests: an extensive program of light "entertainment," legitimated by a modicum of high-profile "public service" programming.

The inaugural evening of commercial programming began with a 15-minute preamble titled "KTLA: A New Public Servant," which featured addresses from a variety of local civic dignitaries, foregrounding the station's responsibilities and advantages to the local community. After Cecil B. DeMille and Landsberg gave inaugural addresses, Bob Hope, under contract to Paramount but also a longtime professional in radio, served as master of ceremonies for the subsequent 60-minute variety program: Even though holding his script, he misread the station's call letters but later correctly read a commercial, as did William Bendix. Other members of the cast included Dorothy Lamour, Jerry Colonna, William Demarest, Ann Rutherford, Peter Lind Hayes, Eddie Bracken, the DeCastro Sisters, and the Rhythmaires.

The program's length and scale proved to be rather unwieldy, especially when compared to the station's regular fare to that time. Reportedly using six cameras, nearly 500 people were involved in the telecast, which was produced by Landsberg with the assistance of Leon Benson of the J. Walter Thompson advertising agency, who represented the chief sponsor for the evening: Lincoln-Mercury dealer Tupman Motors paid $4,000, supplemented by four other minor sponsors.

Inside the studio, guests included representatives from New York advertising agencies and several East Coast television directors. The evening's events were reportedly amateurish—due to the Petrillo ban, prerecorded music was necessary for the singing acts, but the synchronization was off. *Daily Variety*'s review labeled the performers alternately "cold," "scared," and "lacking in warmth."[16] Jack Hellman's "Light and Airy" column in that paper (which focused on the broadcast media) began "You can't make a producer out of an engineer any more than you can make an engineer out of a producer." Complaining about the lack of showmanship in the telecast, Hellman ultimately tempered his critique of Landsberg but nevertheless concluded that the telecast "left the 350 auditors dubious of television's advance and completely unsold on production technique so necessary to its ultimate success. Engineers have done their part ... it now remains for showmen, experts in sight and sound entertainment, to put the shows together and get them ready for the cameras in workmanlike fashion."[17]

The trade paper was more readily impressed the next week with a modest second commercial telecast: a weekly news roundup illustrated by projected slides and narrated by station announcer Keith Hetherington. Although noting that without the pictures the program would have been little different from a radio broadcast of the news (Hetherington's reading was supplemented by "typical newsreel march music" in the background), the review concluded that even "with a lot less than it had on hand" for its first commercial program, the station had "come off with a lot more in the way of a show."[18] This "Telenews" program was at least temporarily sponsored, again by Tupman Motors.

Expensive programs such as the station's premiere did not, of course, become the rule of KTLA broadcasts, and neither did any programming that featured Paramount talent (though it might have if the station had had better success with national ad agencies). Rather, KTLA's foregrounded public-service identification, embellished by Landsberg's programming awards,

16. "Commercial Tele's Debut Here Rates Low as Entertainment," *Daily Variety* (23 January 1947), reprinted in Howard H. Prouty, ed., *Variety Television Reviews, 1923–1988,* vol. 1, (New York: Garland, 1988–1991).

17. Jack Hellman, "Light and Airy" column, *Daily Variety* (24 January 1947), reprinted in Howard H. Prouty, ed., *Variety Television Reviews, 1923–1988,* vol. 1, (New York: Garland, 1988–1991).

18. "Tele Review," *Daily Variety* (3 February 1947), reprinted in Howard H. Prouty, ed., *Variety Television Reviews, 1923–1988,* vol. 1, (New York: Garland, 1988–1991).

was its trump card, extremely important in building the station's reputation as an industry and community leader, qualities highly regarded by the FCC. Because the motion-picture industry (and Paramount in particular) was heavily involved in antitrust litigation, its interests in television were overseen with a jaundiced governmental eye. Paramount's investments in television, covering a wide variety of potential growth markets, served the company's corporate attempts to diversify, and to insure against what ill effects television might have on the motion-picture business. The effect of these investments was to alert the FCC to adopt a position of wary surveillance against further monopolistic practices by the studio within another medium. As a result Paramount found itself in an unenviable economic position: Its early investments were condoned when seen as contributing to the "development of television," in fact absorbing a sizable chunk of the enormous investment that the television industry incurred in its early years. But investments that might have led to an advantage for the motion-picture industry were ruled to be a conflict of interest, for example, in the Scophony antitrust suit against Paramount in 1945, concerning its interest in the manufacturing of a British theatrical television apparatus.

Using Paramount's star talent on KTLA would have meant even greater losses, because their broadcast-appearance fees were considerably higher than early television revenues.[19] But even had they produced "Paramount telefilms," this practice most likely would have raised further questions of conflict of interest. The studio played only a minor role in the content of KTLA's programming, providing occasional settings and props, as well as newsreel shorts. But Paramount's involvement rarely amounted to more than an intriguing location for one of KTLA's many remote telecasts.

The one motion-picture-related staple at the station was Dick Lane. In the commercial era he became the first television "fender bender," selling cars for Central Chevrolet on the "Spade Cooley Show" for years, and actually denting a few during his pitch. Soon the host of the musical variety show "Dixie Showboat," Lane was always best known as the announcer on wrestling telecasts, which for many years were syndicated throughout the country.

---

19. "Paramount TV," *Broadcasting* 34 (28 June 1948): 70.

The Development of
Los Angeles as a Television Market

Although the station's motion-picture-industry ties were not as important to its profile as might be expected, KTLA played a central role in developing the Los Angeles television market. Both in coordination with other corporate entities, and by establishing itself as a provider of integral access to community events and entertainment, the station cultivated television viewing as a habit. The size and importance of the postwar Los Angeles market had been evident for several years. Many servicemen had returned to the area with various electronic and technological skills, creating a labor pool for the local TV industry. But above all, Los Angeles had emerged from the war as a potential commercial and industrial giant. In light of this, television promotion was industrywide in 1947, even with only one commercial station on the air.

KTLA's programming was beginning to serve the area's rising need for entertainment that could be consumed at home. Landsberg obtained the broadcast rights to the Los Angeles Angels baseball games in the Pacific Coast League, and sports continued to play a major programming role. A chatty "man-on-the-street" program, "Meet Me in Hollywood," catered to audience desires to see both celebrities and themselves on the new TV screens, as interviews were conducted with anyone who happened to pass by the corner of Hollywood and Vine. "Shopping at Home" was on the air, as was Lane's variety program, "Hits and Bits."

The impact of covering local news stories was demonstrated on February 20, 1947, when an electroplating-plant explosion leveled several city blocks. Preempting regular programming, KTLA's coverage began before sundown and continued for several hours, with Dick Lane interviewing people at the scene and providing details as they arose. Occurring as it did during the dinner hour, the telecast "scooped" the newspapers and demonstrated KTLA's potential for "live" news reporting, increasing the station's profile as a public servant. The coverage of such "live" local news would eventually become central to the station's reputation.

On the commercial front RCA began preparing its local merchandisers for the sale of television receivers. The Los Angeles Electrical Club sponsored "Television Week" in March 1947, opening with "T-Day," March 10. The promotion was so successful that every available set in the city was sold, and a backlog of orders taken;[20] sets ranged in price from $272 to $2,500.[21] KTLA and W6XAO cooperated with dealers to demonstrate sets, with KTLA expanding its programming to 24 hours per week, including broadcasting a sponsored exhibition baseball game. Landsberg even slyly arranged for 80 hours per week of test pattern to be sponsored, since these patterns were used by dealers and servicemen to demonstrate, install, and repair receiving sets.[22] As a result of the great sales success, the *Los Angeles Times* began a daily log of television programs, and set manufacturers began to buy large shares of local advertising time and space. By September there were an estimated 3,000 sets in use.

As all this indicates, the stakes over commercial television were beginning to rise. A proposed AT&T cable link between Los Angeles and Atlanta, under consideration since 1946, had raised considerable interest but now looked unlikely. Nevertheless, 1947 was a year of growth for KTLA, which was airing 35 hours of programming per week by year's end and had increased its number of sponsors to 24. The station began to advertise its success in such industry magazines as *Television* and even started to associate its activities with the home studio. An ad in the November issue of *Television* features a photo of Lizabeth Scott, hyping her appearance in the Paramount film *I Walk Alone,* and suggesting that everyone in movies and radio "is anxiously watching television to see what effect it will have on his future."[23] Further suggesting that "KTLA sells Hollywood—Hollywood sells the world," it seems clear that the relationship of the ad to Lizabeth Scott was tangential, connotative of glamour, while the real purpose of the ad was to convince national spot advertisers to take advantage of the station's unique address in relation to the Los Angeles and Hollywood markets.

A stronger sense of competition in local Los Angeles television was renewed in 1948, as three more stations received their commercial licenses. On May 6, W6XAO was granted a 90-day temporary license, on condition that Don Lee Broadcasting receive approvals for its license renewals. Difficulties with the radio-industry interests of the company had led to delays in receiving the television license. The station changed its call letters to KTSL, Channel 2. Earle C. Anthony's KFI, Channel 9, began a test period of

20. Susan K. Wilbur, "The History of Television in Los Angeles, 1931–1952: Part II," *Southern California Quarterly* 60 (2) (Summer 1978): 184.

21. "Television Week Opening Fete to Be Held Today," *Los Angeles Times* (10 March 1947): 1.

22. "Telestatus Report: Program Analysis," *Broadcasting* 34 (26 April 1948): 10.

23. KTLA advertisement, *Television* 4 (November 1947): 2.

broadcasts during August. In September, just as the FCC was to begin its "freeze" on station applications, Dorothy Thackery's KLAC, Channel 13, signed on commercially—only two months after breaking ground on the transmitter, and with no experimental test period. KFI began commercial telecasts in October, with a gala premiere featuring Adolphe Menjou as emcee. This gave Los Angeles four independently owned commercial stations (though KFI did act as an NBC affiliate for a few months).

KTLA was at this time both producing more original programming and seeking other sources of revenue. "Pantomime Quiz," one of the biggest hits of early television, was first aired in January, the initial effort at the station by producer (and host) Mike Stokey, whose Stokey-Ebert Productions would create other shows in the months to come, including "Armchair Detective" later that year. In February the station released price-rate information for filming transcriptions of commercials or shows in either 16 millimeter or 35 millimeter.[24] Producers or sponsors could in this way have a record of their television performance, perhaps to be used as a demonstration reel.

As the other stations began to contract for even more sports programming (USC and UCLA football on KLAC, Los Angeles Rams football on KFI, KTSL's continued wrestling and boxing), Landsberg began to seek out alternative program sources. Keying into the region's affection for country-and-western entertainers, he began in July to telecast remote performances of Spade Cooley from the Santa Monica Ballroom—resulting in "The Spade Cooley Show," which would become a KTLA standard for years. The station's director of film programs, Leland Muller, scheduled some old serials starring Hopalong Cassidy, which became so popular that NBC eventually started to run them, revitalizing the career of William Boyd and turning Cassidy into an early 1950s children's icon.

In July 1948 Landsberg televised the local premiere of Paramount's *The Emperor Waltz,* which proved to be a popular success. In an effort to substantiate the station's "news" capabilities beyond such "feature" material, and in answer to KTSL's July agreement with the *Los Angeles Herald Examiner,* KTLA signed a five-year contract with the *Daily News* in September, which "called for the joint development and presentation of outstanding news stories, educational features, and public service programs."[25]

---

24. "Paramount Transcription Rates," *Television* 5 (February 1948): 18.
25. Wilbur, "History of Television," pp. 195, 198.

Network Denial and Affiliate Competition

In December 1948 the FCC decided that Paramount's financial interest in Du Mont rendered the two corporations as one, at least in terms of determining the number of television stations each could own. Since Paramount owned two stations and Du Mont owned three, their joint ownership equaled the total number allowed under the regulations of that time. Neither would be allowed to expand any further, and their pending station applications were denied. The impact of this decision was crippling to the network plans of each corporation and effectively removed them from competition with the powerful radio-network interests. The precise impact on KTLA is somewhat speculative, since no record of its proposed role in a network scheme exists. But it seems fair to suggest that the decision insured that Landsberg's impact on television would remain at a local level, at least for several more years. The degree of this impact would be vividly demonstrated in just a few months.

January 1, 1949, marked the commercial debut of KTTV, Channel 11, the station that would soon become KTLA's chief rival in the local market. Co-owned by the *Los Angeles Times* and CBS (in a 51/49 percentage agreement, with the *Times* as majority shareholder), the station premiered with the telecasting of the Tournament of Roses Parade. The programs on KTTV appeared in boldface in the *Times* TV listings. About a week later the NBC-owned station KNBH, Channel 4, came on the air commercially—thereby converting KFI, Channel 9, into a local independent station.

KNBH was figuring into network plans virtually from the start, building in June an expensive kinescope recording studio in order to enable the distribution of their Los Angeles programs to the East. The kinescopes of NBC's popular Milton Berle program, "Texaco Star Theater," were very successful in Los Angeles and often defeated KTLA's shows for the number-one rating in the area. But KTLA was still the predominant station in Los Angeles, and when the first Emmy Awards were distributed on January 25, 1949—telecast over KTSL, Channel 2—KTLA won three of the six awards presented, including the Outstanding Station Award. It should be noted that since the Academy of Television Arts and Sciences was still such a local Los Angeles concern, most of the awards this first year were won by Los Angeles stations.

A sure sign of the market's new competitiveness was when both of KTLA's other winners—ventriloquist Shirley Dinsdale, who won for Outstanding Television Personality, and Mike Stokey's "Pantomime Quiz," which won for Most Popular Television Program—were almost immediately offered more money from rival stations with network affiliations and wooed away from KTLA: Dinsdale went to KNBH, and "Pantomime Quiz" to KTTV. Landsberg replaced the children's program with a puppet show conceived by former Warner Brothers' animator Bob Clampett. "Time for Beany" (which was kinescoped on 35-millimeter film negative) would become one of the station's biggest hits, eventually syndicated nationally. Stokey's show was replaced by "Movietown, R.S.V.P.," a program that proved successful with a format similar to that of "Pantomime Quiz."

KTLA's prominence in the region was solidified as a result of their 27.5 continuous hours of coverage of the attempted rescue of Kathy Fiscus, a three-year-old child trapped in a San Marino well. The impact of this April 1949 telecast on the area is legendary. The event and its coverage in all of the major media virtually brought the city to a halt and resultantly changed the popular perception of television: Viewers congregated in the homes of neighbors who owned sets or stood crowded around the windows of set merchants all night long. Such an impact was mostly unanticipated and fairly immediate, but the response to the telecast indicated the propensity of television toward this sort of event. Stan Chambers, who along with Bill Welsh reported for KTLA at the scene of the rescue attempt, has suggested that the Fiscus telecast "broke the mold" of television news coverage in its day, which had generally consisted of an anchor reading news-service reports from behind a desk for 15 minutes.[26] The "live" and simultaneous, uninterrupted, and open-ended qualities of this newscast set it apart and left a lingering impression of television's ability to make a certain impact on the daily lives of its viewers.

KTLA's regularly scheduled shows still dominated Los Angeles, as a November survey by Woodbury College in Los Angeles indicated: KTLA was identified as the "station most used" (41 percent of the time) and also featured the two favorite performers of area children—Beany, the favorite of 39 percent, and Hopalong Cassidy, the favorite of 27 percent.[27] An advertisement in the November issue of *Television* indicated that KTLA had

---

26. Stan Chambers, interview with author, 26 January 1989.
27. *Woodbury Television Ratings,* Survey 2 (November 1949).

43 of the top 50 time segments in Los Angeles, as determined by the Hooper "Teleratings" for August and September.[28]

The November issue of *Television* also reported that kinescopes of KTLA programs syndicated by the station (a practice begun only that year) were already circulating to nearly 20 stations across the country.[29] On the national front Los Angeles television began to establish a reputation unheard of for local markets. KTLA syndicated kinescopes of "Wrestling from Hollywood," "Time for Beany," and "Armchair Detective," while KTTV began kinescoping the first network shows from Los Angeles—first "The Ed Wynn Show," and then "The Buster Keaton Show."

By the end of 1949 the Los Angeles area's full complement of seven stations were all actively programming on a commercial basis. The 90,000 sets at the beginning of the year had tripled by year's end.[30] Perhaps as a result of this rapid industrial maturation, rivalries with the established television concerns in New York became manifest. In February 1950 the seven Los Angeles stations formed an association called the Television Broadcasters of Southern California, in response to what they perceived was a takeover of the Television Academy by East Coast TV interests. This disaffection for the eastern control of the Academy would culminate in five of the seven stations withdrawing from the Academy in 1952.

In terms of local programming, however, the most important development of 1950 was the expansion and growth of television news coverage. The outbreak of the Korean War in late June created a keen interest in news, and all of the stations began to implement more newscasts and a higher news profile. In early June three of the seven stations had no regularly scheduled news programs. By late August some 87 different news presentations could be seen over the course of a week.[31]

In terms of industry relations, 1951 was the key transitional year in early Los Angeles television, as stations were realigned in a configuration that would prove more amenable to the emerging three-network control of the U.S. television system. January saw construction begin on the CBS network's "Television City" production facilities at Fairfax and Beverly. Also that month the third annual Emmy Awards—the last to privilege local

---

28. KTLA advertisement, *Television* 6 (November 1949): 2.

29. "Focus," *Television* 6 (November 1949): 5.

30. Susan K. Wilbur, "The History of Television in Los Angeles, 1931–1952: Part III," *Southern California Quarterly* 60 (3) (Fall 1978): 258.

31. James Joseph Rue, "Analysis of Television News Techniques in the Los Angeles Area," master's thesis, University of Southern California, January 1951, pp. 54–55.

Los Angeles shows under consideration—resulted in KTLA winning five awards for its 1950 programming: "City at Night" (Best Public Service), the coverage of Marines departing for Korea (Special Events), "Time for Beany" (Best Children's Show—Beany's second of three consecutive Emmys), the "KTLA Newsreel" (Best News Program), and the award for Station Achievement. Also notable locally was the winning of two awards by Alan Young, whose CBS show was produced at KTTV. ("The Alan Young Show" had first appeared as a summer replacement for "The Ed Wynn Show.")

KTLA stepped up its kinescope syndication in 1951, adding shows such as "Hollywood Reel" (a cross between fan magazines and home movies, produced by cameraman Coy Watson and syndicated Hollywood columnist Erskine Johnson), and "The Spade Cooley Show," among others. New on the air locally was Lawrence Welk, whose Saturday-evening shows were telecast by remote from Lick Pier in Santa Monica. These practices occurred in the shadow of Paramount's final divestiture of its theater chain, and the resultant United Paramount Theatres' plans to merge with ABC.[32]

In an incident that reveals both a naïveté about television's impact and the economic risks of early TV sponsors, a local vitamin company, Thyavals, decided to sponsor nationally the KTLA program "Frosty Frolics," a variety show that featured ice-skating performers, on the ABC network in October. The attempt was short-lived, however, as the company went bankrupt within days after offering free samples of vitamins on the air, flooded by hundreds of thousands of requests. Their demise also affected "The Spade Cooley Show" and Leo Carrillo's "Dude Ranch Varieties" on KLAC, which Thyavals had sponsored locally.

The most prominent example of a local station making a national impact occurred in 1952, when KTLA telecast A-bomb tests from Nevada in April and May.[33] One of Landsberg's final programming coups, these telecasts transformed KTLA into a local source of "network live," as the station's feed was used by all three major networks. Landsberg was the only industry representative willing to undertake the preparations necessary for these telecasts, organizing and building in less than three weeks a complete microwave relay system to Las Vegas via four line-of-sight mountain peaks. KTLA and Paramount had gambled the entire cost of the enterprise, which

---

32. See Timothy R. White, "Hollywood's Attempt to Appropriate Television: The Case of Paramount Pictures," Ph.D. diss., University of Wisconsin–Madison, 1990, pp. 150–200.

33. The most detailed report on the production of these telecasts is the 9 May 1952 speech by Charter Heslep to the Georgia Radio and Television Institute, excerpted as "They Said It Couldn't Be Done" in *KTLA: West Coast Pioneer* (New York: Museum of Broadcasting, 1985), pp. 35–40.

would pay off only if successful. With the use of a Marine helicopter the relay was achieved in time, and the telecast was received nationally.

But KTLA's preeminence in the Los Angeles television market did not endure the rise of a national television culture rooted in the three major networks. To suggest that such a resonant icon as an atomic blast is representative of KTLA's repositioning would, of course, be overdramatizing the case. The station remained at or near the top of station competition in Los Angeles until the mid-1950s and has always maintained its local reputation for news programming and technical and programming innovations. But Landsberg's untimely death in 1956 at the age of 40, after a long battle with cancer, seems somehow indicative of the changes in the local market. Los Angeles would soon become the production center for television, as the NBC and CBS network facilities opened later in 1952. Network "stars" (some of whom were drawn from local shows) as well as network capabilities (such as those demonstrated in news coverage) were now available to Los Angeles "live" and around the clock and soon overtook the local stations' abilities to produce competitive programming. Eventually, KTLA and the whole of Los Angeles's independent television market were forced into a more subservient role, after having produced a dynamic and notable introduction of the allure and ideological project of the U.S. television system to this region.

19

KSL, Salt Lake City: "At the Crossroads of the West"

Donald G. Godfrey, Val E. Limburg, and Heber G. Wolsey

KSL television is flagship station of the Bonneville International Corporation, a wholly owned subsidiary of the Mormon Church—a church with a history in communication enterprises.[1] The Mormons' interest in print made the transition to electronic communications quite natural at the advent of radio and television. According to Bruce L. Christensen, former president of the Public Broadcasting System, "The Church of Jesus Christ of Latter-day Saints [today] is a broadcasting entity."[2]

A good deal has been written about the Mormon Church and the mass-communication business. Donigan has produced the most extensive outline

---

1. The Church of Jesus Christ of Latter-day Saints (Mormons) has been in the communication business since the early 1800s. Its first entry into the field was the production of the *Book of Mormon*, pamphlets and other materials used for proselytizing. The Church's first newspaper, *The Evening and the Morning Star,* began in Independence, Missouri, during the mid-1830s. In Missouri and Illinois prior to the Mormon exodus west, it published hymn books and frontier newspapers including the *Star,* the *Upper Missouri Advertiser*, the *Times and Seasons,* and the *Nauvoo Neighbor*. The first newspaper in Utah was established by the Mormons—the *Deseret News*. All of these publications were, at first, heavily laden with religious philosophy, but there was also a sense of business and economics that developed with their production. James B. Allen, Ronald K. Epslin, and David J. Whittaker, *Men with a Mission, 1837–1841: The Quorum of the Twelve Apostles in the British Isles* (Salt Lake City: Deseret Book Company, 1992), pp. 236–266. See also David J. Whittaker, "Early Mormon Pamphleteering," Ph.D. dissertation, Brigham Young University, 1982.

2. Bruce L. Christensen, "Broadcasting," in *Encyclopedia of Mormonism*, vol. 1 (New York: Macmillan, 1992), pp. 232–234.

history.[3] Limburg and Donigan have both studied the effectiveness of religious programming objectives and Church broadcasting.[4] Wolsey has produced a history of KSL radio, Christensen has discussed WRUL shortwave, and Godfrey has provided an interpretative analysis of Bonneville International Corporation.[5] In addition to these works, Bonneville International has published a set of oral histories featuring interviews with the developers of the system.[6] The Church periodicals and the *Deseret News* have also chronicled developments throughout the years. The topic is of continuing interest to both scholars and the popular press.

KSL radio and television are unusual among the media. They are commercial enterprises owned by a religious entity, a part of Bonneville International Corporation—a growing and influential media corporation. KSL is the earliest centerpiece of the Mormon electronic media.

KSL's Radio Roots

Mormon interest in broadcasting began in 1922 with the construction of KZN radio.[7] It officially went on the air May 6, 1922—as the *Deseret News* radio station. The first words broadcast were "Hello ... hello ... hello ... KZN ... KZN."[8]

---

3. Robert W. Donigan, "An Outline History of Broadcasting in the Church of Jesus Christ of Latter-day Saints, unpublished paper, Department of History and Philosophy of Religion, Brigham Young University, n.d.

4. See Val E. Limburg, "An Analysis of Relationships Between Religious Programming Objectives and Methods of Presentation used by Selected Major Religious Program Producers as Compared to the Church of Jesus Christ of Latter-day Saints," unpublished master's thesis, Department of Communication, Brigham Young University, 1964. Also, Robert W. Donigan, "A Descriptive Analysis of the Effectiveness of Broadcasting by the Church of Jesus Christ of Latter-day Saints in the North States Mission Area," unpublished master's thesis, Department of Communication, Brigham Young University, 1964.

5. Heber Grant Wolsey, "The History of Radio Station KSL from 1922 to Television," unpublished doctoral dissertation, Department of Speech, Michigan State University, 1967. See Christensen, pp. 232–234. See also Donald G. Godfrey, "A Descriptive Analysis and Interpretation of the Bonneville International Corporation," unpublished master's thesis, Department of Speech, University of Oregon, 1969.

6. Bonneville International Corporation, Oral History Series, Conducted by Heritage Associates W. Dee Halverson, Salt Lake City: Bonneville International Corporation, 1992. Hereafter referred to as Bonneville Oral History Series.

7. Donigan, p. 1.

8. Bruce Reese, Bonneville Oral History Series, p. 171.

In KZN's actual inaugural broadcast Mormon Church president Heber J. Grant gave the dedicatory address; the program consisted of speeches and musical selections. Salt Lake City mayor C. Clarence Neslen praised the station and noted that it was made possible by "one of the leading newspapers in the western country."[9]

The *Deseret News* radio actually had gone on the air a few months earlier as an experimental station, with the call sign 6ZM. By March 1922 the experiments had grown into nightly broadcasts. Thus, on May 6, 1922, the *Deseret News* radio, KZN, began broadcasting from an improvised studio on the roof of the *Deseret News* building in Salt Lake City, Utah.

The fact that KZN, like many other stations, was owned by a newspaper was by design. In an era of news competition newspaper publishers were keenly aware of the potential of the instantaneous radio signal. There were even some who feared radio would lead to the demise of the newspaper, and so in the best tradition of the marketplace, the newspaper acquired the competition. In the case of KZN, perhaps none of this really mattered, as both were owned by the Mormon Church.

To the leaders of the Church, and to many Church members, the advent of radio, and later of television, was a fulfillment of prophecy. In 1837 Orson Pratt, a member of the Church's first Quorum of Twelve Apostles, discussed the importance of spreading Christ's word and declared, "There must be something connected with the sound of this trump that is miraculous in order that all nations may hear it ... the sound of that trump will be heard by all people ... in the four corners of our globe. I do not know that the sound will be so much louder than some we have heard, but it will be carried by some miraculous power so that all people will hear it."[10] Church leaders often referred to Pratt's remarks as justification for their commitment to broadcasting, equating the reference to the trump with broadcast technology. His words fostered an enthusiasm for the marvel of electronic media. Just two months before the inaugural broadcast of KZN, the *Improvement Era*, a magazine publication of the Church, editorialized about the potential for the "vacuum tube amplifier" noting, "It is now possible ... that the President of

---

9. "Speeches Given During KZN Inaugural Broadcast, May 6, 1922," Bonneville Oral History Series, pp. 26–28. See Albert L. Zobell, Jr., "radio and the Gospel Message," *The Improvement Era* 50:4 (April 1947), p. 205. See *Deseret News*, May 6, 1922. See also Heber G. Wolsey, "Religious Broadcasting by the LDS (Mormon) Church," unpublished master's thesis, Department of Speech, Northwestern University, Evanston, Illinois, August 1949.

10. *Journal of Discourses*, vol. 16 (Salt Lake City: Deseret Book Company, 1978), pp. 327–328, 336–337.

the Church ... may be able to deliver his sermons in the Salt Lake Tabernacle and be heard by congregations assembled in every settlement of the Church from Canada to Mexico and from California to Colorado."[11]

The excitement over this new instrument as an important sermonizing and missionary tool was evident from the beginning. In October 1924 the Church's General Conference was first broadcast, and the first church service was broadcast shortly thereafter, on November 16, 1924.[12]

The Mormon Tabernacle Choir program, "Music and the Spoken Word," began soon after the station was on the air. This development was not without opposition from the musicians, who questioned the fidelity of radio. In the beginning only rehearsals were broadcast. The first formal broadcast from the Mormon Tabernacle in Salt Lake City was on June 26, 1923. President Warren G. Harding spoke and the choir sang.[13] The choir did not begin its regular schedule until KSL became an NBC affiliate. On July 15, 1929, the first regular network Tabernacle Choir and Organ program was broadcast nationally.

In June 1924 KZN was sold to a radio engineer by the name of John Cope. Cope formed the Radio Service Corporation of Utah with a capitalization of $15,000, and the station's call letters were changed to KFPT.[14] In November of that same year Earl J. Glade joined KFPT to supervise programming, sales, and accounting, and to act as announcer. At that time Glade was a professor in the business school at the University of Utah and had engaged in private advertising in the Salt Lake area. In June 1925 the call letters were again changed, this time to KSL. It was Glade who renewed the interest of the LDS Church and worked out an agreement between the Salt Lake Tribune and the Church for joint ownership of the station. These two organizations maintained their interest in KSL radio and television for approximately 23 years, with the Church's presiding bishop, Sylvester W.

11. Edward H. Anderson, "The Vacuum Tube Amplifier," The Improvement Era 23:5 (March 1922), p. 457.

12. The Improvement Era, 50:4 (April 1947), pp. 205–255. See also Donigan, p. 26.

13. Albert L. Zobell, Jr., "The Tabernacle Choir Marks Its 2,000th Broadcast," Era 70:12 (December 1967), p. 19. See a history of the choir by Charles Jeffrey Calman and William I. Kaufman, The Mormon Tabernacle Choir (New York: Harper and Rowe, 1979). Also J. Spencer Cornwall, A Century of Singing: The Salt Lake City Mormon Tabernacle Choir (Salt Lake City: Deseret Book Company, 1958).

14. "Editor's Table," The Improvement Era 25:8 (June 1949), pp. 735–736.

Cannon, acting as president of the Radio Service Corporation until the *Tribune* sold its interest in order to purchase another station.[15]

On September 1, 1932, KSL changed its affiliation from the NBC network to the Columbia Broadcasting System. As there were relatively few CBS affiliates in the West at that time, the change provided both the station and the network an exclusive western audience.

Television: Will It Work?

As early as 1934 KSL's board of directors began discussing television's potential with KSL's ownership and executives of CBS. The management of the station was encouraged to "keep in touch with this phase of radio work in order that we may be prepared to move along with it from the very beginning."[16] There was even further impetus. Philo T. Farnsworth, one of the developers of television, was a Mormon. His experiments with the transmission of pictures were reportedly making the idea a reality. In the summer of 1936 he wrote KSL radio regarding the outlook for television and suggested that it was a good time in which to make a study of television's possibilities and perhaps "make a set-up for experimental purposes."[17] KSL expressed an interest, but no further action was taken with Farnsworth.

World War II rechanneled the innovative energies of television and the electronic media toward the war efforts. For KSL executives some of the prewar enthusiasm for television seemed to be lacking after the war. Minutes of the board of director's meeting contained a cautionary note: "Television … requires such a tremendous amount of operation equipment and personnel, there appears to be a long way to go before television broadcasting will emerge from the present experimental basis to one based on practical business procedures."[18] However, despite this caveat, the potential of the medium would not be ignored for long.

---

15. This represented the only business venture that the LDS Church and the *Tribune* have embarked upon together except for today's dual newspaper interest in the Newspaper Agency Corporation.

16. Minutes of KSL Board of Directors' meeting, June 18, 1935, KSL Radio, Salt Lake City, Utah.

17. Minutes of KSL Board of Directors' meeting, August 17, 1936.

18. Minutes of KSL Board of Directors' meeting, June 18, 1945.

KSL applied for its license to operate a television station on May 26, 1948—just months before the Federal Communications Commission placed a freeze on television licenses. The FCC granted the construction permit on July 29 of that same year and instructed that KSL-TV begin operations no later than March 22, 1949.[19]

KSL's general manager, C. Richard Evans, made a trip to New York and Washington, D.C., to visit the networks, and before he returned, he had television-contract offers from the American Broadcasting Company, the Columbia Broadcasting System, and the Du Mont Television Network. During the trip he also held a number of meetings with national advertising-agency officials, who communicated enthusiasm for the new medium's potential in Salt Lake City. KSL's national advertising representative, Radio Sales, encouraged the movement toward television, indicating that national accounts were ready to buy time on KSL-TV as soon as it was in operation. Bulova, Chesterfield, Phillip Morris, American Tobacco, BVD, Benrus Watches, Swank Jewelry, Whitman Chocolates, and Polaroid were specifically mentioned.[20]

Following Evans's return from the East on February 14, 1949, he presented three alternatives to the KSL board of directors: (1) proceed according to the issued construction permit, (2) delay construction, which might involve KSL in a local city hearing and possibly mean the loss of the construction permit, or (3) file an amendment to the application for the construction permit asking for a new corporation to handle television, or for a change in location. This would delay the need to file an FCC action for permission to operate until other competing stations had been through the "freeze" and subsequent hearings. The danger in any delay was that KSL might lose its VHF channel designation and end up with a UHF channel, which could not be received on the sets then available.

If management had been cautious in recognizing the powerful potential of television during the war years, that hesitancy was quickly overcome. Less than four months from the time Evans presented his recommendations to the board, KSL television was on the air—June 1, 1949. Three years later, in 1952, KSL repositioned its television transmitter on top of the Oquirrh Mountains overlooking the Salt Lake Valley, making the signal accessible to viewers in Ogden, Salt Lake, Provo, and much of the populated region then served by KSL radio.

---

19. Wolsey, p. 128.
20. Wolsey, p. 129.

A Mormon Station in the Modern World

Despite Church authorities' view of television and radio as a means of carrying the gospel to a wide audience, KSL television and radio operated as business enterprises. They were, from a Church standpoint, investments intended to earn a profit as well as "a factor in the spread of the gospel of Jesus Christ across the world."[21] Balancing these goals has not always been an easy task, as "Church standards" have often been at odds with the economic practices of the day.

An illustration of this dilemma surfaced early when the station's board of directors tried to reconcile a Mormon health doctrine that forbids the use of tobacco and alcohol with the major advertising forces in television at that time. Board-meeting minutes illustrate the conflict, noting that "KSL formerly took beer-sponsored programs and they had been discontinued when [J.Reuben Clark, Jr.] became President of the Corporation [in August of 1938]."[22] KSL radio's refusal to carry beer or wine advertising was carried forward to KSL television and continued for many years, creating both hardship and debate. In 1950 station manager C. Richard Evans "suggested that KSL's policy ... be enlarged to include no demonstration of the operation of a lethal weapon."[23] The dilemma was an interesting one, illustrating the problem of just where to draw the line on anything that might conflict with the religious concepts of the Church. Was it to be drawn in programming, advertising, or both?

Station president J. Reuben Clark, Jr., met with Church officials to consider the alternatives, reasoning that to reject advertising from the network would weaken the station's potential as a mass medium. Viewers could always find what they wanted by moving to competing stations. The question was raised that perhaps the Church should get out of the broadcasting business altogether. However, "to do the latter ... could release the control of the facilities to parties who may not exercise any discrimination."[24] A few weeks later Clark again noted the economic and religious dilemma of refusing advertising and/or programming contrary to religious beliefs and

21. Gordon B. Hinkley, Bonneville Oral History Series, p. 10.

22. Minutes of the KSL Board of Directors' meeting, October 25, 1951.

23. Minutes of the KSL Department Heads' meeting, March 27, 1950.

24. Minutes of the KSL Executive Committee meeting, August 23, 1951. In Salt Lake, KSL's competition was KTVX and KUTV. KTVX, Channel 4, went on the air April 15, 1948. KUTV, Channel 2, joined the competition six years later on September 26, 1954.

said, "It appears that neither KSL nor KSL-TV could be dominant and influential if the Corporation continued to refuse to accept beer programs."[25] Without the programming, he reasoned, the audience would be lost, resulting in reduced advertising, reduced revenues, and considerable difficulty in operating a first-class station.

According to Frank Stanton, CBS-network president, there was sympathy with KSL's position, but it "came down to a question of hard business."[26] The networks were providing an audience for their programs and their commercial accounts. If KSL could not provide that in Salt Lake City, it was possible CBS would change its affiliation. On three different occasions the corporate management had carefully considered the issue and "reluctantly" reached the decision to accept the advertising and the programs, "if approved by the Directors."[27] Almost as a matter of compromise, KSL continued to refuse national spot advertising and local advertising of beer. However, after several years of examining and re-examining its policy, KSL facilities were open to national spot, local, and network advertising of all products, just like any other media corporation in America. The decision was to sacrifice the strict application and interpretation of religious philosophy in order to make the stations profitable and have them provide leadership within local and national media communities. Today KSL does not originate advertising contracts for the sale of alcoholic beverages. However, they do not try to restrict the networks or interfere with network contracts.

While this all seems something of a nonissue from a national perspective, at the time some Church members were clearly upset at the station's compromise and its acceptance of advertising they saw as contradictory to their religion. According to one viewer, "Television is a power we should insist on controlling rather than allow it to control us—even if it means money out of our pockets."[28] However, KSL's operational policy clearly had progressed from one of primarily religious proselytizing to one of business and economics.

Today KSL's policies on all products and programs essentially parallel closely the policies of the majority of other commercial broadcasting stations in America. From the point of view of operating a business for a profit, the policy is sound.

---

25. Minutes of the KSL Board of Directors' meeting, October 25, 1951.
26. Minutes of the KSL Board of Directors' meeting, October 25, 1951.
27. Minutes of the KSL Board of Directors' meeting, October 25, 1951.
28. KSL Public Files, letter from Clearfield, Utah, viewer, April 12, 1953.

Bonneville's Key Station

During the late 1950s KSL television was operating at a loss, and CBS was threatening to cancel its affiliation. Local competitors were outclassing them. According to Arch Madsen, former president of Bonneville International Corporation, "Channel Four had a 450 percent higher rating for their news ... Channel Two was about 200 percent higher." KSL television, Channel 5, was at the bottom of the CBS-network listing. Madsen said that CBS would have dropped its affiliation except for the patience of William Paley. He told Madsen, "We have 190 TV stations on our network ... [and] KSL is in the bottom ten. In fact, they are on the bottom of the bottom ten, because the other nine have a good reason to be there. KSL does not."[29]

The Church had made a clear decision: Its media-enterprise investments were businesses. Over the years the Corporation of the President (of the Church of Jesus Christ of Latter-day Saints) has bought and sold a number of electronic-media properties. It once owned stations in Idaho Falls, Idaho; Cedar City, Utah; and Honolulu, Hawaii. In 1964 all of the Church's expanding broadcast properties and activities were placed under control of a new entity—the Bonneville International Corporation. This corporation provided a "more efficient operation for all companies."[30] The merger left loca' officers and management basically in charge but created a corporate-management operation to oversee and coordinate operations. The individual stations report to Bonneville International Corporation, which in turn reports to Deseret Management Corporation.[31] The new organization brought in new leadership. Arch L. Madsen became Bonneville's president, and, according to Madsen, he was given three charges by Church president David O. McKay: "President McKay made it abundantly clear that they weren't satisfied. He expected me to do things ... emphasizing the need for a substantial budget to build people ... [to build] outstanding public service ... and then, my good friends, we will take care of the profitability."[32]

29. Arch L. Madsen, oral-history interview conducted by Tim Larson, University of Utah, September 1, 1986, Bonneville Oral History Series, pp. 33–36.

30. "Radio, TV Merge by Church," *Deseret News*, September 9, 1964.

31. This is the corporation that manages all of the Mormon Church's commercial assets. For an organizational chart and an explanation of Church holdings see, "Counting Its Blessings," *Arizona Republic* 102:43 (June 30, 1991), pp. 10–11. See also Godfrey, pp. 36, 41–42.

32. Madsen, Bonneville Oral History Series, p. 34.

The primary stations existing when the Bonneville International Corporation was formed were KSL AM-FM-TV, Salt Lake City; KIRO AM-
FM-TV, Seattle; WRUL (shortwave, later WNYW), New York; KID
AM-FM-TV, Idaho Falls; and KBOI AM-FM-TV, Boise. Corporate headquarters were in the KSL television complex. By 1980 the *New York Times*
reported that Bonneville was the "Mormon Business Flagship ... with
revenues of $100 million and a growth rate of at least 15 percent annually
... Bonneville [has a] reputation as an aggressive marketer, an innovative
public service programmer and a leader in television technology."[33] If
Bonneville was the flagship of Mormon business enterprise, KSL television
was the flagstation of Bonneville.

Programming to Serve the Community

The early programming of KSL television had come from the CBS
network and KSL radio. Those local programs carried on radio were trans-
posed to television. The most noteworthy from both a local and national
perspective was that of "Music and the Spoken Word," with the Mormon
Tabernacle Choir, claiming to be the "oldest, continuous sustaining program" in America.[34]

The choir broadcasts made their debut on television less than a year
after KSL had signed on. In 1950 two versions of the program were produced:
A 30-minute program went to CBS radio, and a 60-minute version aired
locally.[35] Both were exactly as the formal title describes: "music and the
spoken word." Music, of course, was the performance of the choir and the
familiar tabernacle organ. The spoken word was provided by a KSL announcer, Richard L. Evans, and consisted of a nondenominational message
of inspiration. On July 15, 1954, the choir appeared on Edward R. Murrow's
"See It Now." So famous was the choir program that the group was invited
to participate in the "first live telecast to Europe."[36] The resultant program

33. "Bonneville: Mormon Business Flagship," *New York Times*, November 24, 1980, p. D4.

34. "Mormons: Singing Saints," *Time*, July 26, 1963, p. 66. See also "KSL Newsman Is Voice
of Choir Broadcast," *Church News* 42:9 (February 26, 1972), p. 14.

35. See *Improvement Era* 63:6 (June 1950), p. 464.

36. *Improvement Era* 65:9 (September 1962), p. 626. See also Christopher H. Sterling and John
M. Kittross, *Stay Tuned: A Concise History of American Broadcasting*, 2nd ed. (Belmont:
Wadsworth, 1990), p. 118.

was the first of the Telstar-satellite relays and featured the choir on location singing from the base of Mount Rushmore. Today the 30-minute television version of the choir is broadcast on the CBS Radio Network, and it is syndicated to 582 independent radio stations, 61 television stations, and 1,550 cable outlets in the United States.

Another program that came over directly from radio to KSL television was the Mormon Church Conference. These biannual events were first televised in 1949, just a few months after sign-on.[37] The program typically features talks by Church authorities, a variety of invited choirs, and the Tabernacle Choir. In 1953 KSL began feeding a small network of stations that agreed to carry conference sessions in their area: KNXT, Los Angeles; KGO, San Francisco; KPTV, Portland; and KTVT, Tacoma. This program, too, has been syndicated to independent stations and cable operations. Today the carrying of the Church Conference by stations beyond KSL-TV has been supplemented by satellite distribution, which relays the sessions to community cable systems and satellite downlink facilities located adjacent to Church meetinghouses. It is translated into 21 languages and distributed globally.

Conference telecasts, the choir, and other religious broadcasts have played historically to a Salt Lake City Mormon audience—a majority of the Salt Lake City–area residents have been Mormon. However, the station and program producers were also conscious of their non-Mormon audience. The "Spoken Word" portion of the choir program was specifically designed to be nondenominational. The station's management walked that line of ethical dilemma again, this time in programming, and they recognized the fact that the non-Mormon audience could not be ignored.

Response to the broadcast of an early Church basketball tournament reflects the wrath of one viewer whose regular programming was apparently pre-empted: "Did it ever occur to you people that you might do a little investigating as to TV viewers' interest before you cut off some of the best programs ... to show ... that damned stupid basketball ... [who] in hell [cares] whether the 4th LDS Mormon Ward of Nephiville [sic] beats the 6th LDS Ward of Mantiville [sic].[38]

With the advent of the Bonneville International Corporation the responsibility for production of the choir and conference broadcasts was taken over by a new Bonneville division called Bonneville Communications. One of the reasons the division was created was to establish a clear line between

37. See *Improvement Era* 66:6 (June 1963), p. 438.
38. Letter in KSL's files from Salt Lake City, Utah, May 9, 1952.

the commercial operation of KSL and the production of Church-related programming. This division of the company became responsible for public-service and foreign-language religious programming—distributed on tape, shortwave, and satellite. The "Home-front" public-service messages are illustrative of this division's work. The spots send nondenominational messages targeted toward teens, families, and "listeners who habitually turned out traditional religious programming."[39] The home-front messages are now in their 20th year of production and claim to be the most widely broadcast public-service campaign in broadcast history. Carried as public-service announcements, they air on the four networks and 740 TV stations in the United States.

KSL was further removed from direct Church telecasting efforts when Bonneville purchased satellite transponder capacity and created Bonneville Satellite Corporation. This "uplink" capability provides the Church with a satellite network reaching from Salt Lake and "downlinked" to satellite receivers installed at Church centers throughout the world. This relieved the Bonneville commercial operations and KSL from philosophical pressures and, at the same time, brought the Church's religious leaders closer to their individual congregations.[40]

Bonneville's Leadership

Many religious entities across the United States own religious radio and television stations. They use the airwaves to seek converts and, as we have seen more recently, to solicit financial contributions. Although the early years of Mormon interest in television and radio may have been to influence conversions, today Bonneville has evolved into what some describe as a "media baron."[41] Others have praised Bonneville's business leadership.[42]

---

39. Whit Wirsing, "Millions Touched by Church Radio-TV Messages," *Church News* 43:31 (July 29, 1972), p. 14.

40. Geoffrey L. Pace, "The Emergency of Bonneville Satellite Corporation: A Study of Conception and Development of a New Telecommunications Service," unpublished master's thesis, Brigham Young University, 1983, pp, 12–79.

41. Nicholas Johnson, "The Media Barons and the Public Interest," *Atlantic Monthly,* June 1968, pp. 43–51.

42. See "Bonneville: Mormon Business Flagship," *New York Times,* November 24, 1980, p. D4.

Like its parent Church, Bonneville has grown from serving the interests of a close-knit, local Mormon population to serving people around the globe.

Bonneville's ownings illustrate its strength and diversity. In 1991 the *Arizona Republic* reported that two television stations (including KSL) in Salt Lake and Seattle, and 16 radio stations—in Salt Lake City, Seattle, New York City, Phoenix, Kansas City, Chicago, Los Angeles, and San Francisco—were owned by Bonneville.[43] At that time Bonneville also syndicated "beautiful music" radio formats and had interests in advertising agencies, production support facilities, and a satellite transmission system.[44] However, of the $300 million the *Arizona Republic* reported coming from these communications companies, an estimated $114.4 million came from KSL television in Salt Lake and KIRO television in Seattle,[45] with the radio stations adding approximately $72 million.[46] As of this writing Bonneville operates seven broadcast-related support companies: Bonneville Communications, Salt Lake City; Bonneville Entertainment Company, Salt Lake City; Bonneville LDS Radio Network, Salt Lake City; Bonneville Satellite Company, Salt Lake City; Bonneville Washington News Bureau, Washington, D.C.; Bonneville Worldwide Entertainment, Salt Lake City; and Video West, Salt Lake City. Bonneville no longer owns KIRO television, but its list of radio properties has grown to include KBIG-FM, Los Angeles; KIRO-AM, KIRO-FM, KNWX-AM, Seattle; KMBZ-AM, KLTH-FM, KCMO-AM, KCMO-FM, Kansas City; KOIT-AM, KOIT-FM, San Francisco; KHTC-FM, KIDR-AM, Phoenix; KSL-TV, KSL-AM, Salt Lake City; KZPS-FM, KDGE-FM, Dallas; WMXV-FM, New York City; and WTMX-FM, Chicago. According to Donald Gale, "Within the industry, Bonneville is considered one of the top ten broadcast groups in the nation."[47]

The reasons for the Mormon interest in media investment have evolved from proselytizing and preaching in the 1920s and 1930s to business enterprise and image advertising. According to former Church president Howard

---

43. KIRO-TV was sold in 1995 to Belo Corporation, Dallas, Texas. It was sold as a result of the network-affiliate shuffling and would have become the independent station. Currently it is an affiliate of UPN.

44. "Mormon Inc.: Finances & Faith," *Arizona Republic*, June 30, 1991, p. A11.

45. In 1994 Bonneville sold its Seattle property, KIRO-TV.

46. "Money in the Media," *Arizona Republic*, July 3, 1991, pp. 1 & A9.

47. G. Donald Gale, vice president news and public affairs, letter to Donald G. Godfrey, January 18, 1996. Dr. Gale indicates that the revenue figures published in the *Arizona Republic* are "far off the track," but could not provide an additional source.

W. Hunter, that evolution has resulted in a broadcast group that is "a voice for Mormonism and its values: family, decency and morality."[48] Today's Church authorities see KSL and Bonneville media as trendsetting, image building, and forward looking. These objectives require practices not always viewed favorably by the KSL audience or other commercial enterprises.

Locally, KSL retains its prohibition of local spot advertisements for alcohol (although it doesn't delete the ads from the network). During the debates over tobacco advertising KSL was among the first stations that chose not to accept such advertising. KSL television has occasionally pre-empted programming it has judged unsuitable. For example, it declined to air such movies as *Dirty Dancing* and *The Graduate*. According to former KSL president Jack Adamson, when CBS was making plans in 1987 to create an animated children's program based on some controversial characters featured on trading cards, KSL rallied the affiliates and family organizations to get the program canceled before its debut.[49]

Critics have charged that these actions reflect the Church's meddling in the daily programming operations of the stations. Critics also object to what they perceive as religious programming favoring the Mormon Church, showing political bias, and slanting the news.[50] But according to Spencer Kinard, KSL television's former news director, "Allegations of church censorship are a crock."[51] These criticisms have sometimes reached the FCC, but KSL and other Bonneville stations have always been granted license renewal. Despite the controversy Mormon ownership attracts, KSL today is not a religious facility; it is a station in business to make a profit, "not to evangelize," Arch Madsen has said.[52]

Summary

The Mormon Church has had an interest in broadcasting since 1922, when it began as radio station KZN. This station, later KSL radio and

---

48. "Money in the Media," p. A9.
49. "Money in the Media," p. A9.
50. Federal Communications Commission, File No. 4081, Petition for Reconsideration of Ethel C. Hale and W. Paul Warton of Renewal of License Granted Station KSL, Salt Lake City, Utah. Washington D.C., 1969.
51. "Money in the Media," p. A9.
52. "Bonneville: Mormon Business Flagship," p. D4.

television, provided the foundation for today's Bonneville International Corporation.

Today's messages from KSL and the Bonneville stations are not those of proselytizing, but of leadership in business and promotion of family values. Although KSL and Bonneville are owned by the Church, the stations are run as any commercial operation. The casual observer would hardly know they were entities of the Mormon Church. KSL and Bonneville do have their share of controversy, however. Commissioner Nicholas Johnson has called them a "media baron" in his *Atlantic Monthly* articles, and the licenses of KSL television and KIRO television have been challenged several times on the grounds that they exhibit "favoritism" toward the Mormon Church. However, in every instance the stations have weathered the controversy, renewed their licenses, and received accolades in the national and local press from industry and community leaders.

Bonneville and KSL are unusual, according to Rodney H. Brady, current president of Bonneville. They are a "commercial broadcast company owned by a religious organization operated strictly as a business and seeking no special treatment."[53]

---

53. Rodney H. Brady, "Bonneville at Thirty: A Values-Driven Company Composed of Values-Driven People," address delivered at the Newcomen Society of the United States, Salt Lake City, June 9, 1994 (New York: Newcomen Society, 1994), p. 11.

20 San Francisco's First Television Station: KPIX

Steven C. Runyon

KPIX (Channel 5 in San Francisco) is, perhaps, the quintessential prefreeze television station. It is representative of television during the late 1940s and early 1950s, yet outstanding due to a number of factors, including its location in San Francisco, its visionary general manager, Philip Lasky, and an excellent staff of technical experts and creative programmers. KPIX was the San Francisco Bay area's first television station, the fourth on the Pacific Coast, and the 49th in the United States.[1]

KPIX went on the air December 22, 1948, with a live ice-hockey game fed to the station from Winterland Auditorium in San Francisco.[2] On December 24 it broadcast the motion picture *A Christmas Carol*. To create an interest in television among the San Francisco Bay–area populace, the station began a significant promotion campaign months before it went on the air. By early 1948 KPIX was publishing a semimonthly newsletter describing its plans as well as providing information about television broadcasting in other areas of the country. "It distributed this letter to publications, television set dealers, advertisers, educators and others until it had been on the air for many months, and other informational sources were doing the job."[3]

---

1. "KPIX, a Short History," KPIX Press Release, undated, circa 1988, KPIX Public Relations Department files, San Francisco.
2. "KPIX, a Short History."
3. "KPIX 1948–1953," 1954 private report prepared by the station, from personal files of Philip G. Lasky, Hillsborough, Calif. (This is one of two major sources from which information was obtained. Direct quotations and information obtained from other sources are footnoted as appropriate.)

The station built a demonstration-studio facility in one of San Francisco's department stores and fed live programming to various television receivers positioned within the store and to other receivers located in the store's windows overlooking the street. Similar closed-circuit demonstrations were given in local hotels. Once the station went on the air, KPIX technicians provided advice and counsel to help TV-set purchasers properly install and operate their new equipment. Not only did the technicians answer viewers' installation questions, they made "house calls" to viewers' homes when necessary.

KPIX's first broadcast studio and offices were located in converted radio studios at the Mark Hopkins Hotel atop Nob Hill in San Francisco. The station's antenna was mounted on the roof of the hotel. The initial staff of KPIX numbered 20 people. Within three years the staff had grown significantly and the station was in desperate need of larger facilities. During 1951 KPIX built a new structure to house the station. In January 1952 the station moved to this all-new three-story facility on Van Ness Avenue. The main studio in this facility was the first San Francisco television studio able to accommodate audiences.

A new antenna and transmitter, located on Mount Sutro in the geographic center of the city, went into service in July 1952. This antenna, at double the height of the hotel antenna, significantly increased KPIX's coverage area.[4] In 1953 the station boosted its power, providing a 100,000-watt signal to San Francisco and the bay area. In 1954 KPIX installed the necessary equipment to convert its transmitter for the transmission of programs in color. In 1980 the station moved again. The historic building at Battery and Broadway near the financial district, originally a factory and built just after the 1906 earthquake, provided about twice as much space as the Van Ness Avenue site. In 1983 the station opened the Satellite/Earth Receive and Transmit Station in El Cerrito. This facility provided KPIX with the capability to receive and transmit live programming via satellite nationwide.

KPIX was originally owned by Associated Broadcasters, the owners of KSFO radio in San Francisco. The station's first vice president and general manager was Philip G. Lasky, one of California broadcasting's best-known pioneers. KPIX was affiliated with both the Du Mont and the NBC television

---

4. KPIX's surplus studio facilities, transmitter, and antenna were donated to the Bay Area Educational Television Association. This enabled KQED, one of the nation's first and most noted educational television stations, to go on the air.

networks. In 1949 the station dropped its NBC affiliation[5] and on April 18, 1949, became an affiliate of the Columbia Broadcasting System (CBS).[6] KPIX's original broadcast schedule called for two to three hours of programming per day, five days per week. By 1953 KPIX was on the air 16 or more hours per day, seven days per week. The station has been owned by Westinghouse since 1954.

Programming Innovations

After KPIX's first live remote of an ice-hockey game on its inaugural broadcast day, the station followed up with a regular and ongoing schedule of live remote sports broadcasts. On January 1, 1949, just a week after beginning its program service to the bay area, KPIX broadcast live the Shrine East-West New Year's Day football game.

> KPIX endeavored to expand the range of its activities by the coverage of important sports events—boxing, wrestling, baseball, football, horseracing, track and field—and other comparable activities; by broadcasting films of president Truman's 1949 inauguration within 24 hours of the actual ceremony ... by taking its cameras to the scenes of local news and events, whether fire or flood, the Zoo or the Livestock Exposition; by offering local collegiate dramatic productions; by inaugurating the first local live religious program; by telecasting the opera and Shakespeare; by telecasting the first local forum; by showing in a series of programs the construction of a house from the purchase of the lot through the writing of the contract to the landscaping with accompanying discussions of problems confronted and solutions suggested; by presenting children's programs ... by securing the cooperation of local schools, colleges and universities in the presentation of a variety of educational programs; and by sending motion picture crews to military posts to bring back documentaries on training procedures.[7]

KPIX originally defined its programming categories as educational, cultural, and informational; civic and governmental; news and special events; sports; agriculture; religion; children's programs; and entertainment. There

---

5. The NBC affiliation moved to San Francisco's third television station, KRON, Channel 4, owned by the Chronicle Newspaper Publishing Company.

6. "KPIX Facts," undated, circa 1988, KPIX Public Relations Department files, San Francisco.

7. "KPIX 1948–1953," pp. 12–13.

are many innovative and pioneering examples within these various program areas. "California Council Table" was a long-running KSFO radio series. In the spring of 1949 KPIX began to broadcast a television version of the program. From the experience gained in broadcasting this program, KPIX began to broadcast a weekly series, "What's Your Opinion?" in October 1951. It quickly became "one of the established weekly sustaining features of KPIX's permanent programming."[8] For this series KPIX created a public advisory board of community leaders. The board, with the approval of the station, was given the responsibility of selecting the subjects and participants for each program in the series. According to San Francisco newspaper columnist Terrence O'Flaherty, this series was "The Bay Area's most sensibly constructed sounding board for public opinion."[9]

Typical of other KPIX-produced discussion programs during this period were "The Press Club Presents," featuring weekly guests from the club's well-known Friday-night dinners; "Ask the Experts," produced for and including local teenagers; "X Marks the Spot," to encourage people to vote; "Gold Label Round Table," featuring key political figures discussing contemporary political issues; and "Report from the Legislature," weekly reports of legislative activities featuring the Speaker of the California State Senate. Under the direction of manager Phil Lasky, KPIX made a serious commitment to public affairs and community-service programming. George Rosen said about the man in *Variety*, "As CBS-TV's Frisco affiliate, he's loaded down with high-rated entertainment shows, hence he figures why try to compete in that area of programming on a local level. Better spend the money in projecting vital issues to serve the community."[10]

Educational and Information Programs

KPIX made a major commitment to educational, informational, and cultural programming. One innovative early live-studio series highlighted scientific subjects and was produced with the help of the California Academy of Sciences. The station made airtime available for the live broadcast of plays featuring drama students from St. Mary's College in nearby Moraga and from

---

8. "KPIX 1948–1953," p. 14.
9. Unannotated newspaper clipping, circa 1953, reproduced in "KPIX 1948–1953."
10. George Rosen, "Phil Lasky's Phi Beta Video Fillip," *Variety,* 18 July 1956.

the University of California. By July 1951 KPIX employed a full-time education director to work with bay-area educational groups. As a result of this the station produced a number of educational programs and series. The first was "Frontiers of Understanding," a weekly series produced in cooperation with Stanford University. Typical of KPIX's public-service commitment during this period, the series was scheduled during prime time from 9:30 to 10 on Friday evenings. The "New Worlds for You" series spotlighted academic courses available to adults through San Francisco public schools.

In order to provide a television alternative to field trips, KPIX produced "Partners in Progress." This series of half-hour programs attempted to show how particular businesses contributed to the development of California, and the relationships between business and education. In the spring of 1952 KPIX broadcast a half-hour series of 15 programs titled "Come to Order." Viewers who watched the series and completed the assigned work received tuition-free college credit from City College of San Francisco. Another formal adult-education series produced by KPIX was "Discovery," a weekly exploration of modern fine and applied art with well-known guest artists such as Frank Lloyd Wright, Charles Eames, George Lichty, and Barnaby Conrad. The series was kinescoped from a closed-circuit broadcast each Wednesday and telecast on Sunday afternoons directly following the CBS presentation of "Omnibus." Other KPIX educational/cultural programs during this period included "Know Yourself Better," "People, Places and Politics," and "Inquiry." This tradition of innovation continued many years later with the creation of the long-running "Evening Magazine" series. This series was the blueprint for the nationally franchised "P.M. Magazine," and the first field-videotaped program in TV history.[11]

Civic Programming

KPIX made an early and significant commitment to civic and governmental programming. Armed-forces presentations stand out as a major area of public-service programming during KPIX's first half decade of broadcasting. In 1951 the station sent a crew to Pearl Harbor, Hawaii, to film a series of programs supporting WAVE recruiting. In 1953 KPIX sent another crew

11. Harry Fuller (KPIX general manager), memorandum to Lance Lew (KPIX Public Relations Department), 28 February 1995, KPIX Public Relations Department files, San Francisco.

to Pensacola, Florida, to shoot footage of naval-aviator training. Other crews were sent to Marine Corps bases in California, including Camps Travis, Pendleton, San Diego, and Coronado. Programming during this period included "Shooting the Breeze," featuring Navy personnel and activities; "TV Chow Call," presentations of Army menus and recipes by military chefs; "Land, Sea and Air," Marine Corps recruiting; "Present Arms," Marine Corps personnel music and variety acts; and "On Wings of Song," highlighting the Air Force.

In January 1949 KPIX began broadcast of its long-running series "Wanted and Missing Persons." This weekly series, later called "KMA-438" (the call letters of the San Francisco Police Department radio station), was "designed, through interviews, special films and demonstrations, to educate the public in the problems of the police, their activities and operations, crime prevention, traffic control and the like. Not only [did] the program deal with current problems, such as narcotics and juvenile delinquency, but possible solutions for these problems [were] explored."[12] As was typical of many of the leading local stations of the period, KPIX was involved in many community-service campaigns and special programs such as charity telethons and other fund-raisers, safety programs, and the ongoing support of community groups and activities.

News and Special Events

In the areas of news and special-events programming KPIX provided leadership and set the example for bay-area broadcasters. By 1950 the station was broadcasting "William Winter and the News," winner of the San Francisco chapter of the Academy of Television Arts and Sciences award for best news program in both 1950 and 1951. By 1953 Winter's news programs were being broadcast Mondays through Fridays from 10:30 to 10:45 p.m. and on Sundays from 10 to 10:30 p.m. During this period the station committed significant resources to filming and broadcasting important news events from a broad geographic area. Memorable news events covered visually included a 1950 major flood in Reno, a large fire in Modoc National Forest in 1951, the crash of a transcontinental airliner near Decoto, and a 1952 earthquake in Bakersfield. It was typical of KPIX to charter a plane,

---

12. "KPIX 1948–1953," p. 52.

send a film crew to the location of the disaster, then edit and broadcast the coverage within hours of the calamity.

Two major news events of the period show KPIX's leadership in this area. In October 1953 a British Commonwealth Pacific Airlines plane crashed near Half Moon Bay, about 30 miles south of San Francisco. "KPIX's were the first TV newsreel cameras on the scene; the station's reporters spent three hours on the scene photographing the still smoldering wreckage and other aspects of the accident. the film was processed, edited and shown the same evening.... Officials of the BCPA, who saw the KPIX program, asked the station's permission to use the film for study at their headquarters in Australia. KPIX gladly complied by providing a copy of the entire footage it photographed, including the portions considered unsuitable for televising, for permanent reference of the airline."[13] A few weeks later a serious explosion occurred at the Hercules Powder Company in Hercules, California. KPIX was given exclusive permission to film the disaster by company executives because of the station's avoidance of sensational and lurid coverage during the recent BCPA airliner crash. Other exclusive coverage during 1953 included the collision of two ships in foggy San Francisco Bay and the visit of the king and queen of Greece to the bay area. One of the first, if not the first, noon television news program, can be credited to KPIX: "One of KPIX's innovating programmers, Ray Hubbard, came up with a bright idea. He called it, *The Noon News*. There had never before been a half hour of midday news. The anchors were John Weston, 'Channel 5's Guy on the Go,' and Wanda Ramey, 'Channel 5's Gal on the Go.' Wanda was one of the first women news anchors in the country and talented enough to survive the title they hung on her."[14]

Transcontinental Live Feed Via Microwave

In September 1951 KPIX received national acclaim and accolades for its nationwide live broadcast from San Francisco of the Japanese Peace Conference. This landmark event, taking place over five days at San Francisco's War Memorial Opera House, inaugurated transcontinental live tele-

---

13. "KPIX 1948–1953," p. 57.
14. Dave McEllhatton, "KPIX-5 History," undated draft of news script, circa December 1994, KPIX Public Relations Department files, San Francisco.

vision via microwave in America. "KPIX directed, coordinated and produced the nationwide telecast in all network and local transmittals from President Truman's opening speech to Secretary of State Acheson's closing words."[15] To accomplish this feat, KPIX used eight television cameras, seven in constant operation during the conference, two fully equipped control rooms, one as a backup for the other, two complete audio controls to provide sound to five audio networks, 100,000 watts of lighting, and a staff of 75. Sig Mickelson, director of news and public affairs for CBS television, stated in a letter to KPIX manager Phil Lasky: "I have been away from San Francisco long enough now to give what I think is a pretty cold appraisal of the job KPIX did in forming the backbone of the pool pickup at the Japanese Peace Conference. The only conclusion that I can draw is that the job was great. Everyone I have talked to since my return has remarked about the clear picture, the alert camera work and direction, the absence of any bloopers, and a general overall competence and excellence of the performance."[16] In 1979 Phil Lasky, KPIX's first manager, reminisced about the conference broadcast: "I think one of my most memorable experiences was supervising and being a part of putting together that gigantic television operation. Nothing like it had ever been done before; to broadcast to the world the Japanese Peace Conference. The treaty, as you recall, was signed in San Francisco at the Opera House. People from all over the world were here, and it was the occasion of the opening of the transcontinental connection of television in the United States. Which is a milestone of TV in America. It was a memorable occasion; exciting."[17]

Beginning in 1949 and continuing into 1953, KPIX produced "Tele-trips," a quarter-hour series of news-feature and documentary programs. Produced on film, this series of 127 programs featured on-location explorations. Topics and locations within the series ranged from the operation of a Navy flying boat on a flight to Pearl Harbor to remotes shot at a local grammar school and the United States District Court in San Francisco. When the first ship returning American POWs from the Korean conflict entered San Francisco harbor in August of 1953, KPIX was the first station to broadcast interviews with the ex-prisoners to a nationwide audience. By sending a shortwave transmitter directly to the ship via tugboat for audio,

---

15. "And Here Is a Big Story ... Briefly Told," KPIX promotion brochure, circa November 1951, in "KPIX 1948–1953."

16. Sig Mickelson, letter to Philip Lasky, 19 September 1951, reproduced in "KPIX 1948–1953."

17. Philip G. Lasky, oral-history interview conducted by Steven C. Runyon, 13 August 1979. Transcribed audio recording from the personal files of S.C. Runyon, University of San Francisco.

and installing television cameras with telephoto lenses on a San Francisco pier, KPIX scooped all other stations by over an hour and was able to provide interviews and comments before the ship docked.

Sports, Agriculture, and Religion

Like many other television stations of the period, KPIX produced a number of sports, agricultural, and religious programs. As already mentioned, KPIX's first broadcast day featured an ice-hockey game and soon after that the East-West football game. During the next few months KPIX offered the San Francisco Bay area televised coverage of the Sixth Army Boxing Championship from San Francisco's Presidio, San Francisco Seals Pacific Coast League baseball games, University of California Pacific Coast Conference games from California Memorial Stadium in Berkeley, basketball games from Stanford University, and live wrestling from Winterland. In addition to these live remotes KPIX motion-picture-camera crews covered events such as skiing in the Sierra Nevada Mountains and filmed interviews with major sports personalities and coaches. In its first five years of broadcasting KPIX presented the home baseball games of the Seals each season. In 1954 KPIX added home games of the Oakland Oaks Pacific Coast League baseball team, also on an exclusive basis. Both the CBS and Du Mont television networks used KPIX regularly to originate San Francisco sporting events for network broadcast. These included the East-West Shrine football games for Du Mont and professional boxing matches for CBS. By the end of 1953 KPIX had broadcast 172 weekly cards of pro wrestling from Winterland. On Thursday evenings in the early 1950s KPIX broadcast "Boys Club Boxing" regularly. In addition to the sporting events KPIX produced a number of sports-information programs featuring well-known sports personalities. These programs included "All-American Sports Review," hosted by Santa Clara University football legend Frank Sobrero, "Sports with Joe Verducci," featuring this San Francisco State College coach, and sports shows featuring Bob Fouts, prominent bay-area sportscaster, and Chuck Taylor, Stanford University coach.

In the area of agriculture KPIX began its weekly half-hour series "Western Farm and Family" early in 1952. This innovative program was "an experiment in the effectiveness of television in providing information of direct and primary interest to the farmers of Northern California. Again putting the accent on quality, KPIX sought out and obtained the cooperation of the Agricultural Extension Service of the University of California, various bureaus of the United States Department of Agriculture, the State Grange, 4-H Clubs, Future Farmers of America and the United States Weather Bureau."[18] Religious programs at KPIX during this period included the yearly broadcasts of seasonal programs and a varied group of weekly religious series. "KPIX, early in its operation, inaugurated a regular nondenominational sustaining program to serve the spiritual needs of its audience. Originally called *Family Vespers,* then *Family Devotions,* and [finally] *Church in Thy House,* this half-hour program [was] presented each Sunday at 5:30 p.m. and was the first local live televised religious program in San Francisco."[19] In 1952 KPIX invited leaders of the major faiths in San Francisco to advise the station in the creation of a weekly educational religious program. The result was "Your Neighbor's Religion," a half-hour series broadcast on Sundays in 1953. A number of these shows were kinescoped and provided to churches and Sunday schools throughout northern California and Nevada.

Programming for Children

KPIX's children's programming is some of the best remembered in San Francisco television during this period. Just the mention of "Captain Fortune" or "Brother Buzz" brings an immediate smile to the faces of many San Franciscans. Among the key KPIX children's program series during the early days were "Once Upon a Time," a 26-week series produced in 1950 that featured dramatizations of famous fairy tales, and "Junior Genius," broadcast Sundays at 5 p.m. in 1951, which involved both the quizzing of participating children in the areas of literature, history, music and entertainment personalities, and dramatic skits performed by the children.

The best remembered of all these early KPIX programs is a series that began in April 1951. This live Monday-through-Friday program, broadcast from 5:30 to 6 p.m., was "Captain Fortune." Each program began with a San Francisco cable-car ride by a group of children to Fortune House, an old

---

18. "KPIX 1948–1953," p. 69.
19. "KPIX 1948–1953," p. 71.

Victorian house located on one of San Francisco's hills. From this filmed opening the program cut to the live studio set representing the interior of Fortune House, where Captain Fortune (Peter Abenheim) entertained the youngsters and related his world adventures. A regular feature of the show was the appearance of Short John O'Copper, a retired sea cook who lived in a barrel near the Fortune House fireplace. Each afternoon the children would knock on his barrel to get him to come out and entertain them with adventure stores and comical doings. It should be noted that Short John O'Copper was a small puppet. The program featured wholesome entertainment, enrichment, and cleverly disguised education. Along with the stories were special guests and demonstrations, films and filmed activities, the promotion of community events and activities of interest to children, and a daily drawing contest that sometimes brought in over 2,500 drawings by boys and girls in a single week.

In 1952 KPIX began weekly broadcasts of "Brother Buzz." This 15-minute marionette program was broadcast every Monday afternoon at 5:15 p.m. Sponsored by the nonprofit Latham Foundation for the Promotion of Humane Education, this series was sanctioned by the local PTA, approved by the Audubon Society, and used by many grade-school teachers for social-science classes. "Brother Buzz is an elf, transformed by the King of Elves into a bumble bee so that he may venture into the animal and insect world, find out about the lives and habits of the various creatures, and, in particular, their problems resulting from encounters with humans."[20] At the conclusion of each program in this long-running series children were invited to join the Brother Buzz Club and take the pledge of kindness to all living creatures.

On Wednesday and Friday afternoons from 5:15 to 5:30 p.m. KPIX produced "WOLO." WOLO was a puppet that toured Europe and met with amusing misadventures during his travels. The series introduced children to the countryside, habits, and livelihoods of Europeans. On Tuesdays and Thursdays for 15 minutes beginning at 5:15 p.m. "Deputy Dave" was featured. This series for youngsters featured Deputy Dave in western attire introducing his audience to short films and songs. The series stressed that "officers of the law are the friends of children." Other children's programming produced and broadcast by KPIX during its early years included "Storyteller," book narratives with dramatized incidents for preteens; "Kids Kapers," a children's talent program on which finalists competed on the air and winners were selected by mail votes; "Uncle George's Cartoon Club,"

20. "KPIX 1948–1953," p. 81.

featuring art instruction and contests for children; "Youth Steps Out," a music and sports program for high-school students; and "Toyland Party," a Christmas-season children's ballet program.

Another one of the most lauded of KPIX's early children's-program series was "Adventure School," designed for preschoolers, hosted by Marian Rowe, and featuring a small group of nursery-school students on each program. "It isn't the cut and dried A-B-C, 1-2-3-4 type of learning for the kiddies," wrote a contemporary local observer. "It is a new concept, on the basis that children are independent individuals who should be taught the fundamentals of human behavior."[21] Even the *New York Times* reviewed this outstanding series: "It is all in line with the wish of Mrs. Rowe to 'encourage children to express themselves but in ways that are socially acceptable.... You should recognize the unique individuality of each child, but you should encourage a group experience.'"[22]

Entertainment

During the early years of KPIX a significant amount of the station's entertainment programming was produced by the station. The two main categories of local programming were music/variety and women's shows, though KPIX tried many different kinds of entertainment programming. Soon after the station went on the air, it began broadcasts of "KPIX Workshop," an anthology live drama series featuring such productions as "Tell Tale Heart" and "Feathertop," an hour-long variety show featuring professional and amateur talent, and two half-hour talent-search series called "Stars in the Making" and "Talent Spotlight." In December 1949 KPIX premiered "The Del Courtney Show." One of the longest-running local shows in San Francisco television history, it featured the nationally known dance-band leader hosting a variety-show format. "Del knew everybody in the music racket," commented Dwight Newton, years later. "If Joe Reichman, Wayne King, Ted Lewis or Jimmy Dorsey came to town—Presto!—first appear-

21. George Rhodes, "Moppets Go to Nursery School on Television," *San Francisco Call-Bulletin,* 26 December 1953, p. 1TV.
22. "Coast TV Carries Child Adventures," *New York Times,* 6 February 1954, sec. 1, p. 11.

ances would be on Del's show. Del was a quick study in picking up commercial soft-sell techniques.... He was affable, inventive, tireless."[23]

Two other pioneering variety shows were "Ladies Day with Lee," featuring Lee Giroux, and "The Sandy Spillman Show," which replaced it in March 1953. First employed at KSFO radio in 1938, Spillman moved to KPIX upon the beginning of operations and within a year had become the station's program director. He left this position to undertake the show. This show was the first in San Francisco to be performed live before a studio audience. Other live KPIX entertainment programming with a music focus during this period included "San Francisco at Night," featuring remote pickups from well-known San Francisco nightclubs, "The Wishing Well," "Nipper Song Shop," "The Bill Baldwin Show," "The Peggy Mann Show," "Don Regan Sings," "The Patty Prichard Show," and "The Music Album." "Hoffman Hayride" was an elaborately produced series featuring western music. "Search for Songs" highlighted compositions submitted by viewers and performed by Del Courtney's orchestra. "Stag at Eve" was a series in which women had their say in a battle of wits with men. An early audience-participation program at KPIX was "Share a Charade." "The Chef's Club" featured men demonstrating their cooking ability. "Cuppa Joe" was a live drama series centered on the philosophical proprietor of a lunch stand.

Among the programs for women were "Teleshopper," a 1949 series "in which a girl shopper displayed her 'finds' in local stores";[24] "KPIX Kitchen," an early cooking show that began in the middle of 1950; "Stitches in Time," about dressmaking and clothing design; "Design for Living," devoted to interior decorating; "Flower Arrangement"; "Your Beauty Clinic"; and "Gracious Living." "Let's Ask the Men" attempted to get the opinions of a group of men about women's apparel. More general entertainment programming during this period included series on hobbies, gardening, amateur photography, and golf.

23. Dwight Newton, "Early Days on the Tube," *San Francisco Sunday Examiner and Chronicle, California Living Magazine,* 18 December 1977, p. 22.
24. "KPIX 1948–1953," p. 94.

Conclusion

KPIX is San Francisco's pioneer television station. Although this chapter has been devoted to highlights of the station's first half decade of broadcasting, the story of KPIX is the story of nearly 50 years of innovative programming and service. Among the self-proclaimed firsts of KPIX[25] are: first broadcast signal in northern California (November 22, 1948, test pattern sent to TV dealers to help sell sets); first broadcast programming; first woman anchor in western United States (Wanda Ramey, second woman anchor in the country); first station to originate telecasts in northern California for transmission to the east (United Nations Telecast); first to telecast opera and the classics; first to make color-TV tests; first local facilities capable of originating full-scale television production (KPIX production center was heralded by many as one of the best designed in the country); first to bring network TV programs to the West Coast; first to televise morning TV programs; first to carry the East-West football game; first live telecast of open-heart surgery; first broadcast college football game (1951); first San Francisco TV show with a live studio audience; first black reporter on San Francisco Bay–area television;[26] and first black newswoman on bay-area TV.[27] Although some of these "firsts" are subject to question or interpretation, they demonstrate well the pioneering nature of the television work of KPIX in San Francisco.

25. "KPIX 40th Anniversary List of Station Firsts," undated, circa December 1988, KPIX Public Relations Department files, San Francisco.

26. Harry Fuller memorandum.

27. Harry Fuller memorandum.

21 KING-TV, Seattle: King of the Northwest

Val E. Limburg

The Pacific Northwest has a rich heritage of broadcast history. The historic dean of broadcast journalism, Edward R. Murrow, grew up in the picturesque Skagit Valley between the Cascade Mountains and Puget Sound; he attended Washington State University, where the school of communication now carries his name. Bing Crosby of Tacoma is another well-known celebrity, another "local boy makes good." Newsman Chet Huntley is remembered on radio station KPCB-AM, Seattle, as hosting the opera broadcast and commentary. Actor/announcer Art Gilmore, Tacoma born and also a graduate of Washington State University, started on Seattle's KVI radio, before his Hollywood days.

Like many other early-pioneer TV stations, the story really begins with radio. In Seattle during the 1920s the earliest stations were owned by two newspapers, the *Seattle Post-Intelligencer* and the *Tacoma Ledger:* stations KFC and KGB, respectively. No one is quite sure which radio station was "first" in the Puget Sound. But there is little doubt about the Northwest's first television station; it was KING-TV. The story of this broadcast enterprise is colorful and comes from many directions.

The Engineer and the Entrepreneur

The earliest experimentation was in 1929 with the transmission of visual cues using crude handcrafted sets with one-inch screens. Much of this work was done by a then dominant radio station, KOMO, owned by the Fisher family. Because the family owned large interests in lumber, banking, and flour mills, it seemed logical that they be the lead in the development of the most ambitious of new enterprises, television. However, when KOMO's engineer, Francis J. Brott, had problems with some of the transmission equipment, he leaned on a colleague who operated a small radio station, KRSC. The call letters stood for Kelvinator Radio Sales Corporation, a business operated by a name soon to become closely associated with the advent of television in Seattle—Palmer K. Leberman, known to his associates as P.K.[1]

Through the 1930s television remained only a dream, a gadget and an experiment being conducted by some of the larger corporations. Television was ready to turn the corner of wide-scale development when World War II put all designs everywhere on the back burner.

In the meantime Leberman became a communication magnate, publishing *Family Circle* magazine, and strengthening KRSC radio. Later he established the first FM station in the Northwest. His investment with *Family Circle* made it possible for Leberman to have the resources that would later be necessary for establishing the first television station in the Puget Sound area.[2]

Although Leberman was the entrepreneur who established KRSC, its FM efforts, and eventually the first TV station, it was really Robert E. Priebe, a former wireless operator for RCA's Radio Marine Office, who did the engineering. The two became friends, as well as close business associates—a team with the dynamics of capitalism and engineering ingenuity that formed the synergy of successful broadcasting. Before long Leberman left the day-to-day operation of KRSC radio to Priebe, who had the responsibilities of announcing, sales, and engineering—all in a one-man operation.

---

1. David Richardson, *Puget Sounds: A Nostalgic Review of Radio and TV in the Great Northwest* (Seattle: Superior Publishers, 1981), p. 89.

2. Hugh Feltis, oral-history interview conducted by Hugh Rundell, Mar. 1976. Transcribed in Burt Harrison, ed., *They Took to the Air: An Oral History of Broadcasting in Washington* (abridged) (Pullman: Washington State University, Murrow School of Communication, 1991), p. 148. Hereafter referred to as the Harrison transcript.

Perhaps it was this eclecticism that gave Priebe the understanding and insight necessary to set up KRSC-FM, and most significantly to design the television station.[3]

Leberman spent much of his time in New York with *Family Circle*. There he witnessed the development of television by NBC and CBS and got the idea that he could be first in the Seattle area and the Northwest. But he knew that he had to work with some haste before others in the Northwest recognized the promise of this new medium.

Priebe provided the engineering expertise, and Leberman applied for a license in 1948. It was received immediately—just before the freeze on new licenses imposed by the Federal Communications Commission. Leberman bartered with RCA and obtained a transmitter from a failing TV station in Florida. The water-cooled transmitter was bought at the time this new electronic transmission of pictures was just beginning to take hold as an advertising medium.[4] Also fortuitous was the fact that the *Family Circle* magazine he had been directing was owned by Charles Merrill of Merrill-Lynch fame. Merrill loaned Leberman the $100,000 needed to build the station, as banks were reluctant to lend money on such a dangerous security risk as this experimental "tele-vision" (tell-ee vision) station.

The First TV Programs in Seattle

The station—KRSC-TV, Channel 5—went on the air on Thanksgiving Day, 1948. The first broadcast, however, was probably seen by no more than a few dozen households that had managed to buy an upright piece of furniture with an eight- or 10-inch screen. A special television section of the *Seattle Times* on the preceding day told of the upcoming event that was to be the inaugural broadcast: the state football championship between West Seattle and Wenatchee high schools. The game was to be broadcast, remarkably, by a mobile remote unit set up at Memorial Stadium, transmitted to the KRSC-TV studios atop Queen Anne Hill, and then rebroadcast instantly for public viewing. It would also be simulcast on AM and FM, perhaps the first triple broadcast of its kind.[5] Although the remote had been rehearsed for two

---

3. Robert E. Priebe, oral-history interview conducted by Hugh Rundell, June 1977, Harrison transcript, p. 284.

4. Priebe, p. 283. See also Richardson, p. 93.

5. "KRSC-TV Takes Air Tomorrow with Grid Game," *Seattle Times*, Nov. 24, 1948, p. 28.

months of closed-circuit training by the station's remote crew, there were still many unknowns and problems that first day: inexperienced technicians, fuzzy signals, undependable cameras, and miserable rainy Seattle weather. Technical quality was poor, mostly from the rain that began in the second half of the game. But few noticed. Everyone was overcome with the techno-logical marvel of this never-before-seen miracle, television.[6]

The city's newspapers took note of the debut, but mainly because of the opportunity to run a special advertising section for department-store ads selling television sets. The section also ran articles on how sports events are directed, keeping the cameramen busy with both engineering and photo-graphic duties: "Television Requires Fast Make-up Change," "Dim Light Is Advised as Best for Reception of Television," and "Millions of Dots of Light Make up Video."[7] The ads in the section were from such stores as Frederick and Nelson, promising demonstration television shows, to be seen from window number 17, Sixth Avenue. For many it was their first look at the new medium. New sets were $339.95 for a Magic Mirror TV Console with a 10-inch direct-view tube. Smaller table-model TV sets cost $202.50.

The first TV program log was that of KRSC-TV for November 25, 1948, found in the preceding day's paper. The high-school football game began at 2:10 following opening ceremonies. After the game were cartoons and news and weather, followed by "Face the Music" at 7 p.m., then "Paris Fashions." At 8:30 was a film, "Air Power Is Peace Power." At 9 p.m. was "Television Playhouse": "Street Scene," starring Betty Field. The station signed off that first day at 10 p.m. The schedule for that first week of programs had test patterns during the day, followed in the late afternoon by children's programs, news and weather, game shows, and TV dramas. The *Seattle Times* reported that the drama programs were "staged in New York at either the Columbia Broadcasting System or National Broadcasting Com-pany's studios and will be seen in Seattle through the medium of teletran-scription. This is a new process, scarcely months old, that enables television shows to be recorded on 16-mm film while actually on the air in New York. The film is then processed and rushed by air to KRSC-TV with the shows themselves seen in the Pacific Northwest only a matter of hours later."[8]

Because KRSC-TV was the only station in Seattle, it was courted by all four networks—NBC, CBS, ABC, and Du Mont. KRSC-TV could take

---

6. Richardson, p. 92.
7. *Seattle Times*, Nov. 24, 1948, pp. 24–40.
8. "KRSC-TV Takes Air Tomorrow," p. 28.

its choice of the best programs from each network.[9] The networks were not yet as we think of them today; programs were not instantly transmitted but sent from station to station on 16-millimeter film, by mail. One station would play the program, then send it on to the next. These film recordings were taken from the face of the picture tube—kinescope recordings. The quality was poor, full of smears and shadows and often fuzzy. But it was television, and any kind of visual signal held the attention of its audience. As a matter of fact, even such pictures prompted thousands of people to pay hundreds of dollars for television sets, to *see* the world.

Television seemed like such a promising enterprise. But in its early days it had two voracious appetites: One was the daily schedule of programs. Being on the air every day, day after day, required hours and hours of programming each week. Some programs were provided by the networks, others originated by the station. The second appetite was the expensive equipment and money required for local programming and station operations. In order to make a profit, local commercials had to be created and placed within the programs, which meant production crews, announcers, and operation personnel for the airing of advertising alone. This was true even in the early days, when commercials consisted of little more than the showing of a slide, with an announcer extolling the virtues of a product—much as was done already on radio.

These demands meant a continual investment of money. To some it seemed a bottomless pit. Leberman, failing to earn money on his initial investment from Merrill's loan, needed cash. He was still involved with managing *Family Circle* and was persuaded by his superior and loanholder to get rid of this money hole, television. As one acquaintance of Leberman put it, "They told him: 'Look, P.K., you've got to make up your mind. Are you going to live in Seattle with your goofy television station, or are you going to live in New York and run our magazine? You've got just two weeks to decide.' P.K. was frightened. He got on the next plane and came to Seattle."[10] Stuck with the proposition of needing to get rid of the station, but not wanting to lose money in the deal, Leberman sought a monied buyer.

9. Jerry Geehan, oral-history interview conducted by Hugh Rundell, July 1977, Harrison transcript, p. 157.

10. Feltis, p.148.

Dorothy Bullitt Enters the Scene

Here a remarkable businesswoman enters the scene of broadcasting in Washington State. Dorothy Bullitt had, only two years before, bought KEVR radio in May 1947. She had two family fortunes with which to work—her father's and her late husband's. KEVR was not a top station when Mrs. Bullitt bought it, but with renovations—among them, changing the call letters to KING—she began promoting the station and creating a new image for it.

According to one version of the origin of the KING call letters, Mrs. Bullitt thought it seemed logical, given that a radio's call letters must start with *K* and must be four letters, that a station located in King County should carry those letters. Others had had the same idea, but the letters were held by a U.S. shipping-board freighter, the *Watertown*. In one of her first acts demonstrating her shrewd competence, Mrs. Bullitt negotiated with the ship's owners to release the letters. It was only a short time before the new Bullitt property was airing its new name: KING. Before long the enterprising Mrs. Bullitt commissioned Walt Disney to create a KING promotional icon, the cartoon character "KING Mike." It was an image of a cartoon microphone that was to last for more than a generation.[11]

By the time Mrs. Bullitt was confronted with the opportunity to acquire the television station, she had already developed a reputation as a shrewd businesswoman and broadcaster. She called in Hugh Feltis, who had recently come back to the Northwest from New York, where he had worked with Frank Stanton's Broadcast Management Bureau. He knew perhaps as much about audiences and the market value of stations as anyone at that time. His advice for Mrs. Bullitt was simple: "Buy it!" Then the negotiations began. the give-and-take had to be handled with finesse, because the owners of another radio station, KJR, owned by Marshall Field, were in the wings, checkbook in hand.

Feltis let Leberman know that Mrs. Bullitt was a reputable business-woman, and that she didn't want to haggle. Leberman set a price range of $350,000 to $400,000. Because Mrs. Bullitt was prepared to finance quickly, and because Leberman was more than a little anxious to get out from under the station's ongoing debt, Feltis believed Leberman would accept the lower price. Mrs. Bullitt agreed to meet directly with Leberman with that offer. As

---

11. Richardson, p. 96.

it turned out, the timing was critical. The offer was the first for Leberman, and he seemed to think that he probably wouldn't do much better.

According to Feltis, Mrs. Bullitt looked at Leberman and said: "Now, we've talked about this, and we'd like to know exactly what we are talking about—a little more exactly than the $350,000 to $400,000 which Hugh tells me you quoted." Leberman tried the bluff: "How's $375,000?" She looked at him sharply and said, "How's $350,000?" Without much hesitation Leberman agreed.[12] It was the first sale of a television station in the United States.[13]

Later the Marshall Field team admitted that they were up against some aces they couldn't match: Mrs. Bullitt's standing in the community, her reputation as a businesswoman, and her ready cash. So KING-TV sprang up with the support of the strong economic undergirding from Dorothy Bullitt, and the managerial and advertising skills of Hugh Feltis, who became the general manager. Although the station belonged to Mrs. Bullitt, it was run by Feltis, who was considered an autocrat, even a dictator, by some.[14]

Seattle's First—and Only—TV Station

KING-TV continued to be the only television signal in the Seattle area from 1948 until 1952. Feltis's experience in advertising and marketing gave him a strong hand in station programming. His practice was to look at the highest-rated programs on the big stations back east, then get those most popular for airing on KING-TV. He chose from a lineup of five networks: ABC, CBS, NBC, Du Mont, and Paramount. The networks were anxious to get their programs to as many markets as possible. On occasion Feltis reported that they would phone and try to sell him a program. He would have them hold while he looked at the ratings and would accept the offer only if the show had about a 29 or 32 share. He would say to CBS, "I don't like the way Paley spoke this morning so I'm not going to take the *Lucky Strike Hour*. I'm going to take the NBC show at that time." Or he would say to ABC, "That ABC show is not going to pay me enough. I'm going to take the CBS show."[15]

12. Feltis, p. 150.
13. Richardson, p. 96.
14. Geehan, p. 157.
15. Geehan, p. 157.

It was easy to fill a schedule this way, and having a monopoly on program choice extended the program day beyond the prior KRSC schedule of only a few hours. This also set a precedent for other stations in Seattle, which, when they came on the air, were expected to have a full day's schedule, not just a few hours in late afternoon and early evening.

But Would TV Catch On?

Even those with TV sets were not especially fascinated with this new medium, at least not at first—not in Seattle. Skeptical Northwest radio managers tried to analyze the situation: "Who's going to sit in a dark room and look at a picture on a screen? No one around here. Everyone's busy playing golf, and going out on boats and fishing."[16] The social standing of such skeptics seemed evident. But the management at KING took notice of the need to engage its audience. They had to get out and involve the community.

Stations in Los Angeles had demonstrated that getting cameras out into the community, and becoming attuned to community activities, would compel TV viewing. In Seattle, KING-TV tried the idea. One of the things that sparked television interest in Seattle was wrestling matches sponsored by Heidelberg Beer. The matches not only gained an audience but greatly enhanced Heidelberg sales, demonstrating the power of advertising on local TV. Slowly, television became a recognized advertising medium, much to the chagrin of newspaper publishers and radio-station licensees. Television wasn't so much a threat back during its shaky beginnings—but it was a sleeping giant.

As KING-TV became successful, other entrepreneurs had their eye on it as a perfect investment, a kind of money tree. One such person was Saul Haas, who had previously expressed some interest in purchasing the station from Leberman at the time of the sale to Dorothy Bullitt. After the FCC-imposed freeze was lifted in 1952, Haas acquired the license for Channel 7, KIRO-TV, which became the CBS affiliate until 1994. The Fisher family acquired Channel 4, the ABC affiliate, KOMO-TV. According to Haas's widow, Dayee, the story of who applied for which of these licenses is a tale

---

16. Feltis, p. 151.

of two strong-willed capitalists at odds, eventually making their decision with the flip of a coin.[17]

The Fortress of a KING

Soon after Dorothy Bullitt took KING-TV, it became clear that television in Seattle had a strong foothold. KING, being first, had a clear and distinct advantage: The FCC's TV freeze had been imposed, shutting out other licenses for television in that area for nearly five years, until 1952. During this time television exploded as a unique American cultural phenomenon, the number of sets nationwide increasing a hundredfold, from 200,000 to 20,000,000.[18] Seattle reflected that boom. KING seemed to be an apt name.

KING-TV outgrew its old studios on Galer Street on Queen Anne Hill and moved to some roomier quarters, a downtown garage at Second Avenue West and Thomas Street. A few years later the station moved into its Aurora Avenue residence, where it has been since.

Learning by Trial and Error, and the Resulting Programs

KING-TV joined a handful of pioneer stations that experimented their way to the development of current technology, production techniques, and programming. KING-TV performers, many of whom were radio announcers and disc jockeys, soon learned that reading copy in front of the camera was a production taboo. But this was before the era of the TelePrompTer; rough, hand-scrawled prompt cards were used, usually not too effectively. Yet to memorize all the material needed for the voracious appetite of this new medium was nearly impossible. Difficult, too, were the exacting demands of live television, the most evident being live commercials. Mistakes would

---

17. Dayee Haas, interview conducted by Hugh Rundell, June 22, 1976, Harrison transcript, pp. 169–170.

18. *Television Factbook, No. 21* (Fall–Winter, 1955), pp. 239, 426–427, as cited in Sydney Head, *Broadcasting in America* (Boston: Houghton Mifflin, 1956), p. 159.

sometimes reveal themselves as a new, inadvertent humor—"bloopers" was their professional label. And there were plenty of them in KING-TV's early history. Early KING staffers recall live commercials that dared compare the competitor's brand but, in front of the camera's glaring eye, often revealed no difference. Or there were machines that wouldn't start—or those that, once started, wouldn't stop.

It wasn't long before television in Seattle became a kind of "children's community theater" featuring daily children's shows with live audiences—that's where Mom and Dad brought Junior and his friends for his birthday. KING's first live-audience-show host was Tom Dargan. His program was "3:30 at the Norselander." He later had the unenviable task of directing live TV daily in a setting that proved conclusively Murphy's law. Whatever could go wrong often did, and usually during live broadcasting. But, then, perhaps the children didn't notice, nor did most of the viewers at home, who were also probably children. However, there is at least one recorded incident during which Dargan was directing a kids' program and a problem caused him to run out of the control room into the studio, where he tripped and fell headlong before the audience. "Then he uttered one shocking expletive, turned with great dignity and retreated into the control room once more."[19]

The first live musical-variety program at KING was a local imitation of Milton Berle's "Texaco Star Theater." In Seattle it was called "Two B's at the Keys," where Stan Boreson and Art Barduhn, in 1949, teamed up for the music of the day. From that first program the show evolved and changed its format slightly, also changing its name from time to time: "Clipper Capers," "People's Parade," "Open for Business," and "The Starliner." All were popular, simple variety shows; all were typical of the flavor of the culture of very early television, its music and entertainment of the day. Finally the show left the air when the Art Barduhn Trio was formed, a musical group that traveled in its quest for national notoriety.

Boreson and Barduhn were the Northwest's first "daytime talk-show hosts." In an attempt to add as much variety and interest to the program as possible, they would often arrange to have entertainers from other media on the program. This was not an easy task, as the Hollywood attitude toward TV was much different in the 1950s. Television was a cheap imitation, a "corruption and an unholy competition" to the motion-picture industry. Many stars with reputations in that medium didn't want to lower themselves to the gadgetry and cheap environment of a television studio. Yet the two

---

19. Richardson, p. 98.

B's managed to get Gloria Swanson, whose movie *Sunset Boulevard* was playing in Seattle theaters. She came in for an interview that seemed so much more compelling than the usual materials on the show that it overran its designated time period by almost an hour, quite unlike today's talk shows.

Boreson later became a mainstay of KING's afternoon programs, most notably the kids' favorite, "King's Clubhouse." It was one of those programs that had a captive audience—school kids just out of school, in no mood for further school work, and often not able, in Seattle's rainy weather, to play outside. It would be an understatement to say that the program was popular. It was a significant part of Seattle's early television, and of the school kids' culture of that era. Ask any Seattle native who was that age during the 1950s.

"King's Clubhouse" featured the droopy face of a basset hound, "No Mo Shun." The dog did nothing at all but reveal its deadpan comedic face. A quick cut to his expression was always good for a laugh. Part of the magic of the show was simply talking to kids—their silliness, their language, their friends in the audience, all were part of the magic that came into their very own living rooms. But perhaps the most magical thing of all was just being part of the "club." True, membership was not exclusive, but it was free, and you were friends with Stan Boreson, even if somewhat vicariously. But it took a "password" to enter the magic: "Zero dachus, Mucho Crackus, Hallaballooza Bub. That's the secret password that we use at the club."[20]

In 1951 Texas Jim Lewis entertained the after-school KING crowd with rope tricks, a few cowboy songs, some shooting of his ol' "44" after a quick draw from his holster, and live animals.

A later generation of children would remember KING's "Wunda Wunda," a program designed for the younger children, ages four through eight. Starting in the mid-1950s and running through 1972, the show became recognized for its value in shaping the imagination of young children in an era before "Sesame Street." It won a Peabody Award and became widely recognized for its sensitivity to how children learn from television. The show's hostess was Ruth Prins, who would begin the program by peering out of the Wunda House to the song, "Wunda Wunda is my name; boys and girls, I'm glad you came. We'll have fun as I explain how we play our Wunda games." Prins's role on "Story Lady," "Wunda's" predecessor, demonstrated her keen ability to enchant children with her warmth. In "Wunda Wunda" KING's production crew experimented with heretofore untried techniques, including rear-screen projections, miniature sets, and split screens. The set

---

20. Richardson, p. 105.

contained stuffed animals, which "merged" with the live animals that came on to the program, including a lion that was supposed to be tame and trained. It wasn't. During the reading of a story the animal playfully held Prins's arm in its jaws. Later it prowled the studios, spooking camera operators and other crew members. Prins continued the live program calmly. But the kinescope of the program was used that night on the 10 o'clock news.[21]

There were other notable local programs. One was a "homemaking" program, "King's Queen," which included cooking featuring Bea Donovan. Later, other programs tried to fill in all the daytime hours left to the stations by the network. "Telescope" was one such program, on which personalities and local events were discussed.

Very early on KING-TV sought to cover community events, one of those being the hydroplane races on Lake Washington. On one occasion, according to Bill O'Mara, the station's first sportscaster, the hydroplane *Quicksilver* flipped over and sank in Lake Washington during Seattle's first Gold Cup run in 1951. O'Mara, an Irish Catholic, did what seemed natural: He fell to his knees in the broadcast booth, crossed himself, and said an "Our Father" right on camera. The *Seattle Times,* in a 1990 restrospective, reported: "News director Lee Schulman, who was Jewish, frantically directed a cameraman to take the camera off O'Mara and point it to the sky. O'Mara's words continued, with the camera panning the clouds. 'I thought it worked out very well,' he said. 'We got hundreds of letters, and only two were critical. One of the first ... calls I got was from Dorothy Bullitt.' She said, 'You did what you felt, Bill, and I approve of that.'"[22]

KING's Early News Efforts

For many years KING-TV led the local media in its unique news efforts. Energetic news director Charles Herring was at that time more than an administrator. He was an on-the-street reporter, anchor, and editor of the stories that aired every evening. Of course, 1951 was early in the era of TV news, and Herring and a single cameraman constituted the entire news operation of the station. Herring stayed on for many years, his face a familiar object to the Seattle community. Early in his career he moved up to really

21. Richardson, p. 110.
22. Don Duncan, "Pioneers in Broadcasting," *Seattle Times*, Aug. 22, 1990, p. A1.

big time in Hollywood but returned after a few months, because he believed that the integrity of KING's management in giving the news operation full independence was not matched in Los Angeles. In 1957 KING sent Herring to cover news in the nation's capital. He provided live reports in what was then an impressive coast-to-coast hookup effort. This effort drew national attention to the station and helped earn its reputation for good, innovative journalism in a medium that was often pooh-poohed by the established print media of the area. In 1962 Herring was part of an NBC team, with Chet Huntley, in the first satellite-TV linkup between Europe and the United States, Telstar.[23]

Because KING-TV had long been held by the Bullitt family, it could run with fewer economic pressures to escape heavy debt or turn profits quickly. Its reputation for allowing the news operation its autonomy was attributed directly to Mrs. Bullitt. One KING-TV reporter, Jack Hamman, indicated that "the family always stood for commitment to do journalism first. They said let's do journalism and then see what the costs will be."[24]

In 1959 Mrs. Bullitt hired Ancil Payne as her key administrator. He was at first the station's manager, then, in 1972, its president. He verified the notion that Bullitt ran an autonomous operation. "Dorothy Bullitt never told me not to do something because we couldn't afford it. You can't find bosses like that anymore."[25]

Payne was not shy about injecting his own presence and worldview into the affairs of Seattle's events and news. He delivered the first editorials in Seattle at a time when station editorials were not the norm, thereby lending the practice the power, and prestige that could come only from the direct involvement of the station manager.

KING-TV also introduced the first TV commentaries, as well as the nation's first locally produced documentaries. Subjects included race relations in Seattle and Portland, and a series on the environment, before these were popular causes.[26] Later KING developed further innovations in its local newsmagazine shows. In 1970 the FCC implemented the Prime Time Access Rule, taking away a half hour of time from the networks and giving it to local stations for the purpose of encouraging the creation of local programming. Many stations didn't really take advantage of the new 30-minute slot to do

23. Duncan, p. A1.
24. Kit Boss, "It's Time to Grieve, Whoever the New Owner Might Be," *Seattle Times*, Aug. 21, 1990, p. A5.
25. Duncan, p. A1.
26. Duncan, p. A1.

anything but buy nonnetwork packaged programs. KING, however, created a new program that was a kind of extension of earlier children's programming. A magazine show of impressive dimensions, it was called "How Come?" The show was a hybrid of educative entertainment for both young people and adult audiences. This combination of audience demographics gave the program high ratings and kept it in the schedule for nearly two decades. KING's efforts were all local. It was an expensive proposition to have not only a large news staff, but a staff devoted exclusively to just one program, "How Come," whose nightly 30 minutes had great demands for ongoing material. The program brought the producers and staff to exotic places, capturing exciting moments; it was a program that made lasting impressions not only on the Seattle audience, but on the profession. By the mid-1970s KING was the first station in Seattle to go with a full one-hour local newscast in early evening, a significant accomplishment in that day.

By the late 1970s KING-TV production was airing four live programs a day as well as seven weekly programs, all of which were coordinated out of a central production office. These efforts included "Seattle Tonight Tonite," "Seattle Today," "How Come," "I Like Myself," "Great American Game Show," "Evergreen Express," "Another Point of View," "Pleasant Journey," "The Eucharist," "Gardening with Ed Hume," and "Shape up with Sparling."

During this time of great growth and investment KING acquired other stations: KREM in Spokane, KGW in Portland, KTVB in Boise, KHBC in Honolulu, and a UHF station in Twin Falls, Idaho. In addition, KING Broadcasting Corporation held six radio stations, a large cable system in eight western cities, and one of the country's largest mobile production units, Northwest Mobile.[27]

By 1984 total pretax profits had grown to $44.5 million annually on net revenues of $134.7 million. Its annual growth was 12–15 percent. Payne was quoted as saying that although the business was capital intensive, it was very lucrative. "No one ever accused broadcasters of not being able to make money."[28]

Northwest Mobile TV also came to figure highly in KING's overall corporate picture, providing a chance to produce without being attached to a stationary studio. The idea was to have a large TV production facility with two large vans built to send microwave signals back to the studio from any

27. *Electronic Media*, Sept. 9, 1991.
28. *Puget Sound Business Journal*, Oct. 20, 1986.

location in the area. Because KING was the first to create the mobile facilities, the facilities were "shared" until other stations developed their own systems.[29]

By the late 1980s the television scene began to change. Cable had its impact, segmenting the TV audience and eroding the ratings, even those of community-conscious KING. Then, a series of pivotal events began to unfold. In June 1989 Dorothy Bullitt died at the age of 97. Until her demise she continued to lead or inspire the forces at KING. There was great sorrow, not just at her passing, but at the realization that the station could never be what it once was without its founder.

The Post-Bullitt KING

The station's once prestigious news department began to experience intense competition and ratings loss. General manager Sturges Dorrance, who had been with KING for 23 years, resigned, and his replacement, Rick Blangiardi, started cleaning house immediately. Bob Jordan came in as news director in March 1990, and though his efforts seemed to be paying off, it just wasn't the same old KING. "Many news staffers, already demoralized by changes that predated Jordan's arrival, chafed even more at his management style, which some former colleagues described as 'brutal,' 'intimidating,' and 'vindictive." He fired or accepted the resignations of at least a dozen staff members, some of whom had been with the station more than a decade. But others saw the purging as healthy, an "invigorating kick in the pants." Anchor/reporter John Sandifer put a positive spin on the grumbling: "We've begun to think that Mr. Jordan maybe isn't Hitler, just Napoleon."[30] One trade publication reported that KING made "major bonus payments to those leaving in exchange for a three-year silence about the station." [31]

Then came the real shocker. After weeks of rumors the Bullitt family announced in August 1990 that KING and its broadcast properties were being sold. Stories in the Seattle papers described this news being met with "grief" by KING employees. Reporter Bob Simmons learned of the development while out on a story. "Everybody was standing with their chins down to their

29. *Seattle Times*, Nov. 25, 1991.
30. Kit Boss, "Sweeps Bring KING-TV a Ratings Victory—of Sorts," *Seattle Times*, Nov. 30, 1990, p. B1.
31. *Electronic Media*, Jan. 13, 1992.

knees. There's a sort of hush." Another reporter claimed that "the reasons people at KING decline other job offers has always been because we work for the Bullitts. To me, the Bullitt family always stood for a commitment to do journalism first."[32] In February 1992 the sale of most of the KING properties was formally closed. KING majority shareholders Priscilla "Patsy" Bullitt Collins and Harriet Stimson Bullitt, daughters of Dorothy, sold all but KING-AM and KING-FM to the Providence Journal Company. Many Seattlites felt uncomfortable with the idea that someone sitting in the boardrooms of Rhode Island and New York would decide what would be best for the Northwest.

The sale was $355 million, one thousand times its purchase price more than four decades earlier.[33] The Bullitt sisters held on to the two radio stations, eventually selling KING-AM to a rival company, Bonneville Broadcasting, owner of KIRO-TV, the CBS affiliate in Seattle at the time. The question of whether the call letters would be changed, so as not to confuse the community about the relationship between TV station and radio station, was determined later.

KING-FM was donated by the family to the nonprofit Beethoven corporation, which was to benefit the Seattle Symphony, the Seattle Opera, and the Corporate Council for the Arts. Operation of the station was to be under the supervision of KIRO.[34] These moves still followed the general philosophy that the Bullitt-family monies should be used for investment in the community. Another part of the KING property, Northwest Mobile Productions, was sold to three former KING managers, to continue as one of the nation's largest mobile producers, producing and making available sports programs from both college and professional teams.

KING also banded its stations together, under the new Providence Journal leadership, and formed an all-news cable channel for the Northwest. The concept was simple: Pull all the local news-gathering efforts into the channel, which it would focus on the Northwest and local stories. The enterprise was to be headed by KING's former news director, Bob Jordan, though that situation later changed when he left KING to go to Los Angeles.

After the sale the Bullitt sisters established the Bullitt Foundation with their $375 million and decided to use most of the monies for funding environmental causes. This seemed a logical step in keeping with the family

32. Boss, "It's Time to Grieve," p. A5.
33. *Broadcasting and Cable Yearbook, 1993*, p. C-71.
34. Chuck Taylor, "KING-AM Purchase Provides 'Critical Mass'," *Seattle Times*, May 13, 1994, p. E1.

tradition of investing in the community. Ecologists from throughout the country were elated.

In the 1993–94 season programming shifts, such as NFL football going to the Fox network, created shifts in network affiliation. Although KING-TV remained with NBC, competitor KIRO lost the CBS affiliation, and its parent company, Bonneville, decided to sell its Seattle TV holdings. KING-AM would remain a Bonneville property, however.

The stability of television ownership in the Seattle area began to erode with the sale of KING by the Bullitt family. Only KOMO-TV remained with the Fisher-family enterprises. A grand era of elegance and predictability, exemplified by KING and the Bullitt family, had rapidly vanished from the broadcast scene in Seattle.

22 Alaska's Television Frontier: Northern Television, Inc., and the Augie Hiebert Story

B. William Silcock

Alaska's television history orbits around one lodestar—broadcast pioneer Augie Hiebert. He launched the state's first television station, KTVA in Anchorage, followed 14 months later with Fairbanks's first TV station, KTVF. The story of these bipolar twins pulsates as a tale of triumph over engineering experimentation, economic challenge, and fire, flood, and earthquake. Hiebert forged a path of public service across the vast 586,400 square miles of America's last frontier, a territory rich with multicultural diversity. The Aleut Native-American word *Alashka* means "great land." Walter Cronkite, who once anchored the evening news at KTVA on the way home from President Nixon's visit to China, recognized Hiebert as a broadcast pioneer, noting that as much as any single person he brought Alaskans "in touch with one another and with the great outside world."[1]

Database searches uncovered no scholarly histories about Alaskan commercial broadcasting, and few entries in the business press and newspapers. This account of Hiebert's role in Alaska television history draws upon public documents, press accounts, a published family biography by daughter Robin Ann Chlupach, and an oral interview with Hiebert. This chapter is the story of two stations intertwined in one diverse company, Northern Television, and their survival and success in a remote, often harsh, business climate, under the leadership of an entrepreneurial engineer. To understand something of the grit it took to build Alaska's first TV station, one must first look

---

1. Walter Cronkite, Forward to Robin Ann Chlupach's *Airwaves Over Alaska* (Issaquah, Washington: Sammamish Press, 1992), p. 10.

to the apple orchards of central Washington State, where youthful experiences planted in Augie Hiebert the seeds of broadcasting.

Experimenting Engineer

Hiebert, born December 4, 1916, was an asthmatic child who cared little for the fruit-farming business. Attracted to electronics and encouraged by friends, by age 15 Hiebert received his ham-radio license, W7CBF. "First I was a radio ham," Hiebert recalls. "I was attracted to the technical side of it. I did not have money for college but I did get to a technical school, partly correspondence and partly on campus in Los Angeles at a trade school."[2]

His Federal Communications Commission first-class phone license in hand, he began a work pattern that would prove critical to his later success in launching Alaska's first TV station, but it took experience at three radio stations in two other states to prepare him for it. Hiebert calls his early experience "combo jobs." The pattern of small stations, with little capital and a diminutive payroll, was to hire only those who could function in two or three jobs. Lessons of broadcasting's tight bottom line came early. KPQ in Wenatchee, Washington, hired him merely to avoid paying overtime to other engineers. The station fired him from his first job when the chief engineer came back from summer vacation. "I was immediately canned the minute he came back and they hired somebody else," Hiebert says. "I had never done on air work before. I didn't know I was going to have to be an announcer to get into the radio business, so that was a disaster."[3]

Hiebert left Wenatchee, close to his home of Crescent Bar, failing to compete "with fellows with pear shaped tones" but eventually found the right combination at a new station, KBND, under construction near Bend, Oregon. "I realized this was also going to be a combo job, and my voice had not improved any, so I volunteered to do the traffic jobs and go out and sell," Hiebert recalls about his $60-a-month second job. His announcing failed to improve, despite practice sessions reading magazines aloud. He did develop the organizational skills to balance multiple tasks, a trait that, coupled with sales experience, would prove important for his later work in television.

---

2. Augie Hiebert, oral-history interview conducted by B. William Silcock, January 23, 1995, in possession of the author. See also Chlupach, pp. 21–22.

3. Hiebert, oral-history interview, January 23, 1995.

Much of Hiebert's adaptive abilities and engineering knowledge developed while working for Stan Bennett, first in Oregon and later in Alaska. Together the two engineers put KBND, Oregon's eighth radio station, on the air three days after Christmas in 1938. Six months later, still in Oregon, and with a salary now at $120 a month, Hiebert replaced chief engineer Bennett, who had moved on to Fairbanks, Alaska. Bennett was intrigued by the opportunity to build the most remote radio station in America. In July he invited Hiebert to join him as an assistant engineer. In August Hiebert accepted Bennett's telegrammed proposal, including a salary increase to $185 a month. The offer was attractive, as it meant more "than doing combo work and maintaining a little 250-watt station, so off I went to Fairbanks."[4]

The engineering team of Stan Bennett and Augie Hiebert put the thousand-watt KFAR, Alaska's fourth and Fairbanks's first radio station, on the air October 1, 1939.[5] Stan and Augie lived for the next 3½ years inside the station, in a one-bedroom apartment, spinning records during the late-evening hours.

The unfolding of World War II gave Hiebert the opportunity to use broadcast-engineering skills to provide critical public service to the community, a pattern he would later follow in television. The military authorized increasing KFAR's power to 10,000 watts. "When the war came the military needed a station that was on a clear channel for entertainment of their widespread complement of troops and for air navigational purposes." Hiebert recalls, "The FCC issued a special temporary authority to go to 660 kilohertz that was a clear channel signal and duplicated only in New York by the NBC station there."[6]

Wartime public-service programming and news distribution launched Hiebert's eventual excursion into television. Hiebert was the first Alaskan to hear the news of the Japanese attack on Pearl Harbor, December 7, 1941, recording shortwave transmissions at the KFAR and, with Bennett, confirming, then alerting, the commander at Ladd Air Force Base, who notified the Alaska Defense Command.[7] KFAR served to alert military and civilians in Alaska to emergency broadcasts and became a conduit to the world of the expanding war. Between 1941 and 1943, 35 live NBC broadcast bulletins originated from KFAR via shortwave transmitter K7X5. Newscasts updated

4. Hiebert, oral-history interview, January 23, 1995.

5. "KFAR Gives Voice to Interior Alaska," *Fairbanks Daily News-Miner*, September 30, 1939, special edition, pp. 1–2

6. Hiebert, oral-history interview, January 23, 1995.

7. Chulpach, p. 47.

the public about the Japanese inroads into the Aleutian Islands, often with the introduction, "We go to Alaska for a war update."[8] The *New York Times* reported the Japanese had labeled KFAR a "cesspool of information" but for "United States troops on remote, cold assignments it is the last connecting link with civilization, being their primary source of news and entertainment."[9]

World War II eventually separated the engineer team. Bennett served as a research engineer at MIT, and Hiebert took over the position as chief engineer, remaining in Alaska to assist in the war effort. Following World War II there was another opportunity to launch a radio station, this time in Anchorage. This experience, along with Hiebert's first station-management position, provided the seasoning Hiebert needed to venture into television. Midnight Sun, owners of KFAR, sent Hiebert in the summer of 1947 to Anchorage to design and build the second station for Alaska's largest city.

Ten months later, on May 1, 1948, KENI started broadcasting. KENI, like KFAR, in Fairbanks was owned by Austin "Cap" Lathrop. The owner stationed Hiebert permanently in Anchorage in August of 1949. Hiebert would maneuver the new station into stronger profit potential in Alaska's largest city. "I did not like the idea of management, I enjoyed engineering but he asked me to do it so I gave it a try."[10]

Over the next 3½ years Hiebert fine-tuned the skills of sales negotiation, contracts, and trade-outs and learned the importance of interpersonal relationships with the business and political leaders of a community.

In 1952, shortly after the FCC lifted the wartime freeze on television licensing, Hiebert traveled for the Midnight Sun Company to Manhattan to research television options. When he returned his enthusiasm for television received a cold welcome as the company's board of directors worried the new medium might be too competitive, especially for its movie theaters.

During this period Hiebert began to see changes in his relationship with the company that had brought him to the far north. Its visionary founder, Cap Lathrop, died in 1950. Wearing Cap's mantle, Hiebert believed television the next logical step to provide community service to a land and a people so remote from the rest of the world. He envisioned television as a cure for "cabin fever," the intense isolation felt by Alaskans far from friends and loved ones in the lower 48 states.[11] Now professionally mature, with the

---

8. Chlupach, p.48

9. Jack Gold, "Along Radio Row—Mr. Foster of Alaska," *New York Times*, May 23, 1943, sec. 2, p. 7.

10. Hiebert, oral-history interview, January 23, 1995.

engineering background of three start-up radio stations—KBND, KFAR and KENI—and with 12 years of broader-based experience—from early "combo jobs" to later station-management duties—now Hiebert could impel his energy into television. In a letter to his parents he wrote of Alaska, "Living here, working here with accompanying problems and experiences has contributed to my mental development. I think it has done a job a lifetime somewhere else would have failed to do. And it's been of immeasurable value."[12]

The $25,000 willed to him by Cap Lathrop provided the farm boy seed money to grow a new crop of stations in Alaska.

Isolation and Economic Challenge

Scholars and journalists have likened Alaska to a developing nation, challenged by economic hardship and developed through communication technologies.[13] Alaska's isolation creates an inward climate of survival and competition. This competitive nature, manifested from the gold rush days to Anchorage's annual Fur Rendezvous sledge-dog matches, played a critical role in the race to bring television to the far north. The "father of Alaskan television,"[14] Augie Hiebert, filed for the first FCC television license on May 18, 1953, one week before the California-based company, Kiggins and Rollins.

Financial backing for Hiebert's newly formed company, Northern Television, or NTV, expanded from his $25,000 seed money to the support of 25 Anchorage businesspeople. "We started KTVA," Hiebert recalls, "by selling company stock to the public for $125,000. That wouldn't even buy the basic equipment now."[15] Hiebert took pride in his all-Alaskan company and instilled an early company ethos of community service. He set the stride

11. Chlupach, pp. 35, 83.

12. Augie Hiebert, letter to his parents, as quoted in Chlupach, p. 83.

13. See J. M. Fallows, "Alaska: Nigeria of the North," *Atlantic Monthly*, August 1984, pp. 1–22; Beverely James and Patrick Daley, "Origination of State-Supported Entertainment Television in Rural Alaska," *Journal of Broadcasting and Electronic Media* 31 (2), spring 1987, pp. 169–80; and R. J. Madigan and W. J. Peterson, "Television on the Bering Strait," *Journal of Communication* 27 (4), pp. 183–87.

14. I. J. Campbell, "Augie G. Hiebert," *Alaska Business Monthly* 5 (1), sec.1, p. 26.

15. Michael Berger, "Far North TV Hits Prime Time," *Alaska Business Monthly* 10 (7), July 1994, pp. 44–52.

himself serving in community organizations. He assisted in creating the Alaska Festival of Music, held every June from 1956 through 1966. KTVA offered a cost-free education series of music festival lectures.[16]

He received construction permits for the television station in July 1953. Hiebert hired the start-up staff in September. NTV avoided much of the high costs of a tower by placing it on top of the Mount McKinley Building, a 14-floor Anchorage pink apartment complex. KTVA-station studios were housed on the first floor.

The California competition, Kiggins and Rollins, built their studios and offices in the basement of the Anchorage Westward Hotel, also with the tower on top. Their call letters, KFIA, stood for "first in Anchorage." The only race they won was the first to test an on-air signal, which occurred in October. Technical problems resulted in poor reception. Advertiser and viewer confidence would be instilled in the new technology after a successful test on KTVA over the Thanksgiving holidays. On December 11, 1953, KTVA began broadcasting as Alaska's first television station.[17] The transcript from the 6:30 p.m. premiere broadcast marks the public-service pledge Northern Television made from the very beginning to Alaska citizens: "One hundred years from now the citizens of Anchorage will not remember what has happened here at KTVA on this 11th day of December 1953.... However, there will be something begun here today that will be important to them, something with which the people of 2053 will be concerned and with which they will have to deal in their own time. It is the question of whether or not KTVA maintains its integrity as a public servant, its support of civic institutions, civic benefits, local business. Its loyalty to Alaska and unfailing allegiance to the United States."[18]

Programming on KTVA was a mixture of NBC and Du Mont network offerings and locally produced shows. Within two years, on July 23, 1955, Hiebert realigned NTV with the CBS Television Network. He dropped NBC because he considered it unresponsive to smaller stations, a niche he believed allowed him a close relationship with CBS executives in succeeding years. "With top rated CBS and our local programming all the time," Hiebert remarked during the second anniversary of Channel 11, December 11, 1955, "we are sure we will be able to offer more and more of what television really ought to be."[19]

---

16. Chlupach, p. 110.
17. Duane L. Triplett, "Commercial Television in Alaska," in R.M. Walp, ed., *Telecommunication in Alaska* (Honolulu: Pacific Telecommunications Council), pp. 101–104.
18. Chlupach, appendix.

For Hiebert the pattern of what television ought to be came from his radio-programming experience, offering shows of local significance. This included a women's program, "Norma Goodman's Hostess House"; a quiz show, "Pan for Gold"; extension-service and community-activity broadcasts; and children's shows. Later in the 1970s, before public television came to Alaska, Hiebert arranged with PBS and the Children's Television Workshop to broadcast "Sesame Street" on a daily basis. A local version of Dick Clark's "American Bandstand" called "The Varsity Show" began in 1958 and continued weekly for the next 14 years. Only the technician worked for NTV; high-school students performed the remaining production and on-air jobs, with part of the profits deposited in a scholarship fund. Hiebert viewed the show as a legacy, a way of inspiring future broadcasters, as he had been encouraged in his youth.[20]

These locally produced programs relied on inexpensive sets and simple production values, a pattern that remains at NTV in the 1990s. NTV's shows were not slick and often looked folksy compared to the competition. The company's business philosophy centered on survival rather than on sophistication. Scornful of today's market-driven broadcasting, Hiebert viewed the early days of Alaska fondly: "We could do a little bit of everything to please the population, we didn't worry about surveys then."[21]

The Alaskan television market in the 1950s, by many standards, could barely support commercial television. Anchorage was a small town of 35,000. The California partnership competing with NTV went broke in the fall of 1954, selling to the Lathrop company, Hiebert's former radio employer. Lathrop now realized Hiebert's vision of television's possibilities was worth pursuit. The *Fairbanks Daily News-Miner,* a newspaper owned by the Lathrop company, announced plans to bring the first station to this far-north town, population 15,000. Business leaders in Fairbanks encouraged Hiebert to return to his first Alaskan home, bringing NTV's experience in launching a television station with him. Hiebert added a few more stockholders, filed the FCC documents, and obtained the call letters KTVF. His competition in the race for television in Fairbanks was with Midnight Sun Broadcasting, his former employer, who had brought him to Alaska in 1939.

---

19. Augie Hiebert, December 11, 1955, remarks in Chlupach, p. 100.

20. Linda Billington, "Always Time to Help Out: Broadcaster Augie Hiebert Honored for his Contributions to Public Life," *Anchorage Daily News,* November 13, 1985, p. 16. See also Chlupach, p. 104.

21. Campbell, p. 26.

The race for television in Fairbanks began 14 months after launching TV in Anchorage. It differed in several ways. Hiebert's daughter, Robin Ann Chlupach, cities several reasons for the emotionally charged contest, including the smaller market base and the end-of-the-road isolation felt by family and friends in this "last outpost of metropolitan U.S.A."[22] KTVF, the NTV station in Fairbanks, premiered February 17, 1955, beating Midnight Sun's KFAR, which began broadcasting in March.

NTV's second TV station in Alaska's only other competitive broadcast market[23] became a twin to KTVA in Anchorage, right down to the Channel 11 frequency. Hiebert explained his engineering logic in lay terms to the local press: "We find that Channel 11 is entirely free of interference such as is quite frequently experienced on lower channels by ignition noise, amateur radio operation, and commercial shortwave transmitters that are so common near Alaskan cities."[24]

KTVF used similar programming and marketing strategies under the umbrella banner of a local focus to serve the public. Although first in the history books with television in Anchorage and Fairbanks, NTV spent years nipped by competition that often fostered lean times of financial struggle. "Getting competition right away was very difficult," Hiebert recalls. "It would have been easy if we were the only station in town. It was pretty difficult for a long period of time just trying to meet the payroll and get enough equipment to keep up with the game."[25] Profitability would not come for 20 years. Hiebert credits the faith of those original stockholders in Anchorage and Fairbanks seeing NTV through economic challenges. They viewed television as an instrument of stability, a substitution for the amenities lacking in the new, harsh country.

Hiebert's frequent travels outside Alaska to CBS affiliate meetings and the National Association of Broadcasters annual convention, brought him face-to-face with technological changes he could bring back to NTV. He viewed technology as a means to further his aspiration of social stability for Alaska. The new technologies' big-ticket price tags heightened the economic pressure the company faced, especially when imposed by the network. In 1969 CBS told NTV they were replacing 16-millimeter film, programming with two-inch quad videotape. This forced NTV to commit to a $250,000 contract with Ampex Corporation to install one tape machine at each sta-

---

22. Chlupach, p. 98.
23. Berger, p. 44.
24. Chlupach, p. 96
25. Hiebert, oral-history interview, January 23, 1995.

tion—a risky decision. "We would program ourselves so we would have a film show and then a tape show, so we would have time to swap in between. It was a hassle," Hiebert recalls. "We finally were able to get two tape machines and right after that CBS switched to one inch, so we were always behind the eight ball trying to keep up with technology and the demand of the network."[26]

NTV did not win every race. Midnight Sun Broadcasting under the leadership of Al Bramstedt—who, like Hiebert, had worked for Cap Lathrop's KFAR in Fairbanks—proved a formidable competitor. Bramstedt bought Midnight Sun, financed by 50 investors, from the Lathrop company in 1959 for $250,000.[27] Their Anchorage affiliate, KENI-TV, beat NTV and surprised the rest of the state with the first colored television broadcast June 18, 1966.

Air transportation to ship in film and videotapes from Seattle to KTVA, and then to KTVF, incurred high costs. A two-week delay was typical for Anchorage, with Fairbanks viewing the CBS programs three weeks after the audience in the continental U.S. Christmas specials would not be seen until the middle of January. News documentary programs often were several weeks old. Hiebert envisioned satellites as a solution to shipping costs, programming challenges, and a new inroad to the "lower 48" to curb Alaskan isolationism. Often these ambitions intermingled. Hiebert used influence in Washington, D.C., to accomplish them. NTV bought stock in Communications Satellite Corporation, created by Congress to develop satellites. In 1969 Hiebert successfully lobbied Alaska's congressional delegation to authorize an experimental earth station to download the CBS feeds of the Apollo 11 moon landing.[28]

Walter Cronkite's CBS coverage was seen not only on KTVA but on KENI-TV (NBC) and KHAR (ABC) for 30 continuous hours. All three stations simulcast the coverage with no interruptions. Hiebert considers his efforts to bring satellites to the far north his most important legacy. Dismissing the critics then and now, he realistically asserts, "It wasn't worth the cost, but it shortened distances, limited the isolation people felt."[29]

26. Hiebert, oral-history interview, January 23, 1995.

27. Ray Tyson, "Alive O. Bramstedt Sr.," *Alaska Business Monthly* 7 (1), January 1991, sec. 1, p. 38.

28. Margaret Bauman, "For Sale, Used Satellite TV Systems," *Alaska Journal of Commerce* 14 (45), November 23, 1990, sec. 1, p. 1.

29. Campbell, p. 26.

A new pattern of live television from the "lower 48" premiered January 3, 1971, as KTVA broadcast a National Football Conference championship game via an earth station completed six months before. "This is a really significant event for Alaska," Hiebert told the *Anchorage Daily Times,* "because now we have entered an age in television that the other 49 states have had for some time."[30] It would not be until 1984 that lower cost and expanded satellite distribution allowed same-day broadcasting of CBS news, sports, and entertainment programming on KTVA and KTVF.[31]

In 1970 KTVA arranged for a videotape of the "CBS Evening News" to be taped at the Seattle affiliate, KIRO, tossed onto an evening-flight plane, and shown at 11:30 p.m. As local TV news came into stride in the early 1970s, NTV met the vogue by using Hiebert's "combo job" techniques learned in the early days of radio. In Anchorage, news employees worked for both KBYR-AM, promoted as "Newsradio 700," and Channel 11's "Eyewitness News." KTVA's news director since 1986, Steve MacDonald, recalls this small "combo" staff operation of four reporters for both TV and radio and their expansion in the 1980s. "As the need for a good local newscast increased," MacDonald observed, "the news staff grew and our broadcast equipment got better."[32]

Although hundreds of television news broadcasts on both KTVA and KTVF covered such diverse topics as Alaskan statehood, the Native Land Claims Act, the economic impact of the Prudhoe Bay pipeline, and the environmental disaster created by the Exxon Valdez oil spill, no story challenged NTV's staff like the fire, flood, and earthquake that directly impacted the stations. These three different disasters knocked the very stations' signals silent.

Natural Disaster

On a Sunday morning in January 1957, a fire in the Northward Building, the home of two-year-old KTVF-TV, burned 50 feet of the main transmission line. Sustaining water and smoke damage, the station was not destroyed, but knocked off the air for a few days. Water problems a decade

---

30. *Anchorage Daily Times,* January 3, 1971, p.1

31. A. G. Hiebert, Henry Hove, and Julianna Guy, "Northern Television, Inc.—Historical Background," private company papers, revised January 17, 1996.

32. Berger, pp. 44–50.

later proved far more disastrous, keeping KTVF off the air for nearly four months. Cresting floodwaters from the Chena River on August 15, 1967, swirled through downtown Fairbanks. Rising above parking meters, water lapped up through the basement of the Northward Building. Pumps kept the level down until a soft spot in the floor gave way, and like a geyser, pressured gray water gushed up into the station, drowning everything in its wake. The 14 feet of water took two months to recede. Chena floodwaters also knocked off KFRB, the radio sister station to KTVF.

As a result, staff were laid off, programs and their sponsors canceled. Hiebert and a consulting engineer, George Frese, worked to return the radio station to the air a week later, but KTVF's completely destroyed television operation would not return until December 9,1967. The only bright spot was the $146,000 an insurance policy provided for new television equipment, which allowed the station to be the first in Fairbanks to broadcast in color. Insurance funds also paid for KFRB's new radio transmitter.[33] A bank loan secured finances to rebuild on the second floor of the Northward Building and this time to locate both the radio and television station under the same roof.

Between the 1957 fire and the 1967 flood at KTVF in Fairbanks, nature rumbled through the tundra silence and cracked the early-evening city bustle in Anchorage on March 27, 1964. Alaskans often feel minor tremors and occasionally lose a dish or wall hanging, but nothing prepared them for the Good Friday shock waves. The earthquake killed 114.

As the earth rattled, Hiebert's phone conversation with an equipment supplier went dead. All he could do was hope KTVA's tower, high above him on the roof of the 14-story McKinley Building, remained standing. "The thought crossed my mind," Hiebert recalls, "that if the antenna is broken and gone, plus whatever other damage has been done, it is probably the end of Northern TV." The tower was bent, but not broken, and came to symbolize for Hiebert a beacon of hope to rebuild his television station.

Alaska's first television station had survived this century's most severe earthquake in North America, but now the rebuilding had to begin. Broken water pipes damaged broadcast equipment, including the transmitter. Through the rubble and wetness wires were soldered. As KTVA returned to the air, warm studio lights brought extra heat for employees. Oil stoves provided additional heat for NTV to patch concrete and sift through office

---

33. Chlupach, pp. 120–125.

files. Tenants evacuated the apartment complex, leaving the station as sole occupant for the next two years.

During this time Hiebert secured bank loans to relocate the company and build a new station complex in Spenard, an Anchorage suburb. A new 392-foot-tower was raised on a two-acre parcel of land. The new broadcast center was dedicated in 1966. It included KTVA, the Muzak franchise, and KNIK-FM, Alaska's first FM station, which Hiebert had launched September 15, 1960, under the call letters KTVA-FM. Before the broadcast center's dedication NTV completed purchase of Anchorage AM radio station KBYR. The deal also added KFRB radio in Fairbanks as a sister station to KTVF television. In 1990 NTV acquired a dormant FM station, obtaining the call letters KXLR and thus expanding Hiebert's empire to two television and four radio stations, AM/FM combinations in both Anchorage and Fairbanks.

Reigning over NTV, Hiebert—known for pulling episodes of popular network programs like a CBS episode of "Maude" that dealt with abortion[34]—feels embarrassed to be in the television business in the 1990s. "The network programming that we have to take as part of our contract is crummy, most of it, except the news and some documentaries," Hiebert says.[35]

Summary

Alaska's first television station, KTVA, and its twin KTVF, were forged through the vision and vigor of Augie Hiebert. Their history of engineering feats, economic survivals, and triumphs over nature seems event driven, but Hiebert would disagree. Despite the fact that his fingerprints "have been all over Alaska broadcasting from the first live sports broadcast to satellite communications,"[36] Hiebert quickly, proudly, points to the people, the employees, whose careers were instrumental to the stations' operations.

The story of Alaska's first television company is retold hundreds of times in the histories of former employees who once began in a "combo job" at NTV. As they move on to other stations in the lower 48, working side by side with other specialists, Hiebert believes "they are heads and shoulders ahead of them because they know what the rest of the broadcast game is all

34. Hiebert, phone interview, January 26, 1996. See also Campbell, p. 26

35. Hiebert, oral-history interview, January 23, 1995.

36. Linda Billington, "Always Time to Help Out: Broadcaster Augie Hiebert Honored for His Contributions to Public Life," *Anchorage Daily News*, November 13, 1995, p. 1E.

about."[37] It's a game the old engineer never tires of playing. Quickly he'll shed his usually modest demeanor and, grinning, share names and success stories of broadcasters who learned their trade under his tutelage. The history of the establishment of KTVA and KTVF are part of Alaska's heritage in the quest to develop a community tied to the lower 48 states. The success of these communication links is the result of the stamina and determination of Augie Hiebert and the support of Alaska's business community.

37. Hiebert, oral-history interview, January 23, 1995.

Selected Bibliography

BOOKS

Abramson, Albert. *The History of Television, 1880–1941.* Jefferson, N.C.: McFarland, 1987.
———. *Zworykin: Pioneer of Television.* Urbana: University of Illinois Press, 1995.
Aronson, Charles S., ed. *International Television Almanac, 1958.* New York: Quigley, 1958.
Balderston, William. *Philco: Autobiography of Progress.* New York: Newcomen Society, 1954.
Balio, Tino, ed. *Hollywood in the Age of Television.* Boston: Unwin-Hyman, 1990.
Banning, William P. *Commercial Broadcasting Pioneer—The WEAF Experiment, 1922–1926.* Cambridge: Harvard University Press, 1946.
Barnouw, Erik. *Tube of Plenty: The Evolution of American Television,* 2nd rev. ed. New York: Oxford University Press, 1990.
Bilby, Kenneth. *The General: David Sarnoff and the Rise of the Communications Industry.* New York: Harper and Row, 1985.
Boddy, William. *Fifties Television: The Industry and Its Critics.* Urbana: University of Illinois Press, 1990.
Boyer, Peter J. *Who Killed CBS? The Undoing of America's Number One News Network,* paperback ed. New York: St. Martin's, 1989.
Carson, Clayborne, David J. Garrow, Vincent Harding, Darlene Clark Hine, eds. *Eyes on the Prize: America's Civil Rights Years.* New York: Penguin Books, 1987.
Carter, Hodding. *Their Words Were Bullets.* Athens: University of Georgia, 1969.
Dicken-Garcia, Hazel. *Journalistic Standards in Nineteenth-century America.* Madison: University of Wisconsin Press, 1989.
Dunlap, Orin E., Jr. *The Future of Television.* New York: Harper and Brothers, 1947.
Everson, George. *The Story of Television: The Life of Philo T. Farnsworth.* New York: W.W. Norton, 1949.
Ewbank, Henry L., and Sherman P. Lawton. *Broadcasting: Radio and Television.* New York: Harper and Brothers, 1952.
Farnsworth, Elma G. *Distant Vision: Romance and Discovery on an Invisible Frontier.* Salt Lake City: Pemberly Kent, 1989.
Godfrey, Donald G., comp. *Reruns on File: A Guide to Electronic Media Archives.* Hillsdale, N.J.: Lawrence Erlbaum, 1992.
Goldenson, Leonard H. *Beating the Odds.* New York: Charles Scribner's Sons, 1991.
Gorman, Joseph Bruce. *Kefauver: A Political Biography.* New York: Oxford University Press, 1971.

Gunther, Marc. *The House that Roone Built.* Boston: Little, Brown and Company, 1994.
Hawes, William. *American Television Drama.* Tuscaloosa: University of Alabama Press, 1986.
Hawver, Walt. *Capital Cities/ABC The Early Years: 1954–1986: How the Minnow Came to Swallow the Whale.* Radnor, Pa.: Chilton Book Company, 1994.
Head, Sydney W., and Christopher H. Sterling. *Broadcasting in America.* Boston: Houghton Mifflin, 1982.
Hinds, Lynn Boyd. *Broadcasting the Local News: The Early Years of Pittsburgh's KDKA-TV.* University Park: Pennsylvania State University Press, 1995.
Inglis, Andrew F. *Behind the Tube: A History of Broadcasting Technology and Business.* Boston: Focal Press, 1990.
Kefauver, Estes *Crime in Ameria.* Garden City, N.Y.: Doubleday, 1951.
King, Larry *Larry King.* New York: Simon and Schuster, 1982.
Kittross, John M. *Bibliography of Theses and Dissertations in Broadcasting, 1920–1973.* Washington, D.C.: Broadcast Education Association, 1978.
Lichty, Lawrence W., and Malachi C. Topping, eds. *American Broadcasting: A Source Book on the History of Radio and Television.* New York: Hastings House, 1975.
Long, Stewart Louis. *The Development of the Network Television Oligopoly.* New York: Arno, 1979.
McArthur, Tom, and Peter Waddell. *The Secret Life of John Logie Baird.* London: Century Hutchinson, 1986.
Porterfield, John, and Kay Reynolds, eds. *We Present Television.* New York: W.W. Norton, 1940.
Powers, Ron. *The Newscasters.* New York: St. Martin's Press, 1977.
Quinlan, Sterling. *Inside ABC.* New York: Hastings House, 1979.
Reinsch, J. Leonard. *Getting Elected.* New York: Hippocrene Books, 1988.
Rivera, Geraldo *Willowbrook.* New York: Random House, 1972.
Rubin, Bernard *Political Television.* Belmont, Calif.: Wadsworth, 1967.
Rubin, Ellis. *Get Me Ellis Rubin: The Life, Times and Cases of a Maverick Lawyer.* New York: St. Martin's, 1989.
Smart, Samuel Chipman. *The Outlet Story, 1894–1984.* Providence: Outlet Communication, 1984.
Sterling, Christopher H., and John M. Kittross. *Stay Tuned: A Concise History of American Broadcasting,* 2nd ed. Belmont, Calif.: Wadsworth, 1990.
Tiltman, Ronald. *Baird of Television.* London: Seeley Service, 1933.
Udelson, Joseph H. *The Great Television Race: A History of the American Television Industry 1925–1941.* Tuscaloosa: University of Alabama Press, 1982.
Walley, David G. *The Ernie Kovacs Phile.* New York: Simon and Schuster, 1987.
Welcome South Brother. Atlanta: Cox Broadcasting, 1974.
Westin, Av. *Newswatch.* New York: Simon and Schuster, 1982.
Wood, William *Electronic Journalism.* New York: Columbia University Press, 1967.

SELECTED ARTICLES

"ABC Opens Probe of Disc Jockeys." *New York Times*, November 18, 1959, pp. 1, 18.

Alexander, S. L. "May the Good News Be Yours: Ralph Renick and Florida's First TV News." *Mass Communication Review* 19 (Winter–Spring) (1992): 72.

"Ambitious ABC Planning." *Broadcasting*, February 16, 1953, pp. 27–29.

Amster, Betty Lou. "News and Documentaries: Immediate Journalism and the Longer View." *Louisville Magazine*, September 20, 1967, p.17.

Anderson, Jack. "Miami TV: In the Beginning." *Miami Herald TV Preview*, June 16, 1964, p. 3.

"Anything Goes ... on Charlotte Peter's Show." *TV Guide*, April 28–May 4, 1956, p. A37.

Ashdown, Paul G. "WTVJ's Miami Crime War: A Television Crusade." *Florida Historical Quarterly* 58 (July 1979–April 1980): 427.

Atkinson, Morgan. "The News Wars." *Louisville Magazine*, December 1986, pp. 73–75.

Barrett, Bill. "Memories of 25 Years Ago Stirred by 25th Anniversary of WEWS in Cleveland." *Scripps-Howard News*, January 1973, p. 18.

Bedell, Sally. "Can Minor League Anchorman Make It in Majors?" *New York Times*, July 12, 1982, late ed., sec. C, p. 15.

Bednarski, P. J. "Bob Braun the Overlooked Institution." *Cincinnati Post*, August 11, 1981, p. 1B.

"Behind 30 Minutes of TV, 50 Hours of Preparation." *Washington Sunday Star,* Pictorial Supplement, July 1, 1951, pp. 14–15.

Berger, Michael. "Far North TV Hits Prime Time." *Alaska Business Monthly* 10 (7) (July 1994): 44–52.

"Best in Video Fare Promised by Reinsch." *Atlanta Journal*, September 28, 1948, p. 1.

Billington, Linda. "Always Time to Help Out: Broadcaster Augie Hiebert Honored for His Contributions to Public Life." *Anchorage Daily News,* November 13, 1985, p. 16.

Birdwhistell, Terry L. "WHAS Radio and the Development of Broadcasting in Kentucky, 1922–1942." *Register of the Kentucky Historical Society* 79 (Autumn 1981): 333–53.

Blair, William M. "'Outraged' Over Video at Hearing, Carroll, Bet Expert, Defies Senators." *New York Times*, February 25, 1951, p. 1.

"Bonneville: Mormon Business Flagship." *New York Times*, November 24, 1980, p. D4.

Boss, Kit. "It's Time to Grieve, Whoever the New Owner Might Be." *Seattle Times*, August 21, 1990, p. A5.

Brechner, J. "Were Broadcasters Color Blind?" *Television Quarterly*, June 1966, pp. 98, 101–02.

Bryan, Wright. "When Can We Look at Television? The Answer Is Now—on WSB-TV." *Atlanta Journal*, September 30, 1948, p. 28.

Calloway, John D. "Chicago's TV News: Testing." *Chicago Scene* 5 (2) (1964): 15–16.

"Cancer Patient to Go on TV." *Louisville Courier-Journal*, May 12, 1953, sec 1, p. 6.

"CBS Will Appeal Jacobson Decision: Walter Jacobson Libel Suit." *Broadcasting,* December 16, 1985, p. 108.

Chandler, Bob. "TV in Lubbock Keeps Pace with Growth of Texas 'Wonder Town.'" *Variety,* April 15, 1953, p. 25.

"City Sets Example in TV Broadcasts." *Cleveland Plain Dealer*, December 18, 1949, p. 11E.

Clark, Rocky. "TV Begins Daytime Schedule." *Bridgeport Post*, September 22, 1948, p. 36.

Condon, George. "The Day Our Lives Changed." *Cleveland Plain Dealer Sunday Magazine*, December 17, 1967, p. 4.

————. "WEWS Rates Big Cheer for Trying Bold Experiment." *Cleveland Plain Dealer,* January 18, 1958, p. 16.

Cosford, Bill. "Gleason in Florida: How Sweet It Was." *Miami Herald*, June 25, 1987, pp. 10AA–11AA.

Coto, Juan Carlos. "Veteran Anchor Ralph Renick Dies." *Miami Herald*, July 13, 1991, p. 1A.

Covert, Colin. "KARE 10 p.m. News Takes 1st." *Minneapolis Star Tribune*, August 20, 1987, p. 1A.

Crafton, Patrick. "Cleveland Due to Become Focal Point of Television Industry, Official Says." *Cleveland News,* October 29, 1948, p. 21.

"Crime Inquiry Attracts Crowds Like World Series." *St. Louis Globe-Democrat*, February 24, 1951, p. 1.

Deeb, Gary. "At ABC, the Net's Set for Happy Talk." *Chicago Tribune*, February 4, 1976, p. 10.

Deeb, Gary. "Bill Kurtis: Everybody's Friend Moves on to New York and the Challenge of Befriending a Nation." *Chicago Sun-Times*, February 28, 1982, Show sec., p. 8.

Dickson, Terry. "Even Strangers Believe They Know Him." *St. Louis Post-Dispatch*, October 3, 1953, p. 1G.

Diehl, William, Jr. "Crosley's Clear Channel Colossus." *Cincinnati Magazine*, March 1968, p. 28.

"Don Lee Television Passes Another Milestone." *International Photographer*, October 1936, p. 12.

Doolittle, Lewis L. "WNHC's Television Arrival Remarkable Achievement." *Bridgeport Herald,* June 20, 1948., n.p.

Einstein, Paul. "Cameras on Corruption." *The Quill,* May 1967, pp. 12–13.

"The Eisenhower Radio-TV Talk." *Kansas City Times*, September 20, 1952, p. 14.

Feder, Robert. "More Viewers Staying Tuned." *Chicago Sun-Times*, March 7, 1993, final ed., p. 18.

Federal Communications Commission. "The Evolution of Television 1927–1943." *Journal of Broadcasting* 4 (3) (Summer 1960): 199–207.

Ferretti, Fred. "CBS Memo Sets TV Reporting Rules." *New York Times*, October 31, 1969, p. 89.

Fields, Gregg. "Channel 7's Owner Attacks NBC's Plans." *New York Times*, March 12, 1987, sec. 4, p. 9.

Frankel, Jim. "WEWS Gets Pat on Back for Grade-A Local Show." *Cleveland Press*, circa January 1958, WEWS-TV Collection.

Goldwyn, Samuel. "Hollywood in the Television Age." *New York Times Magazine*, February 13, 1946, pp. 15, 44, 47.

"Good Local Programming for New York." *Broadcasting*, March 13, 1950, pp. 46–47.

Gysel, Dean. "TV Showed Chicago Like It Is." *Chicago Daily News*, August 30, 1968, p. 37.

Hannon, Robert E. "Putting Together the Charlotte Peters Show...." *Pictures Magazine, St. Louis Post-Dispatch*, January 28, 1962, pp. 2–5.

"Happy Talk." *Newsweek,* February 20, 1972, p. 46.

"Henry Morgan Broadcast to Open Television Chain." *Washington Evening Star*, April 18, 1948, p. 17A.

Hofer, Setphen F. "Philo Farnswroth: Television's Pioneer." *Journal of Broadcasting* 23 (2) (1979): 153.

Hoglin, Richard. "All the News That's Fit." *Time,* June 20, 1994, p. 55.

Holly, Dan, and Reinaldo Ramos. "The Great One Is Dead at 71." *Miami Herald*, June 25, 1987, pp. 1A, 10AA.

Holston, Noel. "Dave Moore Nearing Final 6 p.m. Sign-Off." *Minneapolis Star Tribune,* November 16, 1991, p. 1A.

Howard, Herbert H. "Cox Broadcasting Corporation: A Group Ownership Case Study." *Journal of Broadcasting* 20 (2) (Spring 1976): 209–32.

Howard, T. J. "Channel 2 Manager Leaving: Architect of Tabloid Format Moving to L.A. Station." *Chicago Tribune*, June 19, 1993, Sports Final, Business, p. 1.

"Inside Television." *Variety,* October 12, 1949, p. 33.

"Inventor Describes His Radio Motion Pictures. Televisor Lets Radio Fans Look In as Well as Listen." *New York Times*, April 25, 1926, sec. 9, 17:1–3.

"ISU's Role in Atomic Bomb helped Spawn WOI-TV." *Des Moines Register*, June 10, 1984, p. 3B.

Jicha, Tom. "WTVJ Looks Back at Its Many Firsts." *Fort Lauderdale Sun Sentinel*, March 25, 1995, p. 3D.

"Joe Bartelme, Newschief of Channel 4, Dies." *Minneapolis Star Tribune*, September 6, 1991, p. 4B.

Johnson, Nicholas. "The Media Barons and the Public Interest." *Atlantic Monthly*, June 1968, pp. 43–51.

Jones, Will. "WTCN to Begin TV Shows Today." *Minneapolis Tribune,* July 1, 1949, p. 18.

Kasindork, Jeanie. "King Maker." *New York* 25 (42) (October 26,1992): 56–59.

"KDUB-TV's Start: Switch Thrown Thursday." *Broadcasting and Telecasting*, November 17, 1952, p. 70.

Kitman, Marvin. "Another Day, Another Million." *Washington Journalism Review* (September 1983): 39–42, 58.

Klein, Paul. "Happy Talk, Happy Profits." New York, June 28, 1971, pp. 60–61.

"KRSC-TV Takes Air Tomorrow with Grid Game." *Seattle Times*, November 24, 1948, p. 28.

Ladd, Bill. "After a Slow Start and Lots of Troubles, WHAS-TV Begins to Get out of the Doldrums." *Louisville Courier-Journal*, April 2, 1950, sec. 5, p. 11.

LaFayette, Jon. "CBS Eyes the Prize, Network Focuses on O&Os' Lagging News Ratings." *Electronic Media*, August 1, 1994, p. 20.

Litvig, Irving. "Golden Age of St. Louis Radio." *St. Louis Post-Dispatch*, March 12, 1969, p. 3F.

Lohman, Sidney. "Three New Stations for New York." *New York Times*, June 12, 1948, p. 16.

"Louisville TV Grows Up." *Louisville Magazine*, Fall 1950, p. 19.

MacArthur, Harry. "News of Television and Radio." *Washington Sunday Star*, January 29, 1950, p. 8C.

Manning, Ric. "WHAS Television: Once Stable Station Wracked by Turmoil." *Louisville Courier-Journal*, July 14, 1991, pp. E1, E4.

Mathisen, Chris. "Television's Magic Carpet Beckons Eager Washingtonians." *Washington Sunday Star*, March 18, 1946, p. 3C.

Mazingo, Sherrie. "Home of Programming 'Firsts.'" *Television/RadioAge,* March 1987, p. A10.

McKee, Robert. "WSB Gives Eyes to Dixie." *Atlanta Journal*, September 28, 1948, p. 1.

————. "WSB-TV Raises the Curtain on Dramatic Era of Television." *Atlanta Journal*, September 30, 1948, pp. 1–2.

Morris, Joe Alex. "Home-town TV Makes a Hit." *Saturday Evening Post*, September 3, 1955, p. 50.

"Mr. Crosley Recalls WLW's Start in '21." *Cincinnati Post*, September 27, 1960, p. 21.

Murray, Michael D. "Frank Eschen Gave for Twenty Years: A Profile of a Pioneer Newsman." *St. Louis Journalism Review*, January 1987, p. 8.

————. "KSD Veteran Roedel Retires." *St. Louis Journalism Review*, February 1986, p. 23.

"Mutual's Larry King: Five Years of Questions and He's Still Curious." *Broadcasting* 104 (February 1983): 103.

"Nancy Craig—Interviews." *TV Guide*, April 3, 1953, p. A-16.

"NBC Is Leading in Emmy Race." *St. Louis Post-Dispatch*, August 1, 1986, p. 2A.

Newton, Dwight. "Early Days on the Tube." *San Francisco Sunday Examiner and Chronicle, California Living Magazine,* December 18, 1977, p. 22.

Nielsen, Ted. "Television: Chicago Style." *Journal of Broadcasting*, 9 (4) (Fall 1965): 305–12.

Nusbaum, E. "ISU's Secret Past: From Radio-activity to Television Activity." *Des Moines Register,* September 20, 1993, Today sec., p. 1.

Nyne, G. S. "Wometco's WTVJ/Miami: 25 Years of TV Pioneering." *Historical Association of South Florida Update 2,* December 1974, pp. 2, 6–8.

Platt, Adam. "The World Series of Shamelessness." *Twin Cities Reader*, October 30, 1991, p. 9.

Pollock, Jim. "WOI Has Lively, Controversial History." *Des Moines Register*, March 2, 1994, Metro sec., p. 1.

Powers, Forrest. "News Scrap Continues—It Figures." *Minneapolis Star*, March 9, 1973, p. 23A.

Preston, Marilyn. "Chicago Connection: If You Want to Make It in TV, Get a Windy City Résumé." *Chicago Tribune Magazine*, July 21, 1985, p. 48.

"Profile: The Long Arm of the News—WTVJ Miami's Ralph Renick." *Broadcasting,* January 5, 1976, p. 121.

"Putting the 6 p.m. News into Neat, Small Packages." *Washington Post,* February 10, 1977, p. D1.

Rahn, Pete. "KSDK Sweeps the May Ratings." *St. Louis Globe-Democrat,* June 27, 1986, p. 10C.

Reis, Jim. "The TV Era Ushered in by Advertising." *Kentucky Post,* June 21, 1993, p. 4K.

Renick, Ralph. *News on Television: A Report of an Investigation Carried out under the Terms of a Fellowship of the Kaltenborn Foundation.* Coral Gables, Fla.: May 1950.

Ropp, T. "Philo Farnsworth: Forgotten Father of Television." *Media History Digest* 5 (2) (Summer 1985): 42–58.

Roth, Morry. "O'Leary's (Sacred) Cow Updated as Flynn and Daly Duo Start Another Great Chicago Fire Under Chi News Via WLS-TV." *Variety,* February 11, 1970, pp. 37–38.

Ryan, William J. "Which Came First? 65 years of Kansas City Broadcasting." *Missouri Historical Review* 82 (July 1988): 408–23.

Shiers, George. "Television 50 Years Ago." *Journal of Broadcasting* 19 (4) (Fall 1975): 387–99.

"Six O'Clock and All Is Well." New York: Museum of Radio and Television, 1977.

Smith, Robert R., and Paul T. Prince. "WHDH: The Unconscionable Delay." *Journal of Broadcasting* 18 (1) (Winter 1973–74): 85–96.

Summers, Harrison B. "Programming for Television." *Quarterly Journal of Speech* 31 (1945): 44–47.

"Televised Lung-cancer Operation May Have Been 'World Premier.'" *Louisville Courier-Journal,* April 23, 1953, sec. 1, pp. 1, 7.

"Television Debut Here Marks First in Dixie." *Atlanta Constitution,* September 30, 1948, p. 22.

"TV Gives Front-Seat View of Crime Inquiry." *St. Louis Post-Dispatch,* February 24, 1951, p. 2A.

"TV News: Behind the Scenes." *Encyclopedia Britannica.* San Diego: KUSI Collection, 1973.

Wallace, Richard, and Mary Voboril. "TV, Radio Personality Arthur Godfrey Dies: 79-Year-Old Entertainer and Aviator Made Miami a Household Word." *Miami Herald,* March 17, 1987, pp. 1A, 10A.

"WDAF-TV in New Hands." *Kansas City Times,* May 19, 1958, pp. 1, 4–5.

"WHAS-TV and WAVE Honored for Programming." *Louisville Magazine,* May 20, 1956, p. 19.

"WHAS-TV Will Show Open-Heart Surgery." *Louisville Courier-Journal,* February 21, 1960, sec. 1, p. 27.

Whitehead, Ralph, Jr. "There's No Biz Like News Biz." *Chicagoan,* March 1974, p. 63.

Wilbur, Susan K. "The History of Television in Los Angeles, 1931–1952." *Southern California Quarterly* 60 (2) (Summer 1978): 184.

Wilbur, Susan K. "The History of Television in Los Angeles, 1931–1952." *Southern California Quarterly* 60 (3) (Fall 1978): 258.

"WJZ-TV Debuting Daytime Airing." *Variety*, May 18, 1949, p. 26.

"WMAL Launches TV Service." *Washington Evening Star*, October 4, 1947, p. 12A.

"WMAL-TV Covers the Game." *Washington Sunday Star,* Pictorial Magazine, December 7, 1947, p. 18.

Wood, Mary. "Sale of WLW Marks End to Broadcasting Era." *Cincinnati Post*, June 11, 1975, p. 23.

"WTVJ Sets Dedication." *Miami Herald*, March 21, 1949, sec. A., p. 57.

UNPUBLISHED MATERIAL

Betzold, Don. "Racing Toward Tonight: The History of a TV Newsroom." Unpublished thesis, University of Minnesota, 1972.

Donigan, Robert W. "A Descriptive Analysis of the Effectiveness of Broadcasting by the Church of Jesus Christ of Latter-day Saints in the North States Mission Area." Master's thesis, Brigham Young University, 1964.

"Eyewitness News Twenty-fifth Anniversary." Videotape, May 17, 1995, Alan Weiss Productions.

Glick, Edwin L. "WGBH-TV: The First 10 Years." Ph.D. diss., University of Michigan, 1970.

Larson, Allen David. "Integration and Attempted Integration Between the Motion Picture and Television Industries Through 1956." Ph.D. diss., Ohio University, 1979.

"Lee Phillip: Salute to Lee." Videocassette #TV-0025.1, production of WBBM-TV, 15 min., Chicago Museum of Broadcast Communications, circa 1985.

"Lee Phillip Show: 25th Anniversary of Kennedy-Nixon Debate." Videocassette #TV-0025.1, production of WBBM-TV, 30 min., Chicago Museum of Broadcast Communications, 1985.

"Legends of Chicago Television." Videocassette #TV-02748, production of the Chicago Television Academy and Chicago Museum of Broadcast Communications, 1991.

"MBC Seminar: 20 Years Later, the '68 Democratic Convention." Videocassette #TV-02334, production of the Chicago Museum Broadcast Communications, 1988.

Nielsen, Theodore Lynn. "A History of Chicago Television News Presentation (1948–1968)." Ph.D. diss., University of Wisconsin, 1971.

Parker, William N. "Early Philadelphia Television." Unpublished paper, W3XE File, Free Library of Philadelphia, Theatre Collection, May 1987.

Pauly, John C. "Producing Local Television News: An Observational, Historical and Theoretical Study." Ph.D. diss., University of Colorado–Boulder, 1994.

"Ralph Renick Reporting." WTVJ Collection, Louis Wolfson II Media History Center, Miami-Dade County Public Library System, Metro Cultural Center, October 3, 1966.

Rue, James Joseph. "Analysis of Television News Techniques in the Los Angeles Area." Master's thesis, University of Southern California, January 1951.

Russomanno, Joseph Anthony. "The Tyranny of the Majority: The Culture of Conformity in the Local Television Newsroom." Ph.D. diss., University of Colorado–Boulder, 1993.

"The Vision of Ernie Kovacs." Exhibition Schedule and Program Notes, Museum of Broadcasting, New York, May 30–September 4, 1986.

White, Timothy R. "Hollywood's Attempt to Appropriate Television: The Case of Paramount Pictures." Ph.D. diss., University of Wisconsin–Madison, 1990.

"Will Success Spoil?" film, ABC-owned stations promotions, WLS/Capital Cities Archives, Chicago, 1969.

Williams, Mark J. "From Remote Possibilities to Entertaining Difference: A Regional Study of the Rise of Television Industry in Los Angeles, 1930–1952." Ph.D. diss., University of Southern California, 1993.

Wolsey, Heber Grant. "The History of Radio Station KSL from 1922 to Television." Ph.D. diss., Michigan State University, 1967.

Wozniak, Daniel F. "Education's First Television Station." Master's thesis, Iowa State University, 1958.

Yangho, Choi. "Process of Parasocial Interaction in Local Television News Watching." Ph.D. diss., University of Florida, 1995.

ARCHIVES AND SPECIAL COLLECTIONS

American University Archives, Washington, D. C., WMAL-TV source.

Bonneville International Corporation Oral History Series, Bonneville International Corporation, Salt Lake City, Utah, KSL-TV source.

Brechner Center for Freedom of Information Library, University of Florida, Gainesville, Fla., WFTV-TV source.

Broadcast Pioneers Library, University of Maryland, College Park, Md., WMAL-TV source.

Chicago Historical Society, Chicago, Ill., WBBM-TV source.

Cincinnati Historical Society, Cincinnati, Ohio, WLWT-TV source.

Du Mont Collection, Library of Congress and National Museum of American History, Archives Divisions, Washington, D.C., WMAL-TV source.

Dub Rogers Collection, South Plains College, Levelland, Tex., KDUB-TV source.

Dwight D. Eisenhower Presidential Library, Abilene, Kan., WDAF-TV source.

Farnsworth/Meeks Papers, Hayden Library Special Collections, Arizona State University, Tempe, Ariz., WPTZ-TV source.

Farnsworth, Philo T., Marriott Library Archives, University of Utah, Salt Lake City, Utah, WPTZ-TV source.

Free Library of Philadelphia, Theatre Collection, Philadelphia, Penn., WPTZ file.

Kansas City Broadcasting Oral History Collection, Rockhurst College, Kansas City, Mo., WDAF-TV source.

Louis Wolfson II Media History Center, Miami-Dade County Library System, Metro Cultural Center, Miami, Fla., WTVJ Collection.

Mass Communications History Center, State Historical Society of Wisconsin, Madison, Wisc., KCBS-TV source.

Missouri Historical Society, St. Louis, Mo., WDAF-TV source.

Missouri Valley Local History Collection, Kansas City Public Library, Kansas City, Mo., WDAF-TV source.

Murrow School of Communication, Washington State University, Pullman, Wash., The Harrison Transcripts, KING-TV source.

Museum of Broadcast Communications, Chicago, Ill., WBBM-TV source.

Museum of Radio and Television, New York, N. Y., WABC-TV News Film Collection.

National Archives, Washington, D.C., FCC Materials and Experimental Station Files.

New Haven Colony Historical Society, WTNH-TV Oral History Collection.

Northeast Ohio Broadcast Archives, John Carroll University, Cleveland, Ohio.

Southwest Collection, Texas Tech University, Lubbock, Tex., KDUB-TV source.

State of Florida Collection, University of Miami Library, Miami, Fla., WTVJ-TV and WFTV-TV source.

University Archives, Iowa State University, Iowa City, Iowa, WOI Radio and Television File.

University of St. Thomas, Oral History Collection, Minneapolis, Minn., WCCO-TV source.

Western Historical Manuscripts Collection, Jefferson Library, University of Missouri-St. Louis, KSD-TV source.

Contributors

CRAIG ALLEN received his Ph.D. from Ohio University after having spent 15 years in the news business, half of that time as a television reporter and news director. He is currently an associate professor in the Walter Cronkite School of Journalism and Telecommunication at Arizona State University, where he also does research in areas of reporter performance and broadcast management. He is author of *Eisenhower and the Mass Media.*

MARY E. BEADLE is an associate professor of communications at John Carroll University in Cleveland, Ohio. She received her Ph.D. from Kent State University and teaches electronic-media courses with an emphasis in media history, international media, and management. She also founded and chaired the communication department at Walsh University, where she received an Outstanding Educator Award. She has taught communication courses in St. Petersburg, Russia; Buenos Aires, Argentina; and Asuncion, Paraguay.

DOM CARISTI is coordinator of electronic media studies in the Iowa State University Journalism and Mass Communication Department. He received his Ph.D. from the University of Iowa and previously taught broadcasting and managed the television station at Missouri Southern State College. He was a 1995 Fulbright Scholar lecturing on journalism in Slovenia. He is the author of *Expanding Free Expression in the Marketplace: Broadcasting and the Public Forum.* The author wishes to acknowledge the research assistance of Chris Osher and Margaret Pitiris, graduate students in the Iowa State University Department of Journalism and Mass Communication.

GINGER RUDESEAL CARTER is an assistant professor of journalism at Georgia College and State University in Milledgeville, Georgia. She received her Ph.D. from the University of Southern Mississippi. Her research interests include media and the space program and oral history.

JOHN P. FERRÉ is an associate professor of communication at the University of Louisville, where he investigates ethical, religious, and historical dimensions of mass media in the United States. In addition to numerous articles and reviews, he has written several books, the most recent of which is *Good News: Social Ethics and the Press* with Clifford G. Christians and P. Mark Fackler.

MARJORIE FOX teaches in the electronic-media division at the University of Cincinnati. She completed her master's degree at Northwestern University and worked in television for 12 years. Her television assignments included stations in Ohio and Illinois, including

WMAQ-TV, Chicago. She won a National Fellowship in Broadcast Journalism to the Poynter Institute and served as a faculty intern at CNN in Atlanta.

MARGOT HARDENBERGH (Ph.D., New York University) is on the faculty at Marist College and writes on media history and the impact of media on social life. She was public affairs projects supervisor at WTNH-TV from 1974 to 1979. She wishes to thank all those who generously shared their files and memories with her, especially Bill Ellison.

RUSSELL A. JENISCH (M.A., Southern Illinois University-Carbondale, 1986) is Assistant Professor in the Department of Communication, Northern Kentucky University. His interests are in broadcast and educational video production. Yasue Kuwahara (Ph.D., Bowling Green State University, 1987) is Associate Professor in the Department of Communication, Northern Kentucky University. Her research interests include U.S. and Japanese popular culture.

VAL E. LIMBURG is associate professor and head of broadcasting at the Edward R. Murrow School of Communication, Washington State University. His graduate work was completed at Brigham Young University and the University of Illinois. He is author of *Mass Media Literacy* and more recently *Electronic Media Ethics.*

FRAN MATERA is an associate professor at the Walter Cronkite School of Journalism and Telecommunication, Arizona State University. She teaches public relations, media ethics, and writing. Her research interests include history and creative-media projects. Her publications have appeared in *American Journalism, Journalism Quarterly,* the *International Journal of Intercultural Relations*, and *Communication Research.*

MARK NEUZIL is an assistant professor at the University of St. Thomas in St. Paul, Minnesota. He worked for the Associated Press and several other news organizations for 13 years, then received his Ph.D. from the University of Minnesota. His research has been published in *Journalism Quarterly, American Journalism, New Jersey Journal of Communication,* and *Newspaper Research Journal.*

DAVID NIMMER is an assistant professor of journalism at the University of St. Thomas. He received his undergraduate degree from the University of Wisconsin and worked for 15 years at the *Minneapolis Star,* first as a reporter, then as managing editor. For over a decade he served WCCO-TV as a reporter and eventually associate news director. He is the author of a book of short stories and several articles.

LINDA M. PERRY is an assistant professor of communication at Purdue University, where she teaches journalism and mass-communication law. Her research interests include First Amendment philosophy and theory, public opinion, libel, access to government information, fair trial–free press, privacy, obscenity, and confidential sources.

STEVEN C. RUNYON is director of media studies and general manager of KUSF (FM) at the University of San Francisco, where he has held these positions for over 20 years.

Previous to this he worked professionally in San Francisco broadcasting. He codeveloped USF's Media Studies Program and coordinated the acquisition and development of KUSF. He is the recipient of many grants and awards. He received his master's degree in broadcasting from San Francisco State University and is currently completing a doctorate at the University of San Francisco.

WILLIAM JAMES RYAN is associate professor of communication and immediate past chair of the Division of Humanities and Fine Arts at Rockhurst College, Kansas City, Missouri. He is a regional broadcast historian and began the Kansas City Broadcasting Oral History Project in 1985.

B. WILLIAM SILCOCK teaches broadcast journalism at the University of Missouri's School of Journalism where he serves as executive producer for KOMU-TV (NBC). His broadcast career began in 1974 as a film editor/shipper for KTVA in Anchorage. A former Fulbright Scholar to Ireland, his research thrusts include transnational television news, media ethics and cultural studies. The author expresses gratitude to Pat Timberlake, head of Missouri's journalism library and her assistant Sue Schuermann.

JAY A. R. WARREN, a Texas native, graduated from Texas Tech University in 1995 with a M.A. in Mass Communications and from Texas Christian University with a B.S. in broadcast journalism. In 1995, he was a producer and reporter for the ABC and NBC affiliates respectively, in Lubbock, Texas. Currently, Warren is the director of *Campaign '96* for the Washington Center for Internships and Academic Seminars in Washington, D.C.

DAVID WEINSTEIN is a fellow at the George Meany Memorial Archives, Silver Spring, Maryland, and a doctoral candidate in American Studies at the University of Maryland, College Park. He teaches courses on popular music, film, television, and American Studies at several Maryland campuses. His dissertation is a history of television in postwar Washington, D.C. He has written several articles on television theory and history. He thanks Maribeth DeLorenzo, Douglas Gomery, Lawrence Mintz, Barbara Shaw, and Dabrina Taylor for their help with this chapter.

MARK WILLIAMS teaches film and television history and theory in the Department of Film Studies at Dartmouth College. His study of early television in Los Angeles, *Remote Possibilities,* will be published by the University of California Press.

LINDA KOWALL WOAL, an independent historian and museum curator, has written numerous articles on early film and broadcast history.

MICHAEL WOAL is an assistant professor in the Communication/English Department of the University of New Mexico–Gallup Campus.

HEBER G. WOLSEY is a former professor of communications at Brigham Young University.

Index